Central American Literatures as World Literature

Literatures as World Literature

Can the literature of a specific country, author, or genre be used to approach the elusive concept of "world literature"? **Literatures as World Literature** takes a novel approach to world literature by analyzing specific constellations—according to language, nation, form, or theme—of literary texts and authors in their own world-literary dimensions.

World literature is obviously so vast that any view of it cannot help but be partial; the question then becomes how to reduce the complex task of understanding and describing world literature. Most treatments of world literature so far either have been theoretical and thus abstract, or else have made broad use of exemplary texts from a variety of languages and epochs. The majority of critical work, the filling in of what has been traced, lies ahead of us. **Literatures as World Literature** fills in the devilish details by allowing scholars to move outward from their own areas of specialization, fostering scholarly writing that approaches more closely the polyphonic, multiperspectival nature of world literature.

Series Editor:
Thomas O. Beebee

Editorial Board:
Eduardo Coutinho, Federal University of Rio de Janeiro, Brazil
Hsinya Huang, National Sun-yat Sen University, Taiwan
Meg Samuelson, University of Adelaide, Australia
Ken Seigneurie, Simon Fraser University, Canada
Galin Tihanov, Queen Mary University of London, UK
Mads Rosendahl Thomsen, Aarhus University, Denmark

Volumes in the Series
Theory as World Literature, edited by Jeffrey R. Di Leo (forthcoming)
Life Writing as World Literature, edited by Helga Lenart-Cheng and Ioana Luca (forthcoming)
Cavafy as World Literature, edited by Takis Kayalis and Vicente Fernández González (Forthcoming)
German Literature as World Literature, edited by Thomas O. Beebee

Roberto Bolaño as World Literature, edited by Nicholas Birns and Juan E. De Castro
Crime Fiction as World Literature, edited by David Damrosch, Theo D'haen and Louise Nilsson
Danish Literature as World Literature, edited by Dan Ringgaard and Mads Rosendahl Thomsen
From Paris to Tlön: Surrealism as World Literature, by Delia Ungureanu
American Literature as World Literature, edited by Jeffrey R. Di Leo
Romanian Literature as World Literature, edited by Mircea Martin, Christian Moraru, and Andrei Terian
Brazilian Literature as World Literature, edited by Eduardo F. Coutinho
Dutch and Flemish Literature as World Literature, edited by Theo D'haen
Afropolitan Literature as World Literature, edited by James Hodapp
Francophone Literature as World Literature, edited by Christian Moraru, Nicole Simek, and Bertrand Westphal
Bulgarian Literature as World Literature, edited by Mihaela P. Harper and Dimitar Kambourov
Philosophy as World Literature, edited by Jeffrey R. Di Leo
Turkish Literature as World Literature, edited by Burcu Alkan and Çimen Günay-Erkol
Elena Ferrante as World Literature, by Stiliana Milkova
Multilingual Literature as World Literature, edited by Jane Hiddleston and Wen-chin Ouyang
Persian Literature as World Literature, edited by Mostafa Abedinifard, Omid Azadibougar, and Amirhossein Vafa
Mexican Literature as World Literature, edited by Ignacio M. Sánchez Prado
Beyond English: World Literature and India, by Bhavya Tiwari
Graphic Novels and Comics as World Literature, edited by James Hodapp
African Literatures as World Literature, edited by Alexander Fyfe and Madhu Krishnan
Feminism as World Literature, edited by Robin Truth Goodman
Polish Literature as World Literature, edited by Piotr Florczyk and K. A. Wisniewski
Taiwanese Literature as World Literature, edited by Pei-yin Lin and Wen-chi Li

Pacific Literatures as World Literature, edited Hsinya Huang and
Chia-hua Yvonne Lin
Central American Literatures as World Literature, edited by Sophie Esch
Hungarian Literature as World Literature, edited by Péter Hajdu
and Zoltán Z. Varga
(forthcoming)
Kazuo Ishiguro as World Literature, by Chris Holmes (forthcoming)

Central American Literatures as World Literature

Edited by Sophie Esch

BLOOMSBURY ACADEMIC
NEW YORK · LONDON · OXFORD · NEW DELHI · SYDNEY

BLOOMSBURY ACADEMIC

Bloomsbury Publishing Inc, 1385 Broadway, New York, NY 10018, USA
Bloomsbury Publishing Plc, 50 Bedford Square, London, WC1B 3DP, UK
Bloomsbury Publishing Ireland, 29 Earlsfort Terrace, Dublin 2, D02 AY28, Ireland

BLOOMSBURY, BLOOMSBURY ACADEMIC and the Diana logo
are trademarks of Bloomsbury Publishing Plc

First published in the United States of America 2024
Paperback edition published 2025

Volume Editor's Part of the Work © Sophie Esch, 2024
Each chapter © Contributors, 2024

For legal purposes the List of Figures on p. ix and Acknowledgments on p. xi
constitute an extension of this copyright page.

Cover design by Simon Levy

All rights reserved. No part of this publication may be: i) reproduced or transmitted in any form, electronic or mechanical, including photocopying, recording or by means of any information storage or retrieval system without prior permission in writing from the publishers; or ii) used or reproduced in any way for the training, development or operation of artificial intelligence (AI) technologies, including generative AI technologies. The rights holders expressly reserve this publication from the text and data mining exception as per Article 4(3) of the Digital Single Market Directive (EU) 2019/790.

Bloomsbury Publishing Inc does not have any control over, or responsibility for, any third-party websites referred to or in this book. All internet addresses given in this book were correct at the time of going to press. The author and publisher regret any inconvenience caused if addresses have changed or sites have ceased to exist, but can accept no responsibility for any such changes.

Library of Congress Cataloging-in-Publication Data
Names: Esch, Sophie, editor.
Title: Central American literatures as world literature / edited by Sophie Esch.
Description: New York : Bloomsbury Academic, 2023. |
Series: Literatures as world literature | Includes bibliographical references and index. |
Summary: "A first-of-its-kind study on Central American literature that illuminates classics and highlights new pathways by exploring texts and writers that go beyond or against the confines of the nation-state"– Provided by publisher.
Identifiers: LCCN 2023014168 (print) | LCCN 2023014169 (ebook) | ISBN 9781501391873 (hardback) | ISBN 9781501391910 (paperback) | ISBN 9781501391903 (ebook other) | ISBN 9781501391897 (pdf) | ISBN 9781501391880 (epub)
Subjects: LCSH: Central American literature–History and criticism. |
Central American literature–Appreciation.
Classification: LCC PQ7471 .C46 2023 (print) | LCC PQ7471 (ebook) |
DDC 860.9/9728–dc23/eng/20230615
LC record available at https://lccn.loc.gov/2023014168
LC ebook record available at https://lccn.loc.gov/2023014169

ISBN:		
	HB:	978-1-5013-9187-3
	PB:	978-1-5013-9191-0
	ePDF:	978-1-5013-9189-7
	eBook:	978-1-5013-9188-0

Series: Literatures as World Literature

Typeset by Integra Software Services Pvt. Ltd.

For product safety related questions contact productsafety@bloomsbury.com.

To find out more about our authors and books visit www.bloomsbury.com
and sign up for our newsletters.

CONTENTS

List of Figures ix
List of Tables x
Acknowledgments xi

Introduction 1
Sophie Esch

Part I Modes

1 Reorienting the World: Reading Maya Literatures through *Xocom Balumil* 19
   Rita M. Palacios and Paul M. Worley

2 World Literature in Minor Key: The Central American Short Story 39
   Sophie Esch and Ignacio Sarmiento Panez

3 Central American *Testimonio* as World Literature: English Translation and the Canonization of a Genre 63
   Tamara de Inés Antón

4 When Does Central American Literature Become Global?: The Extraordinary (or Predictable?) Case of Eduardo Halfon 81
   Magdalena Perkowska

Part II Constellations

5 Cosmopolitanism and Disillusion in Rubén Darío 103
   Carlos F. Grigsby

6 Álvaro Menen Desleal's Speculative Planetary Imagination 121
Carolyn Fornoff

7 Between Internationalism and Cosmopolitanism: Roque Dalton and World Literature 139
Yansi Pérez

8 Rewriting the Militant Left: Untranslatability and Dissensus in Horacio Castellanos Moya 155
Tamara L. Mitchell

9 Humberto Ak'abal's Pluri-verses: Indigeneity, Cosmolectics, and World Literature 173
Gloria Elizabeth Chacón

Part III Routes

10 Canal Zone Modernism: Cendrars, Walrond, and Stevens at the "Suction Sea" 191
Harris Feinsod

11 Creole Poetics of the Ocean: Carlos Rigby, Ecological Thought, and Caribbean Diasporic Consciousness 207
Tatiana Argüello

12 US Central Americans Writing Global South Spaces 223
Andrew Bentley

13 Caravaneros as Citizens of the World 243
Robert McKee Irwin

Notes on Contributors 259
Index 263

FIGURES

1.1 *Yocts'i*, which is a design highlighting the interior of xocom balumil or *chikin balamil*. Design by María Elena Pérez Hernández (Tsotsil from Ch'enalo), 2020. Reproduced with the permission of the artist 21

10.1 The SS *Kroonland* of the Panama Pacific Line passes southbound through the Panama Canal–Gaillard Cut on October 25, 1923. Wallace and Elsie Stevens are aboard. James Gordon Steese Family Papers. Courtesy of Dickinson College Archives and Special Collections, Carlisle, Pennsylvania 200

TABLES

3.1 Erasure of Flakoll's textual presence in *They Won't Take Me Alive* (1987) 68

3.2 Labeling and Menchú's secrets 74

3.3 Overemphasized representativity in the TT 76

4.1 Translations to English, French, and Dutch—content comparison 87

ACKNOWLEDGMENTS

I would like to thank the many people involved in the sustained intellectual dialogue that brought this edited volume into being: the authors, the anonymous reviewers, and at Bloomsbury, Amy Martin and Hali Han. A special thank-you goes out to Rita Palacios, Paul Worley, Carlos F. Grigsby, Tamara Mitchell, Alexandra Ortiz Wallner, Ignacio Sarmiento Panez, Christoph Müller, Andrea Martínez Teruel, Mauricio Chavez, Marco Ramírez Rojas, Kelly McKisson, and Bren Ram for their contributions and input at different stages of the volume.

The authors and I thank the *Revista Canadiense de Estudios Hispánicos* and *ELN* (Duke University Press) for allowing us to reproduce, in modified form, the articles by Harris Feinsod and Carolyn Fornoff, which were originally published as:

Feinsod, H. (2019). "Canal Zone Modernism: Cendrars, Walrond, and Stevens at the 'Suction Sea'." *English Language Notes*, 57 (1): 116–28. https://doi.org/10.1215/00138282-7309721

Fornoff, C. (2021). "Álvaro Menen Desleal's Speculative Planetary Imagination," *Revista Canadiense de Estudios Hispanicos*, 44 (1): 43–66. https://doi.org/10.18192/RCEH.V44I1.5900

Introduction

Sophie Esch

This volume brings together two elusive categories: world literature and Central America. Novelists and scholars routinely doubt—more or less jokingly—if Central America or its literature even exist (Arias 2007: ix; Liano 2008: 51). The reasons for these rhetorical taunts are the invisibility and marginality of Central American lives and literatures. A widespread lack of familiarity with the region and its cultures means that, as Ana Patricia Rodríguez puts it, for "many people, Central America figures as an unknown, nebulous zone" (2009: 2). When it comes to world literature, however, the elusiveness rises not from marginality but rather from an overabundance of definitions and conceptualizations. World literature has become a bit of a chameleon, shifting color and acquiring multiple and contested meanings over time. Is it a designation or an aspiration, a descriptor or a reification, a paradigm or a field?

Weltliteratur morphed from its earlier iterations of internationally inclined German intellectuals in the nineteenth century such as Johann Wolfgang von Goethe and Karl Marx, who used it to welcome an imminent age of literary production and global exchange that go beyond national borders and literatures, to the idea of a "synthesizing philology" in the twentieth century (Auerbach 1969: 9). Often evoked, under different names, as a utopian concept of world (and self) understanding and interconnectedness via literature—from such diverse writers as Rabindranath Tagore, Léopold Sédar Senghor, and Maxim Gorky (Helgesson/Rosendahl Thomsen 2020: 9–12; Khomitsky 2013), in practice, it often came to mean a narrow Western or "foreign" canon or a few masterpieces of universal appeal. At the turn of the twenty-first century, the term underwent a renaissance and transformation at the hands of a globally minded, yet nonetheless

Anglophone-dominated US and British academia as well as Francocentric French academia (Casanova 2007; Damrosch 2003; Moretti 2000). In these latest iterations, scholars turned their attention to the question of circulation, translation, reception, market, institutions and networks, symbolic capital and unequal power dynamics, and cosmopolitan desires and frustrations. With this, the differences in shade and meaning increased further, and it has become a fiercely debated paradigm in literary studies (Apter 2013).

Even variations in spelling can signal differences in meaning. World Literature (in the uppercase) pays greater homage to the German and thus capitalized origin of the noun "Weltliteratur." Sometimes used to refer to the current field of study, it appears to hint at institutionalization and canon (Literature with a capital "L"). The spelling of the Warwick Research Collective (WReC), world-literature (with a hyphen), is the one that is most overtly and deliberately critical by design, since it defines and critiques world-literature from a Marxist and world-systems perspective as the inherently unequal "literature of the modern capitalist world-system" (Deckard et al. 2015: 15, italics removed from the original). And while world literature (in the lower case and without a hyphen) begs to be read in somewhat less-charged terms, its meaning remains controversial. Franco Moretti hailed world literature as the unfulfilled promise of truly comparative literary studies (2000), whereas many scholars, following the criticism of the WReC, see it precisely as a problematic means for comparative literature departments to "re-inscribe Eurocentrism as a master narrative of [the] literary field" (Sánchez Prado 2021: 1).

Academics in postcolonial literary studies have thus shown a wariness toward the term, while themselves struggling with the continued dominance of English in their midst. Not surprisingly, some of the most productive contributions and challenges to world literary debates have come from scholars working beyond the classic confines of English departments or the traditional European focus of many Comparative Literature departments. Scholars have gone against the persistent and limiting prevalence of English (Mufti 2016; Tiwari 2021), and from the fields of Latin Americanism and Spanish, scholars have pointed out the inadequacy of many mainstream world literature theories, particularly when it comes to adequately accounting for Latin American literature (Sánchez Prado 2021: 2).

While critical of many of the mainstream theories, Ignacio Sánchez Prado, nevertheless, makes an important case for the relevance of engaging in these discussions from the perspective of Latin Americanism (or, even more specialized, Mexican and Central American studies). He advocates for this critical engagement not in a notion of catchup but rather grounded in the singular position of Latin American literature and intellectual disposition and outlook since he finds that world literature theory "provides critical tools to account for the region's complex history of cosmopolitanism, as well as its paradoxical status as belonging both to the Global South (or the Third

World, or the postcolonial world) and to Western culture" (2018: 8). By the same token, Mariano Siskind stresses the multidirectional quality of Latin American writing vis-à-vis "the world" when he argues that "cosmopolitan discourses and maneuvers [by Latin American authors of specific periods] were strategic, self-conscious, calculated attempts to take part in, contest, overwrite, and redirect the global hegemony of modern culture, in deliberate opposition to local forms of nationalistic, Hispanophile or racially based hegemonies" (2014: 21). A proliferation of books in recent years has provided original scholarship that puts Latin American literature in the center of analysis and theorization, expanding the field via concepts such as "deseo de mundo" (Siskind 2014), "strategic occidentalism" (Sánchez Prado 2018), and "the global Latin American novel" (Hoyos 2017) and via detailed analysis of key institutions and presses (Locane 2019; Müller 2021). These contributions to world literary theories from the angle of Latin Americanism move the field forward from the tendency to see world literature as revolving around one single monolithic center (e.g., Paris, English, the West)—also still problematically prevalent in the positions of the WReC and their ideas of one single modernity—and toward a more accurate vision, namely that world literature deals rather with "global interlinkages in a polycentric world" (Müller 2021: 5).

The chameleonic nature of world literature also spotlights other epistemic dimensions: the question of the world itself, the thingness of world and literature, and the position of the reader. What do we mean when we speak of "the world"? Is "world" even a clearly defined and conceivable object? Is there only one or aren't there rather many worlds? In *What Is a World? On Postcolonial Literature as World Literature* (2016), Pheng Cheah has articulated many of these questions, proposing a normative theory of literature arguing that literature itself is engaged in continuous processes of world-making. In a similar vein, scholars have argued against the tendency of "many approaches to world literature [that] conceptualize it as a factually existing object" (Sánchez Prado 2021: 1). Instead, they have insisted on world literature's inherent "constructedness" (Müller 2021: 1). Needless to say, the meaning of world literature, *literatura mundial* or *littérature-monde*, also changes according to the locus and language of enunciation. World literature, and its iterations in other languages, often means merely literature "that is not one's own," meaning the literature of the Other, written in languages and countries not claimed by the reader. As such, in Spanish, historically speaking, *literatura mundial* has first and foremost meant literature that is penned outside of the Spanish-speaking world, signaling an otherness, foreignness, worldliness to be consumed by Latin American audiences via extensive collections of works from all over the globe and periods translated into Spanish.

Augusto Monterroso, the informal patron saint of this volume, illustrates this fickle complexity. In one of his stories, "Cómo me deshice de quinientos libros" (How I Got Rid of 500 Books, included in *Movimiento perpetuo*), the narrator talks about his futile efforts to get rid of part of his extensive personal library. After determining which books will be discarded, he makes piles and labels them. When it comes to works of fiction, he only makes two distinctions: "literatura mundial, 14; literatura hispanoamericana, 86" ([1972] 2002: 77). For him, *literatura mundial* is a clear object. It is also the literature of the Other, of the non-Spanish-speaking and non-Latin American world. In this volume, however, Monterrosso's writing is discussed in the more contemporary conceptions of world literature, focusing on questions of circulation, translation, and networks as well as literary style and innovation. Just before the boom of revolutionary literature facilitated Central American literature's wider circulation across the globe, Monterroso became famous in part by reinventing a classic genre: the fable. In *La oveja negra y demás fábulas*, he created a formidable lineup of deeply afflicted, tragic and hilarious world literary animals: black sheep, scapegoats, failed monkey satirists, fleas dreaming of becoming Cervantes, and color-confused chameleons ([1969] 2004). The fable of the chameleon is a play on the Spanish idiomatic expression "todo es según el color del cristal con que se mira" (attributed to the Spanish aphorist Ramón de Campoamor y Campoosorio), which is similar in meaning to the proverbial "beauty is in the eye of the beholder." The chameleon gets confused when other animals start using colored glass shards to look at it, thus undermining his color adaptions and mimicry. In the end, it no longer knows which color to turn into. Riffing off Monterroso's fables, the chameleon is thus the tongue-in-cheek spirit animal for this volume and the ever-changing colors and contours of world literature. An Afro-Euroasian animal exotic and foreign in the Americas, the chameleon serves as a stubborn reminder of an intriguing conceptual difficulty: What are we talking about when we speak of world literature and where? On what surface, background, context does the chameleon rest? What colored glass shard are we looking through when discussing world literature?

Given the overabundance of definitions, readers of this volume will not find a commonly shared definition of world literature. Instead, as the volume editor, I asked authors to clarify in their individual articles what they mean by world literature or how they engage with the term. Written by a mix of established and up-and-coming scholars on the basis of invitations and an open call aided via an intensive conference-workshop and review process, the contributions find diverse answers and methodologies to the task of approaching key issues of world literary debates through the lens of Central American literature, meaning the literatures of Guatemala, Nicaragua, Costa Rica, Panama, El Salvador, Honduras, Belize, and the Central American diasporas. Via their expertise, this volume explores a range of questions. What does it mean then to think about world literature with and through Central American literatures? How do Central American literatures challenge, expand, or contract the notion of world literature? What is the meaning of world and literary world-making in the context of the heterogeneous Central American literatures?

The Specificities of Central American World Literature(s)

As elusive as the categories of Central America and world literature appear to be, when brought together, insights emerge about Central American literature, about world literature debates, and about the diverse set of angles and dimensions of the specifics of Central American world literature(s).

For one, while often discussed as marginal, what is actually more astounding is the latent (if unacknowledged) centrality of Central America in some of the key books on world literature. David Damrosch, for instance, dedicates an entire chapter to Rigoberta Menchú's writings and circulation in *What Is World Literature?* (2003). And in what is arguably the most important monograph on Latin American world literature to date, Siskind dedicates two of five chapters to Central American fin de siècle writers: the Nicaraguan Rubén Darío (1867–1916) and the Guatemalan Enrique Gómez Carillo (1873–1927). Yet in both books, Central America as a *region* is noticeably and largely absent (as is Central Americanist scholarship). Darío, Gómez Carillo, and Menchú are seen as having outgrown Central America and entered the world/universal. One could say that this is by design, given that Darío and Gómez Carillo themselves often seemed to want to leave the isthmus behind. Didn't Rubén Darío inaugurate this attitude when he portrayed himself as "asqueado y espantado" (disgusted and terrified) by his homeland's lack of social and political life and adopted Argentina as "un magnífico refugio" (a magnificent refuge, quoted in Ramírez 54, my translation)? But the point that this volume aims to make is that Central American authors cannot and often do not want to escape the isthmus; rather, it is the marking identity in how they relate to the world, whatever their world(s) might be. The Guatemalan-Honduran author Monterroso, exiled in Mexico most of his life, could have easily acquired Mexican nationality and status but he did not want to. He chose to be seen and read as a Guatemalan or Central American author. Darío, too, after the swans and princesses of his earlier poetry with its gaze firmly turned toward Europe, whiteness, or European-tinged orientalism, returned later to the profane prose-poetry that denounced US imperialism in Central America. These nuances get lost if critics do not take Central American intellectual constellations and Central Americanist scholarship into account, instead discussing these authors in the realm of the supposed universal, as world literature debates so often do.

Let me take Damrosch's reading of Menchú as an example. His objective of reading not only Menchú's famous 1983 testimonio but also her less-studied and more recent book *Rigoberta Menchú: La nieta de los mayas* (1998, Crossing Borders), over which she had much more authorial control, is commendable. Yet the insights and conclusions he draws are surprisingly trite. For instance, Damrosch presents the following as one of his most important findings about Menchú's work: "the real surprise to emerge from Stoll's research is not that [Menchú's] book is so literary but that it is so *worldly* ... Menchú distilled real-life events into an emblematic, quasi-novelistic account intended to have direct real-world effects, as indeed it did" (2003: 238–9, italics in original). For one, this erroneously credits Stoll's controversial and biased anthropological research with "uncovering" what was always clear to most Latin Americanists, namely that the testimonio genre is an acutely worldly, political literary genre written and produced always with the objective of having a direct impact on the extraliterary world. Second, it shows a lack of serious engagement with Arturo Arias's more nuanced and illuminating analysis of the misreadings of Menchú in the United States (especially those from his 2007 book *Taking Their Word*, all of which were already published in article form in 2002 and 2003, when Damrosch's book came out). In addition, in Damrosch's account, Guatemala appears merely as the place where Menchú, despite being world famous, surprisingly, it seems, still lives, and not as the country to which she has dedicated a life of political struggle: "Rigoberta Menchú is one of the most international of contemporary authors, her work produced for a global audience and often written on her laptop while traveling the globe. Yet she also maintains deeply tied to a small country where she still lives" (2003: 259).

This remark, however, aptly highlights some of the tensions that exist between national and world literatures. In their translations of Auerbach's conceptualization of *Weltliteratur*, Maire and Edward Said call it "a visionary concept, for it transcends national literatures without, at the same time, destroying their individualities" (Said and Said in Auerbach 1969: 1). The question of specificity and transcendence is also what I want to highlight in this volume. Central American literature is, of course, not a national literature; it is a regional literature that encompasses seven nation-states and the diaspora, but it is important to acknowledge and engage with the specificity of this region's literature. What does it mean then to approach the idea and polemics about the world literature paradigm from a Central Americanist perspective?

For one, focusing on Central American world literature means centering different genres than those that usually dominate current world literature debates, in particular the modern and contemporary novel and, to a lesser degree, classical epics or dramas. The novel plays a much less exalted role in discussions of Central American literature (even though there are, of course, key Central American novelists that have circulated widely in translation and beyond the isthmus, especially Miguel Ángel Asturias, Sergio Ramírez, Gioconda Belli, Horacio Castellanos Moya, and Rodrigo Rey Rosa). The genres that stand out when it comes to Central American world literature are poetry, short story, and the testimonio. The importance of poetry indeed shines through in this volume, as it is the most analyzed genre throughout its chapters, be it that of well-known poets Darío, Roque Dalton and Ernesto Cardenal; of lesser-known, but equally important, Black, Indigenous, queer, or migrant voices, such as those of Carlos Rigby, Rosa Chavéz, Humberto Ak'abal, Manuel Tzoc Bucup, Amado Chan, Javier Zamora, and Roy G. Guzmán; as well as of non-Central American poets, Blaise Cendrars and Wallace Stevens. Similarly, the short story is so vital to Central American letters that some of the authors in this volume venture to theorize a "world literature in minor key" by analyzing the strategic and innovative writing of authors who firmly position themselves as speaking to the universal from the smallness and marginality of Central America and through the brevity of a genre considered minor. The importance of these shorter genres can also be seen as a result of the material conditions of the literary field in Central America, where it is easier for authors to publish short pieces in newspapers and magazines than an extensive novel given the region's paltry book industry and middle class. And then there is, of course, the testimonio, the genre that outside of the isthmus has the greatest visibility. The testimonio was the dominant genre of committed literature in the 1980s in Central America, which featured (often mediated) witness accounts by subject positions previously unheard in Latin American literature. Its definition, scope, and aim have long been debated, especially in US academia and the "culture wars" of the 1990s. Next to poetry, the testimonio often became the Central American genre par excellence, especially in the context of the Anglo-American academia and European and US American solidarity movement. The testimonio is also intimately entangled with what Arias has called the "narrative textuality" of the region, underscoring that the divide between subaltern and lettered, oral and written spheres is less pronounced in Central America than in other parts of the world (2007: xiv).

Thinking about Central American world literature also returns the discussion to one of the central tenets of Goethe's conception of *Weltliteratur*, namely that it ushers in a new age of the waning importance of national literatures. In Central American literature, one key challenge to the nation-state and its literary apparatus arises in Indigenous and Black works that question the monolithic and simplistic narratives of Central American nation-states, which are clustered around whiteness, mestizaje, and Spanish. Indigenous and Black literatures from the region often look far beyond the nation-state and instead invoke cosmos, oceans, roots and routes, and languages other than Spanish and thus create fissures and cracks in any monolingual, monocultural, or geographically limited and limiting conception of the region's literatures. And while Central American nations often display or speak from a fervent nationalism (on the background of weak sovereignty and constant imperialist intervention on the isthmus from elsewhere), the lived reality of many of its writers often tells a very different story. It is overly common for Central American authors to have several national allegiances. Many writers were born and raised, or have lived in two different Central American countries or were forced to live in exile or migrate within or beyond the isthmus due to political persecution or personal life choices. Alexandra Ortiz Wallner has thus rightly identified a common tendency in Central American literature of it producing and becoming "literaturas sin residencia fija" (literatures without a fixed abode, 2013). I mention here only a few names as examples of a widespread tendency: Monterroso in Honduras, Guatemala, and Mexico; Castellanos Moya in Honduras, El Salvador, and the United States; Belli in Nicaragua, Costa Rica, and the United States; Claribel Alegría in Nicaragua and El Salvador; Franz Galich in Guatemala and Nicaragua; Mario Payeras in Guatemala and Mexico; Gloria Guardia in Panama, Venezuela, Colombia, and the United States; and Zee Edgell in Belize and the United States. Yet these writers maintain a strong (at times tumultuously) affective relationship with their homeland(s). This is why I continue to find Arias's purposely bilingual conception of Central America as a "space of afectividad" useful and illuminating. Central America is never just a geographical space (even though this is central for Central American positioning within the world) but also a space of "collective affection" and "emotional memory," and "grief, fear, hope, nostalgia, and compassion" are among the feelings that constitute the Central American subjectivities—also in the diaspora (Arias 2007: xx–xix).

The question of affect and politics foregrounds another key dimension of Central American world literature, namely the Cold War as a polycentric, multivocal, simultaneously local, national, and planetary world event and period, in which internationalism, solidarity movements, exile, adherence, and dissidence created new meanings of cosmopolitanism and *littérature engagée* and *dégagé*. Nicaragua, El Salvador, and Guatemala were critical and bloody battlefields of the so-called Cold War, and the impacts of this time continue to profoundly shape the region's literary output and outlook. Worlds were found(ed) and lost in the Cold War, and the literature in Central America is still trying to remake its worlds after the war's end. The close of the Cold War and the guerrilla period was also a loss of the utopian imagination, as Jean Franco pointed out in her now classic study on the Cold War in the Latin America, *The Decline and Fall of the Lettered City* (2002: 260), in which Central American literature—once again—plays a vital role.

And to close with the most obvious and crucial aspect, thinking Central American literature and world literature in the same volume means that questions of inequality, power, and access are particularly pronounced or magnified. On this point, Franco also develops the idea of "peripheral phantasies" and discusses the "deep sense of alienation that comes from being off-center" and "both the desire of the periphery for recognition and the deep sense of futility at the inability to overcome the constitutive exclusion of Latin America from the universal" (2002: 9). While Franco discusses this marginality in relation to all of Latin American literature, nowhere on the continent is the sense of belonging to the periphery more pronounced than in Central America. This is not just because it is the proverbial periphery of the periphery but also because of its exalted position within the world economy, which leads to a simultaneous and particularly searing center-periphery position. On the one hand, it is seen as a forgotten "outpost in the tropics" (Arias 2007: 5) but on the other hand, is a nodal point of world commerce (the interoceanic canal) and intimately tied to the whims of the world market (via cash crops such as coffee, banana, and pineapple). In that sense, if one follows the WReC's conception of world-literature, aren't all the banana and canal novels and poems pivotal pieces of the actual "literature of the modern capitalist world-system," even though the WReC does not discuss them?

Equally, the literary field in Central America is, in general, precarious but this then again contrasts ever more sharply with the high global visibility of some (Darío, Asturias, Cardenal, Menchú, Belli). The region has a limited publishing industry and writers publishing with small presses are pitted against a few writers who tower above the rest due to their international distribution with major transnational publishing houses. Against the splendor and might of Latin America's quintessential lettered cities, Mexico, Lima, Buenos Aires, any notion of the lettered city always appears as tenuous in Central America. In *La république mondiale des lettres* (1999, The World Republic of Letters 2007), Pascale Casanova develops the idea of "small," as in "literarily deprived," regions (2007: 181). And while I bristle at the prejudiced and deterministic sound of this designation, the image of literary deprivation and smallness crops up throughout Central American authors' writings about the region. The lettered city emerges often in the form of a small library in the jungle, fondly curated and cherished yet in a perilous state—be it José Coronel Urtecho's book shelf of US poetry in his finca at the banks of the San Juan River or the small collection of books kept by Payeras and his guerrilla comrades in the Guatemalan jungle, quickly devoured and destroyed by the rain forest's insects, fungi, and humidity. Another image of literary deprivation appears in the limited and autodidactic yet significantly cosmopolitan-canonical literary education of Central American writers. Monterroso, for example, recalls that his education consisted of the few books he could find at the national library in Guatemala, a library so poor that according to him it only had "good books" (meaning, for him, old classics). The Maya Quiché poet Ak'abal narrates that his literary education comes from books that he found in the trash in Guatemala City (many of them foreign or in other languages). These images also underscore inequalities on multiple levels: the lack of resources in the public library, the barriers to education and the differences in opportunities and access to books and formal training between an Indigenous man and a non-Indigenous in early- to mid-twentieth-century Guatemala. Yet all these anecdotes also portray literature as in equal parts precious and precarious in the Central American literary imagination.

Working on the topic of world literature from regions generally less visible in these debates entails stressing and repeating the dominance of the previous scholarship while also forging new critical entry points. In the present volume "the dominating voices in the World Literature pantheon— Pascale Casanova, Franco Moretti, besides the ubiquitous David Damrosch and Emily Apter" appear again and again (de Medeiros 2020: 18). It thus runs the risk of repeating the Euro/US/French centrism of comparative and world literature debates, which often still operate under a problematic paradigm: "On the one side the European tradition in the general humanities holding the place of an exemplary, implicitly universal form from which theoretical models can be generated; on the other side all non-Western languages in the more specialized realm of area studies, holding the place of raw material, as it were, on which these theoretical models can be applied" (Melas 2006: 32). The volume finds its most powerful answers to these issues when it engages Maya and Caribbean theories, be it cosmolectics, textual designs, Rastafarianism, or Édouard *Glissant*'s poetry of relation. It is in these chapters that a polycentric, nonhierarchical, pluricultural vision of world literature emerges that surpasses previous theorizations, informed by the multitude of Central American textual narratives. And in other chapters that do engage explicitly with the theories of the "World Literature pantheon" emerge nuance, clarification, and critique—all of which are desperately needed in the face of the often sweeping claims made by the pantheon's chief telamons and caryatids.

Organization

This volume proposes to think Central American world literature via three themes: modes, constellations, and routes. Instead of a chronological or comprehensive approach, the volume is organized thematically given that the region is comprised of seven pluricultural and multilingual nation-states, diasporas, East-West, and South-North migrations and impacted by the lingering presence of different imperial powers. The volume addresses some canonical authors, precisely those that tower above the rest in terms of international visibility, but it also purposefully invites many readings from the geographical, racial, or linguistic margins of Central American literature to underscore the breadth and depth of Central American world literature. I find that it is in the complex interplay of this literary and theoretical richness that the two elusive categories, world literature and Central American literature, come to shine and illuminate each other.

The volume's first part discusses modes of reading and writing Central American literatures as world literatures. It opens with a powerful appeal and decolonial intervention for reading Maya literatures in Guatemala and Belize, not via Western concepts of world literature but through Mayan concepts and thinkers. Rita M. Palacios and Paul M. Worley propose Xocom Balumil, a cosmolectical Maya textile design and concept meaning "sides of the earth," to analyze the writings and narrative textualities and performances of Rosa Chávez, Manuel Tzoc Bucup, Amado Chan, and Negma Coy. The second chapter then proposes the idea of a world literature in minor key as a literature of extraordinary and strategic originality that harnesses the power of smallness (of genre, region, press, or stature) to circulate via expected and unexpected avenues. Paying special attention to a genre often sidelined in mainstream world literature debates—the short story—Ignacio Sarmiento Panez, and I discuss the stories of Monterroso and those of the contemporary Salvadoran writer Claudia Hernández as paradigmatic examples of this strategy. The third chapter by Tamara de Inés Antón hones in on the genre most associated with twentieth-century writing and reading from and about Central America: the testimonio. De Inés Antón pays attention to an aspect so far largely overlooked in the extensive and controversial discussions on the genre: the question of translation. In particular, she shows how two of the most famous testimonios from the 1980s—Rigoberta Menchú's and that about a female guerrilla fighter named Eugenia in El Salvador by Nicaraguan-Salvadoran writer Claríbel Alegría and US American writer Darwin J. Flakoll—have been severely altered in their English translations in order to cater to reading expectations, preferences, and the limited knowledge of Western English-speaking audiences. The chapter questions to what degree the controversies surrounding the testimonio genre in the United States are owed to not only deliberate (gendered) misreadings but also mistranslations and to nuances lost in translation. The section closes with a discussion of the most recent Central American global literary success story: the autofictions of Guatemalan author Eduardo Halfon. Underscoring the inequality of world literary systems, Magdalena Perkowska provocatively asks whether Halfon's easy insertion within world literary circuits is extraordinary or rather predictable, owing principally to an activation of discourses on memory and the Holocaust, and thus issues of primordial interest in the current cultural imagination of Europe and the United States. She makes this argument via a critical assessment of world literary theory and meticulous attention to differences in edition and translation in the English, French, Polish, German, and Dutch versions of Halfon's stories.

The second part of the volume is dedicated entirely to divergent cosmopolitan constellations. It opens up with an intervention on the meanings of cosmopolitanism in Darío and their subsequent disillusionment during his time in Paris. Darío, who put not only Nicaragua and Central America but all of Latin America on the (world literary) map via his modernista poetry written in Spanish by a poet from the former colonies, is a key figure in Siskind's seminal work on cosmopolitan desires in Latin American literature. With his chapter, Carlos F. Grigsby enters into a sustained dialogue with Siskind's work while also offering important corrections and nuances to his argument, namely that Darío was far more critical of and disillusioned with a francocentric cosmopolitanism than most critics acknowledge. The three chapters that follow are dedicated to cosmopolitan constellations of Central American Cold War literature. Carolyn Fornoff analyzes the speculative short stories of Salvadoran writer Álvaro Menen Desleal, arguing that he constitutes an anomaly in Central American Cold War literature since he preferred speculative, fantastic, and planetary registers in contrast to his contemporaries in El Salvador and Guatemala who favored realist, localized, rural, and leftist-aligned committed literature. Fornoff argues against views that see his work as escapist and apolitical and instead underscores his "speculative planetary imagination" as a different dimension of Central American world and Cold War literature. She thus proposes a potent critique of Central Americanism as tending to favor revolutionary, localized, and realist literature over other modes of literary writing and speculation. This chapter is then followed by an analysis of the postnational political worlds of the prototypical member of the Committed Generation: Marxist poet and militant Roque Dalton. Yansi Pérez positions Dalton's leftist internationalist cosmopolitanism as an example of the "imaginary affective-communal space that proposes alternative forms to understand, feel, and imagine the common." She sees this represented in Dalton's images of leftist outsiders and foreigners meeting in a tavern in Prague in the years just before the 1968 invasion of the country by Soviet and Warsaw Pact countries. And just as Czechoslovakia plays a key role in Dalton's novel, Czech writer Milan Kundera plays a key role in the intertextual universe of Castellanos Moya's dissident literature, as analyzed by Tamara L. Mitchell. Mitchell approaches the work of the Honduran-Salvadoran postwar writer from two critical world literature angles: strategic intertextuality and untranslatability. Mitchell shows how Castellanos Moya establishes hemispheric parity in his work via intertextual references to writers from Central and Eastern Europe. In addition, she shows how changes in different editions and translations of his novel *La diáspora* underscore questions of untranslatability and time. This section on cosmopolitan constellations closes with a reflection on the cosmolectical nature of Indigenous literature, which presents a unique ontology about the relation between society, nature, and cosmos that challenges conventional conceptions of world literature. Gloria Chacón develops this argument via a reflection on the pluriversal poetry and the cosmopolitanism of the Maya Quiché writer Ak'abal.

The third part is focused on the different routes and spatial-affective dimensions of Central American literature as world literature. In the first chapter of this section, Harris Feinsod puts the Panama Canal at the center of his analysis. Via literary texts from authors both from and beyond the isthmus, he proposes the passage through this key area of world trade and US imperialism as having created its own multilingual literature: canal zone modernism. Tatiana Argüello follows with another chapter on the significance of maritime waters in the Central American world literary imagination. She provides an important reading of the notoriously overlooked Nicaraguan Afro-Caribbean poet Carlos Rigby via an appropriately pluricultural theoretical combination of ecocritical approaches, Édouard Glissant's poetics of relation, and reflections on Rastafarianism. These longitudinal routes are then followed by latitudinal routes and more recent dynamics of migration. Andrew Bentley analyzes the ever-growing contemporary corpus of writing by US Central Americans and argues that these create a transnational space of resistance and solidarity via an imaginary of Central America as part of the Global South, negatively affected by war and migration. The book closes with Robert McKee Irwin's discussion of the recent testimonial play, *Caravaneros* written by Douglas Oviedo, one of the Honduran migrants who was part of the 2018 collective mass migrations from Central America to the United States, in which thousands of migrants joined together to walk the perilous journey through Mexico toward the US border. McKee Irwin finds that the actions by these migrants and the text by Oviedo are part of a cosmopolitan world-making from below and that the "stateless genre" of migrant literature transforms the members of the migrant caravan into citizens of the world. As they leave their previous national affiliations behind, migranthood becomes their primary subjectivity. The edited volume thus closes with an outlook that returns to the utopian and humanist dimensions of world literature via that very Central American of literary modes: the testimonial voice and the atypical *letrado*.

The present volume, guided as it is in spirit by the quirks of Monterroso's ever-shifting, slightly color-confused chameleon, also offers other entry points and paths of reading. Even though the articles are organized in these three thematic parts, they also communicate among each other beyond those sections. I thus also invite readers to read in diagonal pairs, for example the peripheral cosmopolitanism and community from below in both Dalton and Oviedo (chapters by Pérez and McKee Irwin), the question of translation in the chapters by de Inés Antón, Perkowska, and Mitchell, or those on indigenous world literary concepts (chapters by Palacios and Worley and Chacón). Both orderly readings and zigzag readings are encouraged as readers delve into this very first book thinking Central American literatures as world literatures in their prismatic complexity.

References

Apter, E. S. (2013), *Against World Literature: On the Politics of Untranslatability*, London and New York: Verso.

Arias, A. (2007), *Taking Their Word. Literature and the Signs of Central America*, Minneapolis, London: University of Minnesota Press.

Auerbach, E. (1969), "Philology and 'Weltliteratur'," translated by M. Said and E. Said, *The Centennial Review*, 13 (1): 1–17.

Casanova, P. (2007), *The World Republic of Letters*, translated by M. B. DeBevoise. First Harvard University Press paperback edition. Convergences Inventories of the Present, Cambridge, Massachusetts London, England: Harvard University Press.

Cheah, P. (2016), *What Is a World? On Postcolonial Literature as World Literature*, Durham: Duke University Press.

Damrosch, D. (2003), *What Is World Literature?* Princeton, NJ: Princeton University Press.

Deckard, S., N. Lawrence, N. Lazarus, G. Macdonald, U. Pablo Mukherjee, B. Parry, S. Shapiro, and W. Research Collective, eds. (2015), *Combined and Uneven Development: Towards a New Theory of World-Literature*. Postcolonialism across the Disciplines 17. Liverpool: Liverpool University Press.

Delgado, L. (2010), "La biblioteca en la selva: modernidad y vanguardia en los relatos autobiográficos centroamericanos," in V. G. Pla and R. Baldovinos (eds.), *Tensiones de la modernidad: Del modernismo al realismo—Tomo II*, 35–56, Guatemala: F&G Editores.

Franco, J. (2002), *The Decline and Fall of the Lettered City: Latin America in the Cold War*, Cambridge, Mass: Harvard University Press.

Galich, F. (2004), "Desde el centro de la periferia de la periferia. Reflexiones de un subalterno letrado," *Istmo. Revista virtual de estudios literarios y culturales centroamericanos*. Available online: http://istmo.denison.edu/n08/foro/centro.html.

Helgesson, S. and M. R. Thomsen (2020), *Literature and the World*, London; New York: Routledge. Taylor & Francis Group.

Hoyos Ayala, H. (2017), *Beyond Bolaño: The Global Latin American Novel*, New York: Columbia University Press.

Khomitsky, M. (2013), "World Literature, Soviet Style: A Forgotten Episode in the History of the Idea," *Ab Imperio* (3): 119–54. Available online: https://doi.org/doi:10.1353/imp.2013.0075.

Liano, D. (2008), "Centroamérica Cultural/Literaria: ¿Comarca, Región, Zona, Naciones?" in W. Mackenbach (ed.), *Intersecciones y Transgresiones: Propuestas Para Una Historiografía Literaria En Centroamérica*, I:51–66, Hacia Una Historia de Las Literaturas Centroamericana, Guatemala: F&G Editores.

Locane, J. J. (2019), *De la literatura latinoamericana a la literatura (latinoamericana) mundial: Condiciones materiales, procesos y actores. De la literatura latinoamericana a la literatura (latinoamericana) mundial*. De Gruyter. Available online: https://doi.org/10.1515/9783110622096.

Medeiros, P. de (2020), "Mia Couto and the Antinomies of World-Literature," in K. Van Haesendonck (ed.), *The Worlds of Mia Couto*, 11–31, Oxford, Bern, Berlin, Burxelles, New York, Wien: Peter Lang.

Melas, N. (2006), *All the Difference in the World*, Stanford: Stanford University Press.
Monterroso, A. (1969), *La oveja negra y demás fábulas*, 10th edition, Mexico City: Ediciones Era.
Monterroso, A. ([1972] 2002), *Movimiento perpetuo*, Mexico City: Punto de lectura.
Moretti, F. (2000), "Conjectures on World Literature," *New Left Review* (1): 54–68.
Mufti, A. (2016), *Forget English! Orientalisms and World Literatures*, Cambridge, Massachusetts London, England: Harvard University Press.
Müller, G. (2021), *How Is World Literature Made? The Global Circulations of Latin American Literatures*. De Gruyter. Available online: https://doi.org/10.1515/9783110748383.
Ortiz Wallner, A. (2013), "Literaturas sin residencia fija: Poéticas del movimiento en la novelística centroamericana contemporánea," *Revista Iberoamericana*, 79 (242): 149–62.
Rodríguez, A. P. (2009), *Dividing the Isthmus. Central American Transnational Histories, Literatures, and Cultures*, Austin: University of Texas Press.
Sánchez Prado, I. M. (2018), *Strategic Occidentalism: On Mexican Fiction, the Neoliberal Book Market, and the Question of World Literature*, Evanston, Illinois: Northwestern University Press.
Sánchez Prado, I. M., ed. (2021), *Mexican Literature as World Literature*, Literatures as World Literature, New York: Bloomsbury Academic.
Siskind, M. (2014), *Cosmopolitan Desires: Global Modernity and World Literature in Latin America*, FlashPoints, Evanston, IL: Northwestern University Press.
Tiwari, B. (2021), *Beyond English: World Literature and India*, Literatures as World Literature. New York: Bloomsbury Academic.

PART ONE

Modes

1

Reorienting the World: Reading Maya Literatures through *Xocom Balumil*

Rita M. Palacios and Paul M. Worley

Scholars and critics of Latin American literary studies often ignore or pay little attention to the literary production of Central America, and Indigenous literatures like those written by Maya peoples in the peripheries of these already marginalized national literatures are further obscured. Moreover, even when included, Central American national literatures tend to reproduce the goals and "vices" of nationalism, which result in the homogenization and erasure (genocide in the worst of cases) of Indigenous voices that do not comfortably fit a nation-state model. In this article we build on the work of the Kaqchikel intellectual Aura Cumes and on our book *Unwriting Maya Literature*, arguing that one can use a Maya textile design for the cosmos known as *xocom balumil*,[1] or the "sides of the earth," to resituate these literatures within processes of literary production that transcend, defy, and even ignore contemporary borders and nation-states. At its core, our work to date has focused on different conceptualizations of what we refer to as "writing" in English, and in our book we use the Maya word *ts'íib* to construct a literary criticism that privileges Maya understandings of "writing," such that diverse texts ranging from textiles to pre-Hispanic codices can be understood as literary works. By looking at xocom balumil, here our focus is the term "world." As xocom balumil is a depiction of the planet Earth oriented toward the sun's movement and horizons of east/west as opposed to the set hierarchical points of north/south, this approach not only allows us to consider Maya literatures from within their own epistemologies and ontologies but offers a framework from which a polycentric, nonhierarchical theory of world literature may be built. It is also important to note that gender is a key dimension of weaving: as we pointed out in *Unwriting Maya Literature*, weaving and embroidery are considered activities almost exclusively performed by women. As creator and interpreter of designs like xocom balumil, each Maya weaver is, in the words of Tsotsil poet Ruperta Bautista, a *jchapanej kuxlejal*, an "artisan, artist, maker, builder, erecter of life" and, we would add, an architect of worlds (Worley and Palacios 2019: 52–61, 80). This follows Aura Cumes's analysis of Indigenous women's struggle, where Indigenous women are not merely fighting for ethnic or gender equality but are in fact "creators of liberating forms of life" (2012: 15). After outlining our approach, we argue that through xocom balumil, we can read the works of Maya authors Rosa Chávez, Manuel Tzoc Bucup, Amado Chan, and Negma Coy as the articulation of a pluri-centered, borderless world.

Xocom Balumil

As noted by Cherokee Nation scholar Jace Weaver, Indigenous worldviews challenge Euro-Western notions that tend to privilege linearity and hierarchy on a global scale. Indeed, he describes Indigenous Peoples as being "polycentric," stating that "a tribe ... did not see itself as having a monopoly on truth." In Weaver's words, "each group believed that they had their original instructions, as did every other tribal group. If each tribe lived in accordance with these instructions, all would be well" (2011: 101). Hemispherically, Weaver's idea that Indigenous Peoples are polycentric, or have many different centers, resonates with the Zapatista slogan concerning their desire for a "Mundo donde quepan muchos mundos" (a world where many worlds may fit), as well as with the fact, as noted by Stefano Varese (unmarked),[2] that Indigenous cosmologies are "*cosmocéntricas* y *policéntricas* basadas en la lógica de la diversidad y en la lógica de la reciprocidad. Este es un cosmos diverso, en el que no hay centro privilegiado, ni singularidad hegemónica" ("*cosmocentric* and *polycentric*, based on logics of diversity and reciprocity"). This is a diverse cosmos in which there is neither privileged center nor hegemonic singularity (2018)). Scholarship concerning Indigenous textiles notes that these same concepts of a polycentric cosmos are found in designs whose shapes even suggest concepts from non-Euclidian geometry and the notion that even the smallest piece of the cosmos is nonetheless a complete reflection of the whole (Gil Corredor 2020: 81–7; Worley and Palacios 2019: 46–7).

Drawing upon this scholarship, we assert that the textile design from the Highlands of Chiapas, xocom balumil, provides us with a graphic representation of what a polycentric understanding of the world looks like, with the world it depicts not so much centerless but filled with the possibility of infinite, moving centers. In the design, the central diamond is flanked on four sides by diamonds, altogether representing the cardinal directions: east, west, north, south, and center. As Walter Morris points out in his book on the iconography of Highland Maya textiles, however, the bands emanating out from the center diamond echo the design for the butterfly, which is itself a metaphor for the sun in movement as it journeys to the underworld (2009: 42). In *Unwriting Maya Literature* we point out

FIGURE 1.1 Yocts'i, *which is a design highlighting the interior of xocom balumil or* chikin balamil. *Design by María Elena Pérez Hernández (Tsotsil from Ch'enalo), 2020. Reproduced with the permission of the artist.*

that this sense of movement implies that the design is a two-dimensional representation of four-dimensional space/time, with the sun simultaneously rising, at its zenith, setting, and at its nadir (Worley and Palacios 2019: 46). Further, the small lines that connect the diamonds at the top and bottom of the design to the diamond in the center cement these as representing both the directions east/west and the path the sun takes on its infinite journey in the sky.

In *Time and the Highland Maya*, Barbara Tedlock (unmarked) notes that "none of the contemporary Mayan directions are precisely equivalent to our Western notion of horizontally fixed cardinal points" (1992: 176). While the notions of east/west in Maya languages refer to the movement of the sun, no specific equivalent terms for north/south have been registered in dictionaries for half of all Maya languages (178). Interestingly, terms referring to north/south directions may be place-specific as they note regional weather phenomena or topography. For the Kaqchikel people of the Lake Atitlán region, for example, *xocomil* denotes both the notion of south and the dangerous afternoon winds that come from that direction and make passage across the lake difficult (176). This conception of placeness in the world provides a sense of universality (the trajectory of the sun) while at the same time integrating a sense of locality or specificity (such as regional weather phenomena).

In many ways, then, the design contests Euro-Western understandings of geography and human existence, much along the lines of what Colombian scholar Miguel Rocha Vivas (unmarked) has referred to as *visiones de cabeza* or mirrored visions, which "represent a particular kind of ideosymbolic production that tends to or aspires to subvert and expose conventional, stereotyped, dominant, or hegemonic perspectives and readings on or about Indigenous peoples" (2021: 26–7). He then goes on to say that the mirrored visions examined in his book, *Mingas de la palabra*, "tend to emphasize disenchantment with modernity, but also images of contrast that appropriate modernity itself" (Rocha Vivas 2021: 27). Similarly, the xocom balumil design resists being reduced to conventional perspectives about Indigenous Peoples and Indigenous thought by suggesting other conceptualizations of place and belonging in terms of east/west as opposed to north/south. That is, it does not simply invert the poles of power and privilege, elevating the south over the north, but upends this almost binary sense of either/or altogether, replacing these with directions that are equally an unbounded horizon and typically defined in terms of natural processes associated with the rising/setting of the sun. Further, unlike north and south, defining east/west as where the sun rises and sets recognizes that these are not, in fact, fixed points throughout the year as the earth tilts on its axis. Xocom balumil thus turns one toward an existence focused on endless process and becoming instead of fixity.

Xocom Balumil and a Many-Centered World Literature

Before looking at how contemporary Maya authors may use the philosophy behind xocom balumil in their works, we would like to reiterate how this design defies how we think of or define "world literature." From its inception, one finds struggles over definitions of the "world" in world literature. In the early 1800s, the German writer Johann Wolfgang von Goethe famously coined the term. And while obviously groundbreaking in terms of his formulation of a global literary tradition that circulates across national boundaries, we would suggest that it is precisely his famous emphasis on the nation and national character as the primary units of affiliation that, among other things, give us pause. Concepts associated with "the nation" are, without a doubt, European notions of knowing, organizing, and defining the "world."

In his somewhat ironically titled *The Cherokee Nation: A History*, for example, the Cherokee Nation novelist Robert J. Conley describes how before the European invasion of the continent, "there was no Cherokee Nation as we know it today. There were simply many Cherokee towns," before going on to state that "[w]e do know that the Cherokees would not have a central government again [after the overthrow of the priest class] until after the arrival of the Europeans, when the Cherokee Nation evolved in reaction to new circumstances and needs" (2005: 11). That is, at least for Conley, Indigenous nations as they are known and understood today are a necessary response to European colonization. For Aura Estela Cumes, the possibility of a nation and a nationalism that includes or comes from Indigenous People is nonetheless a red flag given that it would mean an imitation of existing models:

> I do not agree with the idea of Plurinational States or the creation of Indigenous nationalisms, if what they do is repeat the bad habits of European nationalisms, many of them involving ethnocide and genocide. I am more in favor of an autonomy based on other, more suitable logics. Still, contemporary colonial-patriarchal Nation-States use their tremendous power to forbid these autonomies, and in the best of cases most accept the idea of "inclusion", a lethal trap for the existence of Indigenous, as this is [a] starting point for extending the Western, capitalistic, colonial and patriarchal ways of life.
>
> (Íñigo Clavo 2017)

In other words, the political practices of nations themselves tend to foreclose the very possibility of belonging and affinity outside of nationality, as concepts like "inclusion" are deployed to organize people according to existing national and nationalist paradigms. By doing so, these concepts obscure the fact that other ways of relating and being are not only possible but that they also have existed.

To take it one step further, we can see the anti-colonial calls for self-determination and autonomy of Maya thinkers in a similar light as Adom Getachew's (unmarked) broader understanding of Black Anglophone decolonial projects as "world-making" rather than nation-building, and in this manner reframe the study of Maya literatures through xocom balumil to honor a world that articulates itself according to the logic of its makers (Getachew 2019: 2). The notion of world-making proposed by Getachew sees alternatives to the dominant world system; that is, it envisions worlds not created in the likeness of those that are imposed by the West but worlds that are created to supersede existing models and are anti-imperialist and antistatist (4). Meanwhile, Pheng Cheah's (unmarked) framework of world-making in world literature privileges the idea of temporalization over spatiality, arguing for a common history and temporal thread that have brought us to the present day (2016: 8). While this framework is useful for examining world literatures that articulate themselves as Western or in terms of the West, other literatures articulate themselves following a conception of the world and world-making that respond to their own historical time. Cheah dismisses the possibility of coexisting temporalities (Western and non-Western), given that "[w]e cannot, however, undo the history of Western imperialism and colonialism by nostalgically recuperating romanticized precapitalist pasts" (2016: 12). Here we would argue that while Maya authors may be well attuned to the conditions of a world literature as defined by Cheah, their work does not merely draw on "alternative temporalities ... to contest the world created by different flows of global capital" (2016: 12). Rather, we would assert, these authors inhabit multiple temporalities and vie for multiple worlds in their work. As a textile design xocom balumil does not represent a nostalgic look at the past. Rather, it suggests the ongoing maintenance and development of a worldview whose presence can equally be found on the engraving of Lady Xoc on Yaxchilan's lintel 23, the clothing worn by Maya women today, or in the work of Maya writers who adopt its polycentric worldview.

Returning to the notion of the nation, particularly as a category through which one can understand or know an object like "the world," nations are not so much the natural evolution of human society but an obligation into which colonialism and globalization have forced all humans. As observed by Benedict Anderson (unmarked), far from fading away, "nation-ness is the most universally legitimate value in the political life of our time" (1983: 3). It is so natural that in the words of Ernest Gellner (unmarked), "[a] man must have a nationality as he must have a nose and two ears; a deficiency in any of these particulars is not inconceivable and does from time to time occur, but only as the result of some disaster, and it is itself a disaster of a kind," going on to recognize that "[h]aving a nation is not an inherent attribute of humanity, but it has now come to appear as such" (1983: 6). Given that the study of literature relies on the notion of the nation as an organizing principle from which to understand the world, the field's disciplinary practices tend to reproduce reactionary politics. As Joel Nickels (unmarked) points out at the beginning of *World Literatures and Geographies of Resistance*, these are some of the reasons why "'World literature' and 'resistance' seldom appear together in the same sentence" (2018: 1).

Nonetheless, literature can and does play an important role in resistance movements, particularly as these are related directly from territories in which they originate. Nickels goes on to point out that "[o]utside of the theoretical binaries we have constructed—nationalism on the one hand—there is an entire world of territorially-based struggles aimed at constructing forms of self-government outside of the state, maintaining power based in sustained conflict with the state, or assembling organs of struggle that are state-dystonic" (2018: 2). We would assert that Indigenous literatures, particularly those in Central America, tend to fall outside of these binaries, as well as tend to emphasize themes such as autonomy, sovereignty, and independence, whether we are discussing these in terms of their political, cultural, or linguistic aspirations. We say "tend to," of course, because no one theoretical construct or approach is capable of describing the totality of any given literature, especially one that by its very nature must confront the ongoing hegemony of colonial and imperial languages (Spanish and English in the case of all Central American nations with the exception of Belize, where English is the lingua franca) as well as the erasure of their own autochthonous forms of writing and forms of text, whether these be glyphs as in the case of Maya peoples in Mesoamerica or textual forms ranging from textiles and ceramics to petroglyphs and tattoos. As Nickels's analysis suggests, we must understand that these literatures are not simply struggles for a language, a voice, or a seat at the literary table, even though authors themselves frequently describe their work in these terms and scholars and critics frequently emphasize these aspects of these literatures.

Indigenous literatures and their languages are also inseparable from the territories in which they are created, with knowledge of and about territory being encoded in them, and vice versa. The value and utility of this information are, of course, far from theoretical. One only need recall US-based geographer Peter Herlihy's project to "empower Indigenous Peoples" by creating maps in Zapotec, one of the languages spoken in the Mexican state of Oaxaca, and the fact that it was later revealed that his research was funded by the US military (Araujo 2009). Given that, among other things, place names record the locations of natural resources and other aspects of Indigenous knowledge on the landscape itself, reasons for the military interest in the project and the community's backlash to it are obvious.

Of course, Indigenous connections to and relationships with land are frequently stereotyped throughout the hemisphere, particularly insofar as popular imaginings of "Indigenous ancestors" and the folklorization of Indigenous cultures can be mobilized to justify national projects. The power of such imaginings is perhaps best expressed when non-Indigenous people refer to Indigenous groups as "nuestros pueblos" or "our peoples," as if Indigenous Peoples were somehow a possession of a given nation. This situation, of course, has a profound impact on how Indigenous literatures are read. For instance, contemporary mestizo Mexican writers (such as Valeria Luiselli and those associated with the Crack group) intentionally "model themselves on a group of writers known for resisting the imperatives of nationalist literature" in order to be "exempt … from serving as a native informant of stereotypical Mexicanness" (Sánchez Prado 2018: 5). Yet this would be much more difficult for an Indigenous writer since Indigenous Peoples in Mexico and throughout Latin America are often constructed by their respective nation-states as constituting *the* root of their country's cultural capital and so by definition informants on national culture. The situation in Guatemala is not that much different, as the idea of a Maya indigeneity lies at the core of national identity and its corresponding literature and is key in the state's promise of a multicultural society. And even though postwar Guatemalan literature written by non-Indigenous authors reveals a deep discontent with the state and offers scathing critiques of the nation, an idealized sense of Mayaness remains front and center in most cases. Indigenous writers in Guatemala do not feel represented much less supported by the same state that decades earlier systematically set out to wipe Indigenous Peoples from the face of a mestizo Guatemala and which to date continues to criminalize and target many of the same communities in a push to access and exploit natural resources. Even as Indigenous Peoples are discriminated against and murdered through state policies ranging from neglect to military or police violence, in many ways Indigeneity refracted through ideologies of mestizaje is the very precondition for constructing the mestizo citizen-subject.

In literary terms, Indigenous writers are often seen as avatars of and informants about Indigenous Peoples in their own countries and in many ways set the terms for how the histories of their nations and nation-states are understood on a global stage. This articulation, of course, occurs even though the term "indigenous literature" is itself controversial and disputed among its so-identified, or pigeonholed, authors. For example, in 2019, Tsotsil critic and writer Mikel Ruíz called for moving beyond categories that define literature as Indigenous or not-Indigenous is one example; he was seconded by Nahua poet and cultural promoter Martín Tonalmeyotl who boldly and polemically stated that "La poesía indígena no existe" (Indigenous poetry does not exist) (Ruíz 2019; Tonalmeyotl 2019). For these writers, the label "Indigenous" is harmful and not representative of the many peoples who are the original inhabitants of Abiayala and, in the case of Tonalmeyotl, call for specificity. An example of this is a Facebook post by Tonalmeyotl, in which he repeats over fifteen times "No soy escritor indígena" (I'm not an Indigenous writer) and concludes with the statement "Soy escritor nahua" (I am a Nahua writer) (2021). The post was shared more than ninety times, including by well-known Maya authors who specified the communities to which they belong, privileging their own terms of affiliation and rejecting those imposed by the state. In what follows, we hope that our use of xocom balumil represents a move away from the national and its terms and toward polycentric Indigenous perspectives capable of embracing a wide array of human experience.

Xocom Balumil in the Work of Rosa Chávez, Manuel Tzoc Bucup, Amado Chan, and Negma Coy

To read the work of Rosa Chávez, Manuel Tzoc Bucup, Amado Chan, and Negma Coy through xocom balumil allows the reader to go beyond essentialisms and respect the unique land that these authors respond to and honor in their work. More than that, for Central American literature, and perhaps global literature as a whole, xocom balumil allows us to shift perspectives and gaze toward other possibilities that are more closely aligned with Indigenous thought thereby both acknowledging and discarding the real and symbolic dominance of the minority world in what concerns the creation and perpetuation of canonical literatures. In many ways the works we analyze below could be said to dialogue with Rivera Cusicanqui's understanding of the Aymara concept *ch'ixi*, a space both real and imagined, something that is and is not, within which lies a great potential for decolonization: "coexisten en paralelo múltiples diferencias culturales, que no se funden sino que antagonizan o se complementan. Cada una se reproduce a sí misma desde la profundidad del pasado y se relaciona con las otras de forma contenciosa" (2018: 70) (Multiple cultural differences coexist parallel to each other, never coming together as they are both antagonistic or complementary. Each one reproduces itself from the depths of the past and is related to others in a contentious way). The work of these authors shows that reading another way is possible, but more importantly it provides the reader with an opportunity to explore the existence of other possible worlds through logics that the reader may not share.

Rosa Chávez: Transforming the Urbanscape

Rosa Chávez (b. 1980) is a K'iche'/Kaqchikel poet who migrated to Guatemala City with her family at a young age. Her experiences in the city as a Maya woman come through in her poetry, as she moves about and transforms the urbanscape to make it her own, recalibrating the city and its parameters. Her work includes the poetry collections *Casa Solitaria* (2005), *Piedra / Ab'aj* (2009), *Ri uk'u'x ri ab'aj / El corazón de la piedra* (2010), and *Quitapenas* (2010), as well as performance, electronic music, and audiovisual work (in 2021 Chávez directed the video of Rebeca Lane and Sara Curruchich's musical collaboration, *Kixampe*). In her poem "Dame permiso espíritu del camino" (Grant me permission, spirit of the path), Chávez calls upon the spirit of the path and living and nonliving beings (birds, plants, stones) to ask for permission and allow for passage, a move that stands in direct opposition of the push for environmental destruction and dominance of all that is nonhuman in the name of progress. Chávez's position before nonhuman kin resonates with the work and philosophy of Indigenous land defenders who understand life on the planet as a complex set of both horizontal and vertical relations that ebb and flow (the sky, humans, animals, plants, water, mountains, etc.) rather than a strict hierarchy where humans are at the top and all else follows. This notion is also reflected in the woven design, reminding us of the greater Maya universe, which is multilayered (it includes the underworld, the earth, and the sky), all its dimensions woven together by the movement of the sun (time): "Mayan directions are not discrete cardinal or intercardinal compass points frozen in space, but rather are horizontal and vertical lines, sides, vectors, or trajectories that are inseparable from the passage of time. They not only map out the flat world of horizon astronomy, but open the sky to coordinate astronomy as well" (Tedlock 1992: 205–6). In the presentation of her second poetry collection, *Piedra/Ab'aj* (2009), Chávez recites "Dame permiso" as she walks down Panajachel's main street and interacts with a woman who mirrors her movements, her double. Her verses and movements transform the space from tourist thoroughfare to a place for her poetry, where stones and animals have a say and a voice. Her journey down the road follows a path of white and yellow petals and culminates in a ceremonial space, a circle of petals with four colored candles that indicate the four cardinal directions.

In the performance "Somos la voz que recupera su canto" (We Are the Voice That Recuperates Its Song) presented at the 2017 Festival Internacional Centroamericano de Performance Forma y Substancia (International Central American Performance Festival, Form and Substance) and held in an urban park in Guatemala City, Chávez stands at the center of a circle made up of unsuspecting passersby and invited guests and opens with a clay whistle.

She scatters handmade instruments all throughout the circle and invites her audience to join in. Soon, audience members create sounds with whistles and hand-held percussion instruments, contributing to an atmosphere reminiscent of K'iche' poet Humberto Ak'abal's collective sensory poetry. As with "Dame permiso" Chávez molds the space to accommodate her movements, or in this case her sounds, in the process making explicit the audience's relationship with the performance, an effect that reminds us of K'iche' poet Manuel Tzoc Bucup's poetic objects (Worley and Palacios 2019: 174). In "Somos la voz," Chávez creates a different world by remapping space and reorienting her audience. She transforms every attendee from passive participant into collaborator, placing herself, a Maya woman in traditional dress, at the helm.

Manuel Tzoc Bucup: Queering the Urbanscape

Manuel Tzoc Bucup (b. 1982) is a K'iche' poet, performer, and book artist whose work pushes the boundaries of human experience. His published work encompasses a wide range of modes of production, from books published through grants and traditional presses like *Escop(o)etas para una muerte en ver(sos) bala* from 2006, *El ebrio mar y yo* from 2011, *Constante huida* from 2016, and *Atómica* from 2018, to handmade books published through Ediciones la maleta ilegal, the independent press he runs with his Chilean-born partner Rodrigo Arenas-Carter (*De textos insanos* from 2009 and *Gay(o)* from 2010), to self-published and self-curated nonlinear book objects (*Polen*, a bottle containing poems that have been rolled into individual gel caps, from 2014; *Cuerpo de niño triste*, a circular stack of poems that comes in a CD-case from 2015; and *Wuj*, an unbound collection of poetry from 2019). This eclectic array of work reflects the fact that Tzoc is a self-taught, fiercely independent writer and performer who makes strategic use of the advantages each of these modes of publication offers as a way to circumvent censorship and assert editorial control over his work. Indeed, throughout his work Tzoc centers his queerness in his body of work (poetry and performance), initiating an important shift away from a colonial heteropatriarchal system that has impacted Indigenous communities as his verses turn inward (personal) that shape his outward experiences (public) and vice versa. In this sense, his, too, is a world-making literature that harnesses xocom balumil's sense of process and many centers, reorienting the reader's compass to vibrant ways of being, existing, and knowing that are suppressed and ignored by dominant globalized culture. For brevity's sake and as a matter of example, we will focus on the poet's relationship to space in the poem "Wuj."

In "Wuj" or "Book," Tzoc complicates the apparent boundaries between urban and rural spaces, opening with the lines, "Ritual urbano / Ixim regado" (Urban ritual / watered corn) (2019: 22). On one level, the introduction of watering corn, an agricultural act, into the globalized urban environment of Guatemala City, recenters concepts of Maya urbanity in which human settlement is tied to and defined by corn and corn fields (Tokovinine 2013: 9–10). On another, the use of the Maya "Ixim" as opposed to simply "maíz" reasserts the poet's linguistic identity within a space, whether that of the city or of the page itself, which all too frequently excludes Indigenous-language expression. It also resonates with one of the original Maya names for Guatemala, Iximulew, or "land of corn." That said, this gesture is neither naive nor utopian. Rather, the fact that most of the rest of the poem is in Spanish reminds one that writers like Tzoc do not necessarily speak their ancestral languages and that nation-states throughout the hemisphere, in the words of the Mixe linguist Yásnaya Elena Aguilar Gil, continue to "murder" them (2019). Further down the line, with "Amor marica de Nah Tunich" (Nah Tunich's queer love) he traces (his) urban Maya queerness to Naj Tunich, the famous cave with pre-invasion homoerotic murals in Poptún, and connects it with the "Pasos del maya urbano" (steps of an urban Maya) which are in turn animated with the "sangre caliente de les abueles mayas" (hot blood of the Maya grandparents) (Tzoc 2019: 22). Collectively these images provide queer urban Maya with a genealogy that stretches back to Classic Maya culture. That is, being queer is not a colonial import but something with its own trajectory with Maya cultures themselves, with the image of the "sangre caliente" encompassing both descendance and desire. Further, the poet's opting for a neutral article and noun "les abueles" signals the existence of a queerness that precedes inclusive language and is just as adaptable as a nawal, in this case, the nawal tz'i, which takes the form of a "peluche rosa," a pink plush toy toward the end of the poem (Tzoc 2019: 22). Completing its reimagining of space, the poem's final two lines read, "Iximulew triste / Renacido AbyaYala" (Iximulew Sad / Abya Yala Reborn) (Tzoc 2019: 22). While many Maya activists and intellectuals identify the territory of Guatemala with that of the Maya polity Iximulew, the poet ends with the rebirth of Abya Yala, the Guna name for the continent as a whole (Keme 2018: 42). In doing so, the poet eschews underscoring nationality and national belonging, even if this were to be cast in terms of Mayaness, in favor of a Trans-Indigenous, hemispheric form of being. This is echoed in the performance with his partner, Rodrigo Arenas Carter, "Reestableciendo Abya Yala" (Reestablishment of Abya Yala, 2016), which, Tiffany Creegan Miller argues, "centers on the politics of queerness transcending geopolitical borders to establish a dialogue among Indigenous communities across the hemisphere" (2022: 103). Ending the poem and the collection with that line, this is the reborn world into which the reader steps at the volume's conclusion.

Amado Chan: Mapping a Maya Presence in Belize

Amado Chan (b. 1965) is a Maya-Yucatec/mestizo poet from San Estevan, Belize, who writes predominantly in English though he also incorporates Spanish and Maya Yucatec. Chan traces his family history to the rebel Mayas of the so-called Caste War in the Yucatán Peninsula in the nineteenth century on his father's side and to a mestizo identity. This mixed heritage, according to Michela Craveri (2019: 92–5), helps explain the poet's penchant for orality and musicality and use of Maya phrases and Spanish in his largely English language texts. His poetry collections include *Speak to me/Háblame* (1999), *Make the Monarch Blush* (2001), and *Slices of Moldy Bread* (2007). His poem "San Estevan Versus Yo Creek" (1999: 6–7) is of interest here as it invites his reader to position themself in Belize's Orange Walk District (known as a largely mestizo area though not without an important Maya presence) and understand the history and cultural dynamics of two villages "12 miles apart": San Estevan and Yo Creek.

Rather than centering the poem solely on the region's colonial past or a singular ideal mestizo present, the poet traces its trajectory "from Maya to Conquistador to Colonial English" as a reflection of a present where these facets can and do exist but he de-historicizes them when he characterizes the region's linguistic landscape of Maya, Spanish, and English as "that circumstantial mixture / of languages," which is manifest in the town name itself: "the Mayan Yo, sound and sense / combined, narrow, as the word itself / and your language, master, / the Creek, so mundane" (1999: 6). Chan's concern with languages and their colonial circumstances impositions surfaces again in the poem "Make the Monarch Blush" in the collection with the same name, where the narrator tells of a young man who "didn't speak queen elizabeth's / english very well" and "he didn't speak king ferdinand's / spanish much" (2001: 8). At the end, the narrator recounts the loss of the young man's voice: "you may wonder what language / this young man did speak / I didn't ever get to know / for his voice / was strangled even before his birth" (2001: 8). Chan's position defies the notion of a monolithic Belizean national identity, which is centered around Afro-Belizean roots, is Anglo-centric, and generally rejects the possibility of Belizean Maya and mestizo identities (Medina 1997: 774–6).

Returning to "San Estevan Versus Yo Creek," we can see how the poet reorients his reader to invite them to conceive of a Belize that includes Maya peoples and even Spanish invaders, dismantling the notion that Maya people (Mopan, Q'eqchi', and Mopan) are not native to the region but are immigrants (Medina 1998: 151). In the third stanza, the mention of Xunantunich, an important preinvasion Classic-period Maya site, reinforces the idea that the place today known as Belize occupies ancestral Maya territory, drawing a direct connection between contemporary Maya activists and Maya activists in the late 1970s who spoke about a return of the original inhabitants to their ancestral lands (Medina 1998: 148–9). When speaking about the important Maya site in Belize, Chan calls out the ineffectiveness and inadequacy of the linearity of Western thought, "so linear / a western thought in dissonance / with the Xunantunich," as well as the imposition of borders and national demarcations, both real and imagined, that has not contributed a multi- or pluricultural society but instead to a society in contention with itself.[3] In fact, when speaking about a Maya presence in Belize, many do so in the past or render it invisible altogether (Shrimpton Masson 2020: 8). Interestingly, in the preceding verse, the poetic voice remarks on the inability of the "European God" to speak Maya or more specifically to "speak the Baax ka mentik." *Baax ka mentik* translates as "what are you doing," which in this case, serving as a noun and pairing it with the Western God's inability to speak it, makes a commentary on a Western value system that cannot effectively account for the everyday in the lives of the villagers and, perhaps more critically, its rigidity to imagine other worlds beyond itself. Using xocom balumil as a lens from which to read Chan's verses, we can glimpse the poet's own universe, a world made to include a Maya presence and a history in an English-speaking world that is set on effacing aspects of it for its own design of a nation.

Negma Coy: The Cardinal Directions of Writing

When compared to Chávez, Tzoc, and Chan, the poet and artist Negma Coy (b. 1980) may at first gloss seem to correspond to the stereotyped images of Indigeneity that globalization has imposed on Indigenous Peoples worldwide, and Maya peoples in particular, insofar as she still lives in her hometown of Chi Xot (Comalapa, Guatemala) as opposed to a larger urban center, she frequently wears *traje* and speaks Kaqchikel in addition to Spanish. Her work nonetheless challenges the ongoing impact of colonialism and speaks to a host of alternative relationships between humans and other-than-human beings that are manifested throughout the natural world. In other words, and as with the other writers seen here, read via xocom balumil we find that her work leads to a different understanding of the world we already inhabit and which does paradoxically contain multiple worlds. As we shall see, an important part of this project is her advocacy for a Maya literacy that includes Latin script alongside Maya glyphs and publication in a codex-style format that asks many readers to acknowledge both the impact of colonization and their own illiteracy when confronted by these Maya sign systems. In addition to being an accomplished visual artist, Coy has published several collections of poetry, including *XXXK'* (2016) and *Tz'ula'/Guardianes de los caminos* (2019), as well as a book of stories and poems, *Kikotem: Historias, cuentos, poesía del pueblo maya kaqchikel* (2019). We will analyze the poem "Rumuxu'x ri Meq'en ya'/ El ombligo de Meq'en ya'" (Meq'en ya''s belly button) from *Kikotem*, before delving into aspects of the book's presentation and layout.[4]

"Rumuxu'x ri Meq'en ya' / El ombligo de Meq'en ya'" is about a lake near Chi Xot or more specifically its belly button, the symbolic center in Maya cosmovision whether we are discussing humans, towns, or even lakes. The first two lines of the poem read, ""El nacimiento de agua Meq'en ya' tiene un remolino/ en su estómago, yo creo que es su ombligo" (The Meq'en ya' spring has a swirl / in its stomach, I think it's its belly button) (Coy 2019: 29).[5] As the poem itself lays out, the identification of the whirlpool as being the lake's belly button is not personification but the recognition of the lake itself as an other-than-human being, complete with its own agency and will, that is in line with Maya understandings of existence. Further, the water's currents from a spring that feeds the lake are magical beings that steal children's underwear as they swim, and the fish are not simply fish but "el corazón del agua, por eso deben ser libres" (the heart of the water, that's why they must be free) (2019: 39). In turn, other animals' behavior shows humans the natural relationship one should have with the water, as "Las ardillas, por ejemplo: se inclinan ante el / agua antes de beberlo, los armadillos besan el suelo y después / al agua, los pajaritos en cambio le cantan al agua todo el día" (the squirrels, for example, bow before the / water before drinking, the armadillos kiss the ground and then / the water, the little birds sing to the water all day) (2019: 31). Of course, the reciprocal nature of humans' relationship with the water is a kind of intergenerational knowledge, as "las abuelas y los abuelos dicen / que el corazón del agua siente la energía de las personas. Por eso / nosotros le hablamos y le pedimos / permiso antes de sumergirnos" (our grandmothers and grandfathers say / the water's heart feels humans' energy. That's why / we speak to it and ask it / permission before going in) (2019: 33). In other words, here the poetic voice positions her observation about the living lake as coming from her informed perspective as a Maya woman and her ability to use that knowledge to make observations about the world around her. From this perspective, the lake is a living being who relates to people's energy and whose permission people must (and certainly should) request before entering. As if to emphasize that this lake and these relationships are real and exist as part of the same world in which these same things are seen as mere natural resources to be exploited, the poem closes with the poet's advice that "Cuando vengás a Comalapa te puedo llevar / a donde está ese hermoso nacimiento de / agua" (when you come to Comalapa I can take you / to where that beautiful water / springs) where the person, presumably after having asked permission and entered into these same relationships, can swim with these "seres mágicos" (2019: 33).[6]

Any comment upon Coy's work would be incomplete if it failed to mention her commitment to reviving Maya hieroglyphic writing. Although it may be counterintuitive, in many respects her work in this area parallels Tzoc's work insofar as her desire to publish in a bilingual Kaqchikel-Spanish format that also includes the titles of poems and/or entire books in Maya glyphs means that she self-publishes a good bit of her work. That is, given the publishing costs associated with bilingual publication, let alone the costs associated with reproducing Maya glyphs, Coy, like Tzoc, uses self-publishing as a means to circumvent the publishing market's economic censorship and express her work on her terms, distributing photocopies of individual poems, curating pamphlets, and creating small, stapled anthologies. Published by the Maya-centric press Cholsanaj, her *Kikotem* is thus exceptional for its inclusion of Maya glyphs on the cover, the use of the Maya numbering system on each page in addition to the use of Arabic numerals, its use of Coy's paintings, and its codex-style layout. As printed book, the volume itself recalls Cholsamaj's facsimile edition of the *Kumatzin wuj ka'ai*, or Madrid Codex, which, true to the original Maya codex itself, was published as an accordion-style, foldout book. Beyond recalling such Maya manuscripts, *Kikotem* intentionally builds upon efforts to bring these formats to the twenty-first century, demonstrating that such efforts are not simply a matter of preserving ancient aesthetics but of using these to develop Maya arts and literature in the present. The work's use of glyphs, paintings, and Maya numbers further underscores this point by showing how these aspects of Maya writing have been and remain viable ways to assert Mayaness. On the whole, the book itself remaps the Euro-western literary landscape, decentering letters in favor of a broader understanding of literary expression that transcends hierarchies and lets multiple sign systems participate side by side in the book. In doing so, the book signals the existence of Pan-Maya literary traditions that span Mexico, Guatemala, Belize, and Honduras, while finding kinship with other nonalphabetic forms of literacy throughout the hemisphere. That is, as the book decenters national belonging and Latin script, it steers us toward the nonhierarchical, polycentric vision of xocom balumil.

Conclusion

The poets briefly studied here show possibilities beyond the constraints of the nation and its claims to the regulation of spaces, borders, bodies, and identities. The worldviews that inform their work already surpass those constraints because they can encompass both points of contact and contradiction. In the context of Central America, we have framed them within the Maya textile design xocom balumil, which is embodied in woven and embroidered textiles, as a way of describing how they both encapsulate the possibility of multiple worlds and the possibility of multiple ways of being in those worlds. As a way to frame or rethink world literature, xocom balumil thus opens us up to the possibility of moving beyond literary hierarchies of centers and peripheries, the cosmopolis and the provinces, and toward an understanding that all peoples are the "center" of their own lives, stories, and literary traditions, with global literature itself being the recognition of an unbounded trajectory of the sun from the East to the West in an eternal process of becoming.

Notes

1 Though we acknowledge that there are multiple spellings of *xocom balumil*, here we follow the spelling for the name of the design as seen in Morris.

2 We follow Michif/Settler scholar Max Liboiron's move to identify both Indigenous and non-Indigenous people in their book *Pollution Is Colonialism*. Liboiron calls attention to the practices that center and normalize whiteness while excluding and marking others based on their nation, ethnic or cultural affiliation. As a methodological solution, they choose to identify all the people cited in the book but, if the information is not readily available, they present "unmarked" rather than "settler" (2021: 3–4n.10). We adopt Liboiron's strategy in an effort to level out the playing field and not tokenize the Indigenous scholars, artists, writers, and thinkers, among others, by only pointing out *their* affiliation. We do so knowing that this may appear jarring or unorthodox to those who will consequently identify themselves as settlers or unmarked: this is the very effect of the now normalized act of naming to which Indigenous Peoples are subjected with and without consent. Our intent is not to now "tokenize" non-Indigenous People but to make a small contribution to the important anti-colonial work of Liboiron and others that is shifting the terms of engagement in the Western academy.

3 For more on the subject, see Assad Shoman's study "Reflections on Ethnicity and Nation in Belize" (2010).

4 We touch on some of these topics in our article "Las palabras pintadas de Comalapa: Ts'íib en la obra de Negma Coy y Edgar Calel," in which we more specifically examine Coy's work in the context of the Maya concept of *ts'íib*, which can be loosely translated as "writing."

5 The poem is bilingual, but since we are not working with the Kaqchikel version of the poem we will only cite from the Spanish. Our not including it here avoids reducing the Kaqchikel to a mere symbolic adornment in either our own work or the book itself.

6 It would be remiss not to mention that in these lines the poet refers to her hometown as "Comalapa," whereas in the Kaqchikel version of the poem she uses the town's Kaqchikel name, "Chi Xot."

References

Aguilar Gil, Y. E. (2019), "'Las lenguas no mueren, las matan': lo que se esconde tras la extinción de las lenguas originarias en México," *Global Voices*, May 4. Available online: https://es.globalvoices.org/2019/04/05/nuestras-lenguas-no-mueren-las-matan/.

Anderson, B. (1983), *Imagined Communities: Reflections on the Origin and Spread of Nationalism*, New York: Verso.

Araujo, S. (2009), "Zapotec Indigenous People in Mexico Demand Transparency from U.S. Scholar," *Grassroots International*, January 22. Available online: https://grassrootsonline.org/blog/newsblogzapotec-indigenous-people-mexico-demand-transparency-us-scholar/.

Chan, A. (1999), *Speak to Me/Háblame*, Belize City: Factory Books.

Chan, A. (2001), *Make the Monarch Blush*, Belize City: Factory Books.

Chávez, R. (2009), *Piedra/Ab'aj*, Guatemala: Editorial Cultura.

Chávez, R. (2017), "Somos la voz que recupera su canto," [video] filmed by *Barrancópolis*, Festival Internacional Centroamericano de Performance Forma y Substancia, Guatemala City. Facebook, February 26, 17:26. Available online: https://www.facebook.com/watch/?v=1838066003118177.

Cheah, P. (2016), *What Is a World?: On Postcolonial Literature as World Literature*, Durham and London: Duke University Press.

Conley, R. J. (2005), *The Cherokee Nation: A History*, Albuquerque: University of New Mexico Press.

Coy, N. (2019), *Kikotem: historias, cuentos, poesía Kaqchikel*, Guatemala City: Cholsamaj.

Craveri, M. (2019), "La poesía móvil y plural de Belice Amado Chan y el cruce de fronteras," in S. Regazzoni and F. Cecere (eds.), *America: il racconto di un continente / América: el relato de un continente*, 91–105, Venice: Edizioni Ca'Foscari.

Creegan Miller, T. D. (2022), "Queering Abiayala: Personal and Political Cartographies of the Indigenous Americas," in S. A. Day (ed.), *Performances that Change the Americas*, 99–115, London and New York: Routledge.

Cumes, A. E. (2012), "Mujeres indígenas, patriarcado, y colonialismo: un desafía a la segregación comprensiva de las formas de dominio," *Anuario Hojas de Warmi*, 17: 1–16.

Gellner, E. (1983), *Nations and Nationalism*, Ithaca: Cornell University Press.

Getachew, A. (2019), *Worldmaking after Empire: The Rise and Fall of Self-Determination*, Princeton: Princeton University Press.

Gil Corredor, C. A. (2020), *El arte textil maya en los Altos de Chiapas: Devenir de una práctica cultural*, México: Universidad de Ciencias y Artes de Chiapas. Available online: https://repositorio.unicach.mx/handle/20.500.12753/4425

Íñigo Clavo, M. (2017), "Conversation with Aura Cumes on Maya Epistemology, Postcolonial Theory and the Struggle for Identity," trans. Lola García Abarca. *Re-visiones*, 7.

Keme, E. (2018), "For Abiayala to Live, the Americas Must Die: Toward a Transhemispheric Indigeneity," trans. Adam Coon, *NAIS*, 5 (1): 42–68.

(2008) *Kumatzin wuj ka'i'/Códice de Madrid*, Guatemala: Cholsamaj.
Liboiron, M. (2021), *Pollution Is Colonialism*, Durham and London: Duke University Press.
Medina, L. K. (1997), "Defining Difference, Forging Unity: The Co-construction of Race, Ethnicity, and Nation in Belize," *Ethnic and Racial Studies*, 20 (4): 757–80.
Medina, L. K. (1998), "History, Culture, and Place-Making: 'Native' Status and Maya Identity in Belize," *Journal of Latin American Anthropology*, 4 (1): 134–65.
Morris, W. (2009), *Diseño e iconografía Chiapas: Geometrías de la imaginación*, 2nd edition, México City: Dirección General de Culturas Populares.
Nickels, J. (2018), *World Literature and the Geographies of Resistance*, Cambridge: Cambridge University Press.
River Cusicanqui, S. (2018), *Un mundo ch'ixi es posible: ensayos desde un presente en crisis*, Buenos Aires: Tinta Limón.
Rocha Vivas, M. (2016), *Mingas de la palabra: Textualidades oralitegráficas y visiones de cabeza en las oralituras y literaturas indígenas contemporáneas*, Havana: Casa de las Américas.
Rocha Vivas, M. (2021), *Word Mingas: Oralitegraphies and Mirrored Visions on Oralitures and Indigenous Contemporary Literatures*, trans. P. M. Worley and M. Birkhofer, Chapel Hill: University of North Carolina.
Ruiz, M. (2019), "Ruptura de una tradición inventada I," *Tierra Adentro*, August. Available online: https://www.tierraadentro.cultura.gob.mx/ruptura-de-una-tradicion-inventada-i-2/
Sánchez Prado, I. M. (2018), *Strategic Occidentalism: On Mexican Fiction, the Neoliberal Book Market, and the Question of World Literature*, Evanston: Northwestern University Press.
Shoman, A. (2010), "Reflections on Ethnicity and Nation in Belize," *Afrodesc Documento de trabajo*, 9: 1–61.
Shrimpton Masson, M. (2020), "Leyendo Belice: Escritores contemporáneos, entre el Caribe y Centroamérica," *Anuario de Estudios Centroamericanos*, 46: 1–35.
Tedlock, B. (1992), *Time and the Highland Maya*, rev. edition, Albuquerque: University of New Mexico Press.
Tokovinine, A. (2013), *Place and Identity in Classic Maya Narratives*, Washington, DC: Dumbarton Oaks.
Tonalmeyotl, M. (2019), "Poesía indígena sufre de 'inexistencia', afirma Martín Tonalmeyotl," interview by Magdiel Olano, *Leviatán*, December 2. Available online: https://leviatan.mx/2019/12/02/poesia-indigena-sufre-de-inexistencia-afirma-martin-tonalmeyotl/.
Tonalmeyotl, M. (2021), "No soy poeta indígena," Facebook, March 9. Available online: https://www.facebook.com/Tonalmeyotl/posts/10222607597371504.
Tzoc, M. (2019), *Wuj*, Guatemala City: Manuel Tzoc.
Varese, S. (2018), "Los fundamentos éticos de las cosmologías indígenas," *Amérique Latin: Histoire & Mémoire*, 36. Available online: https://journals.openedition.org/alhim/6899

Weaver, J. (2011), "Pluralist Separatism and Community," in H. J. Recinos (ed.), *Wading through Many Voices: Toward a Theology of Public Conversation*, 95–110, Lanham: Rowman and Littlefield Publishers.

Worley, P. M. and R. M. Palacios (2019), *Unwriting Maya Literature: Ts'íib as Recorded Knowledge*, Tucson: University of Arizona Press.

2

World Literature in Minor Key: The Central American Short Story

Sophie Esch and Ignacio Sarmiento Panez

Dedicated to Maureen Shea, who introduced countless students to Claudia Hernández

Obligatory nods to Poe, Kafka, and Borges notwithstanding, the short story rarely features in debates on world literature. Other genres, especially the novel, usually take center stage. A notorious case in point is Franco Moretti's "Conjectures on World Literature" (2000), in which he develops his argument for a true world literary perspective in comparative literature solely based on a discussion of the modern novel. Critics were quick to point out this problematic narrow focus. In his response "More Conjectures" (2003), Moretti explains that he privileged the novel for being the genre and field he knew best and insists that it was just an example. He also adds that this "mistake" could be easily corrected "as we learn more about the international diffusion of drama, poetry, and so on" (173). The short story did not even make it onto Moretti's list and instead appears subsumed under the "so on." Often considered a minor genre or a "starting point" in a writer's career, the short story quickly falls by the wayside—even as it is a central genre across the world. Short story writers have always been painfully aware of this misalignment. Central America's most famous short story writer, Augusto Monterroso, for example, writes about the short story and "this vague and sharp indifference of readers and editors towards this hard-to-grasp genre which through the ages remains stubbornly next to the other big genres which perpetually seem to overshadow and nullify it" (2001: 49, our translation). Despite being considered an art form only few have mastered, the short story always stands in a tenuous relation to other genres and the literary world system, as a short form unloved by publishers yet cherished by a select group of readers one could call literary connoisseurs (generally other writers, scholars, critics, and teachers). As such, the short story points to key topics of world literary debates, including questions of inequality and otherness, mastery and value, and circulation and reception.[1]

In this article, we operate with a relatively conventional definition of world literature, as one that points beyond the national realm and implies wide-ranging circulation and canonicity. While a lot of the current scholarship in world literature debates pretends to move away from the notions of canonicity, masterpieces, and value judgment, we find that "world literature," whichever way you turn it or define it, still has the lingering notion of canonicity, works of quality, works that are or should be read by many (or more cynically, thinking about the market realities of literature, are or should be *bought* by many, or—invoking value and taste judgments once more—by discerning readers). As Paulo de Medeiros from the Warwick Research Collective puts it, world literature "is still, as it has always been, a way of privileging and enshrining works deemed to be central and above others" (2020: 12).

In the inherently unequal world literary system, the notion of minor or small literatures has long been employed as a way to perceive and describe a literature and writerly subject position that occupies a space at the periphery of the big literary players, languages, or countries. This notion is, of course, one that is latently present when thinking and speaking about the literature of Central America, a region often considered minor in a continental and global context. This article looks for answers to the main question guiding this volume—what does it mean or take to write world literature from Central America?—but also adds the question of genre into the mix. What does it mean, then, to write in a small or minor genre from a minor(itized) and small region?

While poetry and testimonio are historically and globally the genres most associated with Central America, we agree with Will H. Corral when he claims that the short story has been the "most consistent" genre in Central American literature (2002). Many Central American authors have been great *cuentistas*. Examples include José Batres Montúfar, Rubén Darío, Salarrué, Rafael Arévalo Martínez, Álvaro Menen Desleal, Alfonso Chase, Carmen Naranjo, Rafael Menjívar Ochoa, Rodrigo Rey Rosa, Jacinta Escudos, Eduardo Halfon, and Denise Phé-Funchal, just to name a few. In this chapter, we concentrate our discussion on two key references in the genealogy of the Central American short story: Augusto Monterroso and Claudia Hernández.

Needless to say, Monterroso (1921–2003) and Hernández (born 1975) represent different generations, trajectories, and patterns of reception. Reading them with and against each other brings out commonalities as well as divergent modes of writing and reading the Central American short story. On the one hand, Monterroso is one of the most read and widely translated Central American authors. Highly acclaimed and winner of many prices, among them the Rulfo, Villaurrutia, and Príncipe de Asturias prize, he has long been hailed by critics for his unique style and wit and, in Spanish, his books are published and republished by big name presses such as Alfaguara, Anagrama, Ediciones Era, and Catédra. His short stories are almost unavoidable for any Latin American high school student and are a must in any Hispanic literature program in the region. In the United States, Monterroso's stories are a staple in intermediate Spanish classes and introductory Latin American literature courses. While Monterroso's fiction is strongly present in many international educational settings, the academic interest on his work has stagnated over the decades, and scholarship on him has been largely confined to Spanish-speaking academia. Claudia Hernández, on the other hand, is still presented as an author who does not receive the attention and circulation she deserves (because she was, until recently, primarily published by small Guatemalan, Salvadoran, and Colombian publishing houses—a deliberate choice by the author). Yet, in many ways, she is a *secreto a voces*, a not-so-secret tip, as one of the major Latin American storytellers of the twenty-first century. She received the Juan Rulfo in 1998 and the Anna Seghers prize in 2004 and was included in Bogotá 39 in 2007. Academic criticism on Hernández's fiction is growing and can be found in equal quantity and quality in both Spanish and English, and incipiently in French. What both writers share is a focus on innovation in the context of unequal world literary system and Central America's marginality within it.

As such, in what follows, we want to discuss Monterroso's and Hernández's short stories as what we call a world literature in minor key. This framing references both the ideas of small and minor literatures and genres as well as the literary and innovative qualities such a literature needs to have in order to become visible and be read. We hereby do not rely on Deleuze and Guattari's controversial and disputed concept of a *littérature mineure* (minor literature) as the inherently political literature produced in a majority language by a minority (1983) but rather more broadly on the idea that minor or small literatures are those that "speak from the cultural periphery and with a marginal, or rather marginalized, voice within the centralized mainstream literary space" (He 2020: 44). In a similar vein, we do not share many of the Eurocentric and Francocentric positions taken by Pascale Casanova, yet we are interested in some of the questions she poses in relation to what she terms *petites littératures* (small literatures, a more appropriate translation of Kafka's notion of *kleine Literaturen* than Deleuze and Guattari's *littérature mineure*) (Casanova 2007: 202–4; He 2020: 34). Even though Casanova in part frames these topics in questionable terms—such as "literarily deprived" regions (181)—what does interest us here is her point regarding a quest for visibility and the ensuing literary strategies and artistic outcomes: "In order simply to achieve literary existence, to struggle against the invisibility that threatens them from the very beginning of their careers, writers have to create the conditions under which they can be seen" (Casanova 2007: 177). She argues that the "creative liberty of writers from peripheral countries is not given to them straight away: they earn it as the result of struggles … by inventing complex strategies that profoundly alter the universe of literary possibilities" (Casanova 2007: 177).

This chapter traces how Monterroso and Hernández employ the minor and small categories to their advantage and use the short story genre and the Central American experience and subject position to create literature of extraordinary appeal. Current world literature theorists—even as they say to have moved on from these categories—hint at certain formulas which are successful for long-lasting world literary appeal: a combination of strangeness and familiarity, a rootedness in place combined with a sense of universality, which creates an intriguing and sustained openness to interpretation (Damrosch 2003: 187, Helgesson and Rosendahl Thomsen 2020: 62). Both Monterroso's and Hernández's writings have these features. What is more, their literature not only operates well at the level of content but also very much at the level of form. We argue that both these authors from a peripheral region (Central America) become visible because of their relentless pursuit of literary originality in terms of form and style, for which they actively employ the short story genre. Brevity, ellipsis, sudden twists, and peculiar narrative voices and tones are some of the techniques they use to write a world literature in minor key: intriguing, complex, and subversive.[2]

Augusto Monterroso: The Literary Giant of the Small Form

As early as 1995, Will H. Corral had already argued that it was about time that academics and critics stop talking about Augusto Monterroso in relation to minor literature or minor genre, since "Monterroso's literature always was and will continue to be major" (11, our translation). Indeed, Monterroso is routinely referred to as one of the greats of Latin American modern letters. No other Central American short stories circulate so clearly and in so many languages beyond their countries of origin as those of Monterroso—if we want to employ, for a moment, Damrosch's broad catchall definition of world literature. His works have been translated into Italian, German, French, Chinese, Arabic, Japanese, Korean, Slovenian,

Swedish, Bulgarian, Hebrew, Finish, Polish, Portuguese, Basque, Catalan, Latin, Greek, Hungarian, and Dutch.³ Notably, he gained this world literary stature despite his famously modest output in terms of number and length of his books. He mostly published short story collections: *Obras completas (y otros cuentos)* (1959, Complete Works (and Other Stories)), *La oveja negra y demás fábulas* (1969, The Black Sheep and Other Fables), *Movimiento perpetuo* (1972, Perpetuum Mobile), *La palabra mágica* (1983, The Magic Word), and *La vaca* (1998, The Cow). He only published one short novel *Lo demás es silencio. La vida y la obra de Eduardo Torres* (1978, The Rest Is Silence: The Life and Works of Eduardo Torres) as well as several autobiographical books, collections of essays, and interviews.⁴ Yet it is precisely this brevity and his obstinate reliance on small and minor forms—short story, fable, conte, haiku, *microrrelato*, flash fiction—for which he became most known. Tiny insects, small-minded humans, human animals with inferiority complexes or bouts of grandiosity also appear throughout his oeuvre. Thus contrary to Corral's request we choose here not to abandon the categories minor, short, and small but rather put them in productive tension with the notions of major, long, and big to discuss Monterroso's work. We see the minor-major tension not as an either/or question or an unsolvable dichotomy but as the unifying thread that captures the modes of production and reception of Augusto Monterroso's writing—especially as they relate to world literature, the short story genre, Central America, and Mexico. The question here is then not *whether* Monterroso's books are world literature or not (by most accounts and theories they clearly would be), but rather *how*—especially as it relates to the questions posed by Casanova on literary visibility for writers from peripheral countries or regions.

Mexico and Central America occupy the pivotal major and minor settings for Monterroso's literary creation and reception, writerly self-conception, and complex positioning within Latin American and world letters. Born in Tegucigalpa to a Honduran mother and a Guatemalan father, he spent the majority of his childhood and adolescence in Guatemala. Due to the political situation in Guatemala, though, he lived most of his adult life exiled in Mexico City. Between 1945 and 1952, he lived in Mexico City periodically before permanently settling there in 1956. He did not return to Guatemala until 1996. Mexico City, one of the major lettered centers of the continent, was key for Monterroso's literary success. In the words of Alejandro Lámbarry: "The Mexican literary field of the mid-twentieth century was consolidated and had great strength: this allowed Monterroso to position himself strategically as a vanguard writer—a type of access which his previous context, Guatemala, would not have provided him" (2018: 93, our translation). Living in the Mexican capital meant that Monterroso lived in close proximity to important lettered circles and developed friendships with many writers. Juan Rulfo, Juan José Arreola, Luis Cardoza y Aragón (another Guatemalan in exile), Rosario Castellanos, Gabriel García

Marquez, Ernesto Cardenal, Sergio Pitol, Jose Emilio Pacheco, and Carlos Monsiváis were among his friends and interlocutors, to name just a few.[5] It meant that he also formed part of the typical heavily male-dominated literary networks across Latin America, which were mutually beneficial for one's writerly career. He published his first books with important Mexican publishers such as Joaquín Mortiz and Era. From there, he made the jump across the Atlantic, publishing first with Seix Barral and then Anagrama, two key transnational Spanish presses for the production of Latin American world literature (Lámbarry 2012: 108; Lámbarry 2019: 217–18; Locane 2019: 99). Thus, from a secret tip author with a small and select group of devoted readers—who Ángel Rama famously called the "the smallest fan club of the continent" ([1974] 1995: 24, our translation) and José Maria Conget a "secret sect" and "clandestine club" ([1996] 2000: 94, 96, our translation)—he was published by the big Spanish corporate publishing houses, and from there literary agents and translations followed (Lámbarry 2012: 108).

Even though Monterroso describes his long exile in Mexico as enriching and happy (González Zenteno 2004: 284; Ríos Baeza 2013: 86), and though it was clearly transformative for his literary career, he always wanted "to be recognized as a Guatemalan author who situated himself explicitly in the Guatemalan and Central American tradition" (Van Hecke 2005: 77, our translation).[6] Since Monterroso is routinely included in many Mexican short story anthologies, his Central American origin and baggage at times get brushed aside, yet it was key for Monterroso's writerly self-conception.[7] Being from Central America came for Monterroso with a strong sense of writing from and for a small and peripheral space. He referred to Central America as the "Fourth World" and spoke of Guatemala as "this tiny territory, almost invisible on the map" (1993: 10; Monterroso 2003: 123, our translation). The notion of smallness relates not only to the objectively small physical size of the region and its countries but also to a perceived weakness, impotence, and marginality in terms of geopolitics and world affairs.

The significance of Central America for his literary creation is particularly evident in Monterroso's first book, which bears the glorious title *Obras completas (y otros cuentos)*. The satirical book is full of both gut-wrenching and hilarious portrayals of inferiority complexes in the face of those perceived as of higher status within the Latin American coloniality of power: white US Americans and Europeans. Examples of this abound in his famous story "Mister Taylor," a bitter satire and allegory of the actions of the United Fruit Company in Central America written in the aftermath of the overthrow of Jacobo Arbenz in 1954, yet set in South America. In this story appears the following scene of an Indigenous man's failed attempt to sell a shrunken head to a poor US American tourist visiting the Amazon: "It is superfluous to mention that Mr Taylor was in no position to purchase it; but since he feigned not to understand, the native felt terribly humiliated at not speaking English well, and made him a present of it while begging his pardon" ([1959] 1980: 17, trans. by John Lyons). Or there is the tragic-comic story "Sinfonía concluida" of a Guatemalan organ player who finds the missing sheets of Schubert's "Unfinished Symphony" in La Merced church in Guatemala City but is frustrated in his attempt to "bring glory to his fatherland" through this extraordinary discovery, especially in Vienna where Schubert specialists treat the "Guatemalan organ grinder" with utter disdain (2002: 31, our translation).

Yet where Monterroso, with tender precision and a wink, expounds inferiority complexes in the face of the colonizer, he also constantly turns these relations on their head. More often than not, the white, European, or American (neo)colonizers are revealed to be the ignorant ones (the Austrian experts do not recognize the Schubert original, the Argentinean Jews do) or to have a poor formation (Mr. Taylor, for example, bases most of his knowledge on his readings of the works of a man named Silliman). In no other story is this turn of the table more evident as in "El eclipse," one of his most anthologized and well-known short stories. Situated in early colonial times in Guatemala (and playing on a similar tale about Columbus and an eclipse in the Caribbean), it tells the story of a Spanish friar who, with a sense of European superiority, tries to trick his Maya captors by predicting an eclipse. Yet the Maya, better astronomers themselves, sacrifice him nonetheless while they recite all the dates of past and future eclipses. While some of today's readers might take issue at the repetition of the much-exaggerated subject of human sacrifice among the Maya, the story nonetheless holds, as it goes against common dynamics of power knowledge and provides a sharp rebuttal of ethnocentrism and eurocentrism. It reveals the colonizer as the ignorant buffoon and inferiority complexes as unwarranted.

It is from this heightened awareness about the epistemological inequality of the world and its literary systems and the coloniality of power that Monterroso constantly reflects on the role of literature and that of the writer, especially those from Latin America. For instance, he insinuates that the Latin American boom might not fundamentally change these power relations reflecting on the boom via the Valladolid debate in "Dejar de ser mono" (Cease to be a Monkey) in *Movimiento perpetuo*: "Over four hundred years ago, fray Bartolomé de las Casas was able to convince the Europeans that we were humans and that we had a soul because we laughed, now they want to convince themselves of the same because we write" (2001: 85, our translation). Even though he was a contemporary of the boom, Monterroso stood for an alternative literary project, one that challenged and undermined the (stereo)typical ways of literary representation from Latin America and one that also constantly challenged the figure of the Latin American *letrado*, his vanity, wordiness, and self-importance (Sánchez Prado 2013: 129, 135, 138). The failed writer is thus a constant in his work, from the monkey who fails to become a satirical writer to the linguistic and intellectual clichés embodied by Eduardo Torres, the protagonist writer of his only novel, *Lo demás es silencio* (González Zenteno 2004: 183).

In the context of this high awareness and high anxiety, Monterroso found a complex answer to the difficult subject position of being a Central American "letrado subalterno" (subaltern man of letters), always seemingly closer to the jungle and the writing monkey position than to the lettered city.[8] Following Casanova's aforementioned idea that writers of small literatures "have to create the conditions under which they can be seen" and thus can "profoundly alter the universe of literary possibilities" (2007: 177), we find five interlaced strategies in Monterroso: a continuous search for originality, a focus on craftsmanship, as well as brevity, an extensive use of intertextuality, and a strategic in/out position in relation to the literary circles and markets. Monterroso was an autodidact with little formal training but an avid reader, and a search for an original and innovative voice characterizes his production. After dabbling and experimenting with different genres and styles, Monterroso developed a peculiar style: witty, crisp, unexpected. His style runs contrary to the more common styles at that time in Latin America, namely the neobaroque and the exuberant boom novels (Van Hecke 2005: 76). Ángel Rama heralded Monterroso as a welcome departure from "literary tropicalism" ([1974] 1995: 25, our translation). To achieve this, Monterroso settled on the small form to practice his craft, which consisted in part of constant editing. He himself is famous for saying—tongue in cheek—that he does not write but he corrects (1987: 29). Settling on craftsmanship meant he took a lot of time to write and publish his books—an act that runs contrary to the literary market machine (and which was probably much easier to accomplish in the 1960s and 1970s than in today's hyperaccelerated literary market). While the word and concept of "mastery" have fallen out of favor (and for good reason, as it often relates to colonialist, racist, and feudal oppressive and exploitative structures; see Singh 2018), it is very hard to talk about Monterroso without invoking the idea of mastery (in the sense of extraordinary craftsmanship). He also became a literal maestro, teaching writing workshops in Mexico; among his disciples were now-famous writers such as Juan Villoro.

Over time, Monterroso became best known as a "maestro de lo breve," a virtuoso of the short form. And, yet another small-big tension, even though Monterroso had a penchant for small animals, especially the flea and the fly, he will forever be associated with the dinosaur (Zavala 2002, 2018). Pun and irony surely intended, his famous shortest short story in the world receives its particular tension and interest from the largest species of reptiles to ever roam the earth: dinosaurs. "Cuando despertó, el dinosaurio todavía estaba allí" (1959: 73, "When he/she/it woke up, the dinosaur was still there," our translation). On the one hand, the short story plays with the grammatical ambiguity of Spanish conjugations, which do not need an accompanying pronoun, and thus leaves the reader to fill in the gap. Problematically so, in translation this indeterminacy is often incorrectly rendered with the masculine singular pronoun "he."[9] Yet in Spanish it is entirely unclear what or who is waking up when the dinosaur is still there. The dinosaur itself? Another animal that lived in the Mesozoic Era? Prey or hunter? What gender does it have? Or could it even be a human time traveler? Furthermore, since the story has a clear sequence (the preterite indefinite of "despertó," and the adverb "todavía," still, together with the verb "estar" in the imperfect), the reader also has to fill in the before and the after of this single sentence. And while not all readers will actively dissect the grammatical ambiguity, they will nonetheless sense it. The story describes a moment where something clearly happened before and something clearly will happen after. Although the story only includes two verbs, it is laden with action and suspense and its interpretive possibilities are infinite.

Intertextuality was another key ingredient of Monterroso's strategies for literary visibility. Using intertextuality strategically, especially if one comes from a region considered minor or lesser in the literary world system (or "literarily deprived," as Casanova would put it), is nothing new, but Monterroso's uses of intertextuality are particularly striking not only in their breadth but also in their originality. An Van Hecke counts 2,652 intertextual references to 1,167 authors in Monterroso's oeuvre (2010: 122). While this might seem like an inferiority complex disguised by or resulting in excessive intertextuality, this aspect of Monterroso's writerly creation is more complex. For one, it speaks of the peculiar education of Monterroso. Self-taught, he relied on his readings at the National Library in Guatemala, about which he said that it was such a poor library that it only had "good books" (1998: 101). With "good books," Monterroso means classics, in this particular case Spanish Golden Age literature, especially his much-favored *Don Quijote*, but also means Greek classics and British literature, especially Shakespeare. In his rather conventional Eurocentric canon of "good books," there is always one exception though: the *Popul Vuh*, which is a key reference for him as part of a long Central American literary tradition. Overall, Monterroso does not use this classical formation to intertextually namedrop but to establish an extensive, sustained, and highly original dialogue with these literatures.[10] Thus, *Oveja negra* is not only a homage to Aesop but also a reinvention and innovation of the fable genre (Kleveland 2002). And while one can see his rewriting of the fable as an aspiration to write oneself into a world literary canon, it is important to note that Monterroso's fables are never a copy (a common worry of Latin American writers at that time) but achieve true originality. Monterroso invented deeply memorable (and perhaps all too human) animals: the relativist giraffe, the flea who wants to be like Cervantes minus the inconvenience of destitution, or the black sheep which was executed and then got a monument erected in its honor. Unsurprisingly, *Oveja negra* is among his most translated works.

His third book, the more challenging *Movimiento perpetuo* is much less translated yet it shows similar strategies in terms of strategic intertextuality, a search for originality, and harnessing the power of smallness. The book is a loose collection of different pieces that escape any clear genre designation: some more essayistic or aphoristic in nature, others more typical short stories. The work acquires a broader and more cohesive structure through the use of a small, routinely despised animal: the fly. Monterroso claims that he always dreamed of publishing an anthology on the fly in literature, and instead he uses the fly here to weave the different texts together and give them additional meaning and world literary dimension (Lámbarry 2022: 58). Again, in a surprising twist of commonly held conceptions, Monterroso writes that in this text there are three universal topics: love, death, and flies. As usual with Monterroso, this is funny and dead serious at the same time since a reflection on mortality is key in his entire oeuvre. This unexpected focus on the fly also challenges the readership to assess their own ignorance. How come they have not paid attention to this small (in)offensive little creature before—especially since all of world literature seemingly has? And here again the intertextuality is telling and strategic since he incorporates fly quotes from Dante, Yeats, Cicero, Apollinaire, Proust, Joyce (no woman, of course) but also Mesoamerican classics. *Movimiento perpetuo* cites two of the key surviving classical Maya texts, the *Popol Vuh* and *Balam Chilam*, as well as Quechua poetry. Maya and Quechua literary flies thus make it into the world canon. Simultaneously, Monterroso inscribes himself into the world canon, becoming himself, in the words of Lámbarry, "la mosca en el canon" (the fly in the canon, 2013, our translation).

Being a fly in the world literary canon means being in the room but not necessarily having a seat at the table. It means that one will not always be perceived, and sometimes misunderstood, yet it nonetheless indicates a persistent presence. As much as this chapter affirms Monterroso's world literary status, it is also important to point out its limits. He was a beloved writer's writer and cherished by a general audience in Latin America, yet there existed constraints in regard to his reception, appreciation, and understanding. For one, his scholarly reception is oddly limited to the Spanish-speaking academia and monographs and volumes published in Spanish (González Zenteno 2004; Lámbarry 2013, 2019; Noguerol Jiménez 1995, with the exception of an extensive chapter on Monterroso in Bell 2014). Latin American writers, Latin American intellectuals, and Latin Americanists in academia understood what Monterroso was trying to do—but did others? An example of the woefully inadequate reception in the United States underscores this lack of comprehension. In 1960, the New York Times Book Review celebrated the publication of *Obras completas* as "a welcome departure from the indigenous manner" (quoted in Lámbarry 2022: 57), which underscores once more the difficulty of the Central American subaltern *letrado* to be not only read but also understood.

Claudia Hernández: Deterritorialization and Otherness in the Indie Press

Claudia Hernández is in many ways a very different writer from Monterroso, of course, and her concerns and topics are other, very much contemporary issues: violence, migration, gender, precarity, and anonymity. Whereas a reflection on literature and the letrado figure is key to Monterroso, Hernández's literature stays far away from the lettered city. While his own life, intertextuality, and other signs of erudition are common in Monterroso's fiction—and a common feature in contemporary Central American writing—Hernández's short stories are written without the by now common autofiction technique nor with any explicit literary references.[11] Her characters do not read books, do not teach at universities, do not travel the world giving lectures, and definitely are not writers. She is much more interested in anonymous and invisible everyday characters and the actions they perform before the most uncommon circumstances. That is the core of her fiction.

Hernández's artistic and cultural life has also been very different to Monterroso's. Born in 1975, she grew up in El Salvador during the civil war (1980–1992), which destroyed most of the artistic networks in the country due to censorship, political persecution, and the exile of numerous authors and creators. During the 1990s, when Hernández completed her secondary and university education, the country was in the process of rebuilding its cultural infrastructure, and only a limited number of works of literature were published in that decade. Consequently, she was not exposed to the same kind of literary circles as Monterroso was in Mexico City in the times of the boom. Unlike many of her predecessors and contemporaries, Hernández is one of the few known current Central American authors who still lives in her home country. Between 2001 and 2013, she published five books of short stories: *Otras ciudades* (2001, Other Cities), *Mediodía de frontera* (2002, Midday of Border) republished in 2007 as *De fronteras* (Of Borders), *Olvida uno* (2005, One Forgets), *La canción del mar* (2007, The Song of the Sea), and *Causas naturales* (2013, Natural Causes). In 2017, Hernández entered a new path in her literary career with the publication of her first novel *Roza, tumba, quema* (2017, Slash and Burn), which was followed by *El verbo J* (2019, The Verb J) and *Tomar tu mano* (2021, To Take Your Hand). While Hernández has published in the last twenty years almost the same number of books of fiction Monterroso published in his whole life, she is not as known yet as Monterroso, nor as widely translated, but we venture to say that she might be eventually. While many of the topics of their stories are different, both Hernández and Monterroso share a proclivity for a world literature in minor key. Just like Monterroso, Hernández has favored the short story genre, as well as innovations in form and style, and she combines the specificity of the Central American experience and subject position with questions of universal concern. In Alexandra Ortiz Wallner's words, talking about Claudia Hernández means talking about condensation and textual concentration, a conscious decision of favoring the "minimum territory of the short story" against the demands of the literary market (2013).

In just two decades, Hernández's short stories have produced an astounding secondary corpus (forty academic articles and counting), which delights not only in her peculiar style and stylistic devices but also in the range of topics and infinite possibilities of interpretation of Hernández's stories, as they touch upon myriad topics of local and global concern. Scholars have predominantly read Claudia Hernández as a Salvadoran writer whose literary work deals with current issues of Salvadoran and Central American societies. Numerous of academic articles and book chapters analyze her short stories in connection to the Salvadoran civil war, the post-conflict society, and neoliberalism (Cortez 2010; Esch 2017; Ortiz Wallner 2013; Perkowska 2019; Rincón-Chavarro 2013; Sarmiento 2016a). The above is particularly relevant and curious because her short stories offer virtually no reference to the Salvadoran civil war and its aftermath. This deliberate or seeming deterritorialization has also been thoroughly discussed. In "Telling Evasions," Misha Kokotovic claims that the silence about El Salvador's reality is nothing but an invitation to look at its recent history and the present (2014: 54). While the above has been the predominant line of interpretation, the fact that Hernández treats topics of universal concern—death, mourning, conviviality—has always been observed (Browitt 2018; Esch 2017; Gairaud Ruiz 2014, 2015; Sarmiento 2017). This tension is then something she shares with Monterroso. Central America is latently present in their work, even though the direction of their work often points beyond it. It is wherein we find one of their formulas for world literary appeal.

Some of the most recognizable features of Hernández's short stories are deterritorialization, anonymity, and the normalization of the absurd, the fantastic, and the abject. In most of her stories, particularly in *Otras ciudades*, *De fronteras*, and *Causas naturales*, the events take place in indefinite places, and extraordinary actions are carried out by mostly anonymous characters that act with normality before the most unsettling situations. This tendency has been present even in her early writings. For instance, in the short story "Color de otoño" (Autumn's Color) included in *Otras ciudades*, Hernández's first book, women named Margarita commit suicide stimulated by autumn: "they get captivated by the autumn's color and they chase it around this time of the year if they are left alone or unattended. They relinquish their lives to reach it" (2001: 10, our translation). The story is narrated by an anonymous man who seeks one Margarita in particular in the ocean of suicidal Margaritas. After an intense search, where time, characters, and situations overlap, the narrator finally finds her, right before she jumps off the balcony.

For Menjívar, Hernández's literature offers a reinterpretation "not only of some aspects of the short story, but of the short story itself" (2007, our translation). One aspect that makes Hernández's stories so intriguing, disturbing, and engaging to readers is the deadpan voice of the narration: the very factual tone in which Hernández's narrators relate the most absurd events. In many cases, the opening lines of the story present a breath of normality right before introducing the readers to unfathomable events. For example, "Missing an arm is uncomfortable when one has a rhinoceros" is the first sentence of the opening story of *De fronteras* (2007: 11, our translation). Another story opener produces a similar estrangement: "When I arrived there was a corpse. In the kitchen. Of a woman. Lacerated. And it was fresh" (17, our translation). Less violent but equally surprising is "The nice thing about being robbed by them was that, a few days after the incident, they would bring back to you whatever they had taken," the first sentence of "Salteadores" (Bandits) from *Causas naturales* (2013: 35). Hernández's characters are always prepared to accept the unimaginable, be it a rain of shit, a woman chasing a ghost of herself, or a little man made out of a handkerchief (2007, 2013). Their impassivity is one of the main features of Hernández's characters.

Another common element of Hernández's distinct style is her use of the conditional and the subjunctive to tell alternative scenarios, displacing the attention from the actions in favor of grammatical complexity and speculation. "Despedida" (Farewell) (included in *Causas naturales*), for example, begins with a long description of the things the narrator would like to tell her boyfriend before transforming into a leopard:

> I wanted to tell him that I would not hold a grudge against him, if, instead of greeting me as always, he decided to run away the next time we would meet. I wanted to tell him that he needed to protect himself from me. In fact, I wanted to suggest to him that he do it, since, even though I had once in a bout of delirium sworn him eternal love, I couldn't guarantee him that I would not try to devour him if we coincided at a street junction.
> (2013: 49, our translation)

After this long description, nevertheless, she simply says, "But he wasn't there when I got there" (2013: 50, our translation). Ellipsis is another common feature in Hernández's stories, especially in the dialogues, where the narration does not only skip time but also jumps from one character to another. In "Molestias de tener un rinoceronte" (Annoyances of Having a Rhinoceros) we find the following passage, where the narrator tries to offer the rhino to everyone who asks him about it in the streets: "Well, it's your lucky day, Mister. My lucky day? Yes, miss: it's yours, I gift it to you. No, I couldn't accept it. Why not, kiddo? It's because the rhinoceros loves you, sir.

But, he seems to be quite taken by you, you'll come to love him, grandpa" (2007: 11–12, our translation).

Hernández also negotiates the question of otherness—but not so much in relation to indigeneity or the coloniality of power and imperialism (as Monterroso does at times), but in relation to vulnerability and conviviality in the Anthropocene and late-stage capitalism. Creatures of particular interest for her are our nonhuman others and those marginalized within human civil society (especially migrants). Because of the former, some critics have started to read Hernández's short stories under the lens of contemporary theories related to animal studies and posthumanism (Buiza 2017; Esch 2017; Pérez 2013; Vásquez Enríquez 2019). These readings have contributed to the understanding of Hernández's fiction from a global literary perspective beyond the pressing issues of El Salvador and Central America. In fact, animals play a major role in Hernández's fiction. *De fronteras* offers several examples of this. Its stories feature a rhinoceros, a stray dog, a vulture, cockroaches, and an ox. Animals, in Hernández's stories, are not secondary characters. They provide support to people in need, they are grieved, and they allow a recurring questioning of the hierarchy between humans and animals.

The topic of migration already appears in *De fronteras* here and there, yet it becomes the main theme in *Olvida uno*. As mentioned above, one of the main features of Hernández's short stories is the anonymity of both characters and places. While this is in general the norm, *Olvida uno* is the only short stories book that breaks with this pattern, at least partially. In this volume, we know that the stories take place in a fictionalized New York City, and in some cases, the characters have a name. Despite the background presence of the city and its immigrants, the book uses many of Hernández's common resources, such as the quotidian presence of the fantastic and the absurd. In Linda Craft's words, "Hernández uses the fantastic and mystical register to translate and sometimes to transcend the dehumanizing aspects of the life of the undocumented migrant who lives in the heart of the globalized capital" (2013: 181, our translation). This is arguably Hernández's most "global" book, at least on the surface. In its pages, people from all over the world—from El Salvador to Bangladesh—interact in the violent and fantastic reality of Hernández's New York City. "La mía era una puerta fácil de abrir" (Mine Was an Easy to Open Door), the story that opens the volume, offers an intimate insight into the lives of thousands of immigrants in the US metropolis. In this story, a newly arrived man moves to a cheap apartment that has no key. As a consequence, numerous random people regularly enter the place to rest, spend some time, and use the bathroom. The narrator welcomes them because they represent the only company he has in the city and are also a source of goods and food, which he often lacks. The end of the story suggests that the narrator, after facing some difficulties with the visitors, has been subtly evicted from the apartment by some of the people who used to regularly enter and use it as their own. "La han despedido de nuevo" (They Have Fired Her Again), Hernández's longest short story, explores the precariousness and invisibility of the immigrants in New York through Lourdes, an undocumented immigrant (presumably Salvadoran). The city's violence forces people from all origins to exhaust their forces in the service industry. Life in the city is particularly challenging for women, who are forced to seek whatever man to secure their legal status, a decent life, and a place to live.

Just as her stories focus on marginal and less visible characters, Hernández opted (or had to opt) for smaller and lesser-known publishing venues and presses. Many of her stories were first shared in the cultural supplements of Salvadoran newspapers like *CoLatino* and *El Diario de Hoy* (Ortiz 2013). This practice, reminiscent of the dissemination of a novel or short story in the nineteenth century, was one of the few possibilities available to a writer in post-conflict El Salvador, where the literary market was almost inexistent. Later on, Hernández's stories began to appear with small local state or independent presses. Her first three books were published in El Salvador. Her breakthrough came with the reedition of one of her short story books in Guatemala. Originally published as *Mediodía de fronteras* in 2002 by the national state-funded Salvadoran press, Dirección de Publicaciones e Impresos, in 2007, the Guatemalan press Piedra Santa issued it as *De fronteras*, which is to date the most well-known edition of the book (and the one often studied). *De fronteras* is a literary success that defied all market odds. For one, the book has an astoundingly ugly cover, which with its odd color combinations, and an image of a winged man gives the book a misleading esoteric or religious tinge. What is more, Piedra Santa is a publisher that predominantly publishes textbooks and literary classics for Guatemalan high school students. Yet while Piedra Santa does not have a wide network to distribute their books, they kept printing copies to keep up with demand, something the Dirección de Publicaciones e Impresos (DPI) never did (a habitual practice of the state press). Other well-known contemporary Central American authors, such as Sergio Ramírez, Gioconda Belli, Horacio Castellanos Moya, Rodrigo Rey Rosa, and Eduardo Halfon, rely primarily on the distribution networks of transnational publishers such as Alfaguara, Penguin Random House, Tusquets, and to a lesser extent, Libros del Asteroide. Hernández, on the other hand, maintains a peripheral presence even as she participates in global literary markets via small and independent publishers across Latin America. Seemingly not interested in becoming a "mainstream" or "best-seller" author, Hernández's version of a world literature in minor key is one that deliberately chooses small publishing venues for her texts but nonetheless aims for a circulation beyond the Salvadoran and Central American borders. This means that even though (or maybe because) she does not publish with the likes of Alfaguara, her literature circulates across Latin America, which is no small feat and should be considered a first major step of world literary circulation.

People not familiar with the Latin American and Spanish literary markets may consider them as a single unit that easily flows across countries and oceans, but nothing could be further from the truth. In reality, these markets are heavily shaped by the author's nationality, and even transnational publishers (such as Alfaguara) do not circulate books outside the writer's country of origin. Therefore, for any writer, especially for a Central American one, having their work published in a different country is a step toward their internationalization, despite how "minor" it may seem from the metropolitan republic of letters. Following the publication of individual short stories in anthologies of Central American short stories (and in digital venues of the Spanish-speaking world) and of *De fronteras* in Guatemala, some of Hernández's stories were translated into English. For example, in 2014, Marguerite Feitlowitz translated the first part of "Hechos de un buen ciudadano" as "Deeds of a Good Citizen" and published it in *Review. Literature and Arts of the Americas*. A complete translation of *De fronteras* into English was done as a senior thesis at Bard College some years ago and also had National Endowment of the Humanities (NEH) funding, but it was never published.[12] In 2016, New York City-based publisher Sangría Editora published Hernández's short story "La han despedido de nuevo," originally included in *Olvida uno* (2005), as a bilingual novella entitled *La han despedido de nuevo* (They Have Fired Her Again) (translated by Aaron Lacayo). The publication of the book was a significant contribution to the spread of Hernández's work, especially in the United States, since its original version, published by Índole editores in El Salvador and never reprinted, is a rare find.[13] In 2016, Puerto Rican independent press Trabalis editores took up *De fronteras* in another reedition. All these movements, always in a minor key, were essential nodal points for Hernández's ever-increasing circulation today.

Given that Hernández now writes novels following a more established and common patterns of rapid circulation and translation, one could claim that her circulation is owed primarily to this more marketable and profitable genre.[14] Yet we argue that the origin of the global circulation of her books is the moment where she breaks the national borders of El Salvador and republishes *De fronteras* with a Guatemalan press, becoming a secret tip author. It is noted, however, that Hernández's switch to the novel came as a surprise since, in 2013, she had declared she was not interested in writing novels (Andreu). Yet we find that her novels actually do not constitute such a clear-cut break with the short story genre since these are shaped and narrated in a similar style to her short stories. Even in this switch from the short to the long from, it is possible to observe numerous commonalities and continuations, meaning Hernández uses the literary innovations that secured her visibility when she was writing short stories to a similar innovating effect when writing novels. So much indeed that one could argue that they are in fact long short stories. One element that is strongly present in both her novels and short stories is the absence of proper names. In *Roza, tumba, quema*, for example, despite being an almost three-hundred-page novel, the characters are only called "she," "the eldest," or "the second of the daughters that lived with her." We find the same in her most recent novel, *Tomar tu mano*, where the characters are called simply "she," "the mother," or "the father." Her novels also rely heavily on the previously described use of ellipsis and switches in dialogues and the subjunctive and conditional mood to tell of alternative scenarios that never happened. This makes for extremely challenging novels that are hard to follow and hard to read. They require the reader to pay attention and to read again. This is then another example of a reluctance to engage in literary market norms in Claudia Hernández. Instead of writing the easily consumable, short novels full of action and dialogue currently in vogue, she presents readers with stylistically, narratively, and syntactically complex and long novels. Thus, to a degree, the main features of Hernández's short stories are still there. Nevertheless, it cannot be overlooked that Hernández's novels introduced some new elements never seen before in her short stories. For example, we find in *Roza, tumba, quema* the first clear references to the Salvadoran civil war and the postwar era. *El verbo J* is a novel that openly discusses issues of gender and migration. Her most recent novel, *Tomar tu mano*, is a powerful narration of gender violence, with some subtle references to the Salvadoran (or Central American) civil war and gang violence. Her novels are, in sum, a more direct approach to the present-day reality, free in many cases of some of the absurd and fantastic situations we normally encounter in her short stories. While the structure and her distinctive style are still present, her novels are clearly a new direction in her literary path yet one that still harbors elements of a world literature in minor key.

Final Remarks

This chapter makes a case for the inclusion of the short story in world literature debates in order to illuminate and complicate certain of its aspects. It is an attempt to think world literature with and against a specific genre and a specific region. By focusing on a literature in minor key and a minor genre, we do not want to idealize these notions. We use them more as descriptors of a reality, and a reality that relates specifically to a region like Central America and to specific genres in the context of world literary debates and circuits. Also, the fact that Monterroso and Hernández have achieved this visibility does not mean that there has been any fundamental change to the inequality of the literary world system(s). In fact, there are many other Central American short story writers that would deserve equal attention: Carmen Naranjo, Jacinta Escudos, Denise Phé-Funchal, Laura Fuentes Belgrave, Luis Báez, Cheri Lewis, and Elena Salamanca.

This chapter proposes the idea of a literature in minor key that relates to genre, form, craftsmanship, origin, and topics. And while it also considers the material and sociological realities of literary markets and circuits, it squarely puts the literary text at the center of the debates. We find that the market, by itself, cannot explain the circulation and reception of some literary works, nor the attention they receive from literary critics and scholars. Furthermore, we underscore the importance of Central America as a region and space for this world literature in minor key written by Monterroso and Hernández. Writing of dinosaurs and rhinos or the business of death, they embrace the universal and seemingly leave the isthmus behind, yet Central America is still there. Their stories derive their urgency and extraordinary insights from the absurdity of living in a place that is both periphery-center—a marginal "outposts in the tropics," as Arturo Arias calls it (2007: 5)—and constantly intervened by colonialism, imperialism, and global capitalism.

Notes

1 The authors would like to thank Mónica Albizúrez, Magdalena Perkowska, and Bren Ram for their comments and corrections on earlier versions of this text.
2 Music theorists will not fully agree, but popular wisdom holds that in the Western tradition music in minor key tends to be (or be perceived as) more dramatic, surprising, suspenseful, interesting, and sad than music set in major key.
3 See Corral (1995: 223–37), as well as Worldcat.
4 These include *Viaje al centro de la fábula* (1981, Voyage to the Center of the Fable), *La letra e: Fragmentos de un diario* (1987, The Letter E), *Los buscadores de oro* (1993, Gold Seekers), *Pájaros de Hispanoamérica* (2002, Birds of Spanish America), and *Literatura y vida* (2004, Literature and, The fauna Life). He also published one book of drawings and paintings, *La fauna* (1992).
5 Centro Virtual Cervantes, "Augusto Monterroso. Cronología 1957–1972." https://cvc.cervantes.es/actcult/monterroso/cronologia/1957_1972.htm
6 For a more detailed analysis of the importance of Guatemalan literature for Monterroso see also Van Hecke 2001. In addition, it should be noted that Monterroso's story of *desarraigo* (uprootedness), *destierro* (exile), and multiple national allegiances is so very typical of Central American lettered circles, e.g., Rubén Darío, Gioconda Belli, Franz Galich, Horacio Castellanos Moya, Rafael Menchívar Ochoa, and Eduardo Halfon, among many others.
7 He features in the *Relatos mexicanos posmodernos: Antología de prosa ultracorta, híbrida y lúdica* (2001) edited by Lauro Zavala for Alfaguara, *El canto de la salamandra. Antología de la literatura brevísima mexicana* (2013) edited by Rogelio Guedea, *El vuelo del colibrí. Antología de la prosa breve mexicana* (2018) edited by Beatriz Espejo. While he is most commonly

referred to as a Guatemalan or Mexican author, sometimes he is also referred to as a Honduran one. In Clara Obligado's *Atlas de Literatura Latinoamericana (Arquitectura Inestable)*, the editor places Augusto Monterroso as a Honduran writer, with a brief summary of his work written by Ana María Shua.

8. The term "subaltern letrado" was coined many years later by Guatemalan-Nicaraguan writer Franz Galich. On the question of the lettered city and the jungle see also Delgado (2010).

9. For examples of this masculinist and anthropocentric bias in translations, see for example translations into English (*Complete Works*) and German (*Der Frosch, der ein richtiger Frosch sein wollte*).

10. Carlos Fuentes captures this notion of a dialogue beautifully when he writes: "Imagine Alice having tea with Borges' fantastic bestiary. Imagine Jonathan Swift and James Thurber exchanging notes. What if a frog from Calaveras County had really read Mark Twain: That is Monterroso" (back cover *La Oveja Negra*, our translation).

11. Eduardo Halfon's and Rodrigo Rey Rosa's literature are salient examples of the uses of autofiction in contemporary Central American literature. Their characters, usually with their same names, live the life of a cosmopolitan man of letters. Literary references abound in their works, too. In Hernández, if there any literary references, they are indirect, e.g., Ionescu's rhinos and Clarice Lispector's cockroaches. She herself has declared that she is unaware of her literary influences. "Entrevista a Claudia Hernández por Rose Marie Galindo y Evelyn Galindo Doucette," p. 194.

12. Email communication by Dr. Nicole Caso from Bard College, September 2022.

13. Curiously, the editors try to hide the publication's origin as a short story and announce it as Hernández's "first novella" translated into English. See https://sangriaeditora.com/archives/1940.

14. *Roza, tumba, quema* was originally issued in 2017 by Laguna Libros, an independent Colombian publisher. It was republished in 2018 by the major Mexican publisher Sexto Piso. In 2021, the book was translated into English and published in the United States as *Slash and Burn* by And Other Stories, an independent, not-for-profit press. Also in 2021, the book was translated into French as *Défriche Coupe Brûle* by Metailié, a French indie press that publishes Latin American fiction. Her second and third novels, *El verbo J* and *Tomar tu mano*, are following a similar path. Published in 2018 and 2021 by Laguna Libros, they have been also reedited in Chile by La Pollera Libros in 2019 and 2021, respectively.

References

Browitt, J. (2018), *Contemporary Central American Fiction. Gender, Subjectivity and Affect*, Eastbourne: Sussex Academic Press.

Buiza, N. (2017), "Trastornando la jerarquía humano-animal: la alienación de la sociedad en la obra de Claudia Hernández," *Istmo. Revista virtual de estudios culturales centroamericanos*, 34. Available online: http://istmo.denison.edu/n34/articulos/07_buiza_nanci_form.pdf.

Casanova, P. (2007), *The World Republic of Letters*, trans. M. B. DeBevoise, Cambridge, London: Harvard University Press.

Conget, J. M. (2000), "El fin de una secta," in M. G. Durán (ed.), *Con Augusto Monterroso en la selva literaria*, 91–7, Mexico City: Ediciones del Ermitaño.

Corral, W. H., ed. (1995), *Refracción. Augusto Monterroso ante la crítica*, Mexico City: Difusión Cultural UNAM; Ediciones Era.

Corral, W. H. (2002), "20th Century Prose Fiction: Central America," *Handbook of Latin American Studies*, 58. Available online: https://memory.loc.gov/hlas/hum58lit-corral.html. Accessed 26 July, 2022.

Cortez, B. (2010), *Estética del cinismo. Pasión y desencanto en la literatura centroamericana de posguerra*, Guatemala City: F&G Editores.

Craft, L. J. (2013), "Viajes fantásticos: Cuentos de (in)migración e imaginación de Claudia Hernández," *Revista Iberoamericana*, 29 (242): 181–94. Available online: https://doi.org/10.5195/reviberoamer.2013.7025.

Damrosch, D. (2003), *What Is World Literature?* Princeton, NJ: Princeton University Press.

Deleuze, G., F. Guattari, and R. Brinkley (1983), "What Is a Minor Literature?" *Mississippi Review*, 11 (3): 13–33.

Delgado, L. (2010), "La biblioteca en la selva: modernidad y vanguardia en los relatos autobiográficos centroamericanos," in V. G. Pla and R. Baldovinos (eds.), *Tensiones de la modernidad: Del modernismo al realismo—Tomo II*, 35–56, Guatemala: F&G Editores.

Domínguez, C. M. (2020), "El regreso de Augusto Monterroso, el breve," Diario EL PAIS Uruguay, October 11, 2020. Available online: https://www.elpais.com.uy/cultural/regreso-augusto-monterroso-breve.html.

Esch, S. (2017), "In the Company of Animals: Otherness, Empathy, and Community in De Fronteras by Claudia Hernández." *Revista de Estudios Hispánicos*, 51 (3): 571–93. Available online: https://doi.org/10.1353/rvs.2017.0057.

Escudos, J. (1997), "La noche de los escritores asesinos," in *Cuentos sucios*, 83–123, San Salvador: Dirección de Publicaciones e Impresos, Consejo Nacional para la Cultura y el Arte.

Espejo, B. (2018), *El vuelo del colibrí. Antología de la prosa breve mexicana*, México, DF: Sextil.

Gairaud Ruiz, H. (2014), "Trayectorias de la muerte en la narrativa de Claudia Hernández," *Revista de lenguas modernas*, 20: 19:39. Available online: https://revistas.ucr.ac.cr/index.php/rlm/article/view/14899/14178.

Gairaud Ruiz, H. (2015), "Rutas de muerte en la narrativa de Claudia Hernández," *Revista de lenguas modernas*, 22: 203–15. Available online: https://revistas.ucr.ac.cr/index.php/rlm/article/view/14899/14178.

García Pérez, D. (2009), "Hacia una poética de Augusto Monterroso: La fábula y el cuento," *Literatura mexicana*, 20 (2): 113–29.

González Zenteno, G. E. (2004), *El dinosaurio sigue allí: arte y política en Monterroso*, México, DF: Taurus.

Guedea, R., ed. (2017), *El canto de la salamandra: Antología de la literatura brevísima mexicana*, Guadalajara: Arlequin.

He, Y. (2020), "Rethinking Minor Literature and Small Literature as Secondary Zone Literature," *Territories: A Trans-cultural Journal of Regional Studies* 2 (1). Available online: https://doi.org/10.5070/T22144835.

Hecke, A. V. (2004), "Guatemala, un espacio imaginario: Monterroso y la literatura guatemalteca," in *Actas del XIV Congreso de la Asociación Internacional de Hispanistas: New York*, 16–21 de Julio de 2001, Vol. 4, 2004 (Literatura hispanoaméricana), ISBN 1-58871-049-1, págs. 677–683, 677–83. Juan de la Cuesta. Available online: https://dialnet.unirioja.es/servlet/articulo?codigo=1220873.

Hecke, A. V. (2005), "Desubicaciones geográficas y fantásticas en Augusto Monterroso," *Revista de Estudios Hispánicos*, 39 (1): 75–99.

Hecke, A. V. (2010), *Monterroso en sus tierras: espacio e intertexto*, Colección Cuadernos 55, Xalapa, Veracruz, México: Instituto de Investigaciones Lingüístico-Literarias, Universidad Veracruzana.

Helgesson, S. and M. R. Thomsen (2020), *Literature and the World*. London; New York: Routledge. Taylor & Francis Group.

Hernández, C. (2001), *Otras ciudades*, San Salvador, El Salvador: Alkimia.

Hernández, C. (2002), *Mediodía de frontera*. San Salvador, El Salvador: Dirección de Publicaciones e Impresos, Consejo Nacional para la Cultura y el Arte.

Hernández, C. (2005), *Olvida uno*, San Salvador, El Salvador: Índole Editores.

Hernández, C. (2007), *De fronteras*, Guatemala: Piedra Santa.

Hernández, C. (2013), *Causas naturales*, Punto de Lectura.

Hernández, C. (2016), *They Have Fired Her Again*, trans. A. Lacayo, Bilingual edition, Brooklyn, NY: Sangría.

Hernández, C. (2017), *Roza tumba quema*, Bogotá: Laguna Libros.

Hernández, C. (2018), *El verbo J*, Bogotá: Laguna Libros.

Hernández, C. (2021). *Tomar tu mano*. Bogotá: Laguna Libros.

Instituto Cervantes (2004), Centro Virtual. "Augusto Monterroso." Available online: https://cvc.cervantes.es/actcult/monterroso/cronologia/1957_1972.htm. Accessed June 15, 2022.

Kleveland, A. K. (2002), "Augusto Monterroso y la fábula en la literatura contemporánea," *América Latina Hoy*, 30: 119–55.

Kokotovic, M. (2014), "Telling Evasions: Postwar El Salvador in the Short Fiction of Claudia Hernández," *A Contracorriente*, 11 (2): 53–75.

Lámbarry, A. (2012), "Augusto Monterroso in the Latin American Literary Field," *The Princeton University Library Chronicle*, 74 (1): 102–9. Available online: https://doi.org/10.25290/prinunivlibrchro.74.1.0102.

Lámbarry, A., ed. (2013), *La mosca en el canon. Ensayos sobre Augusto Monterroso*. México, DF: Fondo Editorial Tierra Adentri.

Lámbarry, A. (2018), "Los nuevos retos del viejo género de la crítica biográfica: El caso de Augusto Monterroso," *Valenciana: Revista de La Facultad de Filosofía y Letras de La Universidad de Guanajuato* (22): 81–100. Available online: https://doi.org/10.15174/rv.v0i22.375.

Lámbarry, A. (2019), *Augusto Monterroso, en busca del dinosaurio*. Barrio del Niño, Tlalpan, Ciudad de México: Bonilla Artigas Editores.

Lámbarry, A. (2022), "Augusto Monterroso y la minificción, de la ruptura a la banalización," *Lejana: Revista crítica de narrativa breve* (15): 53–64.

Locane, J. J. (2019), *De la literatura latinoamericana a la literatura (latinoamericana) mundial: Condiciones materiales, procesos y actores*. De Gruyter. Available online: https://doi.org/10.1515/9783110622096.

Medeiros, P. de (2020), "Mia Couto and the Antinomies of World-Literature," in K. Van Haesendonck (ed.), *The Worlds of Mia Couto*, 11–31, Oxford, Bern, Berlin, Burxelles, New York, Wien: Peter Lang.

Menjívar Ochoa, R. (2007), "Claudia Hernández o la renovación del cuento." Blog. La mancha en la pared. June 2007. Available online: http://lamanchaenlapared.blogspot.com/2007/06/claudia-hernndez-o-la-renovacin-del.html.

Monterroso, A. [1959] (2002), *Obras completas (y otros cuentos)*, 7th edition, Mexico City: Ediciones Era.

Monterroso, A. [1969] (2004), *La oveja negra y demás fábulas*, 10th edition, Mexico City: Ediciones Era.

Monterroso, A. [1972] (2002), *Movimiento perpetuo*, Mexico City: Punto de lectura.

Monterroso, A. (1980), "Mister Taylor," *Index on Censorship*, 1984, trans. John Lyons.

Monterroso, A. (1982), *Lo demás es silencio. Edición de Jorge Ruffinelli*, 2nd edition, Madrid: Catédra.

Monterroso, A. [1983] (1996), *La palabra mágica*, Barcelona: Anagrama.

Monterroso, A. (1986), *Der Frosch, der ein richtiger Frosch sein Wollte: Kurzprosa.* 2., Veränderte Aufl. Belletristik, Bd. 712, Leipzig: Reclam.

Monterroso, A. (1987), *La letra e (Fragmento de un diario)*, Mexico City: Ediciones Era.

Monterroso, A. (1993), *Los buscadores de oro*, Barcelona: Anagrama.

Monterroso, A. [1998] (2001), *La vaca*, Mexico City: Algfaguara.

Monterroso, A. (2000),"Discurso de Augusto Monterroso al Recibir El Premio Príncipe de Asturias." Available online: https://www.ersilias.com/discurso-de-augusto-monterroso-al-recibir-el-premio-principe-de-asturias/.

Monterroso, A. (2002), *Pájaros de Hispanoamérica*, Madrid: Alfaguara.

Monterroso, A. (2003), *Dossier Augusto Monterroso*, Córdoba, Argentina: Ediciones Sur. Available online: https://www.edicionessur.com/producto/dossier-augusto-monterroso/.

Monterroso, A. (2003), *Literatura y vida*, Madrid: Alfaguara.

Monterroso, A., J. Ruffinelli and J. von Ziegler (1989), *Viaje el centro de la fábula*, México: Era.

Moretti, F. (2000), "Conjectures on World Literature," *New Left Review* (1) (February): 54–68.

Moretti, F. (2003), "More Conjectures," *New Left Review* (20) (April): 73–81.

Noguerol Jiménez, F. (1995), *La trampa en la sonrisa: sátira en la narrativa de Augusto Monterroso*. Sevilla: Editorial Universidad de Sevilla-Secretariado de Publicaciones.

Ortiz Wallner, A. (2013), "Claudia Hernández—por una poética de la prosa en tiempos violentos," *LEJANA. Revista Crítica de Narrativa Breve*, 6: 1–10.

Pérez, Y. (2013), "Historias de metamorfosis: Lo abyecto, los límites entre lo animal y lo humano, en la literatura centroamericana de posguerra," *Revista Iberoamericana*, 29 (242): 163–80. Available online: https://doi.org/10.5195/reviberoamer.2013.7024.

Perkowska, M. (2019), "Los archivos del malestar: estética y política de la infelicidad en la ficción centroamericana contemporánea (Ramiro Lacayo Deshón, Jacinta Escudos y Claudia Hernández)," *Revista Canadiense de Estudios Hispánicos*, 44 (1): 183–205.

Poe, E. A. (n.d.), "Review of Hawthorne's Twice-Told Tales." Available online: http://academic.brooklyn.cuny.edu/english/melani/gothic/poe_review.html. Accessed September 30, 2022.

Rama, Á. (1995), "Un fabulista para nuestro tiempo," in W. H. Corral (ed.), *Refracción. Augusto Monterroso ante la crítica.*, 24–9, Mexico City: Difusión Cultural UNAM; Ediciones Era.

Rincón Chavarro, M. C. Catalina (2013), "De violencia, de normalización y De fronteras," *Catedral Tomada. Revista de crítica literaria*, 1 (1). Available online: http://catedraltomada.pitt.edu/ojs/index.php/catedraltomada/article/view/27.

Ríos Baeza, F. A. (2013), "Monterroso, por una literatura menor," in A. Lámbarry (ed.), *La mosca en el canon. Ensayos sobre Augusto Monterroso*, 70–87, México, DF: Fondo Editorial Tierra Adentro.

Sánchez Prado, I. (2013), "Monterroso y el dispositivo literario latinoamericano," in A. Lámbarry (ed.), *La mosca en el canon. Ensayos sobre Augusto Monterroso*, 70–87, México, DF: Fondo Editorial Tierra Adentro.

Sarmiento, I. (2016a), "Claudia Hernández y la escritura de la precariedad," *AFEHC: Asociación para el Fomento de los Estudios Históricos en Centroamérica* (69). Available online: http://afehc-historia-centroamericana.org/index.php?action=fi_aff&id=4297.

Sarmiento, I. (2016b), "Comunidad y catástrofe en la narrativa salvadoreña contemporánea: Horacio Castellanos Moya, Claudia Hernández y Mauricio Orellana," *Transmodernity. Journal of Peripheral Cultural Production of the Luso-Hispanic World*, 6 (1). Available online: http://escholarship.org/uc/item/1fh7d715.

Sarmiento, I. (2017), "¿Qué hacer con los muertos? Claudia Hernández y el trabajo del duelo en la postguerra salvadoreña," *Revista canadiense de estudios hispánicos*, 41 (2): 395–415.

Singh, J. (2018), *Unthinking Mastery. Dehumanism and Decolonial Entanglements*, Durham, London: Duke University Press.

Stavans, I. (1996), "On Brevity: A Conversation with Augusto Monterroso," *Massachusetts Review*, 37 (3): 393.

Vázquez Enríquez, E. C. (2019), "Companion Species in Border Crossings: *Mediodia de fronteras* by Claudia Hernández," *Ciberletras*, 42: 120–32. Available online: https://www.lehman.cuny.edu/ciberletras/documents/8.Medio-Dia-Hernandez-CIBERLETRAS-42.pdf.

Zavala, L. (2002), *El dinosaurio anotado: edición crítica de "El dinosaurio" de Augusto Monterroso*, Mexico: Alfaguara: Universidad Autónoma Metropolitana.

Zavala, L. (2005), *Relatos mexicanos posmodernos: antología de prosa ultracorta, híbrida y lúdica*, México: Santillana: SEP: Comisión Nacional de Libros de Texto Gratuitos.

Zavala, L. (2018), *Variaciones sobre "El Dinosaurio,"* Lima: Micrópolis. Available online: https://www.academia.edu/38034392/Variaciones_sobre_El_dinosaurio_.

Zúñiga Bustamante, J. (2015), "La irrupción de la casa como metáfora de la inmigración en los cuentos de Claudia Hernández," *Istmo* 29–30 (June). Available online: http://istmo.denison.edu/n29-30/proyectos/06_zuniga_jessie_form.pdf.

3

Central American *Testimonio* as World Literature: English Translation and the Canonization of a Genre

Tamara de Inés Antón

Even though key contributions to the field have zeroed in on the fact that world literature exists and gains in translation, it remains a relatively understudied aspect of world literary circulation (Damrosch 2003; Helgesson and Thomsen 2020; Helgesson and Vermeulen 2016). Still, given the reliance on English translation of contemporary Western practices of world literature, it is essential to confront this functioning of both the English language and the practice of translation as "vanishing mediators," rather than treat them as "neutral or transparent" media (Mufti 2016: 16). Considering the rise of English to worldwide preeminence (Mufti 2016) and the asymmetry governing the literary field (Sapiro 2016), alongside the potential for untranslatability (Apter 2013) of languages and cultures, it is key to understand the inherent importance of translation in any conceptualization of world literature. It is equally important to reveal the ways in which translation can further perpetuate (however unwittingly) the very same imbalances it might want to redress (Medeiros 2019: 63).

As long as there is a center that controls the circulation of literary works, that decides the meaning of peripheral works and declares what is to be universal, and therefore, acceptable and accessible to all, the history of canonizations continues to be full of misconceptions and misreadings stemming from the ethnocentrism of the big literary mediators and gatekeepers (Casanova 2004: 20, 154). As such, and through the analysis of two canonical testimonial texts, this chapter develops a concept of canonization defined not only as the "phenomenon of power and exclusion" (Müller 2021: 12) that governs the selection processes by which some texts (and not others) access the world literary canon but also as a process of reframing. Using narrative theory as a framework of analysis, this chapter examines the implications of different (re)framing strategies for the reception of two key Central American *testimonios* in English translation *I, Rigoberta Menchú: An Indian Woman in Guatemala* (1984) and *They Won't Take Me Alive: Salvadoran Women in Struggle for National Liberation* (1987). In this analysis, particular attention is paid to gender aspects of this reframing process since I find that this is a key yet often sidestepped dimension in relation to the marketability, consecration, and academic consumption of each of the two texts.

Testimonio in and as Translation

The genre of *testimonio* inevitably holds a prominent place in any conceptualization of Central American literature as world literature. Even though the production of these politically engaged texts during the second half of the twentieth century sparked an unprecedented interest in Central American literature among international circles, the publication of scholarly works analyzing the genre has been far from steady. According to various scholars, the focus on Central American cultural production during the 1980s was only a momentary flash of enthusiasm followed by a decline in the circulation and study of Central American texts, particularly of those that were not internationally canonized during this period of enhanced interest (Arias 2007; Maier 2004; Nance 2006). Indeed, the brief literature review offered by this section will show that the critical attention that these literary works once received has been dying out since the late 1990s, and most importantly for this project, that very few scholars have discussed in any depth the role that translation played in the reception of these texts.

Nance offers in her book the definition of *testimonio* that informs this chapter: "body of works in which speaking subjects who present themselves as somehow 'ordinary' represent a personal experience of injustice, whether directly to the reader or through the offices of a collaborating writer, with the goal of inducing readers to participate in a project of social justice" (7). She argues that defining the genre in terms of its goals and its means rejects previous notions of *testimonio* as an "spontaneous" text, unlike other forms of literature, which are seen as being "shaped" (Nance 2006: 7). From the point of view of translation and narrative theory, this is particularly important because it encourages a study of *testimonio* as both (i) promoting personal and public narratives of social and political radicalism with a particular readership in mind, I would argue that an international one, and (ii) being shaped by the political, historical, social, and economic context of production that canonized this genre.

Testimonio has been frequently read as concurring with postmodern premises, such as the "subversion of the distinction between elite and mass cultures, the collapse of master narratives, the fragmentation and decentering of the subject, and the affirmation of alterity" (Maier 2004: 7). And still, it is also possible to argue that those subversive elements have been in turn appropriated and assimilated by the Western canon. Taking Menchú's *testimonio* as an example, one can argue that giving voice to an ethnic female subject from Guatemala is indeed proof of subversion within the traditional distinction between elite and mass cultures. However, the fact that this subject needed the collaboration of a Venezuelan French intellectual, not only to help her produce a *testimonio* in written form in a language that was not hers but also to publish it, still maintains the centrality of the intellectual/the elite within the editorial world. In fact, both of the *testimonios* discussed in this chapter are mediated *testimonios*. The mediated nature of this genre, in which the narrator is not always the author of the text, has encouraged academic readings around consciousness-raising and the representation of the Other—approaches undertaken by scholars such as Beverley (1996), Zimmerman (1991), Sommer (1994, 1996), and Gugelberger (1996).

Moreover, the mediation of the ethnographer has raised frequent debates on authority, voice, and subalternity. For example, Arturo Arias (2001) poses again Gayatri Spivak's groundbreaking question "Can the Subaltern Speak?" (1988) to study Rigoberta Menchú's mediated discourse as an ethnicized subject and a subaltern self, and the debate around the factuality of the text (the so-called Menchú-Stoll debate). Arias claims that the "authentic discourse" of the subaltern becomes suppressed, a hidden truth, because of the Westerner's inability to comprehend the speaking subaltern on his/her own terms (Arias 2001: 73). Arias's words on the subject of Western appropriation of the subaltern discourse fit particularly well into any discussion of translation and *testimonio*. In the case of Menchú, whose paradigmatic *testimonio* he continues to analyze in Arias (2007), his words apply first to the construction of Menchú's published *testimonio* in Spanish, which can already be studied as a double layer of translation/mediation: (i) Menchú's retelling of her own story from K'iche' to Spanish and (ii) Burgos's construction of Menchú's narrative into a written *testimonio*; and then (as I will argue below) to the canonization process that this text underwent during its English translation.

With a few exceptions, and regardless of the extensive research on questions of representation and mediation (through the relationship between the editor and the subaltern subject), not a lot of attention has been given to the fact that historians, ethnographers, and translators all face similar issues of representation and truth (Lather 2000: 157). The role of English translation as a new layer of mediation in the construction of *testimonios* as world literary texts remains understudied, and yet it is almost impossible to separate the notion of translation (at least in its most abstract form) from that of *testimonio*. Testimonial narratives—regardless of their temporal and spatial proximity to the events being narrated—are always already mediated/translated by language (Brodzki 2007: 119). Just as the process by which the testimonial subject or narrator memorializes their own trauma can be analyzed as a form of translation in itself, the way in which the writer/ethnographer takes their oral account and puts it into writing can be studied as a form of intersemiotic translation. I could also go on to stress here how any ethnographic project is inherently a project of translation. Since in the words of Brodzki (2007), anthropology as a discipline and as an unequally distributed mode of knowledge production has endeavored itself since its inception in the nineteenth century to render the culture of the Other into the "meaningful" terms of the West (Brodzki 2007: 135).

Furthermore, very few genres might be better catered by translation than that of *testimonio*, a narrative constructed with the main goal of reaching an international audience and gaining their solidarity. If the intended readership of *testimonio* is an international one (Damrosch 2003: 231), then translation acts, in Benjamin and Derrida's terms, as a redemptive force that ensures the living on of a cultural narrative (albeit in a revised or altered form). According to Derrida, the translated text "does not simply live longer, it lives more and better, beyond the means of the [narrator]" (1985: 104). Yet this celebration of the power of translation obscures its material and textual dimensions. The following sections demonstrate the ways in which such a celebration, coupled with an illusion of transparency associated with translation in Anglo-American circles, conceals the importance of location and the translator's role in the crucial reframing of the original narratives, an act that has perhaps enabled a particular reception and consumption of these two particular texts and the genre as a whole.

Location and Reception of *No me agarran viva* and its English Translation

Since developments in world literature have been moving parallel to work in translation studies, scholars in translation studies could and should find in postcolonial and world literature studies some very fruitful theoretical applications (Bassnett 2011: 72) and vice versa. In response to this call for more interdisciplinary communication, this chapter finds that the sociological concept of "location," as developed by Casanova (2010), serves as a compelling entry point when questioning the canonization/reframing of the first *testimonio* of interest here: *No me agarran viva* (1983) as a work of world literature.

Casanova claims that it is necessary to define the position of a text in three ways in order to fully understand its "location" within the world of letters. First of all, one has to describe the position that the source language and the target language occupy within the universe of literary languages. Then the translated author needs to be located within the world literary space in two different ways: firstly, in terms of the place that they occupy within their national literary space and, secondly, regarding the place that this national space occupies within the world system. And finally, the position of the translator and other consecrating agents needs to be determined.

According to these three positions and their centrality or peripherality within the literary field, Casanova designs her study of the different functions of translation, i.e., "translation as accumulation of capital" or "translation as consecration" (296). Due to the peripheral/dominated status of Central American literature, I focus on the latter, which takes place when texts from a dominated language/literary space are translated into a dominating one. In this case, the position of the translated text and its legitimacy will depend not only on the relation between source language and target language or the location of the translated authors but also on the position held by the translator-consecrator (Casanova 2010: 299). In the context of this chapter, the role of the translator-consecrator cannot but remind us of the role of the intellectual/writer "author(iz)ing" and legitimizing the voice of the narrator in mediated *testimonios* (Picornell 2011), doubling down on the level of mediation and reframing needed for the voice of the subaltern to finally be heard by the center.

In the case of *No me agarran viva* (1983) and its English translation, the positions of the source and target language are quite different: Spanish is considered a semi-peripheral language (regardless of its large number of speakers) and English a hyper-central one (Heilbron 2000). Moreover, the location of the authors within the world republic of letters has to be established. The Nicaraguan-Salvadoran writer Claribel Alegría, even within the peripheral position allocated by her status as both woman and Central American writer, has received considerable critical attention and her work has been published both abroad and in her home country (Craft 1997).

Even though her work has been highly recognized within academic circles, it is important to note that her poetry has traditionally received more critical attention than her prose, where she frequently collaborated with her husband Flakoll (Velasquez 2002: 2). Additionally, and even though the works of prose that Alegría co-authored with her husband are among those that have received more critical attention (including the *testimonio* being discussed here), there has been a "collective critical silence" about the role of

Flakoll in Alegría's literary career (Barbas-Rhoden 2003: 23). Barbas-Rhoden goes on to venture the following for this silence: readers might be wrongly attributing the writing to Alegría because topics such as "Salvadoran and women's issues" predominate in their coauthored writings (24).

Interestingly for this study on canonization, this silence runs even deeper and seems much more intentional when one turns to the English translation of this *testimonio*. In *They Won't Take Me Alive* (1987), Flakoll's participation has been completely erased—both textually and paratextually—but the reasons behind this framing strategy have never been openly discussed. Contrary to Menchú's *testimonio*, in *No me agarran viva* (1983), the mediator(s) make the processes of elicitation transparent to the reader. In the source text (ST), both authors make themselves visible by recording some of their questions and intercalating the pronoun "we" periodically. However, only the presence of Alegría is apparent to the Anglophone reader in the target text (TT), as seen in Table 3.1.

Their questions serve to contextualize the story and transition between different topics, but at the same time they indicate to the reader the presence of interviewees who, to a certain extent, control the dialogue, which emphasizes the constructed nature of the history that they are telling (Barbas-Rhoden 2003: 36). This constructedness is also highlighted by the fact that the story is not narrated by its protagonist, but by several interviewees that interpret Eugenia's life in very different manners and embodying a variety of roles: student, sister, *compañera*, mother, wife, *guerrillera*, and political leader. After the first novelistic chapter, in which the last hours of Eugenia are fictionalized, the format of the *testimonio* changes and each chapter is organized around a theme: induction to revolutionary activities, married life, machismo, motherhood, children in the revolution, etc. Alegría and Flakoll contextualize the themes and guide the dialogue to a certain extent, but the text is mainly an account of different individuals that relate anecdotes and complete the story of Eugenia, who can no longer speak for herself. Therefore, this effort of remembering, of narration, is a collective one (Barbas-Rhoden 2003: 38). And it is in this context of collectivity that the disappearance of Flakoll within the English translation is most difficult to understand from an academic perspective.

Turning the attention now to the third level of location posed by Casanova (2010), it should be noted that the English translation of *No*

TABLE 3.1 *Erasure of Flakoll's textual presence in* They Won't Take Me Alive (1987).

ST: "—Dinos algo de la vida de pareja dentro de la clandestinidad—le pedimos" (Alegría and Flakoll 1983: 65).	TT: "Tell me something of a couple's life underground," I asked him (Alegría 1987: 80).

me agarran viva was published in 1987 by Women's Press, an independent publishing company based in London (UK) and dedicated to making available feminist works by women writers from around the globe. The *testimonio* was translated by Amanda Hopkinson who during the decade of 1970s was the editor of the human rights magazine *Central America Report*. In the paratext of *They Won't Take Me Alive* (1987), she presents herself as a writer and journalist who has lived and traveled extensively in Central America and who has been involved in the women's liberation movement since 1968. Thus, it is possible that the very ideology of the publisher and the "translator-consecrator" influenced the editorial decision to erase Flakoll's presence from the TT. From their perspective, it would be easier to market such a politically and sexually subversive text if it is written by a Salvadoran woman, and not by her husband, particularly when this husband is a US citizen, the very country whose Cold War master narrative this book is trying to disrupt.

And to double down in this editorial decision, the textual erasure of Flakoll's presence in the TT is followed by a paratextual one. His name never appears on the cover, and the only time in which his presence is acknowledged is in the section "About This Book" written by Hopkinson (1987: 32). Even there, the TT emphasizes the status of Alegría as the author, who, with the help of her husband's research and testimonies of many of Eugenia's circle, has recounted the story of the life and death of the protagonist of this work. The importance of Alegría as the author is underlined again on the back cover of the TT, where the fact that this story "is told by one of El Salvador's foremost writers" seems to be granting authority to the testimonial voice.

In addition to the TT's paratextual decision to obscure Flakoll's participation, my comparative analysis of ST and translation uncovers a pattern of paratextual strategies that foreground certain political aspects of an already political text. In narrative theory, causal emplotment is an essential feature of narrativity, and it allows people to weight and explain events, so they can form their opinions (Baker 2006: 67). Consequently, it charges any event with moral and ethical significance, allowing people to moralize reality—which is why it is, in my opinion, central to the study of any politically charged genre such as *testimonio*.

In the words of Baker (2006), "patterns of causal emplotment can be subtly changed in translation through the cumulative effect of relatively minor shifts that lend a different weighting to the elements of the original narrative" (Baker 2006: 70). Thus, it is important to note here that I am in no way denying the political nature of the ST, but rather establishing the ways in which shifts in causal emplotment of the translated narrative (i) highlight the role of the United States as facilitator of the violence faced by the people in El Salvador and (ii) emphasize the importance of armed resistance as the only means to end the struggle.

As part of these shifts in causal emplotment, we see framing by labeling. On the one hand, the back cover of the TT emphasizes terms that resonate with the armed struggle such as "comrades-in-arms," "political struggle," "violent confrontation," "military missions," "popular war," "guerrilla forces," "war of liberation," "guerrilla armies," or "soldier." Moreover, this armed struggle is presented as the only alternative in the face of a military regime described "as one of the bloodiest and most brutal ones, even within the aggressively oppressive contexts of many Latin American countries" (Hopkinson 1987: 32). On the other hand, the labeling of the ST centers the narrative in the abnegated role of women that would do and have done everything and anything to liberate their people. The TT is paratextually framed as a narrative of heroism, abnegation, and martyrdom, emphasizing terms such as "entrega total," "abnegación, sacrificio y heroísmo revolucionario," "lucha por la paz y la justicia," "heroínas y mártires," "comprometidas" ["absolute dedication," "self-sacrifice and revolutionary heroism," "fighting for peace and justice," "heroines and martyrs," "committed"].

While the TT features a fairly close translation of the content of ST, it also includes two new paratextual elements written by the translator Amanda Hopkinson, a "Historical Introduction" (1987: 1–19) and a "Preface" (1987: 20–9). Both "Introduction" and "Preface" continue to frame this narrative in the same manner as the paratexts previously discussed. For example, Hopkinson begins her "Historical Introduction" with a reference to the 1932 brutal massacre of Salvadoran peasants. Hopkinson establishes how the legacy of this event has created, promoted, and maintained certain stereotypes from both sides. It allowed the state to disseminate the idea that any tactic was justified against the "[c]ommunist hordes about to overrun the country" (Hopkinson 1987: 1), while creating a profound mistrust of the peasantry against any type of military. Through causal emplotment, Hopkinson frames the current violence in El Salvador as endemic but, most importantly, as caused by first Spanish colonization and then US imperialism. This emphasis on the United States is underlined by the way in which this "Historical Introduction" concludes: "What we want is peace and genuine democracy, not rule by the United States through the armed forces" (Hopkinson 1987: 19).

In addition to this, some of the editorial decisions in the TT, such as obscuring the role of Flakoll—a male US citizen—in the production of the original text, also reinforce a public narrative by which the political radicalism of the narrating voices is authorized by a politically committed intellectual: Alegría—also female and Salvadoran herself. In the TT, it is Alegría herself who denounces to an international audience the suffering of their people at the hands of not only the army but also Reagan's policies. My analysis therefore demonstrates the usefulness of applying Casanova's concept of location to the study of translation and circulation of world literary texts, evidencing that the intersection between gender and politics needs to be considered in any in-depth analysis of the process of canonization. In the case of *They Won't Take Me Alive* (1987), location—understood in terms of publisher, translator, historical context, feminist, and solidarity movements—had a clear impact in how the original narrative was reframed in translation.

The Canonization of *I, Rigoberta Menchú*: The Renarration of a Lost Original

As demonstrated above, translation can be understood as a form of reframing and (re)narration that participates in the construction of a story, rather than merely a process of textual transfer from one language to another. In order to articulate the dialectical relationship between renarration and canonization, this section focuses on Menchú's *testimonio*, a text that serves as the paradigm of canonization of women's *testimonio*, not only for Central America but, some would argue, for Latin America and the postcolonial or subaltern subject as a whole (Mackenbach 2015: 420). It is this prominence as well as the high level of critical attention that this text has received that allows for a particularly fruitful exploration of the concepts of renarration and canonization.

Despite the extensive amount of literature on this paradigmatic *testimonio*, not enough attention has been paid to the role that its translation into English played in the canonization of this text, a translation that for all intents and purposes seems to have taken over the original as part of the world literary canon. A quick literature review on Menchú's *testimonio*, including seminal volumes such as Gugelberger (1996), Arias (2001, 2007), and Carey-Webb and Benz (1996), could suggest that the text being consumed, canonized, and constantly cited is in fact the English translation *I, Rigoberta Menchú: An Indian Woman from Guatemala* (1984), rather than the ST *Me llamo Rigoberta Menchú y así me nació la conciencia* (1983). The constant citing of the TT helps to invisibilize both the ST and the impact of translation, particularly since the TT is mostly being quoted without any explicit consideration to the level of renarration that translation might (and does) entail.

The glaring difference between the two titles—ST and TT—will serve here as a first example of renarration. Due to their highly visible and central position, titles function as a compass that guides the readers through the plot. Titles are regularly and deliberately employed by writers, editors, translators, and publishers to activate particular narrative frames for them to interpret the work at hand. In this case, the reader of the English title will never activate any frame related to revolutionary struggle and the Marxist theories supposed to shape the interpretation of the original, with its use of "así me nació la conciencia." Instead, the English reader will activate a frame through which Menchú's narrative is not merely the personal story of an individual but represents all Indigenous women of Guatemala. Thus, by privileging the study of the TT, critics of *testimonio* could be ignoring and/or depoliticizing a very manipulative practice (that of translation) and at the same time overlooking the scope of the process of renarration that this text has suffered.

The canonization of *I, Rigoberta Menchú* (1984) has given a central position to a heavily mediated text, which has gone through several moments of intervention to give voice to a subject from the periphery. I would argue that there are at least four moments of intervention deserving of study when it comes to this text. The first one would be Menchú's narration of her own story which should be understood both as a form of "cultural translation" (Helgesson and Thomsen 2020: 5) from a K'iche' world to Spanish, which from Menchú's position as an indigenous woman from Guatemala is a highly strategic move (Sommer 1999: 126). The already mediated construction of the ST from a series of interviews between Burgos and Menchú (McEnaney 2020) serves here as the second moment of intervention, which is then followed by a third one: the translation into English, and a fourth one: the consumption and canonization of this text as a paradigmatic example of its genre.

The canonization of *I, Rigoberta Menchú* (1984) does not mean simply its adherence to centrally generated conventions of the genre but also that, by achieving such an iconic status, future texts might need to follow these same parameters (Müller 2021) in order to be read as *testimonio* by academia, thus silencing or homogenizing other marginal voices in the process. Linda S. Maier and Isabel Dulfano discuss this problematic process of canonization and consumption of the *testimonio* by Western audiences, which was quickly followed by disenchantment by Anglo-American academics. Dulfano states that academics have "consumed *testimonio*'s utility and discarded the remains of the discourse" (83). As a "resistant text" (Sommer 1999), *testimonio* has been first translated, and then canonized and consumed by academia, under a certain set of central norms. These norms could not always fit the peripheral nature of the text, thus creating certain resentments, omissions, and tensions.

As discussed by Irene Mathews (2000), the "authority" (truthfulness) of *Me llamo Rigoberta Menchú* (1983) and its "authoring" (narrative responsibility) have a controversial history (104). The controversy behind the authoring of this text can also be explored through a comparative paratextual analysis of ST and TT. The Spanish version includes Rigoberta's name in the title *Me llamo Rigoberta Menchú*, but Elisabeth Burgos is on the cover and title page as author of the book. However, the text published in English shows no "author" on the cover and the text featuring on the title page reads as follows: "Edited and introduced by Elisabeth Burgos-Debray" and "Translated by Ann Wright."

Moreover, the ST *Me llamo Rigoberta Menchú* (1983) includes two paratexts, a preface and an introduction that inform the reader about the mediating presence of Burgos and therefore announce a certain partiality of knowledge when it comes to the text. The English translation *I, Rigoberta Menchú* (1984) does include a translation of Burgos's "Prólogo," but this is preceded by a "Translator's note" where Ann Wright focuses on the fact that Menchú's discourse is that of someone who is not a Spanish native speaker and the difficulty that this presented during the translation process. Ann Wright erases from this "Translator's note" the presence of the ethnographer Elisabeth Burgos to whom she never refers. Ironically, she discusses how she has ventured in some strategic editions to Menchú's words in order to convey clarity, but at the same time she obscures the fact that she is working upon a text that has previously suffered the intervention of an ethnographer who also claimed to have aimed for that same clarity. In fact, Wright's "Translator's note" bears an uncanny resemblance to Burgos's "Introducción" to the first edition in Spanish (Burgos 1983: 7–8), which has been excluded from TT. In brief, the central position of the English translation *I, Rigoberta Menchú* (1984) gives the illusion of a less, rather than more, mediated text and consequently responds to a Western desire of consuming subaltern/peripheral voices, which are ultimately denied a fully authoritative status.

It is this illusion of immediacy between the narrating "I" and the readerly "you" that Menchú seems to personally reject. In carrying out her double duty as a responsible survivor, tasked with denouncing the horrors suffered by her people, and as keeper of her community's secrets, Menchú explicitly and strategically uses both silence and wordy refusals to speak. These protests of silence have survived the editing process from the taped interviews to the written text and remain part of the final product with some explicit mentions to her keeping secrets. Her use of these "secrets" as a strategic tool to keep the distance with her readers was cleverly analyzed by Sommer (1996, 1999).

It can therefore be claimed that the ambiguity that characterizes Menchú's discourse in ST is not only a consequence of the orality of the original discourse, her use of a language that she does not know well (Spanish), or a potential interference from the grammar and discursive practices of her native K'iche', but an intentional textual strategy that keeps her readers from knowing too much, from appropriating and easily consuming her narrative, and from identifying with her. The difficulty the reader needs to overcome when going through this text, the frequent repetitions and halts in the fluency of the narrative, might as well be part of the construction of the text as a political tool (Arias 2001: 77–82). Menchú's secretive privileging of the unknown and the uncertain reflects a general strategy in the text to distance readers and avoid any cultural and political exploitation of her community's worldviews.

TABLE 3.2 *Labeling and Menchú's secrets.*

ST: "Pero sin embargo sigo ocultando mi identidad como indígena. Sigo ocultando lo que yo considero que nadie sabe, ni si quiera un antropólogo, ni un intelectual, por más que tenga muchos libros, no saben distinguir todos nuestros <u>secretos</u>" (1983: 271).	TT: "Nevertheless, I am still keeping my Indian identity a <u>secret</u>. I'm still keeping <u>secret</u> what I think no-one should know. Not even anthropologists or intellectuals, no matter how many books they have, can find out all <u>our secrets</u>" (1984: 289).

Menchú's textual refusals to speak are actually emphasized in the English version by an increase in frequency of their labeling as "secrets" (see Table 3.2). However, these "secrets," i.e., the general lack of fluency of Menchú's narrative that constantly distances her from the reader (Sommer 1996, 1999), have otherwise been carefully wiped out by the translator (Damrosch 2003: 250), producing a TT that is far easier to consume by the international market.

An analysis of this renarration is particularly interesting when it comes to Menchú's accounts of violence, i.e., the chapters on her brother's death and her mother's rape and torture to death. In the ST, the characteristic ambiguity and lack of fluency present in Menchú's discourse suddenly disappear as part of her narration of torture, which becomes very much a matter-of-fact rhetoric with a clear preponderance of details. Menchú does not seek here to horrify her readers and to distance them further; her descriptive narrative and steady tone are aimed to convince. In doing so, Menchú challenges the unspeakability of violence. She provides the reader with a narrative that reads as a whole truth, finally giving them access to uncontested knowledge (regardless of any controversies about its factuality).

Menchú's depiction of torture into English is very close to that of the ST. Indeed, these are passages in which the efforts to create fluency on the part of the English translator were never necessary; thus her presence is not as visible. However, an overall comparison between ST and TT allows me to question how well kept were Menchú's secrets in the TT. If we consider framing ambiguity in the ST as a primarily strategic rhetorical tool, the TT's betrayal of the original's refusal to flow (Sommer 1999: 15) is rather relevant. However, in her "Translator's note," Wright clearly states that Menchú's "spontaneous narrative can leave the reader a little confused as to the chronology and details of the events," and it is therefore the aim of her translation to "retain the vitality" of Menchú's words but achieve "clarity at the same time" (Menchú 1984: vii). This quote should demonstrate how the need and desire of the Western reader to access the Other have encouraged a translation that promotes a much more fluent narrative: one that maintains (and even emphasizes) Menchú's textual references to her silences but frequently betrays her needs for distance.

Similarly, when it comes to the fourth moment of intervention, i.e., the critical reception and consumption of this *testimonio*, one can observe again the imposed needs and preferences of a Western reader in the selection of topics that have been studied in relation to this text. Although hundreds of articles and dozens of very important anthologies and books have been produced on *I, Rigoberta Menchú* (1984), only a relatively small number of scholars have drawn sustained attention to gender representation in this work (Bañales 2014; Bueno 2000; Cantero-Rosales 2003; Fernández-Olmos 1989; Marín 1991; Matthews 2000; Smith 2010; and Sternbach 1991).

Victoria Bañales (2014) questions the reasons behind academia's decision to sidestep (at least in part) the issue of gender when it comes to *I, Rigoberta Menchú* (1984), which seems particularly glaring not only because of Menchú's narrating position as a woman but because of her extensive treatment of gender in her text. Not only does she develop several representations of women throughout her narrative—as mothers, exploited workers, targets of (sexual) violence, participants in the armed struggle, and so on—but her text itself exhibits an incredible ability to actively respond to, resist, complicate, and counter the same contradictions that are present in her construction of gender roles via other representations. In view of the above, Bañales suggests that part of the problem "no doubt stems from the false opposition set up between dominant notions of collectivity (as the overlooking of difference) and differences (as the forfeiting of collectivity)" (Bañales 2014: 365).

It should be noted, however, that there is no need for collectivity (the community) and difference (gender) to be these mutually exclusive categories. The tensions between collectivity and difference had already been observed by Lynda Marín (1991) in her study of Latin American women's *testimonios*, where she claimed that these texts should be read as a complex negotiation between their "stated project"—to speak in a unified way for their struggling and suffering people—and their "unstated project"—to do that while highlighting the inequalities that women endure in their cultures (55). *I, Rigoberta Menchú*'s (1984) emphasis on a collective and communal struggle should have not impeded more gendered analyses of her work. In fact, this has never been the case for other *testimonios* written by Latin American women, which have indeed received gendered readings, i.e., the critical analysis of the representations of gender transgressions in Alegría's *They Won't Take Me Alive* by feminist scholars such as Ileana Rodríguez (1994) or Laura Barbas-Rhoden (2003). Reading Menchú's *testimonio* as both emblematic for a larger community and specific to Maya women's issues is possible (Bañales 2014: 365), and so Western academia could and should have resisted the tendency to present gender and collective indigenous forms of resistance as irreconcilable struggles.

If, as a genre, most *testimonios* literally and figuratively claim to represent not only the experiences of the narrator but those of larger communities,

TABLE 3.3 *Overemphasized representativity in the TT.*

ST: "Me llamo Rigoberta Menchú. Tengo veintitrés años. Quisiera dar este testimonio vivo que no he aprendido en un libro y que tampoco he aprendido sola ya que todo esto lo he aprendido con mi pueblo y es algo que yo quisiera enfocar[...] pero lo importante es, yo creo, que quiero hacer un enfoque que no soy la única, pues ha vivido mucha gente y es la vida de todos. La vida de todos los guatemaltecos pobres y trataré de dar un poco mi historia. Mi situación personal engloba toda la realidad de un pueblo" (1983: 21).	TT: "My name is Rigoberta Menchú. I am twenty-three years old. This is my testimony. I didn't learn it from a book and I didn't learn it alone. I'd like to stress that it's not only *my* (italics NOT mine) life, it's the testimony of my people. ... The important thing is that what has happened to me has happened to many other people too: my story is the story of all poor Guatemalans. My personal experience is the reality of a whole people" (1984: 1).

Menchú's text is no exception. However, in a world constructed through binaries, this tendency to overemphasize the plurality and collectivity often serves as an effective way to efface the individuality (and in this case gender) of the author (Bueno 2000: 119). Menchú's favoring of her identity as representative of her community over her own individuality is a textual strategy that, although present in ST at times, has been further overemphasized in the TT, as exemplified by Table 3.3.

First of all, TT marks in italics the pronoun "my" and emphasizes that this is not only Menchú's life but the testimony of her people. On the other hand, in ST the narrative maintains that this story is a living testimony, one that has grown with Menchú, one that she has learnt as part of a collective adventure with her people. Similarly at the end of the excerpt in TT, it explicitly states that Menchú's story is that of all the poor Guatemalans, while ST highlights that she is not the only one living under these circumstances, that this is the life of all the poor people in Guatemala, and that she is going to tell her part of the story. Thus, without denying the collective and denouncing nature of *testimonio* as a genre, it is important to acknowledge the ways in which the translation into English, or third moment of intervention, has affected the reception of this work and overemphasized the representativeness of Menchú in order for her to fit this image of the idealized witness.

In fact, it is precisely this overly representative phrase, where the TT claims that Menchú's story is that of all poor Guatemalans that was chosen as the title of *Rigoberta Menchú and the Story of All Poor Guatemalans* (Stoll 1999). Stoll's controversial book claimed that Menchú's life narrative contained a number of significant misrepresentations about her and her family, but most importantly to my argument, it sparked an international debate that questioned the nature of the entire genre of *testimonio* (Nance 2006: 5) and possibly changed the way it continues to be read. Without claiming that Stoll or the other participants of the debate relied solely on the English translation of the text, it can still be argued that the consumption of Menchú's story in particular and the overall canonization of *testimonio* as a world literary genre have been necessarily mediated by translation. Canonization, as a key concept in world literature studies, has been brought to the fore by this chapter's comparative and socio-narrative approach. It has been defined as a process of reframing or renarration and then used to explain the narrative shifts that Central American and (potentially) other peripheral works must undergo in order to become part of the world literary canon. Similarly, other relevant concepts in world literature and translation studies, such as location and an overreliance on English translations, have been interrogated here to discuss the ways in which they can be seen to shape the radicalism of these texts, understood both in terms of gender and politics, and their reception as works of world literature.

References

Alegría, C. (1987), *They Won't Take Me Alive: Salvadoran Women in Struggle for National Liberation*, trans. A. Hopkinson, London: The Women's Press.

Alegría, C. and D. J. Flakoll (1983), *No me agarran viva: La mujer salvadoreña en la lucha*, México, DF: Ediciones Era.

Apter, E. (2013), *Against World Literature. On the Politics of Untranslatability*, London: Verso.

Arias, A., ed. (2001), *The Rigoberta Menchú Controversy*, Minneapolis: University of Minnesota.

Arias, A. (2007), *Taking Their Word. Literature and the Signs of Central America*, Minneapolis: University of Minnesota Press.

Baker, M. (2006), *Translation and Conflict: A Narrative Account*, London: Routledge.

Bañales, V. (2014), "Women with Guns: Translating Gender in *I, Rigoberta Menchu*" in S. E. Alvarez, C. De Lima Costa, V. Feliu, R. J. Hester, N. Klahn, M. Thayer, and C. C. Bueno (eds.), *Translocalities/translocalidades: Feminist Politics of Translation in the Latin/a Americas*, 363–80, Durham: Duke University Press.

Barbas-Rhoden, L. (2003), *Writing Women in Central America: Gender and the Fictionalization of History*, Athens: Ohio University Press.

Bassnett, S. (2011), "From Cultural Turn to Translational Turn: A Transnational Journey," in C. Alvstad, S. Helgesson and D. Watson (eds.), *Literature, Geography, Translation*, 67–80, Newcastle: Cambridge Scholars Publishing.

Beverley, J. (1996), "The Real Thing," in G. M. Gugelberger (ed.), *The Real Thing: Testimonial Discourse and Latin America*, 266–86, Durham: Duke University Press.

Beverley, J. and H. Achúgar, eds. (1992), *La voz del otro: Testimonio, subalternidad y verdad narrativa*, Lima-Berkeley: Latinoamericana Editores.

Brodzki, B. (2007), *Can These Bones Live? Translation, Survival and Cultural Memory*, Stanford: Stanford University Press.

Bueno, E. P. (2000), "Race, Gender and the Politics of Reception of Latin American Testimonios," in A. Amireh and L. S. Majaj (eds.), *Going Global: The Transnational Reception of Third World Women Writers*, New York: Garland Publishing.

Burgos-Debray, E. (1983), *Me llamo Rigoberta Menchú y así me nació la conciencia*, Barcelona: Seix Barral.

Cantero-Rosales, M. A. (2003), "Escritura en relación: El discurso testimonial como mediación entre mujeres," *DUODA Revista d'Estudis Feministes*, 25: 37–51.

Carey-Webb, A. and S. Benz, eds. (1996), *Teaching and Testimony: Rigoberta Menchú and the North American Classroom*, New York: State of New York University Press.

Casanova, P. (2004), *The World Republic of Letters*, Cambridge: Harvard University Press.

Casanova, P. (2010), "Consecration and Accumulation of Literary Capital: Translation as Unequal Exchange," in M. Baker (ed.), *Critical Readings in Translation Studies*, 285–303, London: Routledge.

Craft, L. J. (1997), *Novels of Testimony and Resistance from Central America*, Florida: University Press of Florida.

Damrosch, D. (2003), *What Is World Literature?*, Princeton: Princeton University Press.

Derrida, J. (1985), *The Ear of the Other: Otobiography, Transference, Translation*, Lincoln: University of Nebraska Press.

Fernández-Olmos, M. (1989), "Latin American Testimonial Narrative or Women and the Art of Listening," *Revista Canadiense de Estudios Hispánicos*, 13 (2): 183–95.

Gugelberger, G. M., ed. (1996), *The Real Thing: Testimonial Discourse and Latin America*, Durham: Duke University Press.

Heilbron, J. (2000), "Towards a Sociology of Translation: Book Translations as a Cultural World-System," *European Journal of Social Theory*, 2 (4): 429–44.

Helgesson, S. and P. Vermeulen, eds. (2016), *Institutions of World Literature: Writing, Translation, Markets*, New York: Routledge.

Helgesson, S. and M. R. Thomsen (2020), *Literature and the World*, New York: Routledge.

Lather, P. (2000), "Reading the Image of Rigoberta Menchú: Undecidability and Language Lessons," *International Journal of Qualitative Studies in Education*, 13 (2): 153–62.

Mackenbach, W. (2015), "El testimonio centroamericano contemporáneo entre la epopeya y la parodia," *Kamchatka*, 6: 409–34.

Maier, L. S. and I. Dulfano, eds. (2004), *Woman as Witness: Essays on Testimonial Literature by Latin American Women*, New York: Peter Lang.

Marín, L. (1991), "Speaking Out Together: Testimonials of Latin American Women," *Latin American Perspectives*, 18 (3): 51–68.

Matthews, I. (2000), "Translating, Transgressing, Torture ...," in M. Waller and J. Rycenga (eds.), *Frontline Feminisms: Women, War and Resistance*, 85–112, New York: Routledge.

McEnaney, T. (2020), "Rigoberta's Listener: The Significance of Sound in *Testimonio*," *PMLA*, 135 (2): 393–400.

Medeiros, P. (2019), "Translation and Cosmopolitanism," in S. Basnett (ed.), *Translation and World Literature*, 60–74, New York: Routledge.

Menchú, R. and E. Burgos-Debray (1984), *I, Rigoberta Menchú: An Indian Woman in Guatemala*, trans. A. Wright, London: Verso.

Mufti, A. (2016), *Forget English! Orientalisms and World Literatures*, Cambridge: Harvard University Press.

Müller, G. (2021), *How Is World Literature Made? The Global Circulations of Latin American Literatures*, Berlin: De Gruyter.

Nance, K. A. (2006), *Can Literature Promote Justice? Trauma Narrative and Social Action in Latin American Testimonio*, Tennessee: Vanderbilt University Press.

Picornell, M. (2011), "El género testimonio en los márgenes de la historia: Representación y autorización de la voz subalterna," *Espacio, tiempo y forma*, 23: 113–40.

Rodríguez, I. (1994), "*Testimonio* and Diaries as Narratives of Success and Failure in *They Won't Take Me Alive*," in S. Boschetto-Sandoval and M. Phillips McGowan (eds.), *Claribel Alegría and Central American Literature*, 45–60, Ohio: Ohio University Press.

Sapiro, G. (2016), "How Do Literary Works Cross Borders (or Not)? A Sociological Approach to World Literature," *Journal of World Literature*, 1: 81–96.

Sommer, D. (1994), "Resistant Texts and Incompetent Readers," *Poetics Today*, 15: 523–54.

Sommer, D. (1996), "No Secrets," in G. M. Gugelberger (ed.), *The Real Thing: Testimonial Discourse and Latin America*, 130–60, Durham: Duke University Press.

Sommer, D. (1999), *Proceed with Caution, When Engaged by Minority Writing in the Americas*, Cambridge: Harvard University Press.

Spivak, G. C. (1988), "Can the Subaltern Speak," in C. Nelson and L. Grossberg (eds.), *Marxism and the Interpretation of Culture*, 271–313, Urbana: University of Illinois Press.

Smith, K. M. (2010), "Female Voice and Feminist Text: Testimonio as a Form of Resistance in Latin America," *Florida Atlantic Comparative Studies Journal*, 12: 21–38.

Sternbach, N. S. (1991), "Re-membering the Death: Latin American Women's 'Testimonial' Discourse," *Latin American Perspectives*, 18 (3): 91–102.

Stoll, D. (1999), *Rigoberta Menchú and the Story of All Poor Guatemalans*, Boulder: Westview Press.

Velásquez, A. (2002), *Las novelas de Claribel Alegría: Historia, sociedad y (re) vision de la estética literaria centroamericana*, New York: Peter Lang.

Zimmerman, M. (1991), "*Testimonio* in Guatemala: Payeras, Rigoberta and Beyond," *Latin American Perspectives*, 18 (4): 22–47.

4

When Does Central American Literature Become Global?: The Extraordinary (or Predictable?) Case of Eduardo Halfon

Magdalena Perkowska

Which literature, whose world?
—DAVID DAMROSCH, *WHAT IS WORLD LITERATURE?*

It was in Auschwitz.
—EDUARDO HALFON, *THE POLISH BOXER*

In his "Conjectures on World Literature," one of the studies that initiated the revival of the academic discussion on world literature, Franco Moretti observes that the concept implies, at the same time and paradoxically, unity and inequality: "[O]*ne* literature ... or perhaps, better, one world literary system ... but a system ... [that is] profoundly unequal" (2000: 56). Just like international capitalism creates a core, semiperiphery, and periphery, the world system of literatures is organized hierarchically into a core, semiperiphery, and periphery, with asymmetrical and uneven circulation of texts and interferences between them (Moretti 2000: 55–6). Pascale Casanova's Franco-centric perspective in *The World Republic of Letters* ([1999] 2004), which bestows on Paris the regulatory and consecratory power over literatures and their relationships (Siskind 2014: 16–17), is a confirmation of the world literary system's uneven structures, flows, and currents. My point here is not to criticize Moretti's and Casanova's proposals or to engage with them from the standpoint of a Latin Americanist, a task undertaken expertly by others (De Ferrari 2012; Domínguez 2012; Kristal 2002; Müller and Siskind 2019; Sánchez Prado 2006; Siskind 2014), but rather to ponder the issue of unevenness as we consider the position of Central American literature within the world system of literatures. What is its place in this unequal structure? According to Guatemalan writer and scholar Arturo Arias, Central America is one of the areas of the world "that have been doubly marginalized ... both by the cosmopolitan center and by countries exercising hegemony in Latin America" (2007: xi–xii)—a periphery of the periphery, thus; or, the periphery squared. David Damrosch defines world literature as a matter of circulation and reception beyond the country and culture of origin, either in translation or in the original language: "a work only has an *effective* life as world literature whenever, and wherever, it is actively present within a literary system beyond that of its original culture" (2003: 4). The doubly peripheric position of Central American literature means that very few of its writers and their texts will ever transcend and circulate in this "beyond" postulated by Damrosch. Rubén Darío's cosmopolitan desire (Siskind) and trajectory would be one glowing exception. In the twentieth and twenty-first centuries, the Guatemalan authors Miguel Ángel Asturias and Rodrigo Rey Rosa, the Nicaraguans Gioconda Belli and Sergio Ramírez, and the Salvadoran Horacio Castellanos Moya have gained some visibility and recognition in both Latin America and hegemonic centers. However, one may be inclined to suspect that many metropolitan editors and readers reify their stories on past and present violence, corruption, patriarchy, and masculinity as aesthetic expressions that represent the supposed essential truth of some local and cultural particularity (or identity), as happened earlier with magical realism.[1]

When seen from this perspective, Eduardo Halfon's case is extraordinary and intriguing. He is the youngest (b. 1971) among Central American writers circulating in the metropolitan centers. Between 2004 and 2020, Halfon published fifteen books (collections of short stories, novellas, novels, and essays). Three of them were translated into English shortly after their publication in Spanish: *El boxeador polaco* (2008; The Polish Boxer [2012]), *Monasterio* (2014; Monastery [2014]), and *Duelo* (2017; Mourning [2018]). All three have also been translated into French, Dutch, German, and Italian, among other metropolitan languages. *El boxeador polaco* has been translated into more than ten languages. In addition, Halfon's short stories "Signor Hoffman" and "Oh gueto mi amor" from the collection *Signor Hoffman* (2015) were also translated into English and published independently in 2015 in *BOMB* magazine and *Electric Literature* magazine, respectively. Reviews of his books appeared in several languages, and the writer was invited to talk about his fiction and writing in interviews and lectures organized by libraries and editors as well as cultural and academic institutions in Europe, the United States, and Latin America. Not even the pandemic has decelerated this triumphant global trajectory as events became virtual and accessible to readers across the globe. Last but not least, between 2019 and 2020, Halfon penned several essays for *The New York Review of Books*.

What makes for this young author's extraordinary success, especially his greater prominence in Europe and the United States than in most of Central America and Guatemala, where he was born? First, I argue that Halfon's texts translated into English (and other metropolitan languages) elaborate on topics of Jewishness, Jewish identity, experience, and (post)memory, which are of great consequence for post-Holocaust Europe and United States. Second, I examine how his writing explores the genre of *autoficción* that is currently very much *à la mode* in France (where it was first defined), Spain (especially regarding literatures produced in Latin America), and Latin America. To conclude, I take a stance on another crucial question: does Eduardo Halfon's case question or reaffirm world literature as a hegemonic operation of production and reception?

In an article dedicated to the relationship between Jewish literature and world literature, Lital Levy and Allison Schachter (2017: 4) observe that the dominant scholarly discourse on world literature still defines it in terms of "literary competition and exchange between nations." This continued obsession with national affiliation and identity categorization is one of the obstacles for a more even and less hierarchical organization of the world literary system. Writers are never just writers because they must belong to some place and shoulder the equivalent toponymic adjective, which in turn positions them in a corresponding sphere (core, subperiphery, periphery, periphery squared) of the world system of literature. Halfon's family history and his own life story seriously challenge this identity-driven trend. "Guatemalan, Jewish, Lebanese, Polish, American—the narrator is a composite of identities; he comes from a range of places and doesn't quite belong anywhere," states Francine Prose in her review of *The Polish Boxer*, *Monastery*, and *Mourning*, written for *The New York Review of Books* (2018). This loss and/or lack of a stable national, ethnic, and religious identity are partially due to multiple displacements that have occurred in the author's life (Campisi 2018), but they are also a result of his own choice. In the interview with Franco Chiaravalloti for *Revista de Letras*, Halfon (2014a) claims that he does not write "as a Guatemalan or on Guatemalan topics" (my translation). In her review of the French translation of the novel *Canción*, Ariane Singer (2021) quotes Halfon saying, "Quand j'ai commencé à écrire, j'ai eu besoin de détruire les deux colonnes principales de ma maison, le judaïsme et le Guatemala, afin de pouvoir construire ma propre maison" (When I began to write, I had to destroy the two main pillars of my house, Judaism and Guatemala, in order to construct my own home). Therefore, the disbelonging is for Halfon the necessary condition that makes writing possible. Not surprisingly, it is also the general condition of Jewish literature as "a microcosm of world literature in its local and global iterations" (Levy and Schachter 2015: 93) and "a network that traverses multiple geographic regions, political systems, and linguistic frameworks" (Levy and Schachter 2017: 4).

Halfon's declaration quoted above and other similar statements notwithstanding, both Guatemala and Judaism are at the core of Halfon's work, although he insists on the intellectual and emotional discomfort they engender, particularly being Jewish (2014a). Halfon puts a critical distance between himself and any fixed national, geographical, ethnic, or religious affiliation. So, when asked by an indigenous boy on the shore of Lake Amatitlán in Guatemala if he was *not* from there (meaning both Amatitlán and greater Guatemala), the fictional Halfon in *Duelo* (Mourning) answers, "Sometimes" (2018: 105). Sometimes (even often) he is not from there and does not write "as a Guatemalan or on Guatemalan topics" (2014a). But other times he is very much from there, and his writing is from there, evoking experiences and emotions that could not arise in a different place and time. In *Mañana nunca lo hablamos* (2011), a collection of interrelated stories, the protagonist retrospectively narrates his childhood in the violence-stricken Guatemala of 1976–81, which forces his parents to sell their house and relocate the entire family to Miami. The innocent perspective of a child captures and brings to light what an adult character and/or narrator might have hidden: the profound and all-encompassing class inequality and the systemic violence in which the protagonist's well-to-do family inevitably partakes (Perkowska 2017). Violence, poverty, racism, suffering, mourning, and oblivion in the Guatemalan context are also at the center of several short stories, like the beautifully written and politically sensible "Distant" (from *The Polish Boxer* [2012]), or "Bamboo" and "The Birds Are Back" (from *Signor Hoffman* in Spanish [2015b]), as well as the fragments dedicated in *Mourning* to the return of the narrator to the shores of Amatitlán in search of his childhood memories and in order to confront his past imaginings with the knowledge his adult self possesses in the present.

A similar relationship of closeness and distance governs Halfon's approach to Judaism. Although Halfon's character declares in *Monastery*, as the author himself does in interviews, that he has retired from Jewishness or that he is a Jew only from time to time (much like his being "sometimes" from Guatemala), it is undeniable that Jewishness, Jewish history, and memory in relation to various past and present diasporas (Poland, Lebanon, Guatemala, the United States), together with Jewish experiences and religious practices, lie at the heart of Halfon's writing. Indeed, Halfon's literary project displays a paradox. He claims that he had to destroy his

Judaism in order to construct his own literary dwelling (Singer 2021) and his character's Jewishness is contested by humor, irony, and even sarcasm, yet there is no denying that the quest for meaning or, rather, meanings of this heritage shapes the plots, geographical and physical spaces, characters, narrators, and even titles of Halfon's fiction from *El boxeador polaco* on (2008, The Polish Boxer [2012]). The figure of the Polish grandfather—a Polish Jew from the city of Łódź who narrowly escaped death in Auschwitz and whose entire family perished during the Holocaust—is barely visible as a splinter from the past in the first four stories of *El boxeador polaco* (2008). He gains full presence in the homonymous fifth story ("El boxeador polaco"), as he tells his grandson of his harrowing experiences in several concentration camps, and returns thereafter in every book published in the following years. In *Monasterio* (2014c, Monastery [2014d]), Halfon narrates the death of his Polish grandfather together with fragments of his own trip to Warsaw and Łódź in search of the vestiges of the family's prewar life and in order to face the country to which his grandfather didn't want to return because he had felt betrayed. These events are framed by the narrative of a trip to Israel where Halfon arrives to attend the wedding of his sister to an Orthodox Jew, a disturbing experience that prompts a vivid confrontation with his Jewishness and a meditation on the affirmation or negation of one's identity.

A detailed account of the trip to Łódź (and to Auschwitz, during the same visit to Poland) is related in the last story, "Oh gueto mi amor" (Oh, Ghetto My Love), included in *Signor Hoffman* (2015b), which in 2018 was also published as a short book with beautiful illustrations by David de las Heras. Accompanied by a Polish woman (Madame Maroszek) with whom Halfon established an epistolary relationship after she offered her assistance, the protagonist visits the neighborhood, the building, and the apartment where his grandfather's family lived before the war, and from where all were taken to concentration camps. Halfon discovers that the family's apartment is now inhabited by a faded porno actress and her son and that all affective connections with material vestiges of the past are severed. However, just before he leaves Łódź, Madame Maroszek offers him a gift of three books (or their copies), each one of which involves a story of witnessing the unbearable experience of the ghetto or extermination camp, written "*in spite of all*" (Didi-Huberman 2008: 3) and in daring circumstances. The unexpected gift reminds the narrator of the importance of putting one's life in words and sentences, of narrating it "in spite of all" to leave behind a trace that others will discover and try to decipher.

Duelo (2017; Mourning [2018b]) focuses on a secret, and secretly kept guilt, in Halfon's paternal family: the death, at the age of five, of the incurably ill older brother of the narrator's father, abandoned by the family in a New York clinic in 1940. The narrative intertwines the protagonist's remembrance of a story he was told—or he imagined—of a child named Salomon who had drowned in Lake Amatitlán at the age of five, the memories of his own childhood and early adolescence in Miami where his family moved in 1981, his trip to Lake Amatitlán in search of an explanation for the origin of the drowned child's story, and additional details of Halfon's memories of and discoveries about his Polish grandfather. While remembering the Miami period, the narrator focuses on a visit he made with his maternal (Polish) grandfather to a sort of aviation museum, where his grandfather stood for a long time, with an unexpressive face, in front of an old, rusty warplane. The narrator discovers the meaning of that moment thirty years later, during his European trip, when he visits Germany before arriving to Poland. During an unplanned and unwanted visit to Sachsenhausen concentration camp, where his grandfather was imprisoned twice, Halfon discovers that his grandfather might have participated in a resistance movement of Jewish prisoners who, at the end of the war, sabotaged the production of the bomber plane Heinkel.

"Puzzle" is the right word to describe the overall organization and structure of the literary edifice that Halfon began to build with the publication of *El boxeador polaco* in 2008. The Spanish edition consists of six short stories. Four of them have become building blocks for other short stories and/or novels written in later years. *Monasterio* originates from "Fumata blanca" (White Smoke); *La pirueta* (The Pirouette, a novel published in 2010) stems from a story narrated in "Epístrofe" (Epistrophy), while "El boxeador polaco" (The Polish Boxer) and "Discurso de Póvoa" (The Speech of Povoa) initiate the cycle of narrations around the figure of the Polish grandfather, which are woven from fragments recounted in *Monasterio*, *Signor Hoffman*, and *Duelo*, as described above. Other members of Halfon's family (his grandmother, mother, father, and brother) reappear regularly from one text to another, while new characters are people that the protagonist meets during his complex itinerary between Guatemala, the United States, Israel, Italy, Germany, and Poland. Each text can be read independently as an autonomous albeit not entirely complete story or as interrelated fragments of a larger narrative in the making.

Given the thematic and structural relationship between *The Polish Boxer*, *Monastery*, and *Mourning*, it would seem logical, and even convenient, to translate and publish them in sequence. However, the books in translation follow a different logic. They are not only translated but also de- and recomposed or rearranged. Following Damrosch's (2003: 5–6) and Siskind's (2014: 17) suggestions that a world literary critic should explore the networks of translation, circulation, and reception of texts beyond their cultural and linguistic origin, I propose that the details of these modifications offer a clue to Halfon's success in the metropolitan centers of the world literary system.

Table 4.1 facilitates the comparison:[2]

TABLE 4.1 Translations to English, French, and Dutch—content comparison.

Language	Book 1	Book 2	Book 3	Book 4
Spanish	*El boxeador polaco*, 2008, six short stories: "Lejano" "Fumata blanca" "Twaineando" "Epístrofe" "El boxeador polaco" "Discurso de Póvoa"	*Monasterio*, 2014, novel (originates from "Fumata blanca," reproduced with minimal modifications in the text)	*Signor Hoffman*, 2015, six short stories: "Signor Hoffman" "Bambú" "Han vuelto las aves" "Arena blanca, piedra negra" "Sobrevivir los domingos" "Oh gueto mi amor"	*Duelo*, 2017, novel
English	*The Polish Boxer*, 2012, ten short stories: "Distant" (*BP*) "Twaining" (*BP*) "Epistrophy" (*BP*) "White Smoke" (*BP*) "The Polish Boxer" (*BP*) "Postcards" (*LP*) "The Pirouette" (*LP*) "The Speech of Póvoa" (*BP*) "Sunsets" (the grandfather's death, narrated in *M*)	*Monastery*, 2014, eight stories from different sources: "Tel Aviv Was an Inferno" (*M*) "Bamboo" (*SH*) "The Birds Are Back" (*SH*) "White Sand, Black Stone" (*SH*) "White Smoke" (*BP*) "Surviving Sundays" (*SH*) "Prologue at Saint-Nazaire" "Monastery" (*M*)	"Oh, Ghetto My Love," 2015, short story "Signor Hoffman," 2015, short story	*Mourning*, 2018 three short stories: "Signor Hoffman" (*SH*) "Oh Ghetto My Love" (*SH*) "Mourning" (the text published as the novel *Duelo* in Spanish)

(continued)

Language	Book 1	Book 2	Book 3	Book 4
French	*Le boxeur polonais*, 2015, two short stories: "Le boxeur polonais" (*BP*) "L'allocation de Pavoa" (*BP*)	*Monastère*, 2014 novel (published in French before its publication in Spanish)	*Signor Hoffman* 2015 six shorts stories, the same ones as in the Spanish edition	*Deuils*, 2018 novel
Dutch	*De Poolse bokser*, 2019 three books combined: *El boxeador polaco* *La pirueta* *Monasterio* "Ver weg" (*PB*) "Twainen" (*PB*) "Epistrofe" (*PB*) "Tel Aviv was om te stikken" (*M*) "Witte rook" (*PB*) "De Poolse bokser" (*PB*) Ansichtkaarten (*LP*) Spook (*LP*) De pirouette (*LP*) "Toespraak in Póvoa" (*PB*) "Zonsondergangen" (*M*) "Klooster" (*M*)			*Duel*, 2020 combines *Signor Hoffman* and *Duelo* "Signor Hoffman" (*SH*) "Bamboe" (*SH*) "De vogels zijn terug" (*SH*) "Wit zand, zwarte stenen" (*SH*) "Zondagen overleven" (*SH*) "O getto, mijn lief" (*SH*) *Duel* (*D*)

BP—El boxeador polaco (2008), the Spanish edition
M—Monasterio (2014c), the Spanish edition
SH—Signor Hoffman (2015b), the Spanish edition
LP—La pirueta (2010), the Spanish edition

A veritable puzzle, different from the one based on the plot that I have described above, results from this editorial decision to combine translation with de- and recomposition of the fictional storyline components in the Spanish editions of Halfon's books.[3] Fours elements are particularly striking: (i) In some cases, translation and rearrangement lead to a modification of the book's literary genre. In Spanish, *Monasterio* is a novel, while in English and Dutch, it is a collection of stories; (ii) French editions are the closest to the original arrangement in Spanish; (iii) English and Dutch editions of *El boxeador polaco* combine narratives from different collection and/or novels, creating a longer text, which is more sellable and profitable, even if it is less coherent from a purely literary point of view.[4] In both languages, however, the homonymous story dedicated to Halfon's Jewish grandfather's experience in Auschwitz stands in the center of the collection, as if to reaffirm its title. Even as, in fact, they are different books with different content and structure, they, however, maintain the original Spanish title in the new target languages; (iv) in *Le boxeur polonais* (2015a), *Mourning* (2018b), and *Duel* (2020a), the rearrangement combines, in a single volume, texts on the Holocaust, trauma, memory, and affective responses to catastrophic historical experiences that were published separately in Spanish. What does all this, and especially the last point, tell us about publishing practices and strategies, given that out of Halfon's fifteen books, *El boxeador polaco* (2008), *Monasterio* (2014c), *Duelo* (2017), and the story "Oh gueto mi amor" from *Signor Hoffman* (2015b) are the only four books/texts that have been translated into many languages and have entered into global circulation?

In "Conjectures on World Literature" Moretti proposes a new methodology—distant reading—for studying world literature: namely he recommends to focus on "units that are much smaller or much larger than the text: devices, themes, tropes—or genres and systems" (2000: 57). The above summaries of Halfon's fictions translated into "world" languages and their rearrangement after translation help uncover a thematic and structural pattern. All of them interrogate issues of history, (post)memory, and identity in relation to Jewishness and the atrocious experience of the Holocaust. All of them focus on a descendant (the grandson Halfon) who confronts a past trauma warded off by silence and feels compelled to carry out a personal quest for meaning, comprehension, and words even if they prove elusive or only provisional. The figure of the Polish-Jewish grandfather, who kept silent until shortly before his death, stands at the center of the puzzle as its organizing principle and, at the same time, as a spectral presence whose injunction (Derrida 1994) drives his grandson to search for answers, roving through worlds and words, fragments of stories, splinters of memories, and remnants of the past.

It would seem, therefore, that Halfon's publishers in metropolitan centers consider him more interesting and readable for their public as a

Jewish author who happens to have been born in Guatemala and to write in Spanish on issues related to his Jewish heritage than as a Guatemalan author who writes about Guatemala, as many others before him. Let's not forget that *Mañana nunca lo hablamos* (2011), a collection of stories on Halfon's childhood in Guatemala, has not been translated—with the exception of the homonymous story "Tomorrow We Never Did Talk about It," published in *The Massachusetts Review* in 2016. The stories from *Signor Hoffman* that are not related thematically to Jewish identity, history, or memory have been relocated to the eclectic edition of *Monastery* in English, while in Dutch they constitute a thematically rupturing minority in a single volume combining two books dedicated to Halfon's grandfather and family.

This editorial bet on Halfon's Jewishness and Jewish cultural inheritance—which, as mentioned, he himself challenges in his writing through humor and other strategies—replicates a trend observable in the academic and cultural *milieu*, where in the last few years Halfon has achieved a significant presence and visibility through invitations for interviews, conferences, talks, and other forms of intellectual exchange. He has also won prestigious fellowships that offered him time and space for writing. Many of these activities were financed and organized by cultural or academic institutions connected to or depending on the Jewish diaspora in the United States and elsewhere and dedicated to Jewish studies. In 2015, for instance, Halfon was a Sidney Hartman writer-in-residence in the Weissman School of Arts and Science at Baruch College (CUNY). Under his profile on the Sidney Hartman Program's web page we find an excerpt from *The Polish Boxer* that brings to the forefront the connection between the writer, his grandfather, and the Holocaust: "It was in Auschwitz. At first I wasn't sure I'd heard him. I looked up. He was covering the number with his right hand. Drizzle purred against the roof tiles. This, he said rubbing his forearm gently. It was in Auschwitz, he said" (2012: 78). In 2018 the University of Hartford's Maurice Greenberg Center for Judaic Studies named Halfon the Edward Lewis Wallant Award winner for his novel *Mourning*. More recently, in October 2021, Halfon attended a two-day *The Eduardo Halfon Mini-Symposium* that was co-sponsored by the Department of Literatures, Cultures, and Languages and the Center for Judaic Studies and Contemporary Jewish Life at the University of Connecticut. Not coincidentally, four out of five academic articles dedicated to Halfon's narrative delve into diverse aspects of his family history, his Jewish heritage, and the Jewish-Polish (dis)connection (Campisi 2018; Kobyłecka–Piwońska 2021; Marchio 2019; Pridgeon 2017).

A paradox underlies thus not only Halfon's literary project but also its interface with the global literary system as well as editorial and market politics and policies. On the one hand, and using Ottmar Ette's model of world literature as a network beyond the normative binary of world and nation, we can describe Halfon's fiction as a "literature-without-a-fixed-abode" (2016). It configures a decentered space—Guatemala, United States,

Serbia, Poland, Germany, Italy, Israel, Japan—whose many locations, cultural contexts, and idiosyncrasies challenge its protagonist's and the readers' meaning of the "world" and fixed identity. This questioning is best observed in the character's stance toward his own identity, as depicted above: a Guatemalan and a Jew, but at the same time, neither Guatemalan nor Jewish. In order to write, the writer must destroy and *disbelong*. However, this undermining necessarily passes through the issue of belonging, which installs the question of Jewish identity, experience, and memory right in the middle, exposed and available to global culture and market trends.

I would like to argue that the "adoption" of Halfon by Jewish academic and cultural institutions, as well as the translation of his Jewish-themed fictions and their circulation in the metropolitan centers should be examined and interpreted within a larger context, following Moretti's point that a world literature critic should pay attention to waves, representing global trends and market forces, rather than trees standing for national literatures (2000: 66–8). As stated above, Halfon's texts translated into English (and other "world" languages) elaborate on topics of Jewishness, Jewish identity, experience, and memory, which are hugely relevant (even voguish) in post-Holocaust Europe and in the United States, and by this token, prominent in the book market. Indeed, writing during the late 1990s, Andreas Huyssen observes, "[t]he emergence of memory as a key cultural and political concern in Western societies" (2003: 11). He situates the beginning of this "obsession with memory" (3) or "hypertrophy of memory" (6) in the early 1980s, in Europe and the United States, and attributes the explosion of memory discourses to "the ever-broadening debate about the Holocaust (triggered by the TV series *Holocaust* and, somewhat later, by the testimony movement)" (12). Soon after, by 1990s, the Holocaust had become "a cipher for the twentieth century as a whole," "a universal trope of traumatic memory" that extended beyond its original time and space functioning as a "metaphor for other traumatic histories and memories" (13–14) that followed in second half of the twentieth century such as the murderous dictatorships in Uruguay, Chile, and Argentina and the genocide in Guatemala, Rwanda, Bosnia, and Kosovo. Huyssen argues convincingly that the pervasive culture of memory responds not only to the ethical responsibility of remembering or the fear of forgetting; it may also be a consequence of instability created by neoliberal market policies and globalization, an uncomfortable "structure of feeling" (Williams 1977: 128–35) that looks for anchors and fixity amid economic insecurity and increasing social precariousness (2003: 18). But above all, Huyssen affirms, the fixation on the past bears witness to a "fundamental crisis in our imagination of alternative futures" (2).

Writing almost fifteen years later, historian Enzo Traverso manifests a similar position with regard to the emphatic interest in memory and narratives of the past in the contemporary, post-utopic Western culture: "The obsession with the past that is shaping our time results from

[the] eclipse of utopias: a world without utopias inevitably looks back. The emergence of memory in the public space of Western societies is a consequence of this change" (2016: 9). Like Huyssen, Traverso believes that "the memory of the Holocaust plays the role of a unifying narrative" (2016: 14), whose agglutinative force for the West became clearly visible in May 2005, when German Chancellor Gerhard Schröder joined Jacques Chirac, Tony Blair, George Bush, and Vladimir Putin to commemorate the Allied landing in Normandy on June 6, 1944 (2016: 14). Like Huyssen, Traverso interprets the Holocaust and its memory not only as the "paradigm of Western memory" but as "the foundation upon which the remembrance of other ancient or recent forms of violence and crimes should be built" (2016: 16).

This cultural obsession of Western societies with the past, memory, and trauma has been successfully marketed by the culture industry through literature (both fiction and nonfiction: memoirs, autobiography, confessional writing), cinematography (feature films like Steven Spielberg's *Schindler's List* or Roberto Benigni's *La vita è bella*, documentaries, docudramas), TV series, photography books and expositions, comics (like Art Spiegelman's *Maus*), internet sites, museums, and commemorative monuments. Definitely, "the past is selling better than the future" (Huyssen 2003: 20). Huyssen observes that "it is no longer possible … to think of the Holocaust or of any other historical trauma as a serious ethical and political issue apart from the multiple ways it is now linked to commodification and spectacularization" (2003: 18). However, commodification of the past, trauma, and memory does not necessarily entail their banalization since different strategies of representation produce different effects and ethical responses (Huyssen 2003: 18–19). Thus, commercial mythifications of the Holocaust such as Spielberg's *Schindler's List* (1993), or "fairy tales" (Huyssen 2003:18) like Benigni's *La vita è bella* (1997), share cultural space with novels like *W ou le souvenir d'enfance* (W, or the Memory of Childhood) by Georges Perec (France, 1975), *Austerlitz* by W. G. Sebald (Germany, 2001), or, thinking of Latin American contributions, *Lenta biografía* (Slow Biography) by Sergio Chejfec (Argentina, 1990), *Las cartas que no llegaron* (The Letters That Never Came) by Mauricio Rosencof (Uruguay, 2000), and, of course, Halfon's *The Polish Boxer*, *Monastery*, "Oh Ghetto My Love," and *Mourning*.

Given that there is no "outside" to the commodity of culture, Halfon's fiction partakes in its global dynamics, but like other authors listed above Halfon resists the idea of representation and narrativization of a traumatic past for easy consumption and interpretative flattening. The fragmented and elliptical narration of his texts, their convoluted temporality that oscillates between catastrophic experiences situated in the past and the narrator's attempts to comprehend them from a point of view defined by the present, as well as the protagonist's geographical and cultural displacements signify together the workings of memory; the difficulties of comprehension; the limits of words and representation in contrast with the potency of silence, irony, or humor; and the incompleteness of any quest for meaning and belonging. Halfon expresses his encounter with the past and trauma through formal rather than figurative strategies, thus disrupting his readers' unproblematic consumption of the stories he narrates.

At the same time, however, these stories clearly respond to Western societies' obsession with the past and memory, in particular with the Holocaust and the many things it denotes and connotes, from guilt and expiation, through the empathy toward victims and the ethical obligation of remembrance, to "the sacralization of the foundational values of liberal democracies—pluralism, tolerance, and Rights of Man" (Traverso 2016: 15). The grandfather's excruciating experience and his family's tragic fate in Łódź ghetto and extermination camps, the effect of that history on his later life and his new family in Guatemala, his silence and affective negation of Poland and Poles, the affective transmission of his traumatic memories as postmemory (Hirsch 2012) to his grandson Eduardo, the latter's quest for a(n) (impossible) narrative of those events and experiences: all these topics and motives belong to the well-known and widely circulating archive of a multi- and transnational Holocaust discourse, disseminated among readers and spectators alike by Western media culture and its "memory industry" (Huyssen 2003: 22). It is probable, thus, that a Western reader who opens one of Halfon's translated fictions finds comfort in discovering topics she or he feels familiar with through transnational "politics of representation, education, and commemoration" (Traverso 2016: 15) as well as publishing politics that respond to the global cultural market.

It is worth mentioning that both the globally successful authors (Ramírez, Belli, Castellanos Moya, and Rey Rosa) and younger writers belonging to Halfon's generation (Mónica Albizúrez Gil, Claudia Hernández, Vanessa Núñez Handal, Carol Zardetto) are deeply concerned with memory of wars, disappearances, state repression, and genocide in Central America. Since Halfon inhabits several historical and cultural spaces simultaneously, his fictions could bridge the gap between local and global memory. However, only *Mañana nunca lo hablamos* (not yet translated) and *Canción* (the last publication) look into the war in Guatemala, but, interestingly, even these texts don't touch on the genocide committed by the Guatemalan state on its Maya population.[5] Does the author avoid the topic deliberately because at that time he was not in the country and did not experience its trauma? Or is it because of a certain tendency to perceive the Holocaust as a unique event refusing comparisons?

Whatever the case, Halfon's translated texts are familiar not only because of their themes and concerns but also because his writing and approach bridge well into a genre that is currently very much en vogue in the West. This genre is called autofiction and represents a fictional reworking of the author's personal experiences within an overtly metafictional textuality. Annick Louis defines autofiction as narratives "sin pacto previo explícito" ["without a previously explicit pact"], whose meaning (or meanings) is (are) constructed from within their constitutive indetermination between the fictional and the factual (2010: 79). The genre, although not new (some scholars date it back to Dante, for instance), was named and defined in 1977 by the French novelist Serge Doubrovsky in reference to his novel *Son* (Fils). The genre subsequently gained prominence in Europe, in particular in France and Spain, from where it crossed the Atlantic reaching Latin and North America. Several scholars who study autofiction have pointed out that the genre often connects the writing (or fiction) of the self with the exploration of family history (Forné 2022; Gasparini 2012; Louis 2010). Annick Louis, for instance, maintains that autofictions frequently narrate "una búsqueda vinculada a la historia familiar, una suerte de retorno a los orígenes ... el «yo» de estos textos aparece como el eslabón de una cadena que es reconstruida en [el] texto ..." (a search related to a family history, a sort of return to origins ... the "self" appears in these texts as a link in a chain that is reconstructed in the narrative) (2010: 75). In addition, in Spain and Latin America, autofiction often transmits traumatic memories of both the survivors and descendants of the victims of war violence or dictatorial terror, meaning that their storyline and narration combine a critical exploration of the self with memory or postmemory work (Tossi 2020: 93; Prieto 2020: 28). This combination is exactly what the reader finds in Halfon's fictions: on the one hand, the protagonist-narrator examines the issues of his identity and belonging in relation to the family story; on the other, he digs into the traumatic experiences and memories of his maternal grandfather, trying to apprehend the unimaginable. This is a pattern that rides the global autofictional wave (thinking together with Moretti), comforting (potential) readers with a recognizable template and reminding them of other world literary names, like W. G. Sebald and Roberto Bolaño, with whom Halfon is often explicitly compared.

Nonetheless, not everything is completely familiar, and this may be an additional asset for the publishing market: after all, Halfon writes and is published as "a Jewish Guatemalan-American, a Guatemalan-American Jew, or a Guatemalan Jew living in the U.S." (Pridgeon 2017: 105), "écrivain aux origines multiples" (Singer 2021), "de Guatemalteekse Jood" (Keller 2020), or simply "guatémaltèque" (Bensoussan 2014). The toponymic adjective "Guatemalan" always slips into Halfon's introductions, next to his other "origins," be they Jewish, American, or multiple. It is, at the same time, true to reality and conveniently market/reader oriented. Halfon was born in Guatemala, he writes in Spanish, and although Guatemala is not his main topic, he cannot write without being somehow connected to that country.

Nobody buys his books to read about Guatemala, however Guatemala makes him unique. After all, most people will know that thousands of Jewish families emigrated or fled from Europe to, for instance, Argentina. But Guatemala? How many Jewish exiles reached that Central American country known for its indigenous population and culture? "[A] hundred families, they usually say," says the narrator Halfon at some point of *The Polish Boxer* underscoring the minuscule Guatemalan-Jewish community that has to import its rabbis from abroad (2012: 178). If "the past is selling better than the future," as Huyssen declares (2003: 20), the Guatemalan connection, strange and unexpected in relation to Jewishness, draws attention to a talented and original writer, helping promote the translation and dissemination of his work on a global scale.

There is no doubt that Halfon's autofictions on Jewish themes translate and travel well. They are "actively present within a literary system beyond that of its original culture" and have therefore "an *effective* life as world literature" (Damrosch 2003: 4). A collateral question is if Halfon's inclusion into the world literary circuit affects in any way its own structure and working, which Moretti describes as unequal. Confirming Moretti's point of view, Damrosch asserts that "works by non-Western authors or by provincial or subordinate Western writers are always particularly liable to be assimilated to the immediate interests and agendas of those who edit, translate, and interpret them" (2003: 24–5). In a similar vein, Tariq Ali (2013) observes that literary globalization produces and increases cultural conformity and uniformity by exerting the normative force of the dominant Western paradigm. In light of this critique, Halfon's case is as curious as it is paradoxical. On the one hand, his texts challenge metropolitan perceptions of Central American and/or Guatemalan literature as a product of a particular place and culture, representing its local particularity through its content and formal features. In this way, Halfon's fictions thwart the "*expressive* logic" (Siskind 2014: 50) of world literature and its essentializing impulse because they don't fit with the hegemonic image of Central America or Guatemala. They certainly constitute a "thorn" (Moretti 2000: 68) in the one-sidedness of the national conception of Guatemalan literature and also challenge the meaning of "the world" by depicting an itinerary that is geographically and culturally decentered. On the other hand, however, it seems that self-projection, understood here as mirroring in others of one's own concerns, interests, affective investments, and aesthetic values, is fundamental to the core's embracing of Halfon's writing. The *corpus* of his fictions chosen for translation and dissemination in the metropolitan centers deals with themes and issues that match societal and cultural interests of these very centers, without challenging their majoritarian disposition. Becoming global still implies a certain degree of assimilation to a centripetal conception of "the world." Curiously though, Halfon's incorporation into the "global" literary circuit discloses its own operation.

Notes

1 On this "*expressive* logic" in world literature as a discipline and pedagogical practices, especially in university classrooms across the United States, see Siskind (2014: 50–4).
2 It is impossible to provide a comparison that would involve all translations. I have limited it to three languages (English, French, and Dutch) in comparison to the original publications in Spanish. My choice of Dutch over German (German translations were published before the Dutch ones) is due to my knowledge of the former.
3 Halfon (2020b) discusses challenges and gratifications of this process with his Spanish, French, and German editors in "Sobreviviendo a Eduardo Halfon: El trabajo del autor y sus editors," a conversation organized by Indent Literary Agency and held on May 21, 2020.
4 An example: the Spanish edition of *El boxeador polaco* (2008) is 104 pages long, while the Dutch one (2019) is 230. *Duelo* (2017) in Spanish is 106 pages long, while the Dutch edition (2020a) is 147. Lisa Thunnissen, Halfon's Dutch translator, confirmed in a personal communication that the publisher (Wereldbibliotheek) prefers not to publish small books (email message, January 12, 2022).
5 In 2022, in *Lettre International* in Germany, Halfon published a story titled "Beni" that explicitly addresses the genocide in Guatemala, namely the Dos Erres massacre in 1982, in which fifty-eight *kaibiles* (the notoriously cruel counterinsurgent special forces of the Guatemalan military) brutally murdered the indigenous population of Dos Erres village in the Petén region. In typical Halfonian fashion, it interweaves personal and family history, guilt, and implication with a posterior revelation—but in this case with a graphic retelling of the massacre. The story tells of the narrator having to belatedly register for Guatemalan military service in 1989, for which he is aided by a *kaibil*, who was employed by his family to help with official matters—and who also participated in the Dos Erres massacre. "Beni" will be included in the English translation of *Canción*, another example of translation combined with de- and recomposition.

References

Ali, T. (2010), "World Literature and World Languages," [lecture] filmed February 15 for SOAS Globalisation Lecture Series, Brunei Gallery Lecture Theatre, University of London. YouTube, February 15, 2013. Available online: https://www.youtube.com/watch?v=NaP0KEwdGro&t=18s. Accessed December 20, 2021.

Arias, A. (2007), *Taking Their Word: Literature and the Signs of Central America*, Minneapolis and London: University of Minnesota Press.

Bensoussan, A. (2014), "Avènement de Eduardo Halfon," *La République des livres*, June 1. Available online: https://larepubliquedeslivres.com/avenement-de-eduardo-halfon/. Accessed December 20, 2021.
Campisi, N. (2018), "The Dislocation of Cosmopolitan Identities in Eduardo Halfon's *Monasterio*," *Inti: Revista de literatura hispánica*, 87–8: 113–24. Available online: https://digitalcommons.providence.edu/inti/vol1/iss87/10. Accessed October 9, 2021.
Casanova, P. ([1999] 2004), *The World Republic of Letters*, Cambridge: Harvard University Press.
Chejfec, S. (1990), *Lenta biografía*, Buenos Aires: Punto Sur.
Damrosch, D. (2003), *What Is World Literature?*, Princeton: Princeton University Press.
De Ferrari, G., ed. (2012), "Utopías críticas: La literatura mundial según América Latina," special issue of *1616: Anuario de Literatura Comparada*, 2.
Derrida, J. (1994), *Specters of Marx: The State of the Debt, the Work of Mourning and the New International*, trans. P. Kamuf, New York and London: Routledge.
Didi-Huberman, G. (2008), *Images in Spite of All: Four Photographs from Auschwitz*, trans. S. B. Lillis, Chicago and London: University of Chicago Press.
Domínguez, C., ed. (2012), "Literatura mundial: Una Mirada panhispánica," special issue of *Insula: Revista de Letras y Ciencias Humanas*, 787–8.
Ette, O. (2016), *Writing-between-Worlds: TransArea Studies and the Literatures-without-a-Fixed-Abode*, Berlin: De Gruyter.
Forné, A. (2022), "Archival Autofiction in Post-Dictatorship Argentina," *Life Writing*, 19 (1): 145–56. Available online: https://doi.org/10.1080/14484528.2019.1642174. Accessed June 14, 2021.
Gasparini, P. (2012), "La autonarración," in A. Casas (ed.), *La autoficción: Reflexiones teóricas*, 177–209, Madrid: Arco Libros.
Halfon, E. (2008), *El boxeador polaco*, Valencia: Pre-Textos.
Halfon, E. (2010), *La pirueta*, Valencia: Pre-Textos.
Halfon, E. (2011), *Mañana nunca lo hablamos*, Valencia: Pre-Textos.
Halfon, E. (2012), *The Polish Boxer*, trans. D. Hahn, O. Brock, L. Dillman, T. Bunstead and A. McLean, New York: Bellevue Literary Press.
Halfon, E. (2014a), "Eduardo Halfon: 'La incomodidad es un sentir judío,'" interview by Franco Chiaravalloti, *Revista de Letras*, June 16. Available online: https://revistadeletras.net/eduardo-halfon-la-incomodidad-es-un-sentir-eminentemente-judio/. Accessed December 20, 2021.
Halfon, E. (2014b), *Monastère*, trans. Albert Bensoussan, Paris: Quai Voltaire.
Halfon, E. (2014c), *Monasterio*, Barcelona: Libros del Asteroide.
Halfon, E. (2014d), *Monastery*, trans. L. Dillman and D. Hahn, New York: Bellevue Literary Press.
Halfon, E. (2015a), *Le boxeur polonais*, trans. A. Bensoussan, Paris: Quai Voltaire.
Halfon, E. (2015b), *Signor Hoffman*, Barcelona: Libros del Asteroide.
Halfon, E. (2015c), *Signor Hoffman*, trans. A. Bensoussan, Paris: Quai Voltaire.
Halfon, E. (2016), "Tomorrow We Never Did Talk about It," trans. Anne McLean, Amherst: Massachusetts Review, EPUB.
Halfon, E. (2017), *Duelo*, Barcelona: Libros del Asteroide.
Halfon, E. (2018a), *Deuils*, trans. David Fauquemberg, Paris: Quai Voltaire.

Halfon, E. (2018b), *Mourning*, trans. L. Dillman and D. Hahn, New York: Bellevue Literary Press.
Halfon, E. (2018c), *Oh gueto mi amor*, illust. D. de Las Heras, Madrid: Páginas de Espuma.
Halfon, E. (2019), *De Poolse bokser*, trans. L. Thunnissen, Amsterdam: Wereldbibliotheek.
Halfon, E. (2020a), *Duel*, trans. L. Thunnissen, Amsterdam: Wereldbibliotheek.
Halfon, E. (2020b), "Sobreviviendo a Eduardo Halfon: El trabajo del autor y sus editores," [video recording] in conversation with Luis Miguel Solano, Piero Salabè, and Alice Deón, Indent Literary Agency. YouTube, May 21, 1:00:42. Available online: https://www.youtube.com/watch?v=5NrpKTRS7FA. Accessed October 17, 2021.
Halfon, E. (2021), *Canción*, Barcelona: Libros del Asteroide.
Hirsch, M. (2012), *The Generation of Postmemory: Writing and Visual Culture after the Holocaust*, New York: Columbia University Press.
Huyssen, A. (2003), *Present Pasts: Urban Palimpsests and the Politics of Memory*, Stanford: Stanford University Press.
Keller, S. (2020), "Een identiteit onder constructie," review of *Duel*, by Eduardo Halfon, trans. L. Thunniessen, *NRC Handelsblad*, September 18: C9. Available online: https://shira.nl/2020/09/17/een-identiteit-onder-constructie/. Accessed November 5, 2021.
Kobyłecka–Piwońska, E. (2021), "Perturbar el orden de sentido: los viajes polacos de Eduardo Halfon," *Studia Neophilologica*, October. Available online: https://doi.org/10.1080/00393274.2021.1964100. Accessed December 14, 2021.
Kristal, E. (2002), "'Considering Coldly …' A Response to Franco Moretti," *New Left Review*, 15: 61–74.
Levy, L. and A. Schachter (2015), "Jewish Literature/World Literature: Between the Local and the Transnational," *PMLA*, 130 (1): 92–109.
Levy, L. and A. Schachter (2017), "A Non-universal Global: On Jewish Writing and World Literature," *Prooftexts*, 36 (1–2): 1–26.
Louis, A. (2010), "Sin pacto previo explícito: el caso de la autoficción," in V. Toro, S. Schlickers and A. Luengo (eds.), *La obsesión del yo: La auto(r)ficción en la literatura española y latinoamericana*, 73–96, Madrid/Frankfurt: Iberoamericana/Vervuert.
Marchio, J. (2019), "(Pos)Memoria(s) de la diáspora judía en Centroamérica: ¿De un trauma a otro?" *Revista de historia*, 36: 25–40.
Moretti, F. (2000), "Conjectures on World Literature," *New Left Review*, 1: 54–68.
Müller, G. and M. Siskind, eds. (2019), *World Literature, Cosmpolitanism, Globality: Beyond, Against, Post, Otherwise*, Berlin: De Gruyter.
Perec, G. (1975), *W ou le souvenir d'enfance*, Paris: Denöel.
Perkowska, M. (2017), "Infancia e historia: actos de la memoria en *Dios tenía miedo* de Vanessa Núñez Handal y *Mañana nunca lo hablamos* de Eduardo Halfon," *Revista de Estudios Hispánicos*, 51 (3): 595–620.
Pridgeon, S. (2017), "Silences between Jewishness and Indigeneity in Eduardo Halfon's *Mañana nunca lo hablams*," *Revista Canadiense de Estudios Hispánicos*, 42 (1): 99–121.
Prieto, J. (2020), "Autoficción y memoria colectiva: notas sobre el documental en primera persona en Argentina," *Letral*, 23: 24–58.

Prose, F. (2018), "What Can't Be Forgotten," review of *The Polish Boxer*, by Eduardo Halfon, trans. Daniel Hahn, Ollie Brock, Lisa Dillman, Thomas Bunstead, and Anne McLean, *Monastery*, by Eduardo Halfon, trans. Lisa Dillman and Daniel Hahn, and *Mourning*, by Eduardo Halfon, trans. Lisa Dillman and Daniel Hahn, *The New York Review of Books*, November 22. Available online: https://www-nybooks-com.proxy.wexler.hunter.cuny.edu/articles/2018/11/22/eduardo-halfon-what-cant-be-forgotten/?printpage=true. Accessed October 16, 2021.

Rosencof, M. (2000), *Las cartas que no llegaron*, Montevideo: Alfaguara.

Sánchez Prado, I. M., ed. (2006), *América Latina en la "literatura mundial,"* Pittsburgh: Instituto Internacional de Literatura Iberoamericana.

Schindler's List (1993), [Film] Dir. Steven Spielberg, USA: Universal Pictures.

Sebald, W. G. (2001), *Austerlitz*, Munich: Carl Hanser Verlag.

Singer, A. (2021), "Eduardo Halfon: 'Je me sense toujours en danger au Guatemala,'" review of *Canción*, by Eduardo Halfon, *Le Monde*, March 28. Available online: https://www.lemonde.fr/livres/article/2021/03/28/eduardo-halfon-je-me-sens-toujours-en-danger-au-guatemala_6074734_3260.html. Accessed December 18, 2021.

Siskind, M. (2014), *Cosmopolitan Desires: Global Modernity and World Literature in Latin America*, Evanston: Northwestern University Press.

Tossi, M. (2020), "Figuras autoficcionales de la 'memoria herida' en la dramaturgia argentina posdictatorial," *Letral*, 23: 89–117.

Traverso, E. (2016), *Left-Wing Melancolia: Marxism, History and Memory*, New York: Columbia University Press.

La vita è bella (1997), [Film] Dir. Roberto Begnini, Italy: Melampo Cinematografica/Cecchi Gori Group.

William, R. (1977), *Marxism and Literature*, Oxford: Oxford University Press.

PART TWO

Constellations

5

Cosmopolitanism and Disillusion in Rubén Darío

Carlos F. Grigsby

In 1917, one year after Rubén Darío's death, Guillaume Apollinaire (1966) gave a talk in the Théatre du Vieux-Colombier in Paris titled "L'Esprit nouveau et les poètes" (The New Spirit and the Poets), laying out a highly nationalist vision—in fact, Francocentric—of the new direction that modern poetry was to take in the twentieth century. He discussed the role of cosmopolitanism as follows: "A cosmopolitan lyrical expression would give us only vague works with no form or accent, whose value would be those of the platitudes of parliamentary international rhetoric" (903).[1] Apollinaire's notion of a cosmopolitan aesthetics is the opposite of that of the *modernistas*, who through their own marginal cosmopolitanism came to invent a modern tradition of Spanish American literature, independent of the region's former colonial authority. Yet Apollinaire gave this talk during the years of the First Great War—hence the nationalistic impress—in the position of a poet based in Paris who wrote in French.

Originally, the notion of cosmopolitanism was a political and ethical concept which is said to have been coined by the Cynics and developed by the Stoics.[2] It would later play an important role in the thought of the European Enlightenment, notably in the works of Kant and Hegel. By the nineteenth century, with the global growth of industry and commerce, it had also entered the field of aesthetics, as can be seen in Karl Marx and Friedrich Engels's *Communist Manifesto*. In the same paragraph in which the authors describe *Weltliteratur* (world literature), referring to the emergence of a new global market comprised of intellectual products alongside material ones, they also mention cosmopolitanism: "The bourgeoisie has through its exploitation of the world's market given a cosmopolitan character to production and consumption in every country" (2017: 42). At the turn of the century, for Spanish American writers in particular, cosmopolitanism was in the air: Manuel González Prada went as far as writing a poem titled "Cosmopolitismo" and Pedro Emilio Coll founded a magazine called *Cosmópolis*. By the second decade of the twentieth century, however, at least in the eyes of Apollinaire, it was in decline.

I want to use Apollinaire's negative assessment of aesthetic cosmopolitanism as a starting point from which to regard the meaning and importance of the word *cosmopolita* in Rubén Darío's writing. It's only by way of Darío's notion of cosmopolitanism that we can begin to theorize about the place of world literature in his writing and about the place of Darío's writing in world literature. The place from where one speaks—whether it is the center, namely Paris at the turn of the century, or the margins, namely Latin America—is decisive when it comes to how a writer may value cosmopolitanism. For this reason, it's also a crucial concept to understand the history of Spanish American literature vis-à-vis world literature.

Regarding the relation between cosmopolitanism and modernity for *modernismo*, Octavio Paz famously wrote: "The modernistas did not want to be French: they wanted to be modern … In lips of Rubén Darío and his friends, modernity and cosmopolitanism were synonymous" (1965: 19). In a figurative sense Paz was of course right. If we take his words literally, however, slight though significant differences seem to emerge between the two terms. Darío seems to have used the term *modernismo* before he did *cosmopolita* or any of its variants. In the first text in which he uses the former, the *crónica* (chronicle) he wrote on his visit to Ricardo Palma in 1888, the word *cosmopolita* never comes up. Nor is it employed in the whole of *Azul…* (1888) (*Azur…*), despite several obvious occasions for doing so (the style in which "El Rey Burgués" [The Bourgeois King] is written is clearly cosmopolitan, for example). And yet cosmopolitan is precisely how Juan Valera describes *Azul…* in his first letter to Darío: "The book is steeped with a cosmopolitan spirit" (1890: V), he writes, before comparing him to other cosmopolitan Peninsular writers, adding that none of them seems to have such a strong French influence as Darío did, despite never having lived in France at that point in time.

In what would be a typical gesture for Darío, who always incorporated into his writing what critics whom he respected said about his work—thus Jose Enrique Rodó's reading of *Prosas profanas* (Profane Prose) shaped the style of *Cantos de vida y esperanza* (Songs of Life and Hope)—it's plausible to assume that he also appropriated Valera's description of his writing as cosmopolitan. It's a term that captures in one word several of the most important features of his aesthetics.

Historically, in Spanish American literature, to be cosmopolitan or not has been a matter of being able to speak the language of contemporary literature elsewhere; of the self-awareness of marginality and the imagining of its remedies; of weighing the importance of local culture against that of global trends. Specifically, the cosmopolitan discourses of *modernismo* were, in the words of Mariano Siskind (2014: 21), "strategic, self-conscious, calculated attempts to take part in, contest, overwrite, and redirect the global hegemony of global culture." They came to represent a discourse of identity for Spanish American writers throughout the twentieth century, embodying one of the poles in the tension between localism and universalism upon which the tradition of modern Spanish American literature is built.[3] The Cortázar-Arguedas debate of the 1960s, the "Boom," and the more recent case of the reception of Valeria Luiselli are examples of the same tendency.[4] From this perspective, the notion of cosmopolitanism articulated by the *modernistas* inaugurated a discourse of literary subjectivity that was elaborated further, and gradually refined, by later writers throughout the twentieth century, counting among its most eloquent advocates authors such as Alfonso Reyes, Jorge Luis Borges, Julio Cortázar, Mario Vargas Llosa, and Roberto Bolaño.

However, *modernismo* has been largely absent from discussions of global modernism(s) until relatively recently, therefore leading to an image of Latin American literary modernity as one that begins with the "Boom."[5] Unfortunately, whereas modernity itself has been historicized geopolitically, our literary notions of what is modern often remain ahistorical in the same sense. In this regard, Darío's poetry fits poorly with the image of a modernist poet: his writing is not imagistic, it's written in rhyme, etc.[6] Despite their pioneering role as one of the first literary movements to articulate a self-aware artistic response to the experience of modernization, the specific modernity of the *modernistas* (which predates Anglo-European modernism) is not perceived as very modern at all.

On the other hand, within Spanish America, for decades Darío's own canonical status was a point of contention. From the time of Rodó and Groussac's reviews of *Prosas profanas* up until the 1960s, his idiosyncratic cosmopolitan poetics was often perceived as escapist and/or derivatively Eurocentric. Though he was almost unanimously praised for his poetic skill, Darío simply did not read like a poet from the Americas, as Rodó famously wrote. Nonetheless, as is well known, since the publication of Octavio Paz's (1965) essay quoted above and Angel Rama's rethinking of *modernismo* from a sociological viewpoint in the 1960s, there has been a revaluation of the cultural politics of the *modernistas*' cosmopolitanism. What was formerly perceived as frivolous escapism is now recognized as deliberate cultural interventions to become part of Western literature and make sense of the changes brought about by Latin America's entry into the global market of industrial capitalism. In this regard, more recent work by Graciela Montaldo (1994) and Gerard Aching (1997), to name but two examples, show the true extent of the complexity of the *modernistas*' cultural practices.

As for the field of World Literature, Darío has only slowly begun to become part of the conversation. In *La République mondiale des Lettres*

(1999), Pascale Casanova discusses Darío's role in bringing Latin American literature closer to what she calls the Greenwich Meridian, embodied by Paris at the turn of the twentieth century. Comparing him to Danish author Georg Brandes, who similarly "translated" many of French literature's fin-de-siècle innovations for Scandinavian literature, Casanova argues that the significance of both these authors' oeuvres should be construed as a bringing up to date of their literatures, rather than as aesthetic revolution. Therefore, because the work of these writers is one of mediation and renovation, rather than one of innovation, they could not have been consecrated in Paris as such. Insofar as a great deal of Darío's originality comes from his creative imitation of his French counterparts, Casanova is certainly right. On the other hand, however, she ignores the literary complexity and the cultural politics of translation. The teleological and Francocentric model of world literature present in Casanova's otherwise inspiring work flattens out and ultimately reduces the real complexity of the processes by which authors from marginal literatures come to be consecrated in the literary powerhouses of the West. In the case of Darío, for cultural and political reasons, the conditions for the reception of Latin American literature in Paris at the turn of the century were scant, irrespective of their innovative qualities or lack thereof.[7]

More recently, Mariano Siskind has published one of the most stimulating books in the field, thinking of the *modernistas*' cosmopolitanism in terms of the global, interrogating its relation to world literature, and putting forth a refreshing rereading of the *modernista* archive that revalues the place of Gómez Carrillo, Sanín Cano, Emilio Coll, and others within it. Siskind's reading of Darío, however, ignores important aspects of the Nicaraguan's critique of French culture and its marginalization of Spanish American literature which are worth exploring in detail, for they show a keen awareness on the part of Darío of the marginal place that Spanish American literature occupied within the so-called World Republic of Letters.

To be sure, Darío's work provides a challenge to world literature understood in at least two different ways. First, it challenges World Literature (in upper case) understood as a recent field of study that seeks to articulate a transnational or global approach to literary studies.[8] Second, it also challenged world literature (in lower case) as the *modernistas* understood it—it challenged the literature of the *modernistas*' world, the international literature of their time. In the first sense, the obscurity in which Darío's oeuvre remains in the English-speaking world, in stark contrast to his status as one of the most influential writers in the history of Hispanic literature, signifies a challenge for the academic field of World Literature and its representational ambitions.[9] That the discipline is articulated from mostly Anglo-American universities implies that the canon of works to which it aspires is represented in English. In consequence, translation plays a crucial role for the field. Given the complexity of literary translation and its precarious state in the Anglophone book market, this is deeply problematic.[10] Contrary to David Damrosch's definition of world literature as literature that circulates beyond its borders, though Darío has been translated several times in different languages (in English there are at least five different book-length translations published), he remains little known. Moreover, the prosodic characteristics of Darío's poetry defy the commonly held translation practices of our literary culture, especially those carried out from within academia, which prioritize the semantic over other forms of poetic meaning.[11] The situation is compounded further if we take into account how the cultural and specifically literary (postcolonial, exoticist, magic realist, or otherwise) expectations of the Anglophone book market regarding Latin American literature seem to be incompatible with the features of Darío's writing, not to mention the historical distance that separates contemporary readers from it.

However, these facts are not new or entirely unknown. A few scholars and critics have pointed out Darío's obscurity in English, confirming it as a significant gap in the Anglophone representation of Spanish American literature.[12] However, the way Darío challenged world literature in the second sense mentioned above—that is, the *modernistas*' notion of the world literature of their time—has hardly been noticed.

In what follows, I will chart Darío's use of the term *cosmopolita* through a selection of poems and *crónicas*. I will tease out the nuances of the word to apply them to a reading of a shift in Darío's poetics around 1900–1901, which coincides with the profound disillusion he felt toward French culture after moving to the country. Since Darío's cosmopolitanism and his attitude toward Paris as literary center go hand in hand, once his outlook on French literature and culture changed, so did his poetics. After reading closely how Darío uses the term *cosmopolita* in his work, I will look at how he articulated a critique of the marginalization of Spanish America literature within world literature.

Uses of the Word "Cosmopolita"

What is particular about Darío as one of the first ideologues of Spanish American cosmopolitan literary discourse is that, after Valera's letter, he began to employ the notion of cosmopolitanism explicitly. He used it not only as a critical concept by which he categorized contemporary literature in Spanish and beyond, but also as an expressive term in his own poetry, which served to create a poetic persona whose cultural desires were suddenly possible to articulate.

A case in point is "Divagación" (Digression) from *Prosas profanas* (1896). Darío famously described this poem in "Historia de mis libros"

(History of My Books) as "un curso de geografía erótica: la invitación al amor bajo todos los soles, la pasión de todos los colores y de todos los tiempos" (a course of erotic geography: an invitation to love under all skies, to passion of all colors and from all times) (1919: 190). To flesh out what *cosmopolita* means in the poem, it's worth looking at the locations of this cultural excursus and excursion Darío takes us on.

The poem begins with a beckoning, "¿Vienes?" (Are you coming?) (l. 1), followed by a one-sided conversation between the lyrical speaker and his beloved (whose place as addressee is occupied by the reader), in which he invites her to consider different cultural, albeit stereotypical, forms of love, beginning with Ancient Greece "¿Te gusta amar en griego?" (Do you like to love in Greek?) (l. 29). Darío's Greece, however, is explicitly and irreverently seen through a French guise: "Amo más que la Grecia de los griegos / La Grecia de la Francia" (More than the Greece of the Greeks / I love the Greece of France) (ll. 41–2). The speaker then moves on to France, Germany, and Spain, before traveling to the Orient—explicitly orientalized through France: "¿los amores exóticos acaso …?" (Perhaps exotic loves?) (l. 89)—stopping by China, Japan, India, and Israel, for which the *Bible* and *The Thousand and One Nights* are two obvious sources. Clearly, France is the mediator between Darío and the rest of the world beyond Hispanic borders.

Toward the end of the poem, the beloved suddenly breaks free from cultural and national boundaries and becomes one with the wider world, almost indistinguishable from the idea of woman itself and from all women at once. Two adjectives used to convey this erasure of difference are *cosmopolita* and *universal*:

> Amor, en fin, que todo diga y cante,
> Amor que encante y deje sorprendida
> A la serpiente de ojos de diamante
> Que está enroscada al árbol de la vida.
>
> Ámame así, fatal, cosmopolita,
> Universal, inmensa, única, sola
> Y todas; misteriosa y erudita;
> Ámame mar y nube, espuma y ola. (ll. 124–32)

> (A love, then, that can say and sing it all,
> A love that bewitches and surprises
> The diamond-eyed serpent
> Coiled onto the tree of life.
>
> Love me so, fatal, cosmopolitan,
> Universal, immense, unique, one
> and all: mysterious and erudite;
> love me sea and cloud, spume and wave.)

Darío's emphasis on totality in his description of the poem ("todos los soles, la pasión de todos los colores y de todos los tiempos"), despite the text's marked French inflection, is telling of the limitations of his *cosmopolitismo*. The world in "Divagación" is rather narrow. The poem is only on the surface about erotic desire; it would be more precise to say that it is about desire for culture, specifically cultural capital. And though it is a voracious desire, as Molloy (2016) characterizes Darío's poetry, it is a voracity for a world whose limitations are clear to us. While it remains on the level of stereotypes, its passion for them is undeniable, to the extent that there is almost something expansive about its narrowness. The poem stages what Siskind aptly calls Darío's *deseo de mundo* (desire for the world) (2014: 27).

Looking at the use of the term "cosmopolitismo" in the *crónicas* written a few years later, the article titled "Modernismo," written in 1899 and included in *España contemporánea* (Contemporary Spain) (1901), stands out. In his assessment of Spain's cultural stagnation, Darío discusses its provincial conservatism, based on a narrow and traditional idea of Spanishness, as the main cause that led most of the country, except for Catalonia, to lack what he calls cosmopolitan influences: "This blocks the entry of any cosmopolitan influences, as it does any individual expansion ... which is the foundation of modern or modernist evolution" (1901: 311). "Modern" and "cosmopolitan" appear here as clearly distinct though related terms. Cosmopolitanism is the condition for modernism, which goes both for Spain and Spanish America. On the other hand, "cosmopolitan influence" (*soplo cosmopolita* in the original) seems to stand in for specifically international influences. Modernity is something one finds outside of one's nation.

A few years earlier, in conference paper included as an essay in *Los raros* (1896), Darío described the Portuguese symbolist poet Eugénio de Castro as an artist who was "one of the most exquisite in modern European literature, or rather, modern cosmopolitan literature," before adding:

> For today there exists a group of thinkers and men of art who in different climes and under different skies are guided by the same star to the dwelling of their reveries ... Symbolists? Decadents? Oh, fortunately, the time of skirmishes over subtle categories is behind us.
>
> (1896: 224–5)

Used in this passage to describe modern literature, "cosmopolitan" seems to mean something else—proving again, despite Paz's assertion, that they are indeed not synonymous. This use touches on Darío's conception of the world literature of his time. At first glance "cosmopolitan" appears to describe an aesthetics whose influence can be seen across several countries (symbolism and/or decadence).[13] However, "cosmopolitan" here replaces the term "European" when Darío describes "modern literature," as seen in the first qualification he makes before correcting himself: "o mejor dicho, la moderna literatura cosmopolita" (or rather, modern cosmopolitan literature). "Cosmopolitan" expands on "European" to include Latin America (Darío also discusses Brazilian poetry in the text), whereas "modern" specifically describes its symbolist/decadent aesthetics. Therefore, "cosmopolitan" refers to the international dimension—which included a self-awareness and a positive predisposition toward the foreign, going beyond Europe and including the Americas—of the movement of modern literature (i.e., symbolism) at the turn of the century.[14]

This seems to be confirmed in a later *crónica* of 1903 titled "Al Dr. Max Nordau" (To Dr. Max Nordau), in which Darío defends the lasting significance of symbolism against Nordau's critique of the movement. After giving a keen overview of the movement's international importance, Darío mentions symbolism's significance for the literatures of the United States, Latin America, Italy, and Belgium (2006a: 251). The innovations he lists as part of the movement's legacy are similar to those of *modernismo* as he describes them in his autobiography (1918: 196–228). Among other bounties brought by the spread of symbolism to these countries, Darío mentions the development of new rhythms, a revaluation of forgotten classics, and a positive attitude toward foreign literatures (2006a: 252).

Yet the word *cosmopolita* is curiously absent from this description. In an earlier text originally written in 1901, "La literatura hispanoamericana en París" (Spanish American Literature in Paris) included in *La caravana pasa* (The Caravan Goes) (Darío 1902), we see that by then the word had acquired negative connotations for Darío (he had moved to Paris in 1900). Discussing the obscurity in which Spanish American writers lived in the city, cut off from French intellectual life, he writes:

> The *Mercure* opened the *rubrique* of Spanish American letters, no longer active today, given its extreme cosmopolitanism, and M. Finot, editor-in-chief of the *Revue et Revue des Revues,* upon asking me for an analysis of the Argentine intellectual movement, was frank with me in not hiding that he took the matter as pertaining to folklore. Thus, from Malayan literature we pass on to Dominican literature or to the poetry from the Fiji islands. Unfortunately it all comes down to fashion.
>
> (166–7)

Sometime around 1900–1, Darío's enthusiasm for cosmopolitanism had cooled. In the passage above, the term denotes a fad, a result of the commercialism that is taking over Paris. The negative connotation cosmopolitanism has when there is an excess of it (*extremado cosmopolitismo*), in contrast to its idealistic, expansive, and supercharged meaning in "Divagación," reflects Darío's disillusion with Paris.

However, one of Darío's most famous uses of the term comes from a poem written several years later, his well-known poetic self-portrait from *Cantos de vida y esperanza* (1905):

El dueño fui de mi jardín de sueño,
Lleno de rosas y de cisnes vagos;
El dueño de las tórtolas, el dueño
De góndolas y liras en los lagos;

Y muy siglo diez y ocho y muy antiguo
Y muy moderno; audaz, cosmopolita;
Con Hugo fuerte y con Verlaine ambiguo;
Y una sed de ilusiones infinita.

(I was the warden of my dream-garden
full of roses and vague swans;
the warden of turtledoves; the warden
of lyres and gondolas over the ponds;

and very eighteenth-century and very ancient
and very modern; bold, cosmopolitan;
as Hugo strong and as Verlaine ambiguous—
and a thirst for dreams that was continuous.)

(ll. 5–12)

Though it might seem that this is a positive revaluation of the term, it's important to point out that Darío is looking back on his life here, not describing his present self.[15] This point is relevant when we look at the time frame that separates this poem from "Divagación," as the *crónicas* quoted above precede the publication of *Cantos*.

It is a truism to assert that Darío's poetics changed after *Cantos*. What is interesting to note is that part of that change specifically includes his poetics of cosmopolitanism. Darío's Hispanic turn goes beyond espousing pan-Hispanism in the face of US imperialism and performing a poetic persona by which he defined himself as "Español de América y americano de España" (a Spaniard from America and an American from Spain) (1919: 205). As seen in his writings after 1900, it means reformulating cosmopolitanism as universalism. It implies extending his cultural authority across time rather than across space by embracing the works of classical antiquity instead of the novelties of contemporary literature. This shift comes through clearly in his preface to *El canto errante* (The Wandering Song) from 1907:

Fond of classical culture, I have drunk from its source, but always apace with my days. I have understood the strength of traditions in the past, and of foresight into the future ... Woe to the philosophy that comes from Germany, that comes from England or from France, if it is to subtract rather than to add. Let's not forget that many of these splendid imports lie, eaten by moths, in ancient Spanish folios.

(XXI–XXIV)

Unlike the poetic persona of *Prosas profanas*, the one we find in *El canto errante* is not a cosmopolitan traveler but a wanderer who looks onto the past and into the future as he roves about the earth.

Darío's Critique of French Culture

In parallel, through his *crónicas*, Darío articulated a critique of the industrialization and commercialism he found in Paris, as well as the marginalization of Spanish American literature in Europe. His erstwhile awe for the city underwent a profound change in the first decade of the 1900s, acquiring a bitter and ironic self-awareness, which led him to reformulate his cosmopolitanism into a Hispanic-inflected universalism, as seen above. This also had to do with the fact that the only interlocutors Darío found on the other shore of the Atlantic were Spanish, not French.

Little has been written on the international aspirations of the *modernistas* in literally taking Spanish American literature to Paris.[16] More than merely being avid readers of French literature and writers influenced by their French counterparts, many *modernistas* learned or taught themselves French (as was the case of Darío), wrote in French, and moved to Paris to make a life and pursue a literary career there. In Molloy's (1972: 19) terms, the *modernistas* lived in their own literary colony, for they were shunned by Parisian literary society. Rama (1973: 44) even describes them as living in a kind of ghetto, which is perhaps excessive but effectively conveys an idea of how they were cast aside by Parisian intelligentsia.

In his historicization of Darío's aesthetic formation, Siskind treats the period between 1896 and 1905 as a single coherent chapter, during which the *modernista* invented "an expansive poetic subjectivity that can be described as cosmopolitan, even if that cosmopolitanism needs to be qualified" (2014: 185). Nevertheless, as seen in the dates of the texts analyzed above, this cosmopolitanism had already begun to change in as early as 1901. Moreover, Siskind frames the change of Darío's relation to France in psychiatric terms, describing his relation to Paris as a "cyclothymic relation" (185) and a "schizophrenic back and forth between modernist ideological faith and the quotidian experience of cultural rejection and economic need" (219). The connotations of irrationality and instability these descriptions carry over suggest that these changes are not worth examining in more depth. Also, they conveniently offer the advantage of acknowledging shifts in Darío's outlook on French culture without challenging Siskind's main thesis, which is that for Darío "the world is not a plural universe of multiplied difference but rather a uniformly French formation, or a world seen through a French looking glass, divided into modern and premodern camps" (185) and France "not another particular culture, or even a cultural *primus inter pares*; it is a linguistic and cultural body of the universal itself, the condition of possibility of culture as humanity's shared patrimony" (195).

While Darío's Francophilia certainly bordered on a reverence for, and an idealization of, Paris during his Chilean and Argentine periods, once he moved to the French capital, his views thoroughly changed. I have written elsewhere on the multilingual ambitions of the *modernistas* and their failed international campaign to enter the French literary milieu and carve out a space for Spanish American literature there.[17] Suffice it to note here some themes that Darío elaborated in his *crónicas*, which prove that the world was not, for him, a uniformly French formation. In fact, he denounced what French literature ignored and erased from the world. In a text written as early as June 1900, "La exposición: los hispanoamericanos" (The Exhibition: The Spanish Americans), he writes:

> Latin America, for the citizen of Paris, has very few defined contours according to his precarious boulevardian geography ... Ethnographically, it all gets muddled in the distance of vague Venezuelas and unlikely Nicaraguas, even though Hugo's erudition left behind for immortality *The Reasons of Momotombo*.
>
> (1968a: 64)

Nominally, the article was meant to report on an exhibition of French cartoonist Caran d'Ache, in which certain Spanish American representations were exhibited. But the exoticization he found in the works led Darío to reflect on the place of the region's culture as seen through French eyes. In an allusion that bespeaks his idealization of French literature before his arrival, he mentions Victor Hugo's poem on the Momotombo, a Nicaraguan volcano, which appears in *La Légende des Siècles* (The Legend of the Ages) (1882)—as if Hugo's brief interest in the region meant that a wider curiosity existed in Paris. Toward the end of the text, Darío goes further and unmasks, for his readers of the Buenos Aires newspaper *La Nación*, Spanish American sensationalism and idealization of Paris as place of literary consecration, challenging one of the deepest held *modernista* convictions about the world beyond Latin America:

> People barely know about us. The new literature from the Americas has drawn some attention in a few circles, like the *Mercure de France*, but as no one speaks Spanish, except for extremely rare cases, we are completely

ignored ... Now you know, then, to smile every time you read in *El iris decadente* or *La estrella tropical*: "The eminent Spanish American poet Mr. So-and-so, known not only in the Americas and in Spain, but also in Paris ...", etc.

And what about Spain? Spain has no more luck than we do. Here, when it comes to Spain, *olé!* and that's it.

(1968a: 69)

Over the years Darío's critical vision of Western literature developed further, as seen in another piece titled "La Sociedad de Escritores de Buenos Aires" (The Writers' Society of Buenos Aires) in which he celebrates the inauguration of such a society in the Argentine capital. There, he criticizes the then recently created Nobel Prize in the following terms:

There is a Noble prize that knows no borders. Has it ever occurred to anyone that it could ever be won by a writer from Latin America? It's as if we didn't count as civilized nations in that regard.

(2006c: 60)

Darío's ironic use of "civilized" (*civilizadas*) here is postcolonial in its suggestion of European culture's hegemonic position in relation to the other nations it marginalizes for their alleged lack of civilization. He not only challenges the traditional Spanish American view of Paris as international capital of culture, as seen in the previous *crónica*, but questions European culture's dividing of the world into civilized and non-civilized nations. Darío would use the term again in another *crónica* from 1909, "Enrique Larreta," in which he discusses a new translation of a Spanish American novel by Larreta rendered into the French by Rémy de Gourmont:

If Gourmont, aside from translating well, explains to the French something about Latin American intellectuals in general, and presents Larreta as he should, *Don Ramiro's Glory* will enter triumphant into Gaul.

Though, for them to pay attention to Argentine intellectuals, even for the space of a trend, we'd need a good war, a wonderful bloodbath, a brawl with Brazil, with Chile, with both ... In other words, a real display of civilization.

Europeans!

(2006b: 169)

The last passage is striking given its denouncement of the ignorance regarding Spanish America vis-à-vis the sensationalist interests of a Parisian readership eager to consume stories of faraway nations as long as they bear the thrill of war. Darío's ironic use of "civilization" (*civilización*) confirms what was pointed out above regarding his awareness of the marginalization of cultures like his own in the face of European culture's hegemony in the world. This is underlined by the exasperated "Europeans!" (¡Europeos!) with which the *crónica* ends.

Finally, in a later text titled "París y los escritores extranjeros" (Paris and Foreign Writers) included in *Letras* (1911), we see how Paris, in Darío's writing, came to be thematized no longer as the *non plus ultra* of a writer's literary career but as a specifically Spanish American symptom. Darío reflects on what he calls "el embrujo parisiense en el espíritu hispanoamericano" (the Parisian bewitchment of the Spanish American spirit), playfully describing it as a sickness or an addiction which he terms "la parisina" (1911: 9). The main point is to show that the intoxication of Paris has its effect only at a distance—once Spanish Americans reached the city, reality sank in. Consequently, Paris as theme, motif, and setting in Darío's writing acquired the tones of a life-changing disillusion. In the text, Darío goes on to provide an overview of the foreign writers who went to Paris to pursue a literary career there, focusing on those who were Spanish American and found no success. He again broaches the ignorance of Parisians regarding the rest of the world:

> For the Parisian there is no inhabitable place other than Paris and there is no reason for anything to exist outside Paris. Thus we can explain the ancient and traditional ignorance of all things foreign, as well as the curious amazement at any manifestation of foreign superiority.
>
> (1911: 13)

He then discusses the story of French-language Cuban poet Augusto de Armas, on whom he had written in *Los raros*, and who had always fascinated Darío for his ability to write in French. However, his view on Armas's story is different now. Darío uses it to reflect on the history of the place of Paris in his own work. For its revealing content, and its disillusioned self-irony, the passage is worth citing in full:

> When Cuban poet Augusto de Armas arrived in the great city he was already possessed by the madness of Paris.
>
> He wrote admirable poems in French, imbued himself with the spirit of Lutetia, became just another young, long-haired, dreamy French poet of the Quartier Latin—and Paris gobbled him up. There was no careerism then. The poor *criollo* lived believing in the mirage of glory, he dedicated poems to all the big shots at the time, and aside from Banville, who wrote him a kind letter, no one paid him any attention.
>
> Those of us who have moved to Paris have mostly brought with us that same illusion. Yet we have followed different paths. I have been more passionate and have written things that are "more Parisian" before coming to Paris than during my time here. And I always found myself a stranger among these people. And where are the stories of yesteryear now?
>
> (1911: 13–14)

Darío identifies himself with Armas, whose life has acquired the plot of a tragedy, and is no longer the success story it was shown to be in *Los raros*. His reflection on the place that Parisian themes have occupied in his own writing touches on the irony that when he lived farthest from the French capital, his writing was at his most Parisian; when he finally lived in the city, the opposite occurred. Over the years, he articulated a shrewd critique of the lack of conditions for the reception of Spanish American writers in Paris. It would not be until Borges was translated into French by Roger Callois in the 1950s, and the "Boom" took the global literary market by storm in the 1970s, that those conditions changed. Through the self-reflection for which his *crónicas* provided a space, Darío became clear-eyed, if at times bitter and despondent, about his former idealization of the city and how it continued to have the insidious effect of a mirage on Spanish American writers and readers.

The shift in Darío's cosmopolitan poetics and his Parisian disillusion I have so far discussed are summarized in the poem "Epístola" (Epistle) for Mrs. Lugones, included in *El canto errante* in 1907, where Darío again poeticizes cosmopolitanism, though in starkly different terms. Even if the word *cosmopolita* is never used in the poem (Darío had practically dropped it from his vocabulary), it's the background against which the trials and tribulations of his life are set. Paris is poeticized now as "el enemigo / terrible, centro de la neurosis, ombligo / de la locura, foco de todo *surmenage* / donde hago buenamente mi papel de *sauvage*" (the terrible / enemy, center of neurosis, the navel / of madness, the focus of all *surmenage* / where I willingly play the role of *sauvage*) (1907: 63–8).

And yet the city would remain a mystery and a literary precinct the gates of which were closed for Spanish Americans except for extremely rare cases. Despite his bitterness and criticism of Paris, the city never completely lost its allure for Darío. Upon reviewing an Italian biography of Rimbaud, what shocked him about the story of the young rebel, more than being the fact that he had written poetic masterpieces and groundbreaking poetry by the time he was twenty (at which point he decided to abandon writing), was the fact that Rimbaud was able to renounce Paris.[18] This puzzling reading of the text of Rimbaldian biography illustrates the postcolonial anxieties of the *modernistas* at the turn of the century. It throws into sharp relief the marginalized position from which they read, translated, and wrote in full awareness of their predicament, in contrast to Rimbaud, who could give up Paris, where he could have had all a writer could ask for from the world.

Notes

1 All translations are my own. Due to limitations of space, source text quotations have been left out.
2 For more on the history of the term, see Delanty (2012).

3 For one of the most influential theories in the field, in which the historical importance of cosmopolitanism for Latin American literature is fleshed out, see Rama (2019). For a critical discussion of Rama's theory of *transculturación* by some of the leading scholars of the field, see Moraña (2006).
4 In an exchange of articles, Peruvian writer José María Arguedas debated Argentine writer Julió Cortázar on, among other topics, the role of cosmopolitanism for Latin American novelists. Arguedas defended the ethical commitment of art with local culture against what he saw as the superficial and vapid nature of global trends, whereas Cortázar pejoratively dubbed art that was exclusively concerned with the local as narrow-minded and backwards "tellurism." On the other hand, the persistence of the significance of cosmopolitanism can be seen in the reception of Mexican-American writer Valeria Luiselli's work today, which is often characterized as cosmopolitan. At its simplest, the term seems to have become a shorthand for a Spanish American writer whose work includes international (non-Latin American) references, especially European or North American. See Hughes-Hallet (2019) for an example.
5 For a thorough discussion of the topic, see Mejías-López (2010).
6 For an in-depth comparative discussion of modernism and *modernismo*, see Grigsby (2019b).
7 For further discussion of these issues, see notes 15 and 16.
8 For an overview of the field in relation to Latin American literature, see Siskind (2014: 14–19).
9 For a detailed overview of Darío's reception in the Anglophone world and the translational problems it raises, see Grigsby (2019b).
10 It is well known among translation scholars that approximately a paltry 3 percent of all books published in the United States are works in translation. While a surge of interest in translated literature across independent publishers and magazines (Archipelago Books, Deep Vellum, Charco Press; *Words without Borders*, *Asymptote Magazine*, *Granta*, etc.) has recently emerged, deep-rooted and far-reaching problems persist. Anglophone literature, because of its hegemony, continues to be insular. For more information from a translator's perspective, see Post (2019). For a critical account of World Literature's reliance on translation from the point of view of a defense of untranslatability, see Apter (2013).
11 For an exploration of the limits of our translation practices, see Scott (2015).
12 See Díaz (2005), González Echevarría (2006), and Roof (2016).
13 For a discussion of how symbolism eventually superseded decadence as a rubric that designated what was originally understood as two distinct literary movements, see Pittock (1993).
14 Incidentally, this is modern literature before modernism. For a study of the key role that decadence and symbolism played in the making of modernism, see Weir (1995).
15 In that same vein, later we find a *mea culpa* for the *art pour l'art* excesses of his youth, alluding to *Prosas profanas* (see ll. 49–52).

16 See Molloy (1972), Rama (1973), and Darío (2000).
17 See Grigsby (2019a) for a brief reconstruction of the *modernistas* little-known European campaign as seen through Darío's experience in Paris. Some of the *crónicas* discussed in the article are revisited here with a different focus.
18 See Darío (1968b).

References

Aching, G. (1997), *The Politics of Spanish American modernismo: By Exquisite Design*, Cambridge: Cambridge University Press.
Apollinaire, G. (1966), "L'Esprit nouveau et les poètes," in *Œuvres en prose complètes: Volume III*, 900–10, Paris: Bibliothèque de la Pléiade.
Apter, E. (2013), *Against World Literature: On the Politics of Untranslatability*, London: Verso.
Casanova, P. (1999), *La République mondiale des Lettres*, Paris: Editions Seuil.
Damrosch, D. (2003), *What Is World Literature?*, Princeton and Oxford: Princeton University Press.
Darío, R. (1890), *Azul …*, Guatemala: Imprenta de la Unión.
Darío, R. (1896a), *Los raros*, Buenos Aires: La Vasconia.
Darío, R. (1896b), *Prosas profanas*, Buenos Aires: Pablo E. Coni e Hijos.
Darío, R. (1901), *España contemporánea*, Paris: Garnier Hermanos.
Darío, R. (1902), *La caravana pasa*, Paris: Garnier Hermanos.
Darío, R. (1905), *Cantos de vida y esperanza*, Madrid: La Revista de Archivos.
Darío, R. (1907), *El canto errante*, Madrid: Biblioteca Nueva de Escritores Españoles.
Darío, R. (1911), *Letras*, Paris: Garnier Hermanos.
Darío, R. (1919), *Obras completas: El viaje a Nicaragua e Historia de mis libros*, XVII, Madrid: Mundo Latino.
Darío, R. (1968a), "La exposición: los hispanoamericanos," in P. L. Barcia (ed.), *Escritos dispersos de Rubén Darío: II*, 64–9, La Plata: Universidad Nacional.
Darío, R. (1968b), "Un nuevo libro sobre Arthur Rimbaud," in P. L. Barcia (ed.), *Escritos dispersos de Rubén Darío: I*, 308–16, La Plata: Universidad Nacional.
Darío, R. (2000), *La caravana pasa: libro primero*, ed. G. Schmigalle, Berlin: Edición Tranvía.
Darío, R. (2006a), "Al Dr. Max Nordau," in G. Schmigalle (ed.), *Crónicas desconocidas (1901–1906)*, 241–53, Managua: Academia Nicaragüense de la Lengua.
Darío, R. (2006b), "Enrique Larreta," in G. Schmigalle (ed.), *Crónicas desconocidas (1906–1914)*, 160–9, Managua: Academia Nicaragüense de la Lengua.
Darío, R. (2006c), "La sociedad de escritores de Buenos Aires," in G. Schmigalle (ed.), *Crónicas desconocidas (1906–1914)*, 55–62, Managua: Academia Nicaragüense de la Lengua.
Delanty, G., ed. (2012), *Routledge Handbook of Cosmopolitan Studies*, London: Routledge.

Díaz, I. (2005), "Traducciones de la obra de Rubén Darío en la lengua inglesa," in N. Urbina (ed.), *Miradas críticas sobre Rubén Darío*, 281–92, Managua: PAVSA, Fundación internacional Rubén Darío.
González Echevarría, R. (2006), "The Master of Modernismo," *The Nation*, January 25. Available online: https://www.thenation.com/article/archive/master-modernismo/. Accessed March 8, 2022.
Grigsby, C. F. (2019a), "*El fracaso de París*: Rubén Darío's *Modernista* Campaign in France," *Modern Language Review*, 11 (4): 720–39.
Grigsby, C. F. (2019b), "Rediscovering Rubén Darío through Translation," PhD diss., University of Oxford, Oxford.
Hughes-Hallet, L. (2019), "Lost Children Archive by Valeria Luiselli Review—Border Crossings," review of *Lost Children Archive*, by Valeria Luiselli, *The Guardian*, March 15. Available online: https://www.theguardian.com/books/2019/mar/15/lost-children-archive-valeria-luiselli-review. Accessed March 8, 2022.
Marx, K. and F. Engels (2017), *Das kommunistische Manifest: eine moderne Edition*, Hamburg: Argument Verlag.
Mejías-López, A. (2010), *The Inverted Conquest: The Myth of Modernity and the Transatlantic Onset of Modernism*, Nashville: Vanderbilt University Press.
Molloy, S. (1972), *La Diffusion de la littérature hispano-américaine en France au XXe siècle*, Paris: Presses Universitaires de France.
Molloy, S. (2016), "Voracidad y solipsismo en la poesía de Darío," in "Extraordinario: Rubén Darío," special issue, *Zama*: 311–17.
Montaldo, G. (1994), *La sensibilidad amenazada: Fin de Siglo y Modernismo*, Rosario: Beatriz Viterbo.
Moraña, M., ed. (2006), *Ángel Rama y los estudios latinoamericanos*, Pittsburgh: Instituto Internacional de Literatura Iberoamericana.
Paz, O. (1965), *Cuadrivio*, Mexico: Joaquín Motriz.
Pittock, M. (1993), *Spectrum of Decadence: The Literature of the 1890s*, London: Routledge.
Post, C. (2019), "Will Translated Fiction Ever *Really* Break Through," *Vulture*, May 7. Available online: https://www.vulture.com/2019/05/translated-fiction-has-been-growing-or-has-it.html. Accessed March 8, 2022.
Rama, Á. (1973), "Sueños, espíritus, ideología y arte del diálogo modernista en Europa," in R. Darío, *El mundo de los sueños: Prosas póstumas*, 5–55, Río Piedras: Editorial Universitaria.
Rama, Á. (2019), *Transculturación narrativa en América Latina*, Mexico: Nómada.
Roof, M. (2016), "Rubén Darío en inglés: la poesía," *Revista Casa de las Américas* (282, January–March): 10–33.
Scott, C. (2015), *Literary Translation and the Rediscovery of Reading*, Cambridge: Cambridge University Press.
Siskind, M. (2014), *Cosmopolitan Desires: Global Modernity and World Literature in Latin America*, Evanston: Northwestern University Press.
Weir, D. (1995), *Decadence and the Making of Modernism*, Amherst: University of Massachusetts Press.

6

Álvaro Menen Desleal's Speculative Planetary Imagination

Carolyn Fornoff

Read side by side against his contemporaries, the Salvadoran writer Álvaro Menen Desleal (born Álvaro Menendez Leal) appears to be a striking anomaly. Unlike other members of El Salvador's Generación Comprometida (Committed Generation), Menen Desleal wrote speculative and marvelous tales abstracted from immediate sociopolitical concerns. He refrained from thematizing indigeneity or rural life and opposed literature's didactic function. His tales eschewed realism and local color in favor of universal non-places that seemingly transcended geopolitical space and linear historical time.

If at the turn of the twentieth century, *modernista* (modernist) writers like Rubén Darío and Enrique Gómez Carrillo laid claim to Central America's ability to speak to the universal and establish global conversations, the majority of Isthmus authors who followed in their wake rejected this cosmopolitan approach and turned their attention back to the local, foregrounding literature's responsibility to shape and contest regional issues. Most Central American authors of the twentieth century dismissed cosmopolitanism as a Eurocentric posture that was disengaged with what really mattered: the quotidian reality of their readers' circumscribed space. They argued that the Isthmus's cultural particularity was not a sign of "backwardness" that distanced Central American literature from global conversations, but instead a proud marker of originality, a distinguishing feature that should be woven into cultural production in order to stand out.

In parallel fashion, scholars of Central American literature have largely focused on regional specificity and cultural difference as justifications for the region's hemispheric relevance. Consequently, Central American literary studies has attended to what is widely considered exceptional about regional cultural production: such as subalternity, revolution, migration, and indigeneity. Critics have focused on works that illustrate the specificity of the contexts in which they were produced or that actively shaped national political conversations. We might propose that this privileging of local distinctiveness is why Central Americanist scholars have spent more time discussing Rodrigo Rey Rosa's *El material humano* (Human Matter) than his novels set in Africa and Asia (like *La orilla africana* [The African Shore] and *El tren a Travancore* [The Train to Travancore]), or Horacio Castellanos Moya's *Insensatez* (Senselessness) than *Baile con serpientes* (Dance with Snakes). Looking further back, authors like Carlos Martínez Rivas, a contemporary of writers of the Sandinista Revolution, but who did not participate in revolution, has also received less critical attention. In this manner, scholarship has tended to echo the dominant posture of the time that the only literature that mattered was that which actively engaged in national politics. Such an approach perpetuates a narrow view of the political and of literary production and reinforces the centrality of the nation, a view that writers like Menen Desleal actively dispute.

Within this context, Menen Desleal has slipped through the cracks, revealing the fissures of current approaches to Central American cultural production. El Salvador is infrequently the setting of his fiction, which centers instead on protagonists from the United States, the Soviet Union, Asia, the distant historical past, or even outer space. Additionally, while his literature has a political bent, it is not political in the actively engaged sense of contemporaries like Roque Dalton or Manlio Argueta (or, beyond the bounds of El Salvador, Ernesto Cardenal and Sergio Ramírez). His posture is more cautious, cynical of ideology writ large. Further distancing him from his cohort, Menen Desleal avoids realist representational models. Instead he works within genres proper to world literature like sci-fi, which makes him a regional oddity, or within hemispheric genres like the fantastic, placing him more in dialogue with South American authors like Jorge Luis Borges and Julio Cortázar than with his compatriots.

This chapter takes seriously Menen Desleal's global literary engagement and accounts for what I term his speculative planetary imagination. This speculative planetary imagination deploys a scalar framework that zooms out both geographically and temporally. It expansively conceptualizes space and time by moving past the nation to think about the planet, past differences of race and class to think through the category of species, and past the historical moment and toward deep time. This scalar imagination is political but not in the local revolutionary sense that depicts questions of national concern. Rather, it is politicized in calling into question a myriad of projects including space exploration, nuclear power, authoritarianism, and even revolution itself.

I first outline Menen Desleal's disagreements with the Committed Generation, and his assertion that distance from the local context was essential to literary innovation. This celebration of migration, external perspectives, and autonomy is at the core of Menen Desleal's cosmopolitan thought. Second, I highlight the intersection between his cosmopolitanism and interest in speculative genres of world literature. Thinking from a planetary or even galactic perspective allowed Menen Desleal to accomplish several avenues of critique, including the critique of the neo-imperial pursuit of mastery, as well as a critique of the belief that Salvadoran political concerns were unrelated to broader issues of the Cold War. I argue that Menen Desleal's engagement with expansive categories like the planet and the species was not necessarily an escapist gesture but laid claim to the Central American ability to narrate from the universal, and to the isthmus's belonging within capacious ontological categories and global ethical debates. This zoomed-out perspective held for Menen Desleal the allure of freedom from national borders and geopolitical and cultural marginalization, while also foregrounding the inherent fragility of a world imperiled by nuclear war.

Desleal to the Committed Generation

Menen Desleal formed part of El Salvador's Generación Comprometida (Committed Generation), a robust group of budding intellectuals and writers who met throughout the 1950s in San Salvador, and included men who would later participate in the revolution such as Roque Dalton, Manlio Argueta, Roberto Armijo, and José Roberto Cea. The Committed Generation shared the precept that to write literature that was both politically and culturally relevant, it was imperative to decisively break with Salvadoran literary tradition, namely *modernismo* (modernism), *vitalismo* (vitalism), and *regionalismo* (regionalism), which by the 1950s felt outdated. These writers, most of whom were born in the 1930s, were instead inspired by hemispheric cultural trends like the avant-garde and existentialist movements, Mexican muralism, and Pablo Neruda's blending of verse with politics (Melgar Brizuela 2006: 88).

The group began as a literary circle, Cenáculo de Iniciación Literaria (Cenacle of Literary Initiation), which gathered in 1950. Its original congregants, including Menen Desleal, subsequently called themselves the Grupo Octubre (October Group), indicating their ideological affinity with Soviet and Guatemalan socialist revolutions, which both respectively unfolded during the month of October. In 1956, several members including Dalton, Argueta, and Armijo (but not Menen Desleal) broke off to found the Círculo Literario Universitario, based at the Universidad de El Salvador. Throughout these different groupings, members coalesced their energies around the Sunday literary pages of *La prensa gráfica* and *Diario Latino*, and later, the literary magazine *Hoja*.

Although the term "Committed Generation" is now used as a catchall to encompass these varying literary formations, the expansive nature of these groupings meant that in spite of the name, its members never converged around a single goal or ideological point of view. The moniker "Committed Generation" was put forth in 1956 by Ítalo López Vallecillos, inspired by Jean Paul Sartre's vision of the socially engaged intellectual. Other writers did not share this vision and repudiated the name. Menen Desleal was one of the most vehement objectors. Unlike López Vallecillos and the members of the Círculo Literario Universitario (University Literary Circle), Menen Deseal fundamentally disagreed that literature had to serve a social or political purpose. He fashioned himself more in the mold of Jorge Luis Borges, a cosmopolitan writer who envisioned the literary vocation as an endeavor that stretched far beyond the immediate historical moment and geographical context. Menen Desleal preferred to call the group "Grupo Internacional" (The International Group) or "Grupo Espontáneo" (The Spontaneous Group) which respectively referred to its global perspective and the spontaneous way it gathered (Melgar Brizuela 2006: 88).

A biographical blurb for Menen Desleal included in a 1962 issue of *Cultura*, a literary magazine directed by Claudia Lars, humorously noted Menen Desleal's brash repudiation of his supposed membership. It read, "Nos asegura que no pertenece a la llamada 'generación comprometida'—como nosotros habíamos afirmado—ni a ningún grupo que quiera apresarlo por medio de cualquier obligado compromiso ... Según sus propias palabras: pertenece a la vida que evoluciona siempre, y que nunca guarda como nuevas, formas gastadas." (He assures us that he does not pertain to the so-called "Committed Generation"— as we have affirmed—nor to any group who would claim him by way of some compulsory commitment ... According to his own words: he pertains to life as it constantly evolves, which never maintains that overworn forms are new ones.)

As specified in his chosen pen name, which reworks his birth name from Menéndez Leal into Menen Desleal, the lack of allegiance to any one cause, group, country, or aesthetic form was central to Menen Desleal's philosophy. This disloyalty was often presented with performative hubris. He described the other members of the Committed Generation as "casi todos ... con talento" (almost all ... talented) but thought of himself as an autonomous entity (Alcides Orellana 2015). As he once put it with characteristic swagger, if necessary, he could stand in for his entire generation and act as "El 'hombre-generación', el 'hombre-orquesta', en cuyos hombros podría reposar la responsabilidad de la literatura nacional" (The "generational man," the "one-man-band," on whose shoulders the responsibility of national literature could rest) (Alvarenga 2010: 13). Perhaps because of this ambition for singularity exemplarity and posterity, Menen Desleal's fiction always reached past the confines of the local and toward more universal forms and themes.

A believer in the maxim that no publicity is bad publicity, he drew attention to his work through scandals, many of which he sparked himself. In 1963, shortly after winning second place in the Certamen Nacional de Cultura de El Salvador (El Salvadorian National Culture Competition) for his book of short stories *Cuentos breves y maravillosos* (Short and Marvelous Stories), Menen Desleal was accused of plagiarizing Borges and Adolfo Bioy Casares's similarly titled collection, *Cuentos breves y extraordinarios* (Short and Extraordinary Stories). The polemic unfolded in national newspapers with op-eds arguing both sides of the case. As a result, a suit was levied against Menen Desleal, and he was found guilty. Yet despite this, or rather because of this scandal, this book became a bestseller. It broke sales records and was subsequently translated into English and Romanian: a rarity for Salvadoran writers of the era. In 1968, Sergio Ramírez revealed that Menen Desleal had himself unleashed the polemic by penning both the op-ed that accused himself of plagiarism and the subsequent one in his defense (Ramírez 2011). The polemic caught on, and others dove into the fray, spreading the work's visibility. This game of mirrors was furthered by the collection's prologue, which was supposedly written by Borges in praise of the work. This too was apocryphal. Borges, who did not know Menen Desleal, later found out about the scandal and was bemused (Huezo Mixco 2011: 103).

The self-obloquy that shot Menen Desleal's first book to bestseller status exemplified his media-savvy grasp that public interest was best generated through ignominy and buzz marketing. He reveled in the spotlight, stirring the pot with games that blurred the line between plagiarism, appropriation, and dialogue. A firm believer that originality was a chimera, Menen Desleal insisted that good art was born out of imitation. This shrewd understanding of publicity derived from his extensive experience navigating a variety of media outlets, including a pioneering role in the nation's televised news. Throughout the 1950s he worked at *El Diario de Hoy* directing the Sunday literary supplement and writing the column "Paso Doble." He went on to found El Salvador's first independent news programs: the radio program *Tele-reloj* and the television show *Telediario* in 1956. In these organizations Menen Desleal had to constantly negotiate objective reporting while also evading censorship. In one case, he drummed up viewership by challenging president José María Lemus to a boxing match and declared himself the winner when Lemus unsurprisingly never showed. In another, when a censor appeared at the station to review the scripted news before it aired, Menen Desleal offered the official a blank page and then went on the air with black tape covering his mouth, gesticulating in silence for an entire minute. Citing these acts, Jorge Ávalos has argued that Menen Desleal was El Salvador's first performance artist: a person who imbued his actions with political and theatrical meaning (Ávalos 2016).

This more flexible relationship with the existing authoritarian government led contemporaneous intellectuals to find Menen Deseal lacking, if not complicit, in his political stance. Unlike leftists who felt that the state needed to be overthrown, Menen Desleal's prominent role in the media industry throughout the 1950s and 1960s necessitated a more measured stance. Later, during the most brutal years of the Civil War in the 1980s, he worked for José Napoleón Duarte's nondemocratic administration as the Director de Cultura del Ministerio de Relaciones Exteriores (Cultural Director of the Ministry of Foreign Affairs), participating in a world tour that was aimed at improving the regime's image abroad by spreading disinformation about the rebels. Menen Desleal was an active participant in the authoritarian government during the worst years of the Civil War, and for this he was rightfully pilloried. Dalton poked fun at him in his posthumous work *Pobrecito poeta que era yo* (Poor Little Poet I Was) (1976), and Cea accused him in his memoirs of being part of the "Generación Troncometida" (Non-committed Generation) that actively undermined the radical cause. Cea wryly observed that this complicity "no le resta a su estética ningún valor, solamente a su 'moral y civíca' que creía y decía sostener" (does not take away from any of his aesthetic value, only his "morality and civility" that he believed and claimed to uphold) (2003: 124).

In the wake of Menen Desleal's passing in 2000, reassessments of his political waffling have eased, in large part due to the understanding that during the cultural Cold War in Latin America, "there were only troubling options" for intellectuals (Iber 2015: 17). Salvadoran writer and former guerrilla Miguel Huezo Mixco has noted that whereas some intellectuals of the era like Dalton approached politics as if it were a game of Russian roulette, Menen Desleal played it like it was poker (2011: 97).

Although Menen Desleal never took up arms against the state, his work was not apolitical. His short story "Una carta de familia" (A Family Letter), written in 1969, thematizes the vexed practice of writing under censorship and the complicated question of state complicity. Several of his other short stories poke subtle fun at characters who are military men, like "El suicida" (The Suicide) (1961), which narrates a military man's futile attempts to effectively commit suicide. The long speculative collage "El día en que quebró el café" (The Day Coffee Went Bankrupt) (1961) imagines how the successful creation of synthetic coffee would send El Salvador into a tailspin, with regimes recurring to foreign intervention. Unlike other members of the Committed Generation, Menen Desleal didn't restrict his critiques to one ideology but instead found all political ideologies wanting. "Revolución en el país que edificó un castillo de hadas" (Revolution in the Country that Built a Fairy Tale Castle) (1970) critiques how revolutionary projects often end up consolidating power in a few hands and are driven by ideological fanaticism: a veiled dig at the Cuban Revolution.

While the stories mentioned above speak to El Salvador's sociopolitical situation, they do so without explicitly referencing it. As such, these fictions are universalizable; they can be extrapolated to any nation in Central America or to any authoritarian or developing country in the world. The absence of cultural particularity or markers of national difference (with the exception of atypical stories like "El día en que quebró el café" [The Day Coffee Went Bankrupt]) reflect Menen Desleal's forceful rejection of the contemporaneous mandate that Salvadoran writers principally dramatize the domestic in order to move political conversations in new directions. While he wrestled with local politics on a daily basis through his news programs, he viewed literature as an autonomous sphere, a space that could disconnect from these quotidian battles and operate on a larger scale by engaging with universal themes, attracting transnational readers, and reworking cosmopolitan paradigms. This approach exemplifies what Ignacio Sánchez Prado has described as the "time-honored tradition of … Latin American cultural thinkers devoted to challenging the notion that universalism is solely the province of European and U.S. culture, or that the region can only be a permanent source of foreignness and otherness" (2018: 9).

Since most Salvadoran writers of the early to mid-twentieth century were preoccupied with regionalism and *costumbrismo*, Menen Desleal viewed his literary project as one of rupture. Unlike the more tempered approach of colleagues like Dalton who advocated a critical reappraisal of the national canon that kept the good while discarding the bad, Menen Desleal dismissed antecedents like Salarrué and Alberto Masferrer as mediocre.

For Menen Desleal, this national mediocrity was not just confined to the past but also permeated the present. Like Castellanos Moya's protagonist Edgardo Vega in *El asco* (Disgust), Menen Desleal was not just ambivalent about El Salvador's emblematic characteristics but openly mocked them as irredeemably retrograde. As his friend Renán Alcides Orellana noted, "Así era Álvaro … convencido de que aquí no podrá existir jamás el espacio azul que necesitan el arte y la cultura" (Álvaro was like that … convinced that here would never exist the blue space that art and culture need). Consequently, Menen Desleal felt that leaving El Salvador was imperative to intellectual growth, the only way to escape its insular literary scene and suffocating political conditions. In an interview published in *Revista Caracol* in 1974, he described emigration as driving his generation's creativity (Alcides Orellana 2015).

While migration is typically discussed in tandem with the civil war or postwar eras, Menen Desleal's voluntary and involuntary migratory patterns index the longer histories of Salvadoran translocality. He lived in Mexico in the 1950s and served as the Salvadoran consul in Western Germany in the late 1960s and in Algeria in the 1970s. He perceived emigration as a way to access cultural universality but also to reignite the creativity tamped down by authoritarian rule. Cecilia Rivas points out in *Salvadoran Imaginaries* that "the tendency to view emigration as a solution to El Salvador's social ills and personal issues alike" is "a 'very Salvadoran' trait" (2014: 9). Menen Desleal believed that distance from the nation nurtured a certain expansiveness of thought, which, in turn, brought with it literary inventiveness.

He consequently conceived of his personal literary canon as a cosmopolitan constellation of authors whose narrative techniques departed from nationalism and realism. None of his formative influences were Salvadoran, with the exception of Francisco Gavidia, whose play *Ursino* (1887) Menen Desleal later reworked into *El cielo no es para el reverendo* (Heaven Is Not for the Reverend) (1968). He was primarily indebted to authors throughout the Americas and Europe. Borges and Juan José Arreola influenced his early fantastical work, as did sci-fi writers like HG Wells, Isaac Asimov, and Ray Bradbury. He was inspired by existentialists like Franz Kafka and Albert Camus, repeatedly thematizing the latter's proposition that suicide is the fundamental philosophical question. In addition to existentialism, Menen Desleal was intrigued by absurdism: his acclaimed play *Luz negra* (Black Light) echoes Samuel Beckett's *Waiting for Godot* (1953) and dialogues with José Revueltas's *Ensayo sobre un proletariado sin cabeza* (Essay on a Headless Proletariat) (1962) (Camacho Navarro 2011–12: 207). His short stories circle around the fundamental nonsensicality of the universe, framed as a query that transcends geopolitics.

Other members of the Committed Generation scoffed at Menen Desleal's interest in vanguardist techniques and dabblings in absurdism, existentialism, and speculative fiction. For writers like Argueta, Armijo, and Cea, aesthetic play distanced literary creation from the urgent realities of national life (Alvarenga 2010: 21). To their minds, in order to truly transform the status quo, realism was the most effective literary form. The peasantry and the proletariat's vernacular, daily routines, and exploitation needed to be accurately captured in order to awaken the reading public's consciousness. But Menen Desleal found this approach militant and narrow-minded. He was one of only a few writers of his generation alongside Dalton and Waldo Chávez Velasco who utilized avant-garde techniques. Likewise, he made no effort to depict rural life or to recreate the countryside vernacular (Martínez Gómez 1992: 208), grounding his fiction instead in a mestizo, urban, middle-class point of view (although he himself grew up quite poor).

Menen Desleal's open aspiration for cosmopolitan universalism was derided by his peers as escapist. In his memoirs, Cea dismissively described him as having "aires provincianos de Universalismo" (provincial universalist airs) (2003: 129). A chapter in Dalton's *Pobrecito poeta que era yo* mocked a character conspicuously named "Álvaro" with a bourgeois attitude, obsessive desire to kill Salarrué (Dalton 1994: 61), and mercenary ambition to transcend his impoverished past by turning it into a bestselling book. Dalton, who worked for Menen Desleal at *Teleperiódico*, presents his fellow writer's drive to be "cada día menos salvadoreño, cada día más bienaventuradamente cosmopolita" (each day less Salvadorean, each day more blessedly cosmopolitan) (1994: 81) as an opportunistic scheme and not an aesthetic choice. The character Álvaro baldly expresses the self-serving ambition to leave his country behind: "Después uno triunfa escribiendo cuentos cosmopolitas, se va a Londres o a una Universidad norteamericana y se jode para siempre jamás" (After one has success writing cosmopolitan stories, one goes to London or to a North American university and gets the fuck out forever) (40–1). For Dalton and others of the Committed Generation, intellectual detachment from the national project (be it literary or political) was indefensible, and Menen Desleal, a chief reprobate.

Menen Desleal's repudiation of the local and embrace of international characters and milieus indeed reflected his cosmopolitan aspirations. Mariano Siskind has defined cosmopolitanism as a "desire for the world" and a means of escaping "nationalistic cultural formations" (2014: 3). In contrast to the delimited conceit of the nation, the concept of the "world" operates as a discursive "symbolic horizon for the realization of the translocal aesthetic potential of literature and cosmopolitan forms of subjectivation" (Siskind 2014: 3). Cosmopolitanism imagines the literary product and its author to participate in horizontal, nonhierarchical dialogue with other works of world literature on an abstract plane that disregards spatial and temporal modes of production. For Menen Desleal, cosmopolitanism went hand in hand with the refusal to be marginalized from certain themes and forms proper to world literature, such as artificial intelligence and nuclear war, or science fiction, simply because of his country of enunciation. Even if these were conversations or conventions established in the Global North, they nonetheless affected Central America. As an ex-centric writer, Menen Desleal asserted his ability to speak to the universal, to imagine and contest planetary questions of concern. From the Isthmus, he addresses the problematic ethics of the nuclear age, and does so through genres like sci-fi, in ways that empty contemporaneous neo-imperial projects like space exploration of their heroic content.

Speculating the Planet from the Isthmus

For the remainder of this chapter, I focus on a salient aspect of Menen Desleal's cosmopolitanism: his speculative planetary imagination. This narrative technique zooms out temporally and spatially, projecting into unknown futures, or distant galactic spaces and alien perspectives. This expansion outward shifts the conversation away from the here and the now and disrupts normative ways of thinking about space and time. Menen Desleal's planetary speculation enacts what Wai Chee Dimock has theorized as deep time, which regards time as "a set of longitudinal frames, at once projective and recessional, with input going both ways" (2008: 3). This temporal broadening decenters the nation-state by "loosening up [its] chronology and geography," while simultaneously creating planetary temporal coalescence by "binding continents and millennia into many loops of relations, [into] a densely interactive fabric" (Dimock 2008: 4). Such a loosening allows Menen Desleal to approach the intersection of ethics and futurity from a capacious spatiotemporal point of view.

Menen Desleal's disinterest in the nation and disavowal of the responsibility to envision Salvadoran political futurity leads him not to an impasse in which the literary exercise is deemed futile or frivolous but to an affirmation of Salvadoran participation in questions of planetary concern: namely survival in the nuclear age. Rather than appraise his belonging to a peripheral nation as delegitimizing his narrative claim to projects that originate elsewhere, like space exploration or artificial intelligence, Menen Desleal inscribes planetary interconnectivity in order to communicate these projects' scalar consequences for humans as a species. This act of speculating from a planetary perspective encourages holistic thinking, while simultaneously questioning the very nature of this totalizing enterprise by subverting human exemplarity and universal knowledge.

The conceptual shift from the nation to the planetary was particularly resonant within the context of the Cold War. The Cold War has often been framed as a bipolar struggle between the United States and the Soviet Union. This antagonism, however, was not confined to these two nations but extended globally. Nations were divvied up by allegiance to these competing centers into a taut network of relational power. For many Latin American countries, the Cold War was a period of political polarity in which the ideological dispute between the United States and the USSR saturated domestic battles. Such was the case for El Salvador, in which the military-oligarchic state was challenged by revolutionary forces pushing for democratization (Chávez 2017: 9).

Menen Desleal's fiction was uninterested in how these conflicts played out in the domestic sphere. He narrates through characters native to the centers of power: the United States and the Soviet Union, as well as China, Spain, and Germany. His depiction of protagonists from the United States or the USSR does not flesh out the particularities of their opposing ideologies but instead represents their disquieting similarities, like the shared ambition for global domination and unwavering belief in human prepotency. Menen Desleal focuses on manifestations of human hubris that are premised on mastery, such as the nuclear arms race, space exploration, and artificial intelligence, positing these anthropocentric projects portend the species' demise.

A primary preoccupation of Menen Desleal's fiction is the nuclear arms race. In spite of international condemnation of the devastating 1945 US bombing of Hiroshima and Nagasaki, nuclear power remained a coveted defense tool in the escalating Cold War. Throughout the 1950s and 1960s, the United States and the Soviet Union grew their nuclear stockpiles exponentially (Holloway 2010: 387). In the 1950s, both countries developed thermonuclear weapons known as superbombs. While nuclear war was widely seen as unacceptable by citizens and policy-makers alike, these stockpiles were not just a latent threat; in 1953, Eisenhower suggested they might be used to end the Korean War. The United States housed missiles in Turkey and Guam, and the USSR planned to do so in Cuba, sparking the Cuban missile crisis in 1962. Put simply, these weapons had global reach. Any misstep or miscalculation between the principal antagonists could quickly spiral into catastrophe on a planetary scale and would likely be played out first in peripheral regions.

Menen Desleal's short stories about nuclear war concur that its inevitable outcome is ruination: the end of the world, if not the planet. These are apocalyptic narratives of human extinction. In "Hacer el amor en el refugio atómico" (Making Love in the Atomic Shelter) (1972), a German couple survives nuclear war by hiding out in a bunker. In stark contrast to the title, the protagonists decide that without breathable air they have no option but to end their own lives. The sci-fi story "Los vicios de papá" (Father's Vices) (1972) recounts, from the perspective of future artificial intelligence, how nuclear war wiped out the human race. The narrator's mother is a supercomputer that helped the United States "win" the war—a triumph defined by a lone human survivor, who died soon thereafter. The US supercomputer's account of this victory is uttered in a patriotic tone that the narrator flatly observes "no fue escuchada más que por el viento" (was not heard by more than the wind) (Menen Desleal 2013: 28). These stories problematize the notion that there is a way to win world war since the most likely outcome, the end of the species, obviates nations themselves.

In one of Menen Desleal's best-known tales of science fiction, "Una cuerda de nylon y oro" (A Cord of Nylon and Gold) (1965), nuclear war is combined with the exploration of outer space. Written in the wake of China's second nuclear test in 1965, the story reflects Menen Desleal's concern with the emergence of the fifth nuclear power and the reliance on nukes to assert international strength. It is also a meditation on the fragility of the planet and the terrifying interrelatedness of the shared commons. The story is narrated by Henry, a North American astronaut who decides to commit suicide during his twenty-sixth orbit because his wife has been unfaithful. He severs the titular cord that connects him to the shuttle, and floats off into space, where he believes he will perish after depleting his remaining minutes of oxygen. However, like many of Menen Desleal's stories about men who plan to take their own lives ("El suicida" [The Suicide], "El malthusiano" [The Malthusian], "Tribulaciones de un americano que estudió demografía" [Tribulations of an American Who Studied Demographics]), things go awry. Mysteriously, even after Henry's oxygen is gone, he does not die. Suspended in a liminal state between life and death, he orbits the Earth for eternity.

At first, Henry rejoices in his newfound freedom unimpeded by "un planeta que ya me hartaba" (a planet I was already sick of) (Menen Desleal 2013: 74). He enjoys the spectacle of the planet's "mapamundi borroso" (blurry globe) obtained from this omnipotent perspective (2013: 76). He revels in the ability to totally see the planet yet not know anything about it. This seems to actualize the promise of space exploration: transcendence of earthly problems through technological innovation. Henry is a man no longer subject to the Earth's rhythms and logic, able to gaze down upon it as if it were a small object compared to his human form: "a veces la tengo a mis pies, a veces arriba, a veces a los flancos" (at times I have it at my feet, a times above, at times at my sides) (75). This is the ecstatic pleasure of "seeing the whole," described by Michel de Certeau in *The Practice of Everyday Life*, a distant view from above that "allows one to read [the world], to be a solar eye, looking down like a God" (1984: 92).

Yet the pleasure of detached observation sours when something happens that colors the Earth's sky "rojo sangre ... verde ... violeta" (blood red ... green ... violet) (Menen Desleal 2013: 78). In his eternal circumvention, Henry is forced to witness the planet's nuclear annihilation, without knowing what triggered it. His totalizing vantage is not a triumph but a sadness, a realization of planetary interconnectedness that comes too late. He sees a series of flashes, first in Vietnam, then China, "San Francisco, Los Angeles, Detroit, Nueva York, Washington ... Y otros cien al sur, sobre México y Panamá y Río y Buenos Aires; y otros al norte, sobre Montreal y Ottawa" (San Francisco, Los Angeles, Detroit, New York, Washington ... And another hundred to the south, over Mexico and Panama and Rio and Buenos Aires; and others to the north, over Montreal and Ottawa) (2013: 78). The list goes on, piling up cities East and West. From Henry's satellite perspective, the mushroom clouds look serene, a proliferation of blooms that appear to join hands "en macabra ronda infantil" (in a macabre ring-around-the-rosy) (2013: 78). The dark side of the earth turns even darker, "oscuro con una fosforescencia de ultratumba" (dark with a ghostly phosphorescence) and the green woods on its light side fade to grey (2013: 78). For Henry, the nuclear disaster is a spectacle: a calamity full of dynamic coloration and transformation, devoid of graphic carnage. Henry embodies the aerial view of the bombs themselves that survey the expanse below as an abstracted cartography. The spectacular aerial view of total planetary destruction encapsulates in one image the horrific conclusion of human scientific achievement. However, this aerial view is also opaque and limited. It offers the viewer no way to understand the causes behind the event or the human bodies beneath the smoke: the information that exists beyond the limits of visibility.

Although Henry is a spectator of this disaster and not a participant, he is not altogether detached from its ethical consequences. He is embroiled in what Gennifer Weisenfeld terms the "participatory encounter" of spectatorship, in which the spectator is morally implicated in the observed event (2012: 83). This participatory observation is evidenced by a list that Henry repeats to himself, an inventory of events that unfolded on the day that he cut the cord. The events range from the political, to the cultural, to the personal: "Había un presidente llamado Johnson, de Gaulle amenazaba con un ataque a la OTAN … Von Braun seguía haciendo ciencia ficción. Río de Janeiro recién había cumplido cuatrocientos años de fundada. San Salvador acababa de ser semidestruida por un terremoto … Ciento ochenta mineros japoneses morían dentro de su mina derrumbada … Mi hijito John tenía rota la nariz" (There was a president named Johnson, de Gaulle threatened to attack NATO … Von Braun kept performing science fiction. Rio De Janeiro recently had celebrated 400 years since its establishment. San Salvador had just been half-destroyed by an earthquake … a hundred-eighty Japanese miners died in a collapsed mine … My little son John had broken his nose) (Menen Desleal 2013: 75). This montage of spatially disconnected yet temporally concurrent events acts as an archive of the moment and provides a kaleidoscopic view of planetary time. The recurrent list counteracts the potential homogenization of the planet as a uniform space that the abstracted satellite view suggests. The narrative reveals what exists underneath the totalizing image. The story thus scales both up to a planetary view and down to quotidian dramas, layering visual information with the language of memory, to grasp the concept of planetarity: the planet as a "world commons" grounded in ethical relation (Elias and Moraru 2015: xviii). Yet this relationship between human and nonhuman, memory and planet, is inherently unequal. The end of this world, the world as Henry remembers it, is not the end of the planet. Though grayed, the planet persists, continuing to rotate, with Henry captured in its orbit.

Henry was likely modeled after the astronaut Edward White, the first North American to successfully walk in space. While accomplishing this feat during the 1965 *Gemini 4* voyage, White famously joked to his mission partner that he did not want to reenter the spacecraft, calling it "the saddest moment of [his] life" (1965: 39). *Life Magazine* celebrated the achievement with a huge color spread that featured the astronauts' onboard dialogue and pictures of White floating in front of the curve of our blue planet. The spread declared the mission a "triumph" of human engineering (1965: 26). White died two years later during a preflight test of *Apollo 1*. Fatal spaceflight-related accidents were common for astronauts of the era. Those that joined the profession were seen as heroes or as men harboring a death wish—or both, martyrs in pursuit of the final frontier.

In "Una cuerda de nylon y oro" (A Cord of Nylon and Gold), White's assertion that he wasn't "coming in" from his spacewalk is reimagined as a literal refusal to return to life on Earth. Henry chooses to die at the pinnacle of his success, in the ecstatic moment of planetary escape and observation. Yet this ambition—of dictating death and scientific mastery—is subverted. Menen Desleal frames technological innovation as a sign not of future possibility and mastery but of mass extinction. The astronaut does not represent the start of a new era of human achievement but its end. Henry is rendered an impotent observer, a passive object caught forever in Earth's orbit. The totalizing cosmic view reveals Earth to be dangerously interconnected, a fragile ecosystem.

Menen Desleal's narration from the vantage point of protagonists who are supposedly heroic in the Western tradition (like the astronaut) in order to undermine them enacts what we might describe as a decolonial gesture. It complicates and fractures the human project of mastery: mastery over Earth, which can be viewed from the outside as a discrete object, an external view that solidifies the role of the human as subject and the Earth as object. This enterprise is subverted as Henry is caught in the deadened Earth's eternal orbit, which reinstantiates his status as an object caught in the dynamics established by his home planet. He has no control over the planet, his species, his wife, or even over his own life: shattering the illusion of human agency. The story thus empties the narrative of mastery that saturated Cold War discourse and disputes. The invention of powerful superbombs is not decisive proof of human power but an invention that becomes more agential than its creator, culminating in the end of the human species. The competition for mastery that unfolded during the Cold War as a project of dominion, subordination, and control folds back upon itself and is revealed to be both absurd and self-exhausting.

Menen Desleal notably elaborates this critique of the neocolonial ambition for mastery through the Global North genre of science fiction. Sci-fi circulated regularly in the United States (albeit as a less-prestigious genre) and to a lesser extent in neighboring Mexico, but its use was totally anomalous in the isthmus. Menen Desleal was an outlier, as well as El Salvador's pioneering science fiction writer (Bell 2004: 126). His appropriation of the genre manifests what Sánchez Prado calls "strategic Occidentalism," the purposeful divergence from national norms and use of Western forms in order to perform them "back at Western culture as a form of intellectual decolonization" (2018: 19). This gesture of appropriation lays claim to the Central American ability to narrate questions of ethical and political concern through other aesthetic modes that deviated from the realism of the Committed Generation. It also thematizes the impossibility of thinking about the future, specifically, the political future of the nation, without also engaging the global context in which those futures unfold.

Menen Desleal's entire oeuvre can be effectively situated within the supercategory of speculative fiction due to its consistent engagement with a variety of nonmimetic narrative strategies: sci-fi, magical realism, absurdism, and the fantastic. The term "speculative fiction" has risen to prominence as a more expansive alternative to these subgenera in reference to any nonrealist mode of imagination. While speculative fiction is often oriented toward the future, futurity is not a requisite component. Regardless of its temporal or ideological orientation, speculative cultural production is any form of artistic expression that does away with the rules of reality. The departure from consensus reality allows authors to interrogate existing norms and sociohistorical conditions and rewrite the possible. Speculative recastings encourage readers to imagine how things could change for the better or to confront the eventualities of current trajectories. Nonrealist speculation provides distance from what is, so that the status quo might be questioned.

It is not the case, according to Menen Desleal, that speculating from a cosmopolitan or planetary perspective is a facile way to overcome the myopathy of local or national epistemologies. By abstracting out to galactic settings or foregrounding alien narrators, Menen Desleal concludes that there is no perspective from which accurate universal knowledge can be created. This is because knowledge is always indelibly linked to the body that articulates it and cannot be delocalized. The presumption that one's perspective is universal leads to epistemological blind spots; it cannot anticipate its own failings.

Just as Henry's totalizing view of the Earth occludes more than it reveals, several other short stories also dramatize the fallacy of perception. These are tales that operate at the level of species and are narrated from the perspective of alien life forms that encounter Earth. These accounts of humanity from the perspective of a nonhuman species stage the impossibility of cosmic knowledge or of transcending ontology. In "El animal más raro de la Tierra" (The Rarest Animal on Earth) (1961), a Martian scholar concludes that the rodent is the most notable species on Earth, erroneously attributing human actions (like the invention of the mouse trap) to the rat. Likewise, in "Primer encuentro" (First Encounter) (1966), an alien runs away in disgust after first glimpsing the barbaric form of the human body. Both tales ask readers to see the world askew, to denaturalize what we take for granted.

A similar message is at the heart of the short story, "Memorandum sobre el tercer planeta" (Memorandum on the Third Planet) (1964). As in "El animal más raro de la Tierra" (The Rarest Animal on Earth), this piece adopts the format of an official state document written by an alien bureaucrat, the Acting Commissioner of the Milky Way, and addressed to the "Tercer Intuidor Emérito de Venus" (The Third Intuitor Emeritus of Venus) (Menen Desleal 1969: 83). In this document, the Acting Commissioner summarizes the findings of a longer report analyzing the possibilities of life on the Third Planet of the Solar System, or as we call it, Earth. The Commissioner writes that the team has concluded that life is impossible on this third planet, given its large bodies of water, "elemento impropio para el desarrollo de la vida" (an inadequate element for the development of life), and its "atmósfera letal" (lethal atmosphere) (1969: 83). However, he notes, the planet's molten core offers amenable conditions for the development of life, "gracias a su densidad y temperatura cálida" (thanks to its density and warm temperature) (1969: 83). The author furthers that such a possibility is remote, given that the planet appears to be rapidly cooling. This refers to nuclear winter, the climactic result of nuclear war, which goes unmentioned in the text.

Through narrative inversion, Menen Desleal underscores that ontology drives epistemology. As humans, we consider the geosphere to equal the absence of life. We consider the biosphere, the parts of the planet above the earth's surface, as containing the conditions that allow our ecosystem to flourish. This supposition is turned on its head: it is in the Earth's core that the aliens find the promise of life. Here Menen Desleal pokes fun at contemporaneous ambitions to find life in outer space, pointing out that the search is based upon the premise that all life looks the same and relies on the same conditions. The second message of the story is more melancholic, buried beneath the story's humorous play with point of view. The momentous arrival of alien life to Earth occurs right after humans have brought their species to extinction through nuclear war.

Menen Desleal utilizes galactic settings and nonhuman narrators to decenter the human from the epicenter of narrative and planetary history. The story of the Earth, Menen Desleal cautions, is longer and more expansive than that of humans. The Earth is inherently out of human grasp: defined by the irrational and the absurd. Menen Desleal echoes Albert Camus's belief that any attempt to understand the world is doomed because the universe has no discernible meaning or rational logic. Consequently, the pursuit of knowledge is futile. This is not only a human problem but a problem for any life force that attempts to understand the world. As Camus puts it in *The Myth of Sisyphus*: "those categories that explain everything are enough to make a decent man laugh" (1955: 21). For Menen Desleal, this disorderly universe will go on long after we are gone, a demise he speculates that we will bring about ourselves, driven by the injudicious quest for mastery.

The resolute pessimism and cosmopolitanism that defined Menen Desleal's aesthetics was out of place amid the Committed Generation's utopian search for better politics and more expansive representations of El Salvador. Yet its sardonic disenchantment with literature's didactic responsibility anticipated trends in contemporary literature from the isthmus, which has grown weary of literature's nation-building charge. An ex-centric writer with complicated politics, Menen Desleal's speculative fictions questioned the endgame of nuclear war and the obsession with human exceptionalism. The global magnitude of settler technological hubris, he demonstrated, had implications for every continent on the planet.

References

Alcides Orellana, R. (2015), "Menen Desleal y su motivación a emigrar," *Diario CoLatino*, April 18. Available online: https://www.diariocolatino.com/menen-desleal-y-su-motivacion-a-emigrar/.

Alvarenga, L. (2010), "La Generación Comprometida de El Salvador: problemas de una denominación," *Istmo: Revista virtual de estudios literarios y culturales centroamericanos*, 21. Available online: http://istmo.denison.edu/n21/articulos/11-alvarenga_luis_form.pdf.

Ávalos, J. (2016), "Álvaro Menén Desleal: agente provocador," *La Zebra*, August 1. Available online: https://lazebra.net/2016/08/01/jorge-avalos-alvaro-menen-desleal-agent-provocateur-cronica/.

Bell, A. (2004), "Álvaro Menén Desleal (pseudonym of Álvaro Menéndez Leal) (1931–2000)," in D. B. Lockhart (ed.), *Latin American Science Fiction Writers: An A-to-Z Guide*, 126–8, Santa Barbara: ABC-CLIO.

Camacho Navarro, E. (2011–12), "Rev. of *Luz negra* by Álvaro Menen Desleal," *Cuadernos Americanos*, 136: 206–8.

Camus, A. (1955), *The Myth of Sisyphus*, trans. J. O'Brien, New York: Vintage Books.

Castellanos Moya, H. (2010), *El asco*, Barcelona: Tusquets.

Cea, J. R. (2003), *La generación comprometida: unos documentos y testimonios para su historia social, ética y estética*, San Salvador: Canoa.

Chávez, J. M. (2017), *Poets and Prophets of the Resistance: Intellectuals and the Origins of El Salvador's Civil War*, Oxford: Oxford University Press.

Dalton, R. (1994), *Pobrecito poeta que era yo*, San Salvador: UCA.

De Certeau, M. (1984), *The Practice of Everyday Life: Volume One*, Berkeley: University of California Press.

Dimock, W. C. (2008), *Through Other Continents: American Literature across Deep Time*, Princeton: Princeton University Press.

Elias, A. J. and C. Moraru (2015), "Introduction: The Planetary Condition," in A. J. Elias and C. Moraru (eds.), *The Planetary Turn: Relationality and Geoaesethetics in the Twenty-First Century*, xi–xxxvii, Evanston: Northwestern University Press.

Holloway, D. (2010), "Nuclear Weapons and the Escalation of the Cold War, 1945–1962," in M. Leffler and O. A. Westad (eds.), *The Cambridge History of the Cold War*, 376–97, Cambridge: Cambridge University Press.

Huezo Mixco, M. (2011), "Tocarle el hombro a Borges," *Cuadernos Hispanoamericanos*, 737: 95–103.

Iber, P. (2015), *Neither Peace nor Freedom: The Cultural Cold War in Latin America*, Cambridge: Harvard University Press.

Lars, C., ed. (1962), "Colaboran en este Número," *Cultura: Revista del ministerio de educación*, 26.

López Vallecillos, Í. (1964), *El periodismo en El Salvador*, San Salvador: Editorial U.

Martínez Gómez, J. (1992), "Tres aproximaciones al cuento salvadoreño contemporáneo," *Anuales de literatura hispanoamericana*, 21: 203–14.

Melgar Brizuela, L. (2006), "La Generación Comprometida," *Cultura: revista del consejo nacional para la cultura y el arte*, 93: 86–106.

Menen Desleal, Á. (1963), *Cuentos breves y maravillosos*, San Salvador: Ministerio de Educación Dirección General de Publicaciones.

Menen Desleal, Á. (1969), *Una cuerda de nylon y oro y otros cuentos maravillosos*, San Salvador: Dirección General de Cultura.

Menen Desleal, Á. (1967), *Luz negra*, San Salvador: Ministerio de Educación Dirección General de Publicaciones.

Menen Desleal, Á. (1971), *Revolución en el país que edificó un castillo de hadas y otros cuentos maravillosos*, San José: EDUCA.

Menen Desleal, Á. (1972), *Hacer el amor en el refugio atómico*, San Salvador: Editorial Universitaria Centroamericana.

Menen Desleal, Á. (2013), *La ilustre familia androide*, San Salvador: Biblioteca Básica de Literatura Salvadoreña.

Ramírez, S. (2011), "Dos premios literarios en un mes para Álvaro Menén Desleal," *Carátula*, 44, Available online: https://www.caratula.net/dos-premios-literarios-en-un-mes-para-alvaro-menen-desleal/.

Rivas, C. M. (2014), *Salvadoran Imaginaries: Mediated Identities and Cultures of Consumption*, New Brunswick: Rutgers University Press.

Sánchez Prado, I. M. (2018), *Strategic Occidentalism: On Mexican Fiction, the Neoliberal Book Market, and the Question of World Literature*, Evanston: Northwestern University Press.

Siskind, M. (2014), *Cosmopolitan Desires: Global Modernity and World Literature in Latin America*, Evanston: Northwestern University Press.

"The Glorious Walk in the Cosmos" (1965), *Life Magazine*, June 18: 26–40.

Weisenfeld, G. (2012), *Imaging Disaster: Tokyo and the Visual Culture of Japan's Great Earthquake of 1923*, Berkeley: University of California Press.

7

Between Internationalism and Cosmopolitanism: Roque Dalton and World Literature

Yansi Pérez

There are many possible genealogies for the concept of the "international" but the one most relevant in my chapter stems from the various workers' organizations that began to form throughout Europe after the French Revolution and eventually formed the First Communist International. I conceptualize the "international" before it becomes the ideology of state of the Soviet Union and later in all the other countries where communism was imposed. In this chapter, I propose the "international"[1] as a concept that attempts to define a space of production, circulation, and reception for literary texts. To define this space, it is important to establish a critical dialogue with the two spheres of circulation that monopolize the dissemination of texts: the national and the global/world. To better explain my use of the concept, I will begin with a reflection about how a notion of production and circulation beyond the national borders began among workers. Their goal was the defense of workers beyond their own countries as Ernest Jones, a Chartrist leader, states below:

> "For us, nation is *nothing*, man is *all*," he declared. "For us the oppressed nationalities form but one: the universal poor of every land, that struggle for life against the nation of the rich, that mighty race of which every man gives health, labour, life unto society."
> (quoted in Braunthal 1967: 78)

Most relevant for me in this workers' movement is this organization's capacity to generate forms of affiliation, solidarity, and community that go beyond national borders and defy the global order imposed by capital on the world (then and now): "We begin tonight no mere crusade against an aristocracy. We are not here to pull one tyranny down only that another may live the stronger. We are against the tyranny of capital as well" (quoted in Braunthal 1967: 78). The new type of relation this international workers' movement foments is solidarity among all workers, a bond that exceeds any national bond, trade union, or guild, as well as any racial[2] or gender differences. In 1848, George Julian Harney, a British union leader, presented to some German communists his concept of international solidarity based on the following terms:

> "I appeal," he declared, "to the oppressed classes in every country to unite for the common cause." But what was the common cause? Was it the liberation of Poland from Russian rule, or the freedom of Italy from Austria? Harney explained that "freedom from the Russian and Austrian yokes is not the end of the matter. We do not need a King Czartoryski. We need no kingdom of Italy. We need the sovereignty of the people in both countries." But who were "the people"? The people, he continued, were the workers and peasants, and the cause of the people was "the cause of labour, of labour enslaved and exploited ... In all countries there are people who grow corn and eat potatoes, who make clothes and wear rags, who build houses and live in wretched hovels ... Do not the workers of all nations have the same reasons for complaint and the same causes of distress? Have they not, therefore, the same just cause?"
>
> (quoted in Braunthal 1967: 67)

These workers' movements advocated for a type of alliance that surpassed the political and ethical demands of the nation-state while at the same time it did not have, until that moment, any formal recognition at the international level. This capacity to supersede the national borders while at the same time defying the world order is what will characterize the concept of the "international" that I propose in this chapter through my reading of Roque Dalton.

Pheng Cheah in his book *What Is a World? On Postcolonial Literature as World Literature* (2016) affirms that we only properly speak of world history after the emergence of a global market. This perspective complicates any attempt to assimilate the Marxist position to any Enlightened efforts by figures such as Kant or Goethe which propose cosmopolitanism as a space that allows the expansion and transcendence of national borders at the juridico-political levels as well as in the cultural and literary spheres. Cheah writes that what defines a world is not merely geographical extension but rational-purposive human relationality; the connections and intercourse that unite people and places for the determinate end of production to satisfy human needs. Material relations of production cannot be reduced to their physico-spatial dimension because they involve rational human ends. Second, Marx's definition of the world as a system for the universal satisfaction of needs leads to a distinction between true and alienated forms of human production. The world market is the function and field of the production of commodities for profitable exchange instead of production for the direct satisfaction of needs. Accordingly, the world market is not a true world. It is certainly not the only world that is possible, but merely an alienated world, a world that the bourgeoisie has made in its own image.

(2016: 65)

The world, from this perspective, requires a different mode of restraining and coercion that is just as rigid, if not more so, than the one implemented by each nation inside its borders. The "international" allows us to go beyond the national order but it does not assimilate to the world order imposed by commodities or geopolitical orders. The concept of the "international" that the Salvadoran poet Roque Dalton employed will help us to understand better new forms of affiliation and communities not recognized within the national sphere and defies the ones imposed by the world's global capitalist order.

The concept of the international that the Salvadoran poet Roque Dalton postulates in his work will produce a distancing effect with respect to the concepts of national and world literature as well as present a reinvention of forms of affiliations and communities that were not recognized in the geopolitical and economic order of his time.[3] In this chapter I will explore, through the study of Dalton's poetry, this other space of signification, of affinities and phobias that the international proposes. The "international," as I understand it in this chapter, is an imaginary affective-communal space that proposes alternative forms to understand, feel, and imagine the common. This chapter is inspired by theories of the common by Pierre Dardot and Christian Laval (2019), of the community by Roberto Esposito (2009), Jean Luc Nancy (1991), and Jacques Rancière (1999), and by critics who have tried to do a genealogy of the concept of the commune such as Kristin Ross (2016) and Bruno Bosteels (2021) in an attempt to find alternatives to the neoliberal order after the fall of Real Socialisms. I propose the concept of the "international" as central in these debates.

In the first section of the chapter, I study the poem "Taberna" (Tavern) that is part of the poetry book *Taberna y otros lugares* (Dalton 2000; Tavern and Other Places), where the poet imagines and invents a new type of community that resists the geopolitics imposed on the world during those years, 1966–9, where the East and the West (divided by the Iron Curtain) outlined two models of existence, two types of regimes that were in constant dispute over the hegemony of the globe.[4] The international community that Roque Dalton created in his book does not align with either of these two blocs fighting to impose their model for the state, their ideal form of community, and relation between the economy and politics. In this book, Dalton challenges the limits that defined the private, the public, and the common during one of the most critical periods of the Cold War. In his poem "Tavern," Dalton imagined a space where all those who could not find a place in their respective nation-states or the global order of those years could find a home.

In the second section of the chapter, I focus on another of Dalton's poetry books, *Las historias prohibidas del Pulgarcito* (2002; The Banned Histories of Tom Thumb) where the poet rewrites El Salvador's national history by stripping it of all mythology about its autochthony, its chauvinistic patriotism, and all the foundational myths that feed these ideologies. In this book, Dalton redefines and reinvents through the signifier of People and the concept of the poor, the political history of his community outside the parameters of the national as well as beyond the narratives of the world or global that his historical moment permitted.

In this section of my chapter, I owe a tremendous debt to Ernesto Laclau's book *On Populist Reason* (2005). In this text, the identity of social actors gets configured around the claims-demands made to a system. Due to the system's inability to meet these demands, a certain homologation occurs among the different heterogeneous demands that configure a claim around a symbolic name, an empty signifier, which grants a name to the collectivity that arises from it. This empty signifier symbolizes two things: the name of the collective identity that is instituted by a lack (the proletariat, the poor, the dispossessed) and the social actors that come to be known as the enemy, the ones that block access to justice (the oligarchy, the bourgeoisie, a caste). When the demands exceed the ability of institutions to meet them, the figure of the People is created and it requires a total restructuring of the existing symbolic order so that these demands can be fulfilled. The People becomes the master signifier: an area of the common that is not recognizable in the known discursive spheres and which exceeds the meanings considered legitimate in an existing order. The People unites all the social actors that emerge against the status quo.

The questions and problems that will guide my study of Dalton's *Historias prohibidas del Pulgarcito* are: How is the collective subject of the People constructed if you simultaneously reject the pedagogical, political, and civic instruments that a national community implements for its own formation? What space, what place, what agency correspond to all those whose claims and demands are not satisfied or recognized by the institutions that configure the political reality of a nation and which are also not acknowledged by the legal apparatus administered by international institutions? What part, to use Rancière's words, corresponds to all those who are not included in the existing order, to all those without a part?[5] How do we name that part of the common, of the collective, that has been expelled from all discursive communities and for which we cannot find an intelligible meaning or zone of legitimacy? What must we do to create a new relation between sense and those areas of the common that have been excluded from all normativity in order to create a new common sense?

I

One language, in itself, can form a fork, not only by nature, but also by will and art. In private or in public, those who speak a language retain their capacity to draw from their knowledge of its grammar the elements of a new and cryptic variety of speech …
It seems that human beings not only speak and speak languages. They also break and scatter them, with all their reason, in the sounds and letters of tongues made multiple and dark.

(HELLER-ROAZEN 2013: 17)

The poem "Taberna" (Tavern), included in the book *Taberna y otros lugares* (2000; Tavern and Other Places), which won the prestigious Casa de las Américas Prize in 1969, is written with the following assumption: the poet transcribes conversations that he hears by chance in a tavern, U Fleků, in Prague during 1966–7. These conversations contain the voices of young Czechs, Western Europeans, and some Latin Americans. One can imagine a murmur of voices that flow in many different languages and tones to which the poet grants a *lingua franca* (shared language). It is not likely that the poetic voice understood all the languages spoken at the long tables of the tavern, a fact that necessitates that the shared language be reproduced not just with translations but also by transcribing gestures, intentions, suppositions, and imaginary dialogues.

The language of the poet creates a tower of Babel. The new "cryptic variety of speech," to cite Heller-Roazen (2013: 17), heard in U Fleků is what Dalton will attempt to transcribe in his poem. The linguistic differences are erased but without making them homogenous. The prosody of the poem is plural, dispersed throughout it we see alternating italics with cursive letters, some verses appear entirely with capital letters, and different fonts and sizes are used. In the poem, all the voices speak the same language but the tone, the expressivity, the diction, the accent, are all different. The *collage* nature of the poem breaks its unity both at the level of expression and intentionality. The world fits in one language under the condition that this language is atomized: islands of meaning appear that sometimes configure small archipelagos and at other times float in their expressive and semantic singularity. The transcriber, the poet, declares:

> El autor solamente ordenó el material y le dio el mínimo trato formal para construir con él una especie de poema-objeto basado a su vez en una especie de encuesta sociológica furtiva. En el conjunto de opiniones recogidas no hay ninguna que pueda atribuirse completamente al autor y por ello éste las presenta en el seno del poema sin ninguna jerarquización, ni frente a la verdad, ni frente a la bondad moral o política.
> (Dalton 2000: 146)

> All the author did was put the material together and give it a little formal structure to make it into a kind of poem-object based, in turn, on a kind of undercover sociological study. None of the opinions found in the poem can be attributed to the author alone and that's the reason they are arranged here without any particular order as regards their truthfulness or their moral or political worth.
> (Dalton 1996: 155)

The author claims that he does not "create" his material; instead he limits himself to organizing it, giving it a form, in order to compose what he calls a poem-object. The legal, economic, politico-national anchoring that the authorial signature grants a discourse gets reduced to its minimal expression in this text. The poem offers refuge, shelter, to voices that do not find a welcome reception in the bipolar geopolitics that divides the world in those years. We also must remember that what Dalton claims to transcribe is what was said in the most cosmopolitan of taverns in Prague, one year before the Russian tanks entered to "correct" the former Czechoslovakia's misalignment with the orthodoxy imposed on the countries from the Eastern Bloc. Many of those who speak in the poem did not belong to Western European countries, indelibly separated by the Iron Curtain, but they did not necessarily allow themselves to be inscribed in the monolithic space that was the Eastern Bloc of those years; it is this "misalignment" that the Russian tanks would "correct" with their invasion a year later in 1968. The ensemble of opinions gathered in the poem, Dalton alerts us, has not been put in any particular hierarchy. They are isolated inside the poem not to subdue them but in order that they can continue to exist in their extra-territoriality with respect to the two poles, and their corresponding orthodoxies, that dominated the political geography during those years.

Those who came from the other side of the Iron Curtain and during those years spent time in the tavern did not find a comfortable home in their respective countries. Among the proper names that Dalton mentions in the short prologue to his poem we find Régis Debray who would later find himself incarcerated in Bolivia for being involved in Che Guevara's guerrilla, Alicia Eguren, a Peronist militant who was later disappeared during the Argentinean dictatorship in the 1970s, José Manuel Fortuny Arana, a Guatemalan communist militant who was forced to go into exile after the coup that ousted Jacobo Árbenz in 1954, Saverio Tutino, a fighter in the antifascist Italian resistance and the only European journalist allowed to report from Cuba during the Cuban Missile Crisis and who then turned to *guevarismo* (follower of the guerrilla warfare option) after he read Debray's book ¿*Revolución en la revolución*? (Revolution in the Revolution?). The two Cubans mentioned, Hugo Azcuy and Aurelio Alonso, wrote in the journal *Pensamiento crítico* (Critical Thought) that attempted to present a Marxist position beyond the Stalinist orthodoxy, inspired by Gramsci, Lukács, and Latin American thinkers. This journal that existed between 1967 and 1971 was cancelled by the government and those who collaborated in it were condemned to ostracism during the years from 1971 to 1978, the period of Stalinization of the Cuban Revolution.

The voices that this poem brings together are varied: Guevarists, Peronists, Latin American communists, young Czechs that tried to imagine another way of living not subject to the Soviet orthodoxy. All are affiliated with the revolutionary Left but, at the same time, are persecuted and silenced by the ideological orthodoxies that dominate the world they live in. The world fits in the poem but not the entire world or the coordinates used to organize the globe during those years. The principal form of affiliation for a great percentage of the world's population during the years from 1945 to 1989 was not nationality but belonging to one of two blocs, the Communist or the Western capitalist world, each fighting for world domination. The East and the West are codified, first and foremost, by two distinct ideologies.[6] Affiliating with the wrong bloc in this geopolitical divide could mean the loss of all rights, incarceration, and even death. It is interesting to note that Roque Dalton does not mention by name any of those present in the tavern that were from the Eastern Bloc, except the Czechs. The poetic voice speaks of "conversations heard by chance between young Czechoslovakians, Western Europeans and a smaller number of Latin Americans" (Dalton 1996: 155). I venture two possible explanations for this absence though I have no source to cite: (i) It is possible that the presence of people from other European communist countries was reduced due to the political openness circulating in the ex-Czechoslovakia during the years prior to 1968. (ii) It is plausible to think that U Fleků was a place forbidden for citizens from these countries because of the types of conversations that occurred there and because of the great number of foreigners that circulated there. It is well-known how suspicious the countries from the Communist Bloc were about their citizens being exposed to any foreign influences. This non-aligned space created in the poem through the diverse perspectives and voices presented made the community of people that gathered at the tavern and the conversations that the poem collects a utopian space that rewrites the cartography of the world that surrounded them.[7]

The international dimension that Dalton proposes for his poem is written against the grain, counter to how the globe, at that particular historical moment, organized its coordinates and political affiliations. The voices that populate these poems don't just live in-between, inter-nations; as the word "international" indicates, they find asylum in the face of how the global, the world, is conceived at the time. The "international," in order to find its own voice, needs to invent for itself a utopia where other forms of affiliation, other geopolitical forms of organizing, of community not recognized (or accepted) by the world that surrounds it are possible. The Communist International, since its foundation in 1864,[8] was formed to imagine and foment other ways of belonging not accepted by the established global order. The "international" exceeds the national space but cannot conform to the world because the world always requires a certain geopolitical order, a rigid hierarchy in the order of affiliations which often forbid belonging to more than one of these orders. The space of "international" enunciation that the poem proposes is situated beyond the nation and outside the world, at least the way in which the world was conceived by the capitalist logic that dominated the globe since the nineteenth century.[9] In his poem "Tavern," Dalton attempts to configure an international community for those who, paraphrasing Bataille, do not have a community or do not find it in the bipolar map that the Cold War created for the planet.

This poem does not try to produce a new Esperanto, a universal language made of all the existing languages but without the flavor of a single one: artificial without murmurs, onomatopoeias, body language, or its own accent. Socialist Realism aspired to do this, Dalton affirms in his poem, and it failed. The conversations are torn asunder, like Heller-Roazen (2013) proposes in the quote above, from their original languages and they are circumscribed in dark tongues:[10] sectarian or conspiratorial jargon, the words of the excluded. It is a language full of clues, codes that only the co-conspirators inside the poem understand. It is the language spoken by those that aspire to belong to a guerrilla:

la única organización pura que
va quedando en el mundo de los hombres
es la guerrilla.
Todo lo demás muestra manchas de pudrición

(Dalton 2000: 162)

The one sure thing I can tell you
is that the guerrilla
is becoming the only pure organization ...
All the others show signs of going bad.

(Dalton 1996: 169)

It is the language of partisans, of guerrillas, that hopes that the Party, as the poet states in another verse, has a sense of humor. Even if that means, as stated in another moment in the poem, and with capital letters: "Getting the party mixed up with Andre Breton!" (Dalton 1996: 159). The poet writes, "*Esta conversación podría recogerse como un poema*" "*This conversation could fit into a poem*" and another voice responds with capital letters that shout: "¿PARA QUÉ? ¿CREES QUE ASUSTARÍAS A ALGUIEN" (Dalton 2000: 156) "WHAT FOR? DO YOU THINK YOU'D SCARE ANYBODY?" (Dalton 1996: 163). Transcribing this conversation, even if it is in poem form, can only be perceived as a threat or treason. The jargon of the conspirators aspires to conceal a great secret. Translating it to uninitiated ears can only be conceived as a form of desertion. There has never been a better occasion for the phrase: *Traduttori traditori* (translators traitors).

The imaginary community that this poem founds does invent not only its own cartography but also its own axiological axis, its own values: forgetting is a source of perfection; madness a source of confidence; the only appropriate form to speak of politics is by risking your life for it; things are named, following Sartre, to denounce them. The list could go on but what is of interest is that the moral code presented in this community includes its own subversions; the ideal contains its own caricature. "Todo podría ser tan sencillo" "Everything would be so simple," the poetic voice affirms, "si no insistiera el hombre / en discutir su asunto con el bien y el mal" (Dalton 2000: 154) "if a man did not insist / on discussing his battle with good and evil" (Dalton 1996: 161). Morality[11] is only stupendous when "UNO NO TIENE GANAS DE NADA" (Dalton 2000: 163) "YOU DON'T FEEL LIKE DOING ANYTHING" (Dalton 1996: 169).

When the ex-Soviet Union invades the ex-Czechoslovakia in 1968, Roque Dalton is no longer in Prague and finds himself living in Mexico among other party activists and intellectuals. Carlos Monsiváis, in a chronicle about the events of that year, narrates Dalton's reaction to the Soviet invasion, pronounced at a gathering in the artist Vicente Rojo's house:

> Le indigna la prepotencia soviética y está seguro que de producirse la intervención armada, la condenará Fidel Castro. A los dos días, Castro emite su larguísima apología de la operación soviética a la que elogia sin medida: "Hay que salvar al país socialista." Veo a Roque, que comenta lacónico: "Extraordinaria argumentación la de Fidel."

(Monsiváis n.d.)

He finds the Soviet arrogance shameful and is sure that if an intervention occurs, Fidel Castro will condemn it. Two days later, Castro broadcasts his very long justification of the Soviet operations which he praises without measure: "We must save the Socialist country." I see Roque, who comments laconically: "Extraordinary reasoning by Fidel."

(my translation)

The poet will never be able to reconcile his affiliations inside and outside the poem. He will constantly be split between the international inclination of his poetry, always capable of creating new forms of community[12] that turn upside down the geopolitical order of the world and the imposed decision to take sides with one of the blocs in existence in the world that he inhabited. This tension between his political biography and his artistic practice, between the political and artistic avant-garde, with often contradictory demands, ends up having a tragic consequence in his life. Roque Dalton is assassinated in 1973 in El Salvador by his own comrades. He was accused of being, simultaneously, an agent of the Central Intelligence Agency and the Cuban secret service.

The accusation that causes his death, being a double agent, betraying both blocs that are confronting each other and, particularly, betraying his comrades in arms, puts Dalton in an impossible position with respect to the world. And this position is antithetical to the one he constructs in his poem. The ones who kill him are members of the guerrilla, the organization he believed to be the only form of legitimate community during those days. Aurelio Alonso (2007), in a text written in 2006 in honor of Kiva Maidanik, a Soviet academic who coincided with him and Dalton in Prague in 1967, remembers fondly the conversations and shared ideals they discussed at that time, especially about the armed revolution:

> We were in Prague when we learned that Che was fighting in Bolivia. For Roque, Hugo and me that was like a decisive turn towards continental revolution although this may seem naïve now. We received discreet smiles from our brothers of the east and the majority of Latin American communists working in the magazine, even from those who had some hope took care to avoid being identified with that adventure. Only from Kiva did we receive some encouragement of our enthusiasm although probably not of our optimism.

The inoperative community and unavowable community as defined by Nancy (1991) and Maurice Blanchot (1988), respectively, only existed inside the pages of his poetry.[13]

II

For Dalton, writing requires a certain form of treason against the homeland. In his novel, *Pobrecito poeta que era yo* (Poor Little Poet that I Was), Dalton includes the following epigraph which is a quote by Lawrence Durrell: "It is the duty of every great patriot to hate his country creatively" (Durrell 1958: 112). This creative hatred, this productive treason of his language and his homeland, requires an inevitable dialogue with multiple "foreign" literatures as well as a radical rewriting of the literary sphere that citizenship designates as ours.

In *Las historias prohibidas del Pulgarcito* (The Banned Histories of Tom Thumb), a collage poem made up of historical texts, some real, others apocryphal, poems and *bombas* (a type of limerick popular in El Salvador), Dalton disrupts the national discourse to discover a notion of "the People" that exceeds in a political as well as symbolic and legal manner the concept of nation-state. In this book, Dalton appears to tell us that it is only through the questioning and the destruction of the foundational myths and of patriotism, the love of the homeland, that one can construct a notion of "the People" that goes against the grain of all nationalist mythologies and even of the Marxist concept of social class. The first text in the book is an excerpt of a letter written by Pedro de Alvarado to Hernán Cortés where he describes his first defeat in the territory of Cuzcatlán (present-day El Salvador). This fragment has a dual role: as a foundational text and as the beginning of the genealogy of the concept of the People[14] that this text puts forth. Both roles are closely tied to each other. This letter (*carta de relación*) is a foundational text because it is through this letter that Dalton begins to configure the notion of "the People" that he wishes to propose: the popular identity does not exist prior to the existence of its enemy. Unity is only conceivable through the destruction of what you oppose. In the antagonistic structure that configures every social sphere, the presence of the other-enemy impedes social identities from being whole, from being themselves entirely. It is the impossibility of being a whole/complete community, a tribe, an ethnic group, a nation, that constitutes the "People," since "People" is always defined against an enemy, an Other.

Dalton's most well-known poem in this book and in his entire oeuvre, at least in El Salvador, "Poema de amor" (Love Poem), has come to represent for many a second national anthem. However, if we read it carefully, we notice that it is inscribed in one of the sections of the book where the collage, understood as a rhetorical apparatus that dismantles the traditional discourse of the nation, is very prominent. The section of the book where we find this poem is entitled: "La guerra es la continuación de la política por otros medios y la política es solamente la economía quintaesenciada" (War is a continuation of politics by other means and politics is only the quintessential economy). This bricolage that Dalton creates between Clausewitz (*War as Politics by Other Means*) and Marx makes explicit a notion of antagonism that exceeds the Marxist conceptual geography of the class conflict. In this fragment, Dalton recreates the ill-named "guerra del fútbol" (soccer war) that was fought by fostering and fomenting the chauvinist patriotism of both Salvadorans and Hondurans. Dalton shows through various newspaper fragments and his own reflections how this love for the homeland is manipulated by both El Salvador and Honduras to create a war whose only objective was to produce a false national unity and to distract both populations from other real problems.

The "Love Poem" functions in the book not only as a celebration of the homeland but also as a demonstration of the miserable and dark corners of the Salvadoran reality. Only through hostile and precarious conditions that Salvadoran history has created for its citizens can one name "the People." Only through the creative hatred can one reinvent a sense of belonging that after the founding of the Communist International came to be known as the *International*. The counter-hegemonic articulation that the master signifier "People" makes possible is constructed through an affective modality that inverts the foundational cliché of all national mythologies—love of country—and invents a sense of the international that unites all those left without being a part of anything, without belonging to their places of origin. The construction of a counter-hegemony requires work with affects that configure collective subjects. The singular nature of the work that Dalton proposes is that he places the emphasis on the need to dissolve collective configurations that national discourses create in order to configure new collective international subjects that make explicit their precarious existence. The signifier that Dalton proposes to counter the two national subjects in conflict in the soccer war is the empty signifier: "el pobre," "the poor." The strength of this signifier is that it defines the collectivity that it names not by its social class, historical, national, or cultural traits but by its precarious nature in the symbolic chain and power sphere in which it belongs.

The people as an entity is configured through a series of exclusions, negations, marginalizations, and exploitations: "los que se pudrieron en las cárceles de Guatemala, / por ladrones, por contrabandistas, por estafadores, / por hambrientos, / los siempre sospechosos de todo" (Dalton 2002: 200) (those who rotted in prisons in Guatemala, / Mexico, Honduras, Nicaragua / for stealing, smuggling, swindling, / for starving / those always suspected of everything) (Dalton 1984: 47). This subject "People" is defined not by its unity but by its virtue of having been denied everything, of having been expelled from everywhere. The People is created when there is a certain form of the common that exceeds all the normative and recognizable forms known in a determinate historical moment. Only when we expose the myths of a national history, when we destroy their enchantment, does the real subject of history rise: the poor, the People. It is a naked subject, anonymous, that lives crossing borders, that we can only see when we destroy the illusion of nationality. Dalton, in the final fragment of this section that is entitled "Algunos resultados del conflicto (hasta la fecha)" (Some Results of the Conflict [until now]), summarizes the meaning behind the poorly named soccer war, "decenas de miles de salvadoreños vagando con su hambre a cuestas, de Honduras a El Salvador y de El Salvador a Honduras. En Honduras ya no tienen tierra, en El Salvador no tienen tierra ni trabajo. No son ni salvadoreños ni hondureños: son pobres"[15] (Dalton 2002: 215) (hundreds of thousands of Salvadorans roaming with their hunger on their backs, from Honduras to El Salvador and from El Salvador to Honduras. In Honduras they no longer have land; in El Salvador they don't have land or work. They are neither Salvadoran nor Honduran: they are poor [my translation]). The positioning of this subject is defined by the universality of the condition that makes evident what it lacks. This subject lacks all the master signifiers that configure and position, anchor, in a territory and a concrete history almost all identities: land (nation, culture, ethnos, language) and work (money, property, one's place in the means of production, power). That they exist without land and work, displaced outside and inside all borders, is what encompasses them in the empty signifier of "poor" and grants an international character to their struggle. But it is the empty signifier that grants them a new location anchored in the universality of the "lack" that defines them. The poor is the signifier that defines all those who have fundamental needs whether they be economic, symbolic, spiritual, or a mix of all of them. The heterogeneous nature of the multiple demands of the subjects that configure this group is subsumed in this emblem of a "universal lack" that is the signifier "the People." This emblem of the universal lacking upon which a new form of belonging is founded is what the concept of the "international" attempts to shelter. It is through "the People" that we can grant meaning to certain semantic areas of concepts such as cosmopolitanism and universalism. It is only through this signifier, according to Dalton, that we can grant meaning to the concept of world literature. World literature would be, in Dalton's case, the literature of those that don't have a land that they can define as their own or work that allows them to live with dignity. World literature begins in that place where national literatures collapse and a world order, different from the one that dominated the planet then and now, fails to impose its legitimacy.

Notes

1 For a study of the international as an ideology of the state see Franz Borkenau's book *World Communism. A History of the Communist International* ([1938]).
2 The support of the English working class of the American slaves during the American Civil War (1861–5) came at great personal hardship for the English

workers. By supporting the fight for emancipation of the Southern slaves, they provided an example of the type of solidarity that the workers' movement aspired to achieve. See Braunthal (1967: 86–7).

3   I am referring to the concept of *Verfremdungseffekt* (distancing effect) coined by Bertolt Brecht. Consult Luis Alvarenga's book *Roque Dalton: La radicalización de las vanguardias* (2011; Roque Dalton: The Radicalization of the Avant-Garde) to study Brecht's influence on Dalton.

4   This reconfiguration of the established social order that Dalton proposes in his poem is not so distant from the Paris Commune that Kristin Ross studies in her book *Communal Luxury. The Political Imaginary of the Paris Commune*: "The Commune's working existence that so impressed Marx was in this sense nothing more than a concerted practice of *importation*: of models and ideas, phrases and slogans from distant lands and from distant times, to be reworked in the feverish atmosphere of the clubs and the Commune" (2016: 29). The revolutionary effervescence the young Dalton and his Latin American and Eastern bloc comrades lived during the years 1966–7 are condensed in this book, particularly the poem "Tavern," which attempts to recreate the revolutionary spirit of the time.

5   The complete quote from Rancière's book *Disagreement: Politics and Philosophy* is as follows: "Whoever has no part—the poor of ancient times, the third estate, the modern proletariat-cannot in fact have any part other than all or nothing. On top of this, it is through the existence of this part of those who have no part, of this nothing that is all, that the community exists as a political community—that is, as divided by a fundamental dispute, by a dispute to do with the counting of the community's parts even more than of their 'rights.' The people are not one class among others. They are the class of the wrong that harms the community and establishes it as a 'community' of the just and the unjust" (1999: 9).

6   There were non-aligned countries that did not belong to NATO or the Warsaw Pact. However, the solidarity that many of them declared to the Palestinian cause as well as their condemnation of Israel created a clear polarization with Western nations' unconditional support of Israel. Cuba, in the conference of nonaligned countries celebrated in Algeria in 1973, severed diplomatic relations with Israel. Many countries ended relations with Cuba when it was ousted from the Organization of American States but the only country with which Cuba has ended diplomatic relations is Israel. The Palestinian-Israeli conflict marked another clear form of bipolarity that placed many nonaligned countries together with the Eastern Bloc.

7   Mariano Siskind argues in his essay "The Globalization of the Novel and the Novelization of the Global: A Critique of World Literature" that the radical potential of the globalization of the novel lies in its ability "to imagine the world as the global space, determined by bourgeois culture, in which the novel, or rather the global novel, will inscribe itself" ([2010] 2013: 359). The radical potential of Dalton's poetry, as we will see later, is its ability to imagine through poetry a world that questions the status quo within communist

societies that have already passed the revolutionary period and imagine a new cosmopolitanism, a different global order.

8   For a complete history of the International, see *History of the International Vols. 1 and 2* by Julius Braunthal (1967).

9   In "The Communist Manifesto" Marx and Engels define the new global order: "The bourgeoisie has through its exploitation of the world market given a cosmopolitan character to production and consumption in every country. To the great chagrin of Reactionists, it has drawn from under the feet of industry the national ground on which it stood. All old-established national industries have been destroyed or are daily being destroyed" ([1848] 2013: 17).

10 Here I am appropriating the title of Daniel Heller-Roazen's book (2013).

11 The English translation of the poem by Jonathan Cohen and Hardie St. Martin translates "la moral" to "morale" (Dalton 1996: 169), but I believe a more correct translation of the text is "morality" and will use my own interpretation of the original in this case. In modern usage, "morale" refers to the confidence or enthusiasm an individual feels at a given time. I interpret Dalton's words to refer to the set of rules that indicate virtuous conduct.

12 "Community" and "the common" have an ample bibliography. The most relevant texts for my use of the terms are *The Inoperative Community* (1991) by Jean Luc Nancy and *Communitas. The Origins and Destiny of Community* (2009) by Roberto Esposito.

13 This ability to create a possible third space through literature is similar to Cheah's (2016) proposition on the power of literature to *make a world* and not merely reflect it.

14 The concept of the People has a long tradition. For a more complete review of how this concept has evolved see *Communication, Culture and Hegemony* by Jesús Martín-Barbero (1993).

15 Douglas Oviedo's book *Caravaneros* (Caravan Members) has certain passages that are striking due to the similarity in sentiment they have with Dalton's poem. For instance, "Aquí en México ustedes dejaron de ser salvadoreños, nosotros dejamos de ser hondureños, guatemaltecos, nicaragüenses para ser migrantes, que no se te olvide que eso somos: migrantes" (2020: 115) (Here in Mexico you stopped being Salvadoran, we ceased being Honduras, Guatemalans, Nicaraguans, to become migrants, don't forget that's what we are: migrants). Instead of the signifier "People" we see "Migrant" but the conditions that lead to these signifiers are similar. See also Robert McKee Irwin's chapter in this volume, "Caravaneros as Citizens of the World."

References

Alonso, A. (2007), "Un recuerdo de Kiva Maidanik," *Rebelión*, January 2. Available online: https://rebelion.org/un-recuerdo-de-kiva-maidanik/. Accessed January 14, 2021.

Alvarenga, L. (2011), *Roque Dalton: La radicalización de las vanguardias*, San Salvador: Editorial Universidad Don Bosco.
Blanchot, M. (1988), *The Unavowable Community*, trans. P. Joris, Barrytown: Station Hill Press.
Borkenau, F. (1938), *The Communist International*, London: Faber and Faber Limited.
Bosteels, B. (2021), *La comuna mexicana*, trans. S. Pinet, Ciudad de México: Akal.
Braunthal, J. (1967), *History of the International 1864–1914. Vol. 1*, trans. H. Collins and K. Mitchell, New York: Praeger.
Cheah, P. (2016), *What Is a World?: On Postcolonial Literature as World Literature*, Durham and London: Duke University Press.
Dalton, R. (1984), *Poems*, trans. R. Schaaf, Willimantic, CT: Curbstone Press.
Dalton, R. (1996), *Small Hours of the Night: Selected Poems of Roque Dalton*, ed. H. St. Martin, trans. J. Cohen, J. Graham, R. Nelson, P. Pines, H. St. Martin and D. Unger, Willimantic, CT: Curbstone Press.
Dalton, R. (2000), *Taberna y otros lugares*, San Salvador: UCA Editores.
Dalton, R. (2002), *Las historias prohibidas del Pulgarcito*, 10th edition, San Salvador: UCA Editores.
Dardot, P. and C. Laval (2019), *Common: On Revolution in the 21st Century*, trans. M. McLellan, New York: Bloomsbury.
Durrell, L. (1958), *Balthazar*, London: Faber and Faber.
Esposito, R. (2009), *Communitas: The Origin and Destiny of Community*, trans. T. Campbell, Stanford: Stanford University Press.
Heller-Roazen, D. (2013), *Dark Tongues: The Art of Rogues and Riddlers*, New York: Zone Books.
Laclau, E. (2005), *On Populist Reason*, New York: Verso.
Martín-Barbero, J. (1993), *Communication, Culture and Hegemony: From the Media to Mediations*, trans. E. Fox and R. A. White, London: Sage.
Marx, K. and F. Engels ([1848] 2013), "Communist Manifesto (1848)," in T. D'haen, C. Domínguez, and M. R. Thomsen (eds.), *World Literature: A Reader*, 16–17, London and New York: Routledge.
Monsiváis, C. (1968?), "Pido la palabra, compañero." Available online: http://www.hechohistorico.com.ar/Trabajos/Valores_Socioculturales/nvas.lecs/1968-monsi/mc0289.htm. Accessed September 21, 2022.
Nancy, J. L. (1991), *The Inoperative Community*, trans. P. Connor, L. Garbus, M. Holland and S. Sawhney, Minneapolis: University of Minnesota Press.
Oviedo, D. (2020), *Caravaneros*, Mexico City: Festina Publicaciones.
Rancière, J. (1999), *Disagreement: Politics and Philosophy*, trans. J. Rose, Minneapolis and London: University of Minnesota Press.
Ross, K. (2016), *Communal Luxury: The Political Imaginary of the Paris Commune*, New York: Verso.
Siskind, M. ([2010] 2013), "The Globalization of the Novel and the Novelization of the Global: A Critique of World Literature (2010)," in T. D'haen, C. Domínguez, and M. R. Thomsen (eds.), *World Literature: A Reader*, 329–53, London and New York: Routledge.

8

Rewriting the Militant Left: Untranslatability and Dissensus in Horacio Castellanos Moya

Tamara L. Mitchell

Published a decade and an ocean apart, Honduran-Salvadoran author Horacio Castellanos Moya's *El asco: Thomas Bernhard en San Salvador* (1997; *Revulsion: Thomas Bernhard in San Salvador*) is a literary restaging of Austrian novelist Thomas Bernhard's *Auslöschung* (1986; *Extinction* [1995]).[1] In *Extinction*, narrator Franz-Josef Murau recalls anti-Austrian tirades delivered to his Italian student, Gambetti, railing against the most despised aspects of his homeland: Catholicism, art, music, literature, Fascism, the family, and class divisions, among others. *El asco* is markedly similar to Bernhard's text in terms of plot and tone. Both are jaded monologues by cynical ex-patriots forced home after nearly twenty years due to deaths in the family. Both novels hinge on the conflict that arises when the sole heirs of each work, Murau and Edgardo Vega, must decide how to dispose of the family home: the Wolfsegg Estate in *Extinction* and the Miramonte house in *El asco*. This proves a source of tension in each, as both men divest themselves of the estates against their siblings' wishes. There are also significant formal similarities, as the two works lack paragraph or chapter breaks, and their content is spewed in serpentine, run-on sentences laced with repeated phrases. Like Bernhard's Murau, Vega despises his homeland and obsessively criticizes its culture, government, and people. Both protagonists live abroad (Rome and Montreal, respectively) and avoid visiting "home" at all costs.

Yet *El asco* is not mere pastiche or acritical parody of Bernhard's infamous style, which "hammers away at the reader's nerves with endless repetition and elaboration of a few basic themes" (Kuehn 1997: 550–1). For one, while *Extinction* is told from Murau's first-person perspective, *El asco* is recounted by Vega's interlocutor, Moya, and thus related from a third-person perspective.[2] Likewise, the details and objects of critique—local cuisine (e.g., *pupusas*), Salvadoran rock bands, and national soccer—are culturally specific to El Salvador. Most importantly, while *Extinction* synecdochally thematizes the last gasps of Austrian aristocracy, Castellanos Moya critically resituates Bernhard's aesthetic devices in the Salvadoran context to problematize a different epochal turning point: El Salvador's shift from a military state entrenched in decades of civil conflict to a farcical neoliberal "democracy" nearly over night. In this milieu, in which "un sicópata criminal que mandó a asesinar a miles de personas en su cruzada anticomunista se haya convertido en el político más popular" ([1997] 2018: 30–1) (a psychopathic criminal who assassinated thousands in an anticommunist crusade transformed himself into the most popular politician) (2016: 16), there is no accountability for the violent excesses of the civil war, which continue into the neoliberal present. As Nanci Buiza (2018: 101) observes, the novel "is a literary slap in the face" that seeks to jolt traumatized readers into "perceiv[ing] their own degraded situation." To do so, Castellanos Moya's narrative dialogues with and reimagines the literary tradition that precedes it, adapting Bernhard's scathing, antinationalist prose as a means of critiquing notions of modern development and nationhood that structure postwar El Salvador.

I rehearse *El asco*'s intertextual conversation with and debt to Bernhard to tease out a trend in the Central American author's oeuvre, namely the persistent intertextual and metaliterary dialogue he maintains with an expansive world literary archive. Below, I discuss how he often invokes works of Central and Eastern European literary giants as a means of positioning Central America in relation to a broader (post-)Cold War context. This sets up a sort of hemispheric parity—the periphery of the Americas in dialogue with the European periphery—that challenges the accepted literary canon and indexes parallels among the small states of Europe and Latin America as minor nations affected by global struggles for political, economic, and cultural power. In its examination of this sustained intertextual dialogue, the present chapter has two principal objectives. First, I read the persistent exchange established in Castellanos Moya's prose—what, thinking with Ignacio M. Sánchez Prado (2018), we might call "strategic" intertextuality—as a means of positioning Central American politics and letters in relation to a global context.[3] Second, I undertake a close reading of Castellanos Moya's first novel, *La diáspora* (The Diaspora, 1989), to consider a specific example of this strategic intertextuality. My analysis bears on a sustained debate in world literature criticism regarding the relationship between the cosmopolitan center and the provincial periphery, and I show how *La diáspora* at once establishes parallels to world literature while insisting on a linguistic and geopolitical specificity that resists reduction to the world literary canon.

From *literatura centroamericana* to *Weltliteratur*

Castellanos Moya's narrative fiction has received ample scholarly attention for its candid portrayal of the Cold War—a misnomer in Central America given the civil and dirty wars of the era—and its violent aftermath in Central America. His relentless narrative treatment of inequality, greed, consumerism, and sociopolitical violence of the late twentieth and twenty-first centuries has been described in scholarship as neoliberal noir (Kokotovic 2006), an aesthetics of cynicism and disenchantment (Cortez 2009), and "frictional" works that challenge the limits between fiction and nonfiction (Ortiz Wallner 2012). Moreover, Castellanos Moya's status as an author of global renown has been recognized broadly. Cristina Carrasco (2016: 47), for instance, situates the Central American novelist alongside Roberto Bolaño as authors that have been embraced and commodified on the global book market due to their portrayal of Latin America as a space of violence. This association with Bolaño goes deeper, as the Chilean author published a short piece praising Castellanos Moya's work in *Entre paréntesis* (2004; Between Parenthesis), which publishers have gone on to use in online reviews and as a book jacket blurb on the Central American writer's work ever since. Despite this success, critics have noted that the Central America of Castellanos Moya's novels is still perceived as part of "peripheral modernity" (López 2004: 96), the "[p]eriphery of the periphery" (Dove 2015: 188), and Carrasco (2016: 47) finds that, overwhelmingly, his texts propagate "los estereotipos exotizantes de siempre" (the same old exoticizing stereotypes).

It is generative to revisit this notion of the periphery in light of Castellanos Moya's persistent return to Central and Eastern European authors like Bernhard (Austrian), Elias Canetti (Bulgarian-British), Emil Cioran (Romanian-Franco), and Milan Kundera (Czech-Franco)—authors who, in the European context, pen (semi-)peripheral literatures but, at the same time, have been consecrated as part of the world literary canon. By establishing a sustained dialogue with such thinkers, Castellanos Moya situates Central American letters in relation to major works of world literature and recognizes the shared sociopolitical and ideological realities of the two regions, particularly regarding the Cold War and its aftermath. This dialogue and concomitant aesthetic and political parity emerge in various ways. First, Castellanos Moya's narrative fiction employs intertextuality, such as the above-mentioned stylistic affinities between *El asco* and

Bernhard's antipatriotic literature or, as will be discussed below, in relation to Kundera's prose. Second, Castellanos Moya often thinks with and against these authors, developing an understanding of politics, violence, and aesthetics alongside writers of peripheral European nations. In essays, interviews, and narrative works, the Honduran-Salvadoran author teases out the ways in which the reality of Central and Eastern Europe in the post-Second World War and Cold War eras coincides with the experience of the Central American isthmus in substantive ways.

Of note is that, like Castellanos Moya, each of these authors experiences a sort of exile—Canetti, Cioran, and Kundera live in linguistic and territorial exile, while Bernhard enacts an aesthetic exile—from which emerges a shared distance from and critique of nationalism in their disparate works.[4] This connection becomes salient when Castellanos Moya invokes these authors to question the notion of the homeland, such as in the essay "La metamorfosis del sabueso" (The Metamorphosis of the Sleuth/Hound), in which he draws on the legacy of Canetti to meditate on writing, language, and history: "La patria de un escritor es su lengua: afirmación propia de escritores desterrados, apátridas, de aquellos a quienes les ha tocado padecer extremismos nacionalistas o étnicos. Elias Canetti quizá sea el postrero de los narradores centroeuropeos de la primera mitad del siglo XX, testigos del desmoronamiento del Imperio austrohúngaro" (Language is the writer's homeland: affirmation of exiled, stateless writers, of those who have suffered from nationalist or ethnic extremism. Elias Canetti may be the last of the Central European storytellers of the first half of the twentieth century, witnesses to the collapse of the Austro-Hungarian Empire) ([1996] 2011: 57). At the time the essay was first published, in 1996, Castellanos Moya was experiencing a similar collapse—that of the Salvadoran Leftist project, which, following the 1992 Chapultepec Peace Accords, had been institutionalized in the Frente Farabundo Martí para la Liberación Nacional (FMLN, Farabundo Martí National Liberation Front) political party that was defeated by the right-wing Alianza Republicana Nacionalista (ARENA, Nationalist Republican Alliance) in postwar presidential elections. Although their political experiences diverge in meaningful ways—Castellanos Moya critiques an increasingly authoritarian Left that fought a repressive military regime, whereas his European interlocutors often critique those in power of a dogmatic Soviet Bloc entrenched in decades of authoritarian rule—Castellanos Moya's persistent turn to authors of marginal Central European nations may be understood as seeking refuge and understanding in works created from similar moments of decadence and political peril.

Apropos of the present volume, from Central Europe to Central America, a meta-discourse emerges regarding how great works of peripheral literature fit into that privileged classification of world literature. In what I venture to call an anxiety of recognition, authors of the periphery frequently turn to Goethe's concept of world literature to question the reception of their works in the cosmopolitan center. Castellanos Moya is no exception. In "El lamento provinciano" (The Provincial Lament), the Honduran-Salvadoran writer examines the anxiety of recognition experienced by geographically marginal writers, noting: "Una peculiaridad del escritor que procede de un país pobre y periférico, cuya tradición nacional carece de resonancia en el concierto de la literatura mundial, es el lamento por sentirse marginado, la queja por no ser tomado en cuenta, el complejo por no ser reconocido allende las reducidas fronteras de su patria. Es lo que llamo 'el lamento provinciano'" (A peculiarity of the writer who comes from a poor and peripheral country, whose national tradition lacks resonance in the concert of world literature, is regret for feeling marginalized, resentment at not being noticed, the complex about not being recognized beyond the narrow borders of their homeland. It is what I call "the provincial lament") ([2005] 2011: 42). He concludes by invoking Kundera alongside the progenitor of world literature, Goethe, noting that a certain maturity arrives when marginal authors feel "a gusto en lo que Goethe y Kundera llaman la Weltliteratur" (at home in what Goethe and Kundera call world literature) ([2005] 2011: 45).

This frequent turn to the European tradition does not exist at the expense of Latin American literatures, as Castellanos Moya invokes these traditions alongside Central American thinkers. For instance, complementing his theorization of *el lamento provinciano* through Goethe and Kundera, he addresses how Central American literary greats like Rubén Darío, Augusto Monterroso, Miguel Ángel Asturias, and Roque Dalton overcame the anxiety of recognition. Moreover, Dalton is omnipresent in Castellanos Moya's work. This is evidenced in protagonists' engagement with Dalton's oeuvre, such as one character's decision to write a dissertation on the poet in *La diáspora*, a plot point that becomes quasi-autobiographical when Castellanos Moya publishes *Roque Dalton: correspondencia clandestina y otros ensayos* (2021), a nonfictional meditation on Dalton's life, writing, and death. It may even be argued that Castellanos Moya's very engagement with Central and Eastern European writers relates to Dalton's legacy, as the late poet served as a correspondent in Prague in the 1960s, where he penned *Taberna y otros lugares* (1969) and interviewed Miguel Mármol about the 1932 Salvadoran uprising. Finally, Castellanos Moya practices a Daltonian credo when he critiques aspects of Central America in his fiction. This gesture, as Yansi Pérez (2009: 11) has discussed, reflects the epigraph from *Pobrecito poeta que era yo* (Dalton 1982) citing Lawrence Durrell: "Es una obligación de todo patriota odiar a su país de una manera creadora" ("It is the duty of every patriot to hate his country creatively" [Durrell 1958: 112]). By liberally drawing on authors from both traditions, Castellanos Moya emphasizes how Central American letters are already on par with Europe's.

Castellanos Moya's oeuvre does not just dialogue with authors of world literary status; his works undeniably belong to the world literary canon.

Initially published by small presses in Central America, such as Universidad Centroamericana Editores and Editorial Arcoiris, at the turn of the twenty-first century, Castellanos Moya enters into an agreement with Tusquets that sees many of his past works reissued and future novels released by the elite Barcelona publishing house and its partners in Latin America. Beginning in 2008, his novels have been rendered into multiple languages, with one of the most sought-after translators—Katherine Silver—undertaking English editions for New Directions Publishing. Most recently, in 2018, Castellanos Moya's world literary status was cemented when *Moronga* debuted with megapublisher Penguin Random House. Penguin then began reissuing many of his novels in Spanish and released two collected volumes of his essays. Finally, there is a host of robust scholarship on Castellanos Moya's oeuvre, including two contributed volumes—*El diablo en el espejo* (2016), edited by María del Carmen Caña Jiménez and Vinodh Venkatesh, and *Tiranas ficciones* (2018), edited by Magdalena Perkowska and Oswaldo Zavala—featuring work by major Latin Americanist scholars.

Thus, in terms of availability and reception in both popular and scholarly spaces, Castellanos Moya's corpus has proved cosmopolitan not only in content but also in translation and dissemination. This brief look at the material circulation of Castellanos Moya's work is not merely to establish his bona fides as an author of world literature but also pertains to the below analysis. I now turn to a comparative reading of Castellanos Moya's first novel, *La diáspora*, originally published in 1989, with its reedition by Penguin in 2018, to three ends. First, I posit that alternative archives, both musical and literary, foment dissensus in *La diáspora*, which opens a space for a Left that exists outside of the militant revolutionary project that developed in civil war El Salvador. Second, I analyze how the intertextual archive that the novel deploys in its critique of Left decadence—most notably Kundera's *Žert* ([1967], *The Joke* 2001)—situates the narrative in relation to major works of world literature. Finally, I undertake a close reading of *La diáspora* alongside Emily Apter's (2013) notion of *untranslatability* to think within the framework of world literature but against the universalizing drive of its critical apparatus.

Intertextuality and an Archive of Dissensus

Penned in the tumultuous 1980s and published in the closing years of the Salvadoran civil war, *La diáspora* revolves around a troubling historical failure of revolutionary politics and meditates on the aftermath of the 1983 murder-suicide of Comandantes (Commanders) Ana María and Marcial (pseudonyms of Mélida Anaya Montes and Salvador Cayetano Carpio, respectively), the leaders the Fuerzas Populares de Liberación (FPL, Popular

Liberation Forces). The novel reflects on the suspicious nature of these two deaths, which echo the 1975 murder of Roque Dalton by comrades in the Ejército Revolucionario del Pueblo (ERP, People's Revolutionary Army). These events cast a dark shadow on the movement and lead to a loss of faith in leadership and an exodus of sorts by insurgents. The novel draws on these historical events as multiple narrators question the integrity of the revolutionary project from their exile in Mexico City. The novel's critique has two principal targets: the atmosphere of suspicion cultivated inside the revolution and the guarded control that guerrilla leadership maintained over information, particularly in relation to intellectual and artistic material. *La diáspora* self-consciously rejects the stranglehold of the Left by creating a constellation of narrators in varying stages of turning their backs on the Salvadoran revolutionary project.

In terms of plot, not much happens in *La diáspora*. The narrative begins on the first day of 1984 with protagonist Juan Carlos's arrival to Mexico City after his break with the revolution. He must remain in Mexico as he waits for refugee status and a visa to travel to Canada (1989: 17). He stays with friends, Carmen and Antonio, a Mexican couple sympathetic to the Salvadoran insurgency. At one point, Juan Carlos is kidnapped, roughed up, and questioned about his responsibilities with the Communist Party in El Salvador. Part Two tells the story of Quique López, a blindly loyal guerrilla whose early participation in the war is more a matter of happenstance than ideological commitment. He must flee the country after a failed military assault, which lands him in Mexico City, working in *Presal*, the Party's propaganda office, as he anxiously awaits his return to the front lines (1989: 104). Part Three focuses more sharply on the deaths of Ana María, Marcial, and Dalton and introduces the figure of an Argentine journalist named Jorge Kraus. Perhaps an allusion to Montonero leader Mario Firmenich's staged participation in the Sandinista Revolution, Kraus is a coward and opportunist who times his travels to war-torn locations to overlap with the end of conflict, when the danger has passed. Finally, Part Four presents el Turco, the most embittered member of the eponymous diaspora. A musician that once performed around the world to gain international solidarity for the cultural arm of the Salvadoran Revolution (1989: 176), el Turco abandons the cause in 1981 due to the Party's zealous control of his band (1989: 180–1). The closing pages narrate one drunken night when el Turco quits his job as a pianist in a bar and then joins Juan Carlos at a party in the home of el Negro, the bourgeois Director of *Presal*.

Critics are in agreement about the thematization of political crisis and of a shifting sociopolitical system that permeates *La diáspora*. Sophie Esch (2020: 466) characterizes the text as a "dissident novel" that "highlight[s] the utter lack of moral and political convictions among guerrillas and militants." This dovetails with Héctor Miguel Leyva Carias's (1995: 387) analysis, which underscores how the novel criticizes guerrilla insurgency from within, demystifying revolutionary exceptionalism and challenging the utopic vision of *testimonios*. Likewise, José Luis Escamilla (2012: 63) argues that *La diáspora* functions as a bridge between the ideological writing initiated in 1970s Central America and a future generation that seeks to distance itself from revolutionary writing. Teresa Basile (2015: 201) posits that, rather highlighting heroic deeds of the Left, *La diáspora* goes against the grain by focusing on "las memorias perturbadoras" (perturbing memories) associated with internal betrayals. Related to these betrayals, Alberto Moreiras (2014) reads *La diáspora* in a tragic key, rejecting redemptive or cynical interpretations of the novel and instead locating in it an attempt, through mourning, to think a political and aesthetic future by grappling with the wreckage of the past. Finally, Alexandra Ortiz Wallner (2013: 154) homes in on the diasporic nature of the narrative, emphasizing the geopolitical "dislocation" that once-committed militants seek out as they become disillusioned with the revolution.

My reading of *La diáspora* coincides with these evaluations in many ways. However, what I find most noteworthy in Castellanos Moya's text does not relate to national or political boundaries, but rather to artistic ones. *La diáspora* is a tale of escape. The first-order escape is geographical and political—Juan Carlos and the rest of the ex-revolutionaries put physical distance between themselves and El Salvador to make a life outside of the Party and civil war. However, there is also a second-order escape that proves even more revealing—an aesthetic escape—which is undertaken by nearly every character in the text. Here, I read *La diáspora* through its internal artistic archive, which, I contend, points to how the novel thinks outside of Left-Right dichotomies through archival dissensus. I contrast the consumed and produced archives of the truly diasporic characters of the novel—Juan Carlos, Gabriel, and el Turco—with those of the characters that are attempting to return to or enter El Salvador—Quique and Kraus. Contrasting these two archives reveals the ways in which the former seeks an opening, an inclusion of more voices and more modes of telling that challenge revolutionary dogma, whereas the latter seeks a closure in the form of a totalizing political and literary consensus.

Notably, the two characters with the most constrained archives are the most dedicated to the ideals of the revolution: Quique López and Jorge Kraus. Quique, who works as a *teletipista* for *Presal*, the Mexico City arm of the press agency in charge of disseminating the Party's ideological materials and spin on what is occurring in El Salvador, copies communiqués that he frequently does not understand, and he refuses to think too much about the internal conflicts of the revolution to avoid trouble (1989: 86–7). When he is ordered to return to El Salvador, his supervisor asks him to write out his responsibilities so that his replacement has a guide. In Quique's estimation, this is the worst task imaginable given that "no hay peor trabajo que ponerse a escribir algo propio, le cuesta un mundo" (there is nothing worse than writing something of one's own, he finds it impossible) (1989: 87). Later, he must enlist the help of a colleague to pen a brief report on the military situation in El Salvador—a situation that he hopes not only to join, but in which he aspires to serve as a military leader—and he admits that "está cabrón que ni siquiera pueda exponer un análisis sobre eso" (it's messed up that he can't even put forth an analysis about it) (1989: 90).

Like Quique, Kraus is solely interested in pleasing revolutionary command. He is an opportunistic would-be novelist whose "pluma siempre estuvo dispuesta a colaborar en lo que el proceso revolucionario le exigía" (pen was always ready to collaborate in what the revolutionary process demanded of him) (1989: 119). Kraus understands that the "official story" surrounding the deaths of Comandantes Ana María and Marcial is suspect at best and likely an out-and-out lie, but he doesn't care (1989: 128). His endgame is to write the story that gets him access, which, he believes, will lead to fame and wealth. So he sets off to portray as fact whatever the Party asks of him: "él partiría de lo que [el Partido] consideraba 'la verdad' y su trabajo consistiría precisamente en demostrar que esta verdad era absoluta, hasta en los mínimos detalles" (he would begin with what the Party considered "the truth" and his job would consist precisely of demonstrating that that truth was absolute, down to the smallest details) (1989: 139). The opportunistic Kraus aims to cash in on his support of the party line.

Contrary to Quique and Kraus, ex-militant protagonists Gabriel, Juan Carlos, and el Turco aim to expand their intellectual and artistic archive, including texts and music that are deemed anti-communist, taboo, or Western. Gabriel is writing a dissertation on Dalton's death at the hands of his ERP comrades, a topic that casts the revolution in a negative light. Juan Carlos is portrayed as in the process of shedding the ideological confines of the insurgency, and he consumes novels and films out of line with Party ideals by artists like Ingmar Bergman, Marguerite Yourcenar, Heinrich Böll, and Milan Kundera. Eventually, after expanding his consumed narrative archive, Juan Carlos contemplates penning his own novel about the most forbidden of topics—the suspicious nature of Ana María's assassination and Marcial's suicide (1989: 41), which would constitute a direct challenge to the official narrative of the Party. El Turco proves the most rapaciously anti-revolutionary in terms of his artistic tastes, which is a result of the Party having censored his own artistic output when he labored on their behalf. His is principally a musical archive, and he rejects any genre associated with revolutionary communism. He derides leadership's preference for "la cancioncita antes del discurso" (1989: 36; the little ditty before the speech) and refuses to play "cancioncitas pendejas puestas de moda por los cubanos" (37; stupid little songs popularized by the Cubans). Instead, he wants to form a jazz band, which becomes meaningful in multiple ways.

Marked by improvisation and a polyphonic ensemble style, jazz allows an individual musician to stand out during intricate solos. The musician then rejoins the ensemble, making space for a different instrument to take the lead. Likewise, jazz is characterized by polyrhythm, which is the simultaneous presence of two or more conflicting rhythms that are not obviously derived from one another. Finally, jazz is a diasporic music, arising in African American culture in the late nineteenth and early twentieth centuries, and during the Cold War, jazz was deemed countercultural to both Soviet and US ideological paradigms (Borge 2018; Kofsky 1998). This final characteristic is of particular import, as jazz constitutes a key thread between Castellanos Moya's novel and one of its central intertextual archives: Kundera's *The Joke* ([1967] 2001), which narrates the decadence of twentieth-century communism from the perspective of various current and former Party members in the declining Eastern Bloc of the 1950s and 1960s. In both novels, jazz becomes central to disrupting intellectual and aesthetic consensus.

In *The Joke*, militant young musician Ludvik Jahn praises jazz's melodic specificity and ability to innovate and affect hegemonic Western music from the periphery. However, this same narrator cautions that, unlike jazz soloists, socialist musicians should sacrifice individualism to the collective ([1967] 2001: 140). From this effort, Stalin's "new art" would emerge, which encompasses "socialist content in national form" (141). This new art, in *The Joke*, is traditional folk music updated with lyrics that reflect socialist values. However, after a decade of forced labor as a miner, this same narrator, disillusioned with the Stalinist tendencies of the Communist Party, describes folk music as nothing more than empty propaganda (155). The novel closes with a spirited performance by Ludvik's disillusioned bandmates, reunited after a long separation following an ideological fallout. During the performance, each bandmate, moved by the music, improvises a solo. The band thus performatively breaks with the Stalinist ideology that insists that "in the folk song, one does not stand out from others but joins with them" (140). Analogously, *La diáspora* closes with el Turco, reeling from a night of partying, imagining a reconciliation with his militant younger brother in El Salvador, who, after hearing the jazz band, would forgive and accept the decision that resulted in el Turco "tronando con el Partido" (Casellanos Moya 1989: 181; breaking with the Party).

The anti-dogmatic potential of music is just one of myriad connections between the two novels. In addition to the overt intertextual reference mentioned above, Kundera's novel serves as a formal and thematic inspiration for *La diáspora*. The later novel implements a similar formal structure to its Czechoslovakian forebearer, with shifts among different narrators—both jaded intellectuals and dogmatic working-class militants—across different parts. Both novels include fictionalized primary source archival material, and there are echoes across specific scenes, such as the closing passages of abjection that take place in an outhouse (in *The Joke*) and el Negro's bathroom (in *La diáspora*), dwelling on laxative-induced defecation and alcohol-induced vomiting, respectively. Thematically, the unifying thread of each work is the way in which revolutionary dogmatism and Left decadence lead to the collapse of the viability of the socialist project. Likewise, machismo and the arbitrarily cruel treatment of women are important elements in both texts. In this way, *The Joke* proves the key intertextual touchstone in *La diáspora*.

The parallels that exist between *La diáspora* and *The Joke* serve a variety of ends. Castellanos Moya's debt to Kundera positions the Central American novelist in relation to an author whose discontent with nationalism, socialism, and revolutionary poetics rendered him (in)famous worldwide and domestically. In dialogue with Kundera, Castellanos Moya critiques dogmatic Left-Right dichotomies and decries Left authoritarianism at a time when it is dangerous to do so. Moreover, this intertextual gesture situates Central American literature of the Cold War period as part of a broader world literary exchange—a world to which, as *La diáspora* makes clear, the region already belonged in terms of geopolitics. Finally, by dialoguing with a national tradition that, as Kundera himself has lamented, forms part of the perceived "small nations" ([2005] 2013: 290) of "Central Europe" (295), a critique of the center-periphery binary emerges, which becomes especially ironic considering how central these peripheral nations were to ideological battles of the Cold War era. Beyond mere critique, through strategic intertextuality, Castellanos Moya effectively introduces dissensus into world literature as an author at the periphery of the periphery who claims a place in the canon. However, as gestured at above, parity with works of world literature is not the same as conflation. In the closing section, I undertake a close reading of *La diáspora* to show that, despite Castellanos Moya's insistent dialogue with the canon, attention to aesthetics—the deeply literary aspects of *La diáspora*—serves to index the geopolitical and linguistic specificity of Central American letters.

Untranslatability, Incommensurability, and Semantic Excess

A revealing semantic tic arises in *La diáspora*, namely the marked prevalence of the verb *tronar* (to thunder) across the narrative. Unwieldy and polysemic, *tronar*, I contend, falls under what Apter (2013), following Barbara Cassin, has named the untranslatable. Thinking against what she calls world literature's "reflexive endorsement of cultural equivalence and substitutability" (2), Apter describes the untranslatable as "a linguistic form of creative failure with homeopathic uses" (20). Untranslatable terms, such as the Portuguese *saudade* or Greek *mimesis*, are often polysemic and culturally specific, and they are notoriously difficult to render outside of their local language and context. According to Cassin, in an interview with Marc-Alexandre Reinhardt and André Habib, the untranslatable

> points less to that which we do not translate than that which we do not cease to (not) translate. Untranslatables are "symptoms" of linguistic difference, in other words, manifestations that can't be added up nor essentially identified. These symptoms we come across in those passionate and impassive translators' notes; that we encounter, that arrest and confront us ... They are therefore signs of an open-ended, virtually infinite, ongoing work-in-progress.
> (Reinhardt, Habib, and Cassin 2015: 6–7)

Cassin and Apter identify the play of homonymy as a particularly tricky space for translation. Homonyms are, of course, words that are either spelled the same (homographs) or pronounced the same (homophones) but boast different meanings. And they are ripe for designation as untranslatables because this feature—identical spelling or pronunciation with multiple meanings—is most often lost when rendered in translation.

Due to its semantic slipperiness and the cultural specificity of its rich polysemy in Salvadoran parlance,[5] *tronar* is a homonym whose multiple connotations in *La diáspora* are difficult, if not impossible, to render in translation. *Tronar* in El Salvador and the region is at once and imperfectly: to thunder, to lose one's cool, to fight, to have sex with a woman, to rant, to fail, to storm off, to break with, to break up with, to fire, to kill, to gun down (*Diccionario de la lengua española* 2014). Incredibly, *tronar* is deployed in almost all of these connotations, either explicitly or in abstracted form, in *La diáspora*: el Turco constantly loses his temper; a comrade is killed by government snipers during a protest; Carmen and Antonio's relationship is falling apart; el Turco is fired from his job; Gabriel fights with his former boss; the male narrators relentlessly try to sleep with women. Without a doubt, though, the most persistent and overt use of *tronar* relates to the titular diaspora's falling out with the revolutionary Left. From the first page of the text, when Carmen greets Juan Carlos, declaring "Tronaste con el Partido" (You broke with the Party) (1989: 13), to the final section, when el Turco reminisces about the dissolution of the cultural arm of the revolution, musing "la mayoría de artistas acabó tronando con el Partido" (the majority of artists wound up breaking with the Party) (1989: 181), the verb appears nearly a dozen times in the characters' discussions about why individuals are leaving the Party (1989: 13, 15, 20, 21, 29, 31, 55, 181). The omnipresence of this verb becomes a semantic symptom of the period, a time when ideals were being sacrificed, supporters suppressed, and the revolutionary project of the Left was falling apart, failing, *tronando*.

By insisting on the untranslatable, Apter holds space for undecidability, mistranslation, and incommensurability in translation and world literature.

Tronar, as untranslatable, underscores how, even as a work of world literature situated within the context of the global Cold War, an obstinate geopolitical and linguistic specificity endures in *La diáspora*. Intriguingly, this obstinacy goes further, extending to an epochal specificity, which becomes evident in a comparative reading of the 1989 original alongside Penguin's 2018 reissue of the novel. An author's note precedes the 2018 reedition, stating "Me he atrevido a cepillar el lenguaje, pues el paso de los años dejaba al descubierto bordes romos, superficies con frases descascaradas" (I have ventured to polish the language, as the passing of the years exposed blunt edges and crude phrasing). Beyond these changes, Castellanos Moya asserts that he has not altered the plot, "ni ciertas imprecisiones históricas, ni los personajes" (nor certain historical inaccuracies or the characters).[6] A comparison of the two editions shows that, notably, one of the most persistent revisions is the almost systematic substitution of occurrences of *tronar*. In the original text, there are over a dozen instances of *tronar* and its variants (*truenes* [fights], *tronazón* [break up], etc.), while in the reedition, a third of these are substituted with synonyms and reworkings. For instance, "Carmen le había asegurado que *estaba a punto de tronar* con el Comité de Solidaridad y también con el Partido" (1988: 15, my emphasis) shifts to "Carmen le había asegurado que *estaba a punto de salirse* del Comité de Solidaridad y también del Partido" (2018: 16, my emphasis).[7] This revisionist gesture becomes uncannily suggestive of the untranslatable; *tronar* as spirit and sign of 1980s El Salvador is not only linguistically and geopolitically specific but also temporally specific, and untranslatable in a present-day reworking of the text by its own author.

Interpreted as an untranslatable, the erasure of *tronar* in the twenty-first-century reedition becomes symptomatic of a shift in political discourse. Indeed, Castellanos Moya revisits and edits *La diáspora* after the Left is no longer the opposition party to ARENA's rule, as the FMLN is institutionalized with the election of Mauricio Funes to the presidency in 2009. The FMLN that selects former CNN journalist Funes as its presidential candidate—the first non-guerrillero nominee for the party—is far removed from the dogmatic ideologues that Juan Carlos and the other "deserters" criticize in the pages of *La diáspora*. These revisions aesthetically silence an element of the earlier version, and the resounding absence of *tronar* in the reedition indexes a shift away from the dominant zeitgeist of the original context.

Across the years, Castellanos Moya, while celebrated and internationally successful, has also stirred controversy and been criticized for penning antipatriotic novels (Castany Prado 2012: 18) that denigrate Central American letters and communities (Cortez 2014),[8] as preferring to "mirar hacia afuera e incorporar recursos de otras tradiciones en sus textos, aunque hable de Centroamérica" (Carrasco 2016: 60; look abroad and incorporate resources from other traditions in his texts, even if he addresses Central America). While these assessments have merit, it is also true that Castellanos

Moya's turn to authors of semi-peripheral or peripheral European nations establishes a parallel between Central European and Central American experiences during the Cold War and productively situates Salvadoran literature as part of a broader world literary exchange. Akin to the enduring engagement with Dalton across Castellanos Moya's oeuvre discussed above, *La diáspora*'s generative untranslatability, as evidenced in the homonym *tronar*, shows how his literary corpus does not merely turn to world literature to comprehend and amplify Central America's role in the Cold War but also insists on a singularity that refuses conflation with the European tradition with which his novels often thematically and formally engage. Against world literature and, generatively, against the twenty-first-century reedition of *La diáspora*, the *tronar* of the original novel generates a semantic and aesthetic excess that can only be (*un*)*translated* with attention to the geopolitical and historical specificity of 1980s El Salvador.

Notes

1. See Quirós (2016) and Thornton (2014) on affinities between *El asco* and Bernhard's oeuvre. See Ribeiro (2016) and Werner (2020) for more on intertextuality between *El asco* and *Extinction*.
2. Correspondingly, Castellanos Moya renders a famous formal device from *Extinction*, the oft-repeated phrase "habe ich zu Gambetti gesagt" (I said to Gambetti), in the third person: "me dijo Vega" (Gambetti told me). This stylistic change may be interpreted in relation to the genre of *testimonio*. See Thornton (2014).
3. Indeed, Castellanos Moya could be read as an heir to Sergio Pitol's "heterodox cosmopolitanism" (Sánchez Prado 2018: 25), as both authors turn to "an archive of heterodoxies" (2018: 32) from the Eastern European tradition.
4. By "aesthetic exile" I allude to Bernhard's infamous "posthumous literary emigration" in which he prohibited the publication of his works in Austria (Honegger 2001: 306).
5. In the entry for "tronar" in the *Diccionario de la lengua española* (2014), El Salvador appears as the most frequent geographical location for the multiple meanings of the verb and as the only country with its own regionally specific locutions: "Dicho de un hombre: tener relaciones sexuales con una mujer" and "inmediatamente" (for "tronando y lloviendo").
6. Curiously, and perhaps tellingly, no such author's note accompanies the reedition of *El asco*.
7. Two additional examples include (my emphasis in each): "Le preguntaron cuáles eran las causas de *su truene* ..." (1989: 21) is changed to "Le preguntaron cuáles eran las causas de *su ruptura* ..." (2018: 22; They asked him the reasons behind his departure). And "la mayoría de artistas *acabó tronando* con el Partido" (1989: 181) becomes "la mayoría de artistas *acabó saliéndose* del Partido" (2018: 153; the majority of the artists wound up breaking with the Party).

8   The critique I reference comes from an editorial titled "¡Adiós, Horacio!" in which Beatriz Cortez (2014) affirms "después de ver repetido el mismo retrato una y otra vez, de leer una y otra vez a una voz demasiado similar regodearse de la misoginia, burlarse de la pobreza, celebrar el racismo y el imperialismo cultural, retratar repetidamente a nuestro país desde una perspectiva colonialista, y renegar de todos los escritores nacionales, le perdí interés poco a poco" (after seeing the same depiction repeated over and over again, after reading time and again an all too familiar voice delighting in misogyny, poking fun at poverty, celebrating racism and cultural imperialism, repeatedly portraying our country from a colonialist perspective, and repudiating all national writers, I lost interest little by little).

References

Apter, E. (2013), *Against World Literature: On the Politics of Untranslatability*, London: Verso.
Basile, T. (2015), "Las memorias perturbadoras: revisión de la izquierda revolucionaria en la narrativa de Horacio Castellanos Moya," in T. Basile (ed.), *Literatura y violencia en la narrativa latinoamericana reciente*, 195–212, Argentina: Universidad Nacional de la Plata.
Bernhard, T. (1995), *Extinction*, trans. D. McLintock, New York: A. Knopf.
Bolaño, R. (2004), "Horacio Castellanos Moya," in *Entre paréntesis*, 171–3, Barcelona: Anagrama.
Borge, J. (2018), *Tropical Riffs: Latin America and the Politics of Jazz*, Durham and London: Duke University Press.
Buiza, N. (2018), "On Aesthetic Experience and Trauma in Postwar Central America: The Case of Horacio Castellanos Moya's *El asco* and Claudia Hernández's *De Fronteras*," *Hispanófila*, 184: 99–115.
Caña, J., M. del Carmen, and V. Venkatesh, eds. (2016), *Horacio Castellanos Moya: El diablo en el espejo*, Valencia: Albatros.
Carrasco, C. (2016), "De Macondo a San Salvador: la recepción de la narrativa de Horacio Castellanos Moya en España," in M. D. C. Caña Jiménez and V. Venkatesh (eds.), *Horacio Castellanos Moya: El diablo en el espejo*, 47–62, Valencia: Albatros.
Castany Prado, B. (2012), "Literatura antipatriótica," *Quimera* (348): 12–19.
Castellanos Moya, H. (1989), *La diáspora*, San Salvador: UCA Editores.
Castellanos Moya, H. ([1996] 2011), "La metamorfosis del sabueso," in *La metamorfosis del sabueso: Ensayos personales y otros textos*, 57–64, Santiago: Ediciones Universidad Diego Portales.
Castellanos Moya, H. ([1997] 2018), *El asco: Thomas Bernhard en San Salvador*, Barcelona: Penguin Random House.
Castellanos Moya, H. ([2005] 2011), "El lamento provinciano," in *La metamorfosis del sabueso: Ensayos personales y otros textos*, 42–5, Santiago: Ediciones Universidad Diego Portales.
Castellanos Moya, H. (2016), *Revulsion: Thomas Bernhard in San Salvador*, trans. L. Klein, New York: New Directions.

Castellanos Moya, H. (2018), *La diáspora*, Barcelona: Penguin Random House.
Cortez, B. (2009), *Estética del cinismo: Pasión y desencanto en la literatura centroamericana de posguerra*, Guatemala: F&G Editores.
Cortez, B. (2014), "¡Adiós, Horacio!," *ContraPunto*, October 27. Accessed September 23, 2017.
Dalton, R. (1982), *Pobrecito poeta que era yo*, San José: Editorial Universitaria Centroamericana.
Diccionario de la lengua española (2014), s.v. "tronar," 23rd edition, *Real Academia Española*. Available online: https://dle.rae.es/tronar. Accessed January 4, 2022.
Dove, P. (2015), "The Allegorical Machine: Politics, History, and Memory in Horacio Castellanos Moya's *El sueño del retorno*," *The Yearbook of Comparative Literature*, 61: 174–201.
Durrell, L. ([1958] 1991), *Balthazar*, New York: Penguin.
Escamilla, J. L. (2012), *El protagonista en la novela de posguerra centroamericana desterritorializado, híbrido y fragmentado*, San Salvador: Editorial Universidad Don Bosco.
Esch, S. (2020), "Uneven Battles: Central American Cold War Literature," in A. Hammond (ed.), *The Palgrave Handbook of Cold War Literature*, 451–70, Cham: Palgrave Macmillan.
Honegger, G. (2001), *Thomas Bernhard: The Making of an Austrian*, New Haven: Yale University Press.
Kofsky, F. (1998), *John Coltrane and the Jazz Revolution of the 1960s*, 2nd rev. edition, New York: Pathfinder.
Kokotovic, M. (2006), "Neoliberal Noir: Contemporary Central American Crime Fiction as Social Criticism," *Clues*, 24 (3): 15–29.
Kuehn, H. (1997), "On Reading Thomas Bernhard," *The Sewanee Review*, 105 (4): 541–53.
Kundera, M. ([1967] 2001), *The Joke*, New York: Harper Perennial.
Kundera, M. ([2005] 2013), "Die Weltliteratur (2005)," in T. D'haen, C. Domínguez, and M. R. Thomsen (eds.), *World Literature: A Reader*, trans. L. Asher, 289–300, London and New York: Routledge.
Leyva, C. and H. Miguel (1995), "La novela de la revolución centroamericana (1960–1990)," diss., Universidad Complutense, Madrid.
López, S. L. (2004), "National Culture, Globalization and the Case of Post-War El Salvador," *Comparative Literature Studies*, 41 (1): 80–100.
Moreiras, A. (2014), "The Question of Cynicism: A Reading of Horacio Castellanos Moya's *La diáspora* (1989)," *Nonsite*, 13: 46–64. Available online: https://nonsite.org/the-question-of-cynicism/#.
Ortiz Wallner, A. (2012), *El arte de ficcionar: la novela contemporánea en Centroamérica*, Madrid: Iberoamericana.
Ortiz Wallner, A. (2013), "Literaturas sin residencia fija: Poéticas del movimiento en la novelística centroamericana contemporánea," *Revista iberoamericana*, 79 (242): 149–62.
Pérez, Y. (2009), "Odiar a la patria de forma constructiva: Roque Dalton, Horacio Castellanos Moya y El Salvador de posguerra," paper presented at *Northeast Modern Language Association*, Boston, MA, February 27.

Perkowska, M. and O. Zavala, eds. (2018), *Tiranas ficciones: Poética y política de la escritura en la obra de Horacio Castellanos Moya*, Pittsburgh: Instituto Internacional de Literatura Iberoamericana.

Quirós, D. (2016), "'Este no es un país de escritores': *El asco*, Thomas Bernhard y la literatura centroamericana en la época neoliberal," in M. D. C. Caña Jiménez and V. Venkatesh (eds.), *Horacio Castellanos Moya: El diablo en el espejo*, 33–45, Valencia: Albatros.

Reinhardt, M. A., A. Habib, and B. Cassin (2015), "The Untranslatable: A New Theoretical Fulcrum? An Exchange with Barbara Cassin," *SubStance*, 44 (2): 6–14.

Ribeiro, H. J. (2016), "A *Extinção* da América Latina: *Asco*," *Remate de Males*, 36 (1): 259–73.

Sánchez Prado, I. M. (2018), *Strategic Occidentalism: On Mexican Fiction, the Neoliberal Book Market, and the Question of World Literature*, Evanston: Northwestern University Press.

Thornton, M. (2014), "A Postwar Perversion of *Testimonio* in Horacio Castellanos Moya's *El asco*," *Hispania*, 97 (2): 207–19.

Werner, J. (2020), "Thomas Bernhard's *Extinction*: Variations/Variazioni/Variaciones," in S. Dowden, G. Thuswaldner, and O. Berwald (eds.), *Thomas Bernhard's Afterlives*, 207–37, New York: Bloomsbury Academic.

9

Humberto Ak'abal's Pluri-verses: Indigeneity, Cosmolectics, and World Literature

Gloria Elizabeth Chacón

"In the 'beginning' was the word, ... and the word was God." This divine logic in its putative veracity, predicated on its mediterraneo-centric wisdom, projected a limited vision of the world outside the trade crossroads of the Middle East. In naming the continents of Europe, Africa, and Asia as constituting the totality of the world, this cartographic trinity not only summarized the circumference of the globe but naturalized its existence. The absence of any references to Indigenous Peoples from the Americas in one of the most disseminated texts of Western literature, *The Bible*, contributed to rampant ignorance about their existence. Centuries after their encounter with the colonizer's forces, Indigenous Peoples' written expressions remained impenetrable, excluding them from the notion of "people of the book." In this cultural mapping of writing and the book, Indigenous Peoples continued to be absent from historical and geographical conceptions of the world, shaped by colonial discourses that came to dominate in the Western hemisphere. A knowledge deficit about Indigenous Peoples' lands in Judaic, Christian, and Muslim teachings led to the historical farce of "discovery" in the fifteenth century. Haunted by the partial knowledge generated about their own writing systems and books, Indigenous nations remain misread and mistranslated. The rise of contemporary Indigenous writers insist on their existence beyond the three continents and continuously grapple with the West's incomplete rendering of the world. Through their verses and narratives, Indigenous writers propound an alternate vision of infinite pluri-verses at variance with the institutional limitations of "new world" discovery discourse and modern cartography.

In this piece, I will discuss Humberto Ak'abal's work from the Maya K'iche' nation as representative of an Indigenous literature that invites readers to imagine other ways of relating beyond political geography or postcolonial literature overtures. Through Ak'abal's poems, interviews, and a short story, the discussion revisits and interrogates the tenets of world literature like cosmopolitanism, globality, literary market circulation, and translation as well as theoretical frameworks that contribute to world reading practices (Moretti 2000). I argue that Indigenous literatures are not simply a corrective to world, global, planetary, or universal literatures. Rather, these textual practices offer what I term a cosmolectical literature. Based on my previous scholarship, *Indigenous Cosmolectics: Kab'awil and the Making of Maya and Zapotec Literatures* (2018), I define cosmolectical literatures as those cultural productions that engage in a dialogue with the cosmos, understood as an animate world that includes ontologies not always accounted for in other literatures, and one that manifests a temporality that conjures the past and present at the same time. In that context, I argue that this literature performs "a double gaze," an optic that duplicates and generates more than a thesis, antithesis, and synthesis. It is a gaze that straddles the past and the future simultaneously generating multiple visions. Cosmolectical literature can be observed in other literary traditions, but I point out its definitive trait in Indigenous literature and, particularly, in Humberto Ak'abal's work, as he asserts, "yo veo el futuro a través del pasado" (I see the future through the past); his work deploys this double gaze with memory at its fulcrum because "no hay olvido" (there is no forgetting) (Ollé 2004: 221, my translation).

My discussion and analysis of Ak'abal's formative years as a reader and his evolution as a writer illustrate his literary trajectory as grounded in a conversation between his social experience and the cosmos writ large. At the same time, his poetry and narrative forge a literary system that takes us beyond first and third world dichotomies. Ak'abal's work is an ontological affirmation about being human and being in relation with other nonhumans. Similar to what Nickels defines as "non-state" geography, Ak'abal advances a corpus that rises above nation-state boundaries against settler colonialism and a redrawing of cartographies based on other notions of kinship, language, nature, and the pluri-verses. Collectively his texts represent an original and self-sustained historical and philosophical contribution to theories of world literature.

Undoing Cosmopolitanism

Indigenous literature as part of world literature in the ways it was first imagined by Goethe and the cosmopolitan aspects of his formulation proves to be counterintuitive, paradoxical at best. Indigenous Peoples are simply not interpellated as readers or producers of literature. In interviews with Marie-Louise Ollé, Juan Sánchez, and Gerardo Guinea and in his memoir, *El sueño de ser poeta* (The Dream of Being a Poet), published posthumously in 2020, Ak'abal describes an unexpected encounter with books. In narrating the difficult circumstances that led to his flight from a village in the mountains to Guatemala City, he poignantly recalls a relationship to books that must be understood from his position as an Indigenous person in dialogue with 500 years of colonial history. As an Indigenous man searching for a job in the City—penniless—he spent many of his days rummaging through refuse in Guatemala City's largest dumpster. It is in this undesirable, marginal place that blatantly exposes capitalist excesses and needless waste where he came across books he terms as "world classics." He states, in the interview with Ollé,

> Pero de alguna manera fue como una suerte haber vivido en la basura algunos días porque encontré muchos libros ahí. Supongo que libros que dejaban algunos turistas que estarían de paso … eran autores que no fácilmente se consiguen, o se conseguían en Guatemala.
>
> But somehow it was kind of lucky to have lived in the garbage for a few days because I found a lot of books there. I suppose there were books left by some tourists who passed through … they were authors who are, or were, not easily obtained in Guatemala.
>
> (Ollé 2004: 208–9, my translation)

The singularity of Ak'abal's encounter with "universal" literature in the city's largest landfill is not isolated from the global capitalist forces and cosmopolitanism that makes Guatemala a tourist attraction. Although he offers a variation of this memory in his interviews and in his book, *El sueño de ser poeta*, the experience of becoming acquainted with books by authors like Samuel Beckett in the city's dumpster remains consistent. Ak'abal questions the citizen of the world rhetoric that allows tourists to discard books in a nation that is at the losing end of the capitalist world system and undergoing a major ideological challenge crisis in the 1980s. Cosmopolitanism as a desirable bourgeois value gets stripped from any romanticism in Ak'abal's account, critiquing it as motivated by the power of capitalism and consumerism. At the same time, Ak'abal reveals his astonishment at finding classics published in Spanish that would contribute to the expansion of his treasured personal library. Due to settler colonialism and advanced capitalism, Guatemala represents an "under-developed" society for Mayas. That is, Maya people struggle to survive in a system that is alien to them and continues to dispossess them, particularly in the capital where they are exploited for labor. This chapter in Ak'abal's life patently illustrates the deep social, racial, and cultural divide in Guatemala wherein Indigenous populations are denied access to knowledge in all languages. His consuming desire to read reflects what at the time UNESCO describes as a "hunger for books" in the developing world. Coincidentally. it was UNESCO that funded the anthology *Ajkem tzij/Tejedor de palabras* (Weaver of Words) where most of his oeuvre is gathered.

Indigeneity and World Literature

Theorizations of world literature as a political and economic system resonate with the conditions that have historically suppressed Indigenous authors in Central America. The Warwick Research Collective's proposal of "world literature" as an extension of comparative literatures "after the multicultural debates and the disciplinary critique of Eurocentrism" (2015: 4–5), for example, describes to a degree the emergence of Indigenous literatures from Central America. Regionally, these textual expressions suffer from limited circulation compared to that of non-Indigenous authors in established publishing houses. Nonetheless, Indigenous literary expressions have always had a cultural place in Latin America, albeit one that is subjected and subordinated to the purview of the "lettered city." Indeed, the rise of Latin American letters depended on an epistemological bet that speculated on the disappearance of Indigenous worlds. The alleged triumph of the lettered city over Indigenous orality is a given in Latin American letters and a motif in novels such as Mario Vargas Llosa's *El hablador* (The Storyteller) or Miguel Ángel Asturias's *Hombres de maíz* (Men of Maize) to name some of the most well-known novels. Aside from the limits of circulation, another main deviation of Indigenous literature from economic and political world literature system theories inevitably takes us back to the colonial encounter as a fundamental epistemological divide. Considering these historical and cultural legacies, Indigenous literatures cannot be imagined in isolation. Nonetheless, even post-1990s, a key decade for the decolonization of epistemology in Latin America, the durable connection between land, community, and orality indexed contemporary Indigenous literatures within the local. Time and time again, Latin American literary historiographies tend to imagine them in opposition to globality, cosmopolitanism, or modernity—all defining tenets constituting world literature. Theorizing world literature from Indigenous perspectives and epistemic inversions such as Ak'abal's forces readers and critics to expand their understanding of Indigenous literatures unfettered from local concerns, as they emerge from ongoing relations with multiple Indigenous nations and languages (Warrior, Weaver, Womack 1999). In fact, these surface in dialogue and in tension with global forces, with other traditions, languages, and practices since the fifteenth century (Lyons 2018). For instance, the Maya sacred text, *Popol Wuj* (Book of Council) was immediately translated, circulating in Europe soon after contact (Quiroa 2022) and becoming the most widely known Indigenous piece of literature in the world. Contemporary Indigenous literatures from Abiayala challenge our present understandings of world literature as Western cartography. Instead, Indigenous nations adhere to linguistic mappings that transgress nation-state borders. Theorizing this corpus through Ak'abal's work as a practice that decentralizes a Western logos not only in Europe but in Latin America affords us a constant reminder of multiple worlds and temporalities manifested in alphabetic writing that emerge from a protracted dispute and dialogue about the world since the sixteenth century.

Other Modes of Circulation and Ak'abal

Prior to a global focus on Indigenous rights in the 1990s, Indigenous texts mainly circulated in nontraditional book format via the internet, in compact discs, local journals, and newspapers. Slowly, they entered international circulation in translations; individual poets became better known through other soundscapes in international festivals in Europe and Latin America (Chacón 2018), leading to more exposure. Many of these poets have gained recognition, receiving prizes in Italy, Spain, and France. In their distribution, their texts contested the assumption of a postcolonial era, making evident that colonialism continues for Indigenous communities despite historical breaks with metropolitan powers. Individual authors established high profiles and their publications started to vie for readership in their flow as part of world literature. Collectively, these small editorial productions task the values attached to cosmopolitanism, literary markets, translation, and globalization. Restricted print-runs, unfixed orthographic Indigenous languages transcriptions, these texts require sui generis approaches in dialogue with others analytics such as the "World Republic of Letters" (Casanova 2004), globe (Cheah 2014), and planetary (Nickels 2018). Humberto Ak'abal's works present an understanding of the world and the state of Guatemala as an uneven constitutive process dependent on Indigenous dispossession and tropes of disappearance that limited the world to univocal utterances. His experience with reading and writing literature blatantly demonstrates that the version of the world imposed on him hinges on Maya dispossession and genocide. Although his first publications date to the 1990s, his work is informed by the political upheavals and genocide suffered by Mayan Peoples for centuries. To know Humberto Ak'abal is to understand why global, worldly, planetary approaches fall short in their understanding of his work and why I opt to pursue his cosmolectical "apprehension" (as in to understand with all the senses) of his work.

Ak'abal was born in the municipality of Momostenango in 1951, in a village located in the western highlands of Guatemala. Due to taxing economic conditions, his education was curtailed at the age of twelve. As a young boy, he worked as a sheep herder. His father was a blanket weaver of what is known as a Momostecan poncho. These blankets circulate in global markets and are recognized for their exceptional geometrical designs, colors, and textures. In his youth, he would accompany his father to the city to sell these famous ponchos that require so much time to create, yet whose craftsmanship remains underpaid due to the Guatemalan society's underappreciation of this ancestral craft. His father's death led to an economic precarity that forced Ak'abal to abandon his studies and assume the economic support of his siblings. Yet despite these hardships he pursued his literary vocation as an autodidact and became Guatemala's most renowned contemporary Indigenous poet. His many awards attest to his national and international standing. In 1993, he won the Quetzal de Oro from the Guatemalan Association of Journalists. In 1998, he received the Premio Continental Canto de América from UNESCO, in Mexico, and in 2006, he was the recipient of a Guggenheim Fellowship. In 2003, he was awarded the prestigious Miguel Ángel Asturias National Prize in Literature, which he declined because this literary recognition bore the name of a national author who believed "Indians" were an inferior race. Ak'abal's writing has been translated into various European languages, as well as Hebrew, Arabic, Vietnamese, and Japanese. He was also inspired by diverse literary forms, including the haiku, sonnet, free verse, and oral stories. In his adult years, Ak'abal traveled widely, often times trading long periods of residences between Switzerland and Guatemala. In a rather ironic and tragic twist of events, he fell ill while in Guatemala and passed away in 2019 due to inadequate care.

Indigenous Languages, Spanish, and Self-Translation

Unlike other world literatures in translation, where authors do not typically assume a dual role in the publishing industry, Indigenous writers have traditionally self-translated. This dual writing act reveals the negligible social status of Indigenous languages, a generalized lack of knowledge by

Spanish speakers, and low literacy in Maya languages. Nonetheless, Ak'abal embraces bilingualism as positive in his formation as a reader and writer through Spanish. Ak'abal's bilingualism facilitated his access to canonical texts in Spanish:

> Mi formación autodidacta de la literatura universal ha sido a través de los libros en español, el esfuerzo por aprender a pensar en este idioma me ha servido también para comprender desde otro ángulo a mi propia gente, es como verme de espaldas o verme de lejos, el bilingüismo me ha dado la oportunidad de ver mi entorno desde otra perspectiva.
>
> My self-taught training in universal literature has been through books in Spanish, the effort to learn to think in this language has also helped me to understand my own people from another angle, it is like seeing myself from behind or seeing myself from afar, bilingualism has given me the opportunity to see my environment from another perspective).
> (quoted in Sánchez 2012b: 121–2, my translation)

The political violence in Guatemala of the 1960s and 1970s and the bloody civil war that ensued after 1978 resulted in a genocide that led to two hundred thousand deaths of mostly Indigenous Peoples. Considering this hostile environment writing creatively in an Indigenous language was nearly an impossible endeavor. In an unspoken educational policy of inconsistent instruction in Indigenous languages, most Maya writers resorted to Spanish. Ak'abal notes that one of the obstacles he faced in order to publish was settling for a monolingual version in Spanish. His editor refused to produce a bilingual text due to the costs of production in a country where a quarter of the population was illiterate in Spanish, and only a minority was fluent in Maya K'iche'. In a 1995 interview with Gerardo Guinea, Ak'abal candidly responds to the issue. He noted:

> Los libros bilingües hasta muy recientemente empiezan a circular en el país. Mi sueño más grande es presentarla en k'iche'. Pero la razón de hacerlo en español tiene dos objetivos. El primero, universalizar el pensamiento indio y el otro, descalificar la idea que se ha manejado sobre la incapacidad del indio. Yo mismo he sido analfabeta en mi lengua, y semianalfabeta en castellano.
>
> Bilingual books have very recently begun to circulate in the country. My biggest dream is to present it in K'iche'. But the reason for doing it in Spanish has two objectives. The first, to universalize Indian thought, and the other, to debunk the idea that has been purported about the Indian's incompetence. I, myself have been illiterate in my own language.
> (quoted by Montemayor 1996: 37, my translation)

In effect, the majority of bilingual texts produced prior to the 1990s were mainly technical, consisting of mainly grammars and dictionaries. In the interview with Marie-Louise Ollé, he discusses the controversy of publishing in K'iche' and Spanish and says, "Cuando a mí se me dio esa oportunidad, entonces fue para mí como una puerta y yo aproveché para presentar toda la edición bilingüe de mi obra ya publicada en español en este libro" (When I was given the chance, then it was like an door opened for me and I seized the opportunity to present the entire bilingual edition of my work already published in Spanish in this book) (Ollé 2004: 214, my translation).

After the first editions published exclusively in the Spanish language, Ak'abal deliberately began to integrate more Maya K'iche' language in subsequent publications, self-translating from K'iche' to Spanish and vice versa. These practices differ from the process of translation, circulation, and cosmopolitanism associated with world literature approaches. The social status of Indigenous languages coupled with the reality of a Central American literary market in an uneven literary system determined the fate of his first publications. Another layer to this linguistic dimension of Indigenous literatures means that anthologies translated into French, Italian, or Japanese, are also the final product of multiple linguistic transfers.

Minorities, World Literature Theories, and Indigeneity

Several existing world literature theories elucidate aspects of Indigenous literatures but do not manage to capture their cosmolectical complexity. In the 2017 issue of the *Journal of World Literature*, Moberg and Damrosch propose the "ultraminor" as a new term to think of scale and cultural spaces beyond Deleuze and Guattari's "minor" literature. In Deleuze and Guattari's original proposition, they characterize minor literature as not emerging from a minor language but rather that which a minority creates within a major language and one that it is deterritorialized (1986: 16). With the "ultraminor," Moberg and Damrosch build on this work to announce a new way to broaden center-periphery relations, major and minor languages and spaces (2017: 133). Moberg and Damrosch take into account three important factors in relationship to the "ultraminor": translation, temporality, and space. Due to limited readers, they argue, the "ultraminor" depends on translation, and time is critical as some of these languages may be on the verge of extinction. They also discuss space as another vector of the "ultraminor" as the texts may emerge from a particular ethnic enclave or island. While these characterizations apply to the social and political status of Indigenous production, they cannot broach the process of self-translation, untranslatability, the standardization of Indigenous languages or the political role cosmologies play in the transmission of knowledge, and the solidarity practices that Indigeneity engenders particularly in the academy. Although the "ultraminor" is not about size or demographics, it suffers from the charged connotation of the term "minor." Said differently, the term "minor" is etymologically too close to minority which politically speaking is not the same as Indigenous, particularly in the legal international arena where Indigenous activists distanced themselves from such terms as well as "ethnic," preferring the use of Indigenous Peoples in all international legal instruments such as the Declaration of Indigenous Peoples (Niezen 2003). The "ultra-minor," while useful to a degree, lessens the linguistic and social potential of Indigenous literatures within Central America that vie for equal footing with national and global literature.

Among other world literature approaches that move beyond economic and political systems I find Pheng Cheah's work relevant in analyzing Indigenous works. In *What Is a World: On Postcolonial Literature as World Literature* Cheah "seeks to understand the normative force that literature can exert in the world, the ethicopolitical horizon it opens up for the existing world" (5). In other words, Ak'abal's oeuvre offers readers his perspective of the world as nature and his language as an entry point to this understanding. Indeed, as a global and cosmopolitan "from below" Maya K'iche' citizen, his Indigenous language links him to all sentient beings whether in Paris or Guatemala. Echoing Cheah's insights, Ak'abal's writing shares a new ethico-political horizon for relating with the nonhuman. And, while I find these theories useful in thinking through literature outside the metropolitan centers, cosmolectics more aptly redirect our understandings of the particularities of Indigenous literature, and to better appreciate Ak'abal's reworking of the West's partial ideas of the world. His emphasis on nature does not mean that he sees humans as separate or dominant or that he is uncritical of society, as his defiance toward a world that first denied his existence and then tried to disappear him is palpable, too. Rather, his poems present nature as a force or subject with agency like humans that can address injustice; for instance, in "Libertad" (Freedom), birds enact poetic justice by freely defecating on palaces and cathedrals—two centers of oppressive power for Indigenous Peoples. That poem reflects a cosmolectical engagement, for example wherein the nonhuman acquires agency and intervenes in society.

Cosmolectics and the Languages of Nature

In my book, I make the case that despite the uneven circulation of this literature from the periphery to the center, the most salient characteristic of Indigenous literature is the incessant dynamic between society and cosmos that reorients our gaze beyond the land. Ak'abal's poetry and narrative cultivate a vision that consciously encompasses the West. His relationship to other nations, regions, cosmopolitan centers is through his own Maya language because as Ak'abal asserted time and time again, nature speaks Indigenous languages, "Los barrancos, el viento, el agua, el fuego; todos hablan en nuestras lenguas" (The ravines, the wind, the water, the fire; they all speak in our languages) (quoted in Sánchez 2012a: 52, my translation). In the interview conducted by Ollé, he explains, "Cuando nosotros vemos relámpagos en el sur, sabemos que ya no va a llover y si es a mediados de la época de lluvia, entonces nos está anunciando la canícula, un periodo de dos semanas o de tres semanas en que no habrá lluvias. Y eso es infalible, es un lenguaje natural" (When we see lightning in the south, we know it is not going to rain anymore and if it is in the middle of the rainy season, then it is announcing the heat wave, a period of two weeks or three weeks in which there will be no rain. And that is infallible, it is a natural language) (2004: 211, my translation). Seeing nature as interpretive text, Ak'abal did not place more value on the written word or the book. Indeed, Ak'abal claimed that his first lessons about reading came from his grandparents who first taught him how to decipher or interpret nature. Reading the wind, fire, or bird sounds offers knowledge about the world. He states:

> Y aparte de eso, pues digamos, estoy hablando de un fenómeno en el cielo pero los cantos de los pájaros, los gritos de los animales, el comportamiento del viento, el comportamiento de los animales a parte de su voz, todo eso también tiene un lenguaje
>
> Besides let's say, I'm talking about a phenomenon in the sky but the songs of the birds, the cries of the animals, the behavior of the wind, the behavior of the animals, apart from their voice, all of that also has a language.
>
> (Ollé 2004: 211, my translation)

Furthermore, he did not adhere to a historical and cultural opposition of tradition and innovation, the written and the oral expression. He repeated that it was society that did not allow Indigenous Peoples to thrive culturally or economically in modern society. He repositioned the Indigenous subject as theme in dominant historical discourses to that of Indigenous Peoples as agents in the world. Literary critic, Juan Sánchez argues that Ak'abal is a "sujeto cosmopolita, global y transatlántico, que más allá de su ubicación (Europa, Japón, América) desafía los prejuicios y estereotipos sobre lo regional y lo étnico" ("cosmopolitan, global, and transatlantic subject who beyond his location [Europe, Japan, and America] defies prejudices and stereotypes of the regional and ethnic") (2012a: 122, my translation). While

Ak'abal's position was precisely that literature was universal, he based this assessment on other values that are not necessarily related to circulation or translation. He believed that his Maya K'iche' language facilitated his access and conversation with nature regardless of geography. In his poem "El canto viejo de la sangre" ("The Ancient Song of the Elders") he states that his language "nace de los árboles" ("is born from trees") and "tiene sabor a tierra" (tastes of earth) (my translation). He carried his own universe and connected to others through language. Wherever he traveled, through language.

Ak'abal resisted falling into stereotypical molds. He often said, he was not simply a poet of other literary influences but rather of confluences (Sánchez 2012a). By this assertion, he meant that he thought independently in K'iche' and in Spanish and discovered in the work of self-translation that one language enriched the other. And yet his global perspective cannot be disengaged from the colonial legacy that Spanish represents. In the fourth stanza of "El canto Viejo de la sangre" (The Ancient Song of the Elders), Ak'abal defiantly claims possession of the Spanish language as a right earned by the costly sacrifices endured by his ancestors: "Esta lengua es el recuerdo de un dolor/y la hablo sin temor ni verguenza/porque fue comprada/con la sangre de mis ancestros" (It is a language of painful memory / and I speak it without fear or embarrassment / as it was bought with the blood of my ancestors) (2010: 17, my translation). More than a strictly leftist political edge, his poetry embraces the dialectic between society and cosmos or cosmolectics, as I propose. For example, in yet another of his poems, "La flor amarilla de los sepulcros" ("The Yellow Flower of the Graves") Ak'abal turns to nature to indict injustice and murder against Maya Peoples. The poetic voice exhorts to the sun: "Sol! volvete humo, tizná el cielo,quemá la tierra, estamos de duelo, mi gente, mi sangre, mi pueblo ..." (Sun! turn to smoke, blacken the sky, burn the earth, we are in mourning, my people, my blood, my people ....) In some stanzas, it reads more like an incantation, "¡Que estallen los volcanes! / !Que arrojen fuego! / !Que tiemble, que se raje la tierra / y se trague todo, todo, todo! (let the volcanoes erupt, / let the fire out, / let the earth roar, / let the earth open and swallow it all, all, all!") (Ak'abal 2004: 17–26, my translation).

Other poems reflect the preeminence of nature and complexity of his language. Ak'abal's onomatopoeic poems about birds, wind, and rain prevail. His most famous onomatopoeic poem is "Canto de pájaros" (Bird Songs), which is meant to be heard rather then read in silence. (I recommend the YouTube version.) The poem reproduces the sounds of many birds:

Klis, klis, klis ...
Ch'ok, ch'ok, ch'ok ...
Tz'unun, tz'unun, tz'unun.

(Ak'abal 2000: 28)

The poem exemplifies onomatopoeia but also mirrors his language, that is his language equals nature.

As one of the most widely translated Maya poets in the last five decades, his work moves us through other notions of circulation, such as soundscapes, and other nonhuman subjects, as in this verse, "las piedras no son mudas; solo observan el silencio" (stones are not mute; they just observe silence). Stones here are not simply a poetic device of personification; they represent the Mayan ceremonial centers and stand in for culture, but more important, in the context of this short verse, a cosmolectical understanding of rocks as sentient beings. Ak'abal explains in an interview with Gerardo Guinea: "Bueno, nosotros creemos que cuanto más silencio guarda una persona, más sabiduría tiene …. Asi que al contemplar una piedra, con todo su silencio y mudez, uno concluye sencillamente que hay un universo de sabiduría adentro de ésta." (Well, we believe that the more a person maintains silence, the more wisdom they possess …. Therefore in contemplating a rock, with all of its silence and muteness, one simply concludes that there is a universe of wisdom within it) (quoted in Montemayor 1996: 24). Traditional storytelling, song, and reading nature are all part of his literary practices. In his poetry and narrative publications, there is an indigenization of other intellectual geographies as he offers us a Mayan cosmolectics. Ak'abal once wrote, "mi lectura de la literatura universal no ha sido en vano" (my reading of universal literature has not been in vain) (2010: 11, my translation). He did not reject or deny literary influences. In an interview about his cosmopolitan experiences and writing while residing in a number of countries such as Austria or Japan, he asserts,

> En este tipo de poesía, no obstante escrito en diversos países en los que he tenido la oportunidad de estar, sigo hablando de la naturaleza. Es cierto que aquí no hay cuervos pero hablo de los cuervos de por allá, hablo del coucou de los suizos, estoy hablando de los lobos de Italia.

> In this type of poetry, despite being written in various countries where I have had the opportunity to live, I continue to speak of nature. It is true that there are no crows here but I am talking about the crows over there, I am talking about the cuckoo of the Swiss, I am talking about the wolves of Italy.
>
> (Ollé 2004: 220, my translation)

His works embody the straddling of society and cosmos. In concert with other Indigenous writers, he proposes a vertical and horizontal dialogue between the cosmos and society thereby reproducing a Maya understanding of the universe as a geometric design supported by four pillars.

Maya Textile Influence on Cubist Art

Recognized more for his poetry than for his creative narrative, Ak'abal's short stories disentangle and reorganize the fragile threads that bind the local to the global. In one iconic story, "El Picasso que me asustó" (The Picasso that startled me) included in the collection, *Grito en la sombra* (2001) (Scream in the Shadow), the speaker describes being gripped by a strange sensation while touring a Pablo Picasso museum in Vienna. The poet relates this strange feeling to his Austrian companion who spoke fluent Maya K'iche', and per her suggestion they meander through the museum once more. Suddenly, he states feeling drawn to an untitled painting wherein Ak'abal recognizes his town's blanket /poncho designs. His Austrian companion ensures him Picasso never visited Guatemala. The painting, however, inspires him to track down any connection between Momostenango and Pablo Picasso—who by all accounts had never visited that part of the world. As the story continues in Paris, he relates the encounter with the untitled painting to another friend. Intrigued by the possibilities of Maya influence, they search books on Picasso. One of those books leads them to a postcard from the famous poet, close friend, and later assistant to Picasso, Jaume Sabartés (simply Jaime in the story). The poet had actually lived in Quetzaltenango for many years and had gifted Picasso a Momostecan blanket. The story tacitly links Maya influence on cubism, particularly as that untitled painting in Vienna is one of the first of Picasso's cubism period. Without tautological explanations, this story inverts the gaze of the world, ending with a conversation between friends on "weavings and weavers" and "paintings and painters" (2001: 25). In the short narrative, Ak'abal does not comment on cultural appropriation by the Spanish painter; he simply unveils to readers the hidden but global influence of Maya culture. He demonstrates that despite the fact that there is no acknowledgement of Maya geometric designs in Picasso's experience, the inspiration is undeniable. In effect, he demonstrates Maya influence in the world beyond the discourse of "discovery." Ak'abal provides readers with indelible proof of his local Momostecan ponchos' bearing on a major development in the art world.

Conclusion

Considering Humberto Ak'abal's trajectory as a poet but also in having known him as an incredibly open, curious, and spiritual human being, which can't be separated from his cultural output, I have offered some guiding remarks about approaching his work. His contribution to world literature as nature accessed through Indigenous languages must be read from a more expansive and capacious cosmolectics frame that requires pulling back the horizontal scale and decentering the world as imagined and disseminated by eurocentrism. His poems and short stories invite us toward cosmolectical readings that take the charting of the modern world to his pluri-verses and temporalities that coexist and cohabit. The formation of Humberto Ak'abal is also paradigmatic of an uneven, capitalist, cosmopolitan (from above), and unfair economic and political system that is national and global and yet his work also offers us a zest for life through the networks his language makes for us as readers and critics.

Indigenous writers like Humberto Ak'abal opened and established a growing literary field where they freely exercise their thoughts, feelings, and political agency but also offer a number of possible pluri-verses to dominant and narrow notions of the world. In Central American societies, where the persecution of Indigenous communities persists, Ak'abal had to imagine other worlds, establish international and transnational solidarities and communities of reading. His poem, "No'j/consejo" (Advice), beautifully recapitulates for me all his poetic and ideological work: "–Chattzijon ruj' japachinoq / man kachomaj taj che at mem / xub'ij ri numam chuwe. / ... / rech man kak'ex taj awech." / "Hablá con cualquiera/no vayan a pensar que sos mudo ... eso sí, tené cuidado que no te vuelvan otro" (–Talk to anyone / Lest they think that you are dumb / ... / careful that they don't turn you into an other) (Ak'abal 2004: 91).

Indigenous writers from Central America widen our perception and understanding of the world beyond recent theorizations of world literature through a cosmolectics. Ak'abal's pluri-verses allow us to see the world in the local as in Maya K'iche' aesthetics in a Picasso painting exhibited in Vienna. His poetic contributions carve a place for Indigenous Peoples in historical developments from the vantage point of someone who apprehends the world in its completeness, not from the West's partial gaze. As the speaker's grandfather mandates in the poem, "No'j/Consejo," the speaker must assert their subject position so as not to be minorized. Three years after he passed, in March of 2022, "El ultimo hilo" (The Last Thread) debuted in Denver, Colorado. This tribute to Ak'abal spearheaded by Joel Rinsema and Jake Runestad references his poem. Kantorei and Vocalis brought to life Ak'abal's verses in this choral piece. Renowned composer Runestad and artistic director Rinsema said, Ak'abal's verses spoke to them like no other poet had before. They connected to Ak'abal's words, reminding me that his poems open other ways of relating that engender solidarities where other worlds are possible as the Zapatistas insist.

References

Ak'abal, H. (1990), *El Animalero: Poemas*, Guatemala: Ministerio de Cultura y Deportes.

Ak'abal, H. (1996), "Literatura maya contemporánea." *Blanco Movil*, No. 70 8–9. Available online: http://www.blanconbovil.com.mx/pdf/BlancoMovil_70.pdf.
Ak'abal, H. (1998), *Ajkem tzij/Tejedor de palabras*, 2nd edition, Guatemala: Organización de las Naciones Unidas para la Educación, la Ciencia, y la Cultura.
Ak'abal, H. (2000), *Guardián de la caída*, Guatemala: Artemis Edinter.
Ak'abal, H. (2001), *Aqajtzij/ Palabramiel*, Guatemala: Nawal Wuj.
Ak'abal, H. (2001), *Grito en la sombra*, Guatemala: Artemis Edinter.
Ak'abal, H. (2001), *Ri tzij kek'iyij/Las palabras crecen*, Guatemala: Maya' Wuj.
Ak'abal, H. (2002), *Corazón de toro*, Guatemala: Artemis Edinter.
Ak'abal, H. (2004), *Raqonchi'aj*, Guatemala: Cholsamaj.
Ak'abal, H. (2019), *No permitas que el ayer se vaya lejos*, Bogotá: Universidad Javeriana.
Ak'abal, H. (2020), *El sueño de ser poeta*, Guatemala: Editorial Piedrasanta.
Casanova, P. (2004), *The World Republic of Letters*, tr. M. B. DeBevoise, Cambridge, Ma: Harvard University Press.
Chacón, G. (2018), *Indigenous Cosmolectics: Kab'awil and the Making of Maya and Zapotec Literatures*, Chapel Hill: UNC Press.
Cheah, P. (2014), "World against Globe: Toward a Normative Conception of World *Literature*, New Literary History." SUMMER, 45 (3): 303–29.
Cheah, P. (2016), *What Is a World? On Postcolonial Literature as World Literature*, Durham: Duke University Press.
Deleuze, G. and F. Guattari (1986), *Kafka: Toward a Minor Literature*, trans. D. Polan, Minneapolis: University of Minnesota Press.
Damrosch, D. (2003), *What Is World Literature?*, Princeton: Princeton University Press.
Lyons, S. R. (2018), *The World, the Text, and the Indian. Global Dimensions of Native American Literature*, NY: SUNY Press.
Moberg, R. and D. Damrosch (2017), "Defining the Ultraminor," *Journal of World Literature* (2): 133–7.
Montemayor, C. (1996), "La poesía de Humberto Ak'abal," in H. Ak'abal, *Ajkem Tzij. Tejedor de palabras*, 9–39, Guatemala: Asociación de amigos.
Nickels, J. (2018), *World Literature and the Geographies of Resistance*, Cambridge University Press. https://doi.org/10.1017/9781108581776.
Niezen, R. (2003), *The Origins of Indigenism : Human Rights and the Politics of Identity*, Berkeley: University of California Press.
Ollé, M. L. (2004), "Entretien avec Humberto Ak' abal," *Caravelle*, 82: 205–23. Doi: 10.3406/carav.2004.1469. Available online: http://www.persee.fr/doc/carav_1147-6753_2004_num_82_1_1469.
Quiroa, N. (2022), "The Popol Wuj and Central American Literature: Narratives of Resistance and Cultural Continuity," in G. Chacón and M. Albizúrez Gil (eds.), *Teaching Central American Literature in a Global Context*, 115–26, NY: MLA.
Sánchez, M. and J. Guillermo (2012a), "Detrás de las golondrinas, territorio en expansión: Los libros peregrinos de Humberto Ak'abal," *Revista de Humanidades*, 26 (Julio–Diciembre): 119–42.
Sánchez, M. and J. Guillermo (2012b), *Memoria e invención en la poesía de Humberto Ak'abal*. Available online: http://site.ebrary.com/id/10820742.

Siskind, M. (2014), *Cosmopolitan Desires: Global Modernity and World Literature in Latin America*, Evanston, Il: Northwestern University Press.
Warwick Research Collective (WReC) (2015), "Peripheral Modernisms" Working Papers, November 10, 2015. Available online: https://warwick.ac.uk/fac/arts/english/research/currentprojects/collective/wrec_papers/. Accessed September 7, 2022.
Weaver, J., C. S. Womack, and R. Warrior (2006), *American Indian Literary Nationalism*, Albuquerque: University of New Mexico Press.
Womack, C. (1999), *Red on Red: Native American Literary Separatism*, Minneapolis: University of Minnesota Press.

PART THREE

Routes

10

Canal Zone Modernism: Cendrars, Walrond, and Stevens at the "Suction Sea"

Harris Feinsod

This chapter is a narrowly drawn exercise in the comparison of modernist world literatures at one narrow passage of marine transit—the Panama Canal Zone. I argue that the spatiotemporality of the Canal Zone is a key figure in any history of modernist world literature at sea. To make this argument, I will first elicit the shared concerns of modernist sea literature— as represented by the Portuguese poet Fernando Pessoa—with the theory of world literature proposed by the German philologist Eric Auerbach. Following this account of modernist world literature into the Canal Zone, I will compare literary works by the Swiss avant-garde poet Blaise Cendrars, the West Indian writers Claude McKay and Eric Walrond, the Nicaraguan poet Ernesto Cardenal, and the American modernist poet Wallace Stevens. These writers all glance past one another in their representation of the conflicts, disparities, and experiments in sovereignty that characterizes the Panama Canal Zone as a peculiar choke point of maritime globalization. In choosing not to focus this account on a Panamanian national literature of the Canal, by no means do I mean to discount Panama's own literatures from its claim on world literary space. To the contrary, I suggest that Panama's political geography ought to claim a special purchase on world literature as a whole—in this case, from the French avant-garde to the Harlem Renaissance—once we begin to observe the complex interweave of imperial projects and anticolonial subjects that steam past one another in the Canal's locks and along its banks.[1]

Modernist World Literature at the Great Primordial Wharf

An illusion of cosmopolitan choice accompanies a reader of world literature who contemplates transoceanic modernism's many ports of embarkation and transshipment—Antwerp, Buenos Aires, Colón, Hamburg, Lisbon, San Francisco, Santos, Yokohama, and so on. It is the sort of illusion rhapsodized by Portuguese poet Fernando Pessoa's heteronym Álvaro de Campos, the British naval engineer whose poem "Ode marítima" (Maritime Ode, 1915) praises "O Grande Cais Anterior" (The Great Primordial Wharf) from which he gazes out upon the world (Pessoa 1915a: 71; Pessoa 2006: 168). Intoxicated by modernity's quayside coal fumes, Campos expresses in his expansive odes a futurist fantasy of union with the very engines of oceanic passage and the cargoes they carry: "Içam-me em todos os cais. / Giro dentro das hélices de todos os navios" (I'm hoisted up on every dock. I spin in the propellers of every ship). Even Campos's most conditional, reflective lamentations intensify and broaden his yearning for seaborne totality: "Ah não ser eu toda a gente e toda a parte!" (Ah if only I could be all people and all places) (Pessoa 1915b: 106; Pessoa 2006: 160). In this sort of *saudade* (longing), I cannot help but hear a modernist amplification of the famous Andrew Marvell complaint—"Had we but world enough and time"—that looms large as an epigraph over Erich Auerbach's *Mimesis*, another of the early twentieth century's boldest attempts at a world literary synthesis. And in hearing this echo, it seems to me that Pessoa's poetic predicament—how to write the world poetry of the sea—is linked closely to the problems and methods of comparative literary history as it has sought to account for the nature and structure of world literature. Such a linking certainly makes sense if we understand comparative literary history in Auerbach's terms: as a tension among "diverse backgrounds" converging on a "common fate," accessed by a method that seeks out multiple "points of departure" coalescing around a synthetic or "coadunatory" intuition (Auerbach 1969). A reader of transoceanic modernism, balancing the impulses of Pessoa and Auerbach, might well desire to be hoisted up on every dock and to spin in the propellers of every ship—to take in a synthetic view of a cosmopolitan totality made of human cultures fated, by commerce and technology, to connect as never before.

At the time of its completion in 1914, the Panama Canal represented this connective ideology perhaps more than any other infrastructure of maritime modernity, and many celebrated its role in the spatiotemporal compression of the world. From the standpoint of world literary history, it is therefore just the sort of point of departure around which Auerbach's synthetic intuition could organize comparative literary space. And yet, in the Canal Zone as at so many other zones of transit, modernist writers often confronted obstructions to the synthetic cosmopolitanism desired or observed by Pessoa and Auerbach, obstructions that took such forms as customs houses, immigration bureaus and passport control, deferred wages, toil and illness, state surveillance, and world war. Thus the linking of transoceanic modernism to the question of world literature must account for a system defined at once by intensifying flows of connection and proliferating blockages. The commercial forms and regulatory regimes of transoceanic technologies like the great liner, the tramp steamer, the commerce raider, the canal tug, and the coastal barge each resynthesize the dialectic between free trade and protectionism, fluid and impeded transit. Literary works situated in the micropolitical environments of such ships, or at their various ports of call, do not follow Auerbach's "coadunatory intuition" so much as they express a version of Aamir Mufti's claim that "world literature, far from being a seamless and traversable space, has in fact been from the beginning a regime of *enforced* mobility and therefore of *immobility* as well" (2016: 5). For every Álvaro de Campos, some other character like Claude McKay's Ginger in *Banjo* shows up "on the beach": undocumented, out of work, and booted by immigration bureaus around the Atlantic (McKay 1929: 5).

In all the coastal nations of the modernizing world, often-discarded works of literature and art—proletarian novels, sentimental plays, avant-garde poems, lyric sea diaries, silent films, radical leaflets, photographs, and paintings—attest to this push and pull of connection and blockage and string its tension along several axes of identity and difference. Each work can be understood as a strand in a cat's cradle (Morse 1989: 61–89) of crossings between competing sociopolitical discourses of maritime space, including syndicalism and statism, communism and commerce, exile and empire. Some works may go so far as to allegorize the entire system. However, when the archives of modernism at sea are viewed from the perspective of a given national literature or language tradition, these worldly entanglements tend to appear obscure. This may be true even in our contemporary age of transnational and oceanic scholarly turns, for too often an Anglosphere can be mistaken for the world and an ocean for a transactional arena of fluid connection. In recent years I have sought to articulate a different kind of transoceanic modernism whose worldwide imaginaries do not vindicate the usual language of accelerating connections and simultaneities so much as they trace the outlines of missed appointments, deferred arrivals, lags, collisions (Feinsod 2015), and bad connections (Miller et. al. 2018). In my view, these negative experiences most often frame the expression of maritime modernism, and any given work tropes this comparative problem of modernist world literature (Feinsod 2018). In doing so, this work's discursive situation tends to implicate other disconnected works from within the maritime world system and to draw in even those works that might refuse the very terms of comparison.

For instance, a poem about the economic rationales for migrant labor in the perilous enterprise of canal construction will tend to cast in new light a poem about the speculators and financiers of such an enterprise. Likewise, a story about laboring in the shadows of a great liner will tend to cast in a new light a poem about reveling in a sunny passage on its decks and vice versa. And so here we can begin to chart a contrapuntal Panama Canal Zone according to Cendrars and McKay, Walrond and Stevens.

The Panama Panic

... the Panama Canal, mechanical toy that Messrs. Roosevelt and Goethals managed to make work when everyone else had failed; a lot of trouble for the inhabitants of the two Americas you have dammed up within your giant locks.

—JOHN DOS PASSOS, "HOMER OF THE TRANSSIBERIAN"

"C'est le crach du Panama que fit de moi un poète!" (It's the Panama panic that made me a poet!) exclaims the speaker of Cendrars's long poem *Le Panama ou Les aventures de mes septs oncles* (Panama, or the Adventures of My Seven Uncles) (1918: n.p.; 1931, n.p.). The "crash" or "panic" in question is the bankruptcy and liquidation in 1888–9 of the French Panama Canal Company, directed by Ferdinand de Lesseps. At that time Cendrars was a two-year-old Swiss boy named Frédéric-Louis Sauser, but it is true that the specter of the crash proved a source of childhood anguish to the young "Freddy," whose father had quit his job teaching math in the watchmaking town of La Chaux-de-Fonds to participate in a rash of increasingly risky and ruinous financial speculations of the sort excoriated by Émile Zola's novel *L'argent* (Money, 1891). These included a hotel venture in Heliopolis, Egypt; a German beer export scheme; and an Italian land deal, as well as investments in the canal (Bochner 1978: 16).

In *Le Panama* Cendrars associates the crash's "importance plus universelle" (universal importance) with the shattering of his generation's comfortable youth. "Car il a bouleversé mon enfance" (it turned my childhood upside down), he recalls:

Mon pére perdit les ¾ de sa fortune
Comme nombre d'honnêtes gens qui perdirent leur argent dans ce crach,
Mon père
Moins bête
Perdait celui des autres.

(Cendrars 1918)

My father lost three-fourths of his fortune
Like a number of upright people who lost their money in that crash,
My father
Less stupid
Lost other people's money.

(Cendrars 1992: 34)

While these events are verifiable elements of Cendrars's notoriously cloudy biography, the incendiary personae of Cendrars's poems rarely speak with a strong commitment to autobiographical veracity. Instead, they voice collective and allegorical aspirations for the project of literature in the age of a shrinking, technomodern world—a world conceived of as canalized and crossed by an ever more routine latticework of steamers, railways, and cables.

Accordingly, we might extrapolate from the exclamation "C'est le crach du Panama que fit de moi un poète!" an underdeveloped origin story for the cascading international avant-gardes of the next several decades. By Cendrars's logic, the avant-garde's poetic vocation was structured by financial speculations of roving state-private infrastructure projects in an era when they began to replace formal empire and attentive colonial administrations with neglectful leases, the wobbly legal regimes of "assigned sovereignty" (DuVal 1940: 31), the onset of "petromodernity" (LeMenager 2014; Whalan 2017), precarious migrant labor, the production of civil conflicts (Mufti 2016: 85–134), commodity capitalism stitched together by huge communication and transportation networks, and new, extraterritorial zones of free trade. As the architectural theorist Keller Easterling has noted, the Export Processing Zone (EPZ) and the Free Trade Zone (FTZ) that now dominate the spatial form of capitalism were imagined for Panama's Colón as early as 1917, just three years after the first ship transited the completed canal. They were enacted in 1948 (2014: 29–30).

Therefore Cendrars's exclamation suggests an aesthetic modernism at the dawn of "the zone." To be clear, this is neither Mary Louise Pratt's "contact zone" nor Guillaume Apollinaire's Parisian "Zone" but the Canal Zone itself: scion of "historic entrepots and free ports" and predecessor to contemporary EPZs and FTZs, the typologies that, according to Easterling, have rapidly emerged from a backstage "enclave for warehousing and manufacturing" to become the templates of the "world city" (2014: 25). If Pratt's model of the contact zone asks us to put together our comparative understanding of global modernism through a focus on the relationships between "travelers and travelees" (Pratt 2008: 7–8), the Canal Zone invites us to note the relations of concerns and interests colliding in the teeth of convulsive spatiotemporal and economic logics: booms and busts, annexation and assigned sovereignty, migratory labor and geo-engineering at sublime scales. Hardly the radiant metropolis associated with the historical avant-garde of Apollinaire, the zone is nonetheless the site of an experimental poetry that "beat a rhythm," in Dos Passos's phrase, from an "age of giant machines and scuttleheaded men" (1927: 202). The literature of the zone renders visible the collisions of financial, infrastructural, and labor conditions.

Among the avuncular diaspora of Cendrars's *Le Panama*, none of the uncles works the canal per se, but all seven face their fortunes in the shadows of the infrastructural, planetary transformation it represents. These include the "butcher in Galveston" who "disappeared in the cyclone of 1895"; the cabin boy on the tramp steamer who turns into a gold prospector in California and Alaska; and the railroader in India who becomes a Buddhist anarchist, plotting anti-imperial violence against the British in Bombay. Cendrars's uncles might therefore be regarded as latter-day "heads" on the "many-headed hydra" that, in struggles with the Herculean forces of capitalism, constitute the master trope of the revolutionary Atlantic for the radical historians Marcus Rediker and Peter Linebaugh (2000: 2–6). Correspondingly, any "hydro-criticism" worth its salt will also probably want to be a *hydra*-criticism, attentive to the social histories and foreclosed political futures of stateless sailors, deportees, coalers, wharf rats, and other subjects of dispossession forever emerging in the press of neglectful imperial circumstance (Winkiel 2019).

Cendrars portrays his own vanguard company trailing in the wake of these obliterated people on the speculative fringes of capitalist expansion. His poet belongs to a generation of "Jeunes gens / Qui ont subi des ricochets étranges" (Young people / who experienced weird ricochets), who scrounge their way around the globe shipboard in "la cage des méridiens" (the cage of meridians), to quote one of Cendrars's many ways of deflating the glamour of steamer travel (1992: 38). In his own "baptême de la ligne" (baptism of the line) on a 1912 Atlantic crossing more routine than the one he pictures for his nineteenth-century uncles, Cendrars nonetheless imagined that "j'ai partagé tous les sorts du marin. Beau temps des premiers jours, enchantements, vagues, vents, tempêtes, ouragan, dépontement, avaries, dérive, refuge dans un port de fortune. Je n'attendais pas ces choses au XXe" (Cendrars 1969: 178) (I shared all the sailor's spells. Initial days of fair weather, enchantments, waves, winds, storms, the hurricane, a swerve, damage, drift, the fortunate port of refuge. I did not expect these things in the 20th C). In the fauvist artist Raoul Dufy's cover image for *Le Panama*, a send-up of a railway timetable, Cendrars's name adorns a life preserver, aligning avant-garde authorship with salvage work in a decade defined by maritime disasters from the *Titanic* to the *Lusitania*.

The Slow Cyclone

Beginning with mid-nineteenth-century projects helmed by competing French and American surveyors to cut diverse trans-isthmian routes through Nicaragua and Panama, the story of the Canal Zone is well known to us from histories focused on sublime feats of engineering as well as revisionary labor and colonial history (McCullough 1977). In such accounts, the canal emblematizes the age of the "shrinking world" (Rosenberg 2012) and what Julio Ramos calls "hemispheric compression" (2001)—a swift, commoditized connectivity, often anthropomorphized in boosterist artworks as a "kiss" of the Atlantic and Pacific. Yet, in the framework of transnational and comparative literary history, the shrinking world enabled by the Canal Zone hardly unites the Central American, Caribbean, US, and European vanguardists who variously inhabited it. What would it mean to recompose a literary history of global modernism around the zone, instead of around conventional literary-historical categories of connectivity such as exchange, translation, circulation, intertextuality, and the like? From competing standpoints and historical removes, writers including Cendrars (Switzerland), Stevens (the United States), Walrond (British Guiana), McKay (Jamaica), Cardenal (Nicaragua), Demetrio Aguilera Malta (Ecuador), Malcolm Lowry (England), Olive Senior (Jamaica), and Juan Gabriel Vásquez (Colombia) all investigate the zone's complex temporalities: sometimes luxuriating in swift cruises to and fro, but more often commenting on its slow, grinding excavations, its swelling locks, its rusting hulks among liana vines, its demolished political horizons and laboring bodies.

In his 1954 poem "Greytown" Cardenal charts this desolate century of speculative development projects that has just passed "como un lento ciclón" (like a slow cyclone) at the great primordial "pier of the Americas" (Cardenal 1984: 78–9). Cardenal's poem offers an anti-imperialist reversal of Ezra Pound's historical montage poetics, ironizing the failures of Cornelius Vanderbilt's Nicaraguan canal projects of the 1850s. At first these projects draw in an exuberantly multilingual, migrant labor community: "Americanos, alemanes, irlandeses, / franceses, mulatos, chinos, españoles, / venían, se encontraban aquí, y partían" (Americans, Germans, Irishmen, / Frenchmen, mulattoes, Chinamen, Spaniards, / they'd all come, meet each other here, and leave). But when they rove elsewhere, all they leave behind is one mendicant freebooter who could easily have been one of Cendrars's "uncles": "Edwards E. Brand, de Kentucky, fue el último norteamericano / que se quedó en Greytown, esperando el Canal" (Edwards E. Brand, from Kentucky, was the last North American / who stayed in Greytown, waiting for the canal) (Cardenal 1984: 78–9). Barefoot among the corroded hulls of the paddlewheel steamers that Vanderbilt's concerns have discarded on the shoals of the Mosquito Coast, Brand no longer works as an agent of nascent US imperialism but is fated instead to receive Nicaraguan alms. Cardenal beggars the imperial agencies that arrive at what he calls "the pier of the Americas." Cardenal was therefore uniquely equipped to emerge from retirement for a withering editorial (Cardenal 2014) against President Daniel Ortega's concession of a no-bid Nicaraguan canal project to the Chinese Telecom magnate Wang Jin—part of a new "connectography" (Khanna 2016) and Belt and Road initiative (Chin 2013) that makes our age of capricious interoceanic cuts a cynical replay of the first age of liberal globalization that Cardenal had previously decried.

Within Cardenal's slow century, certain synchronic flashpoints make visible the disparate histories of modernism in the zone, such as the decade or so surrounding the Panama Canal's completion in 1914. To put the works of that decade in dialogue with Cendrars's *Le Panama* is to signal the diverse ideologemes the zone represented for Latin American, Francophone, Afro-Caribbean, and Anglo-American modernisms. It renders the Canal Zone not as a feat of connectivity or connectography but as a site of visibility for the conflicting patterns of representation making up a situation of ongoing cultural and ideological disconnection.

The Suction Sea

McKay's dialect poem "Peasants' Ways o' Thinkin'" (1912) suggests the logics by which West Indian migrant labor assembled at the canal.

> We hea' a callin' from Colon,
> We hea' a callin' from Limon,
> Let's quit de t'ankless toil an' fret
> Fe where a better pay we'll get.
>
> (McKay 2004: 11)

The poem's pursuant pro and con calculations are extensive and precise. According to McKay's speaker, the migrant stands to face a regime of legal discrimination and a society that does not recognize Obeah religion. He faces the incalculably bad trade-off of Jamaican rum for Latin American beer and will suffer the loss of sexual gratification, the comfort of family, the experience of village integrity, and more. He will have to learn a new language, do hard labor without weekends off, and face exposure to tropical disease. But face it he will, for the peasant imagines the possibility of remitting money to his family and the promise of a triumphant homecoming rather than permanent diaspora. McKay's peasant can even resign Black Jamaicans to a lesser lot than "buccra" (white folk), for like the white of an egg, he announces, "we content wi' de outside."

This kind of resignation seemed implausible to some West Indian writers in the zone. Stories such as "The Wharf Rats" in Walrond's *Tropic Death* (1926), which recollects the world of Colón that Walrond witnessed as the child of a "Panama Man," valorize "the motley crew recruited to dig the Panama Canal" as "artisans from the four ends of the earth" (Walrond 2013: 67). And, even if "dusky peon" imperial subjects of the British, French, and Dutch Caribbean supply "the bulk of the actual brawn," Walrond's validation of artisanship over peasant mentality signals an important politicization of Canal Zone labor (Owens 2016).

But as far as the Canal Zone is concerned, Walrond also charts more extreme forms of precarity than McKay. In the simple plot of "The Wharf Rats," a West Indian family lives in a shanty by the Colón coaling station. Whenever the tourist ships arrive, two boys—Philip and Earnest—go out in a little rowboat to dive for coins that wealthy passengers toss into the sea. Finally, owing to a convoluted love triangle, a spurned and vindictive woman named Maffi, who practices Obeah, probably curses Philip to his fate: a death by shark attack as he dives in the murky waters for the tourists' coins. The ship for which Philip performs his final dive is named *Kron Prinz Wilhelm*, a ship with an important history (though one that only tangentially includes the Canal Zone).[2] Walrond peoples the ship's deck with wealthy spectators: "Huddled in thick European coats, the passengers" of the ship "viewed from their lofty estate the spectacle of two naked Negro boys peeping up at them from a wiggly *bateau*" (2013: 80). Here Walrond offers a stark contrast between West Indian migrant labor and a form of tourism that collapses belle epoque and interwar tropes—more stark even than the protocubist class allegory of Alfred Stieglitz's photograph *The Steerage*. For Philip represents a class that does not access steerage passage. Instead, it earns its living from rickety skiffs in the shadows of the imperial liners, and only when passengers are amused by tossing scraps of multinational currency—American pennies and quarters, British sovereigns, Dutch guilders—into the shark-infested waters. Walrond's description of these waters, as the mixed-up currency sinks, makes it plain how they are figures for the maelstroms of investment and ruination that power the spatial typology of the zone: "It was a suction sea, and down in it Philip plunged. And it was lazy, too, and willful—the water. Ebony-black, it tugged and mocked. Old brass staves—junk dumped there by the retiring French—thick, yawping mud, barrel hoops, tons of obsolete brass, a wealth of slimy steel faced him" (2013: 82). The half-submerged ruins of the abandoned project of de Lesseps—where "Iron staves bruised his shins" (2013: 82) —prefigure the Middle Passage chains rolling at the bottom of Édouard Glissant's Atlantic (1997: 6), but Walrond's story is motivated less by the master trope of slavery than by the specific disaster of the "Panama Panic." And here the "yawping mud" deflates the preferred Whitmanian term for voicing New World praise poetry, as if belching a critique of Whitman's celebrations of de Lesseps's Suez Canal in "Passage to India" (2002: 346).

A cruel irony presides over the fact that Walrond's attention to de Lessep's discarded remnants, which linger so menacingly as rusted metal in the dark waters of "The Wharf Rats," would only ever be realized as their own fragmentary ruin. Walrond arrived in Paris in 1928 to continue research on a major work of muckraking Canal Zone history, *The Big Ditch*, supported by a Guggenheim grant and an advance from Liveright. He promised to do for the canal what C. L. R. James would do for the Haitian Revolution. In Paris, Walrond doled out praise on Cendrars, noting his particular esteem for *Le Panama*. Liveright advertised *The Big Ditch* in a 1928 catalog, but by 1930 the press had broken the contract for the hundred-thousand-word book. Walrond later serialized pieces of it as "The Second Battle" in *Roundway Review*, the newsletter of the sanatorium where he resided in the 1950s. They are yet to be republished (Davis 2015: 325–31).

Sea Surface

Stevens is among the best-known writers to take the kind of cruise for which Walrond's coin divers performed. He departed from New York on October 18, 1923, aboard the SS *Kroonland* of the Panama Pacific line, calling in Havana, Colón, Tijuana, and finally Los Angeles. His first and only trip through the canal was also his farthest trip south. His wife, Elsie, kept an elliptical diary on the trip, toward the end of which they conceived their daughter. Stevens also conceived a celebrated poem, "Sea Surface Full of Clouds," venerating the choreography of water and sky off the Tehuantepec peninsula. It was one of Stevens's only poems between *Harmonium* (1923) and *Owl's Clover* (1936). It was also the *Kroonland*'s first trip through the canal since 1915.[3] A photographer captured the ship,

FIGURE 10.1 The SS *Kroonland* of the Panama Pacific Line passes southbound through the Panama Canal–Gaillard Cut on October 25, 1923. Wallace and Elsie Stevens are aboard. James Gordon Steese Family Papers. Courtesy of Dickinson College Archives and Special Collections, Carlisle, Pennsylvania.

newly retrofitted, painted white, and put into use in the trans-isthmian pleasure industry in October 1923, in transit through the Pedro Miguel Lock on the canal, October 25, 1923 (Figure 10.1). Wallace and Elsie can be imagined promenading somewhere in the frame. That same day Elsie describes the "changeable weather" along the canal and a visit ashore to shop for luxury goods in the free zone, ferried about by a "colored driver" who "spoke English as well as any ordinary darky in Hartford" (Lensing 1986). Observing the casual racism of Elsie's account, it should not surprise us that scholars know Stevens to have trafficked in racist codes throughout his career (Galvin 2016), nor that passengers on Panama Pacific cruises participated in blackface pageantry and cross-class masquerades, as visible in the promotional film on the Panama Pacific Line *Over Sapphire Seas* (1934).

In "Sea Surface Full of Clouds" Stevens's readers have observed a postsymbolist exercise in the production of metaphor through the repetitious, narcissistic descriptions of the "obese machine" of sky and ocean, but in his luxuriant pose of touristic description, outrageous moments of cartoonish racial masquerade interrupt placid reflection:

And the sea as turquoise-turbaned Sambo, neat
At tossing saucers—cloudy-conjuring sea?
C'était mon esprit bâtard, l'ignominie.

(Stevens 1997: 85)

Walrond's "suction sea" and Stevens's "sea as turquoise-turbaned Sambo" each are forged in racialized revisions of belle epoque literary aspiration, but they do not reflect or embrace each other as do the sea and sky of Stevens's poem. Instead, they begin to suggest how the Canal Zone's compression of hemispheric space enabled only stark consolidations of racial and class divisions. Walrond's Philip dives to his death for the tourists in the same sea Stevens imagines as a reflection of blackface cruise-line pageantry, cut through with the affectations of the French symbolists, whose language Cendrars had sought to jettison.

Another peculiar fact presides over Stevens's placid transits over the "suction sea." He passes over the ruined subaqueous world of de Lesseps that Walrond makes vivid, content to read the water's glimmering surface as the mirror of his inventive acoustical pleasures. But over the next decades Stevens was no stranger to the risky speculations involved in infrastructural projects on the order of the canal or what he calls the "writhing wheels of this world's business" in his poem "Repetitions of a Young Captain" (Stevens 1997: 273). In fact, Stevens devoted his career to precisely the financial instruments designed to interrupt another "Panama panic." During Stevens's tenure as a bond surety lawyer and later as vice president of the Hartford Accident and Indemnity, the company underwrote construction contracts bonding large-scale transportation and security infrastructure projects, including the Hoover Dam (completed 1931), the San Francisco–Oakland Bay Bridge and the Golden Gate Bridge (completed 1936), the Saint Lawrence Seaway (completed 1959), and the Texas Towers (completed 1958), Cold War radar outposts anchored in the Atlantic for the detection of attacks (Daniel 1960: 267). But earlier, in the reflective, glittering surfaces of Stevens's poetics, he fashioned distinct bulwarks against Walrond's imagination of the coin diver and its knowledge of the social costs of infrastructural finance.

In all, the financing and construction of an infrastructure space like the Panama Canal Zone—a figure for maritime globalization as the spatial form of capitalism—invite us to reassemble a vision of worldwide modernism structured by disparities among destructive French speculators, the acrobatic West Indians who perform their work among jagged ruins, and the Anglo-American tourist-spectators who take in such performances from aloft. This sort of comparative purchase, from the "wiggly *bateau*" down after the guilders and sovereigns toward the submerged ruins of de Lesseps, and then again up toward the decks of the SS *Kroonland*, might be a model for an account of modernism and the sea that rejects the surface view of Stevens in order to work across divides of class, language, and culture and that remains sensitive to colliding stories of money and labor, cosmopolitan mobility and immobility. Such collisions suggest that a "slow cyclone" or a "suction sea" might be maritime figures that reveal more about how worlds come to connect than do a kiss of the Atlantic and the Pacific or a "sea surface full of clouds."

Notes

1 This view of twentieth-century Canal Zone literatures concurs with Dennis Hogan's recent efforts to constitute a comparative archive of the Transit Zones in the nineteenth century, ranging from Mary Seacole and Anthony Trollope to Julio Ardila and Amelia Denis de Icaza. It further chimes with recent efforts by Sophie Esch and Valeria Grinberg Pla to reorganize our understanding of the twentieth-century transit zones in relation to key episodes in world literature. See Hogan (forthcoming and 2021); Esch (2020); and Grinberg Pla (2020). On the Panamanian *narrativa canalera* see also Ana Patricia Rodríguez (2009) and extensive corpus by Luis Pulido Ritter (2013).

2 The actual SS *Kronprinz Wilhelm* never made port near the Canal Zone during its tenure as one of the great prewar German passenger liners. In 1914 the German Imperial Navy requisitioned it as a commerce raider, in which role it captured and sank fifteen British ships off the coast of Brazil in the year before low supplies forced it to dock at then-neutral Newport News, Virginia, where nearly one thousand crew members and officers from the captured ships

remained as "guests," building a scrap village called Eitel Wilhelm. The SS *Kronprinz Wilhelm* was rechristened the USS *Von Steuben* and commissioned as a US naval auxiliary vehicle involved in troop transport, leading to its only stop in the Canal Zone to recoal in 1918. The young Walrond might well have seen it on that occasion while working as a journalist for the *Panama Star*, even if it was no longer sailing under the German flag. Walrond's anachronistic placing of the *Kronprinz Wilhelm* in the zone therefore links the relations in maritime history between prewar Euro-American passenger tourism, wartime commerce raiding, and US military involvement.

3   Christened in 1902, the SS *Kroonland* served twelve years, running from Antwerp to New York for the Belgian Red Star Line. Reflagged as an American ship in 1911 for preferential tax purposes, it was put briefly into use as a Canal Zone mail carrier. Repainted in dazzle camouflage, it served as a troop transport ship from 1917 to 1920 and thence returned briefly to the Red Star Line before two years in the Panama Pacific Line. After this it spent two years running from New York to Miami, but the same hurricane of 1926 that Hart Crane experienced on the Isle of Pines destroyed the tourist market the SS *Kroonland* served, and it was scrapped in 1927.

References

Auerbach, E. (1969), "Philology and *Weltliteratur*," trans. Maire Said and Edward Said, *Centennial Review*, 13 (1): 1–17.

Bochner, J. (1978), *Blaise Cendrars: Discovery and Re-creation*, Toronto: University of Toronto Press.

Cardenal, E. (1984), *With Walker in Nicaragua and Other Early Poems (1949–1954)*, trans. J. Cohen, Middletown, CT: Wesleyan University Press.

Cardenal, E. (2014), "La monstruosidad del Canal," *La prensa: El diario de los nicaragüenses*: January 11. www.laprensa.com.ni/2014/11/01/columna-del-dia/216594-dla-monstruosidad-del-canal.

Cendrars, B. (1918), *Le Panama ou Les aventures de mes sept oncles*, Paris: Sirène.

Cendrars, B. (1931), *Panama; or, The Adventures of My Seven Uncles*, trans. J. D. Passos, New York: Harper and Brothers.

Cendrars, B. (1969), *Inédits secrets*, Paris: Club Français du Livre.

Cendrars, B. (1992), *Complete Poems*, trans. R. Padgett. Berkeley: University of California Press.

Chin, T. (2013), "The Invention of the Silk Road, 1877." *Critical Inquiry*, 40 (1): 194–219.

Conniff, M. L. (1985), *Black Labor on a White Canal: Panama, 1904–1981*, Pittsburgh, PA: University of Pittsburgh Press.

Daniel, H. (1960), *The Hartford of Hartford: An Insurance Company's Part in a Century and a Half of American History*, New York: Random House.

Davis, J. (2015), *Eric Walrond: A Life in the Harlem Renaissance and the Transatlantic Caribbean*, New York: Columbia University Press.

Dos Passos, J. (1926), "Homer of the Transsiberian." *Saturday Review of Literature*, October 16.
DuVal, Commander M. P., Jr. (1940), *Cadiz to Cathay: The Story of the Long Struggle for a Waterway across the American Isthmus*, Stanford, CA: Stanford University Press.
Easterling, K. (2020), *Extrastatecraft: The Power of Infrastructure Space*, New York: Verso, 2014.
Esch, S. (2020), "Passages, Transits, Flows: Thinking Central American Literature across Space, Time, and Capital," *Revista de Estudios Hispánicos*, 54 (1): 7–24.
Feinsod, H. (2015), "Vehicular Networks and the Modernist Seaways: Crane, Lorca, Novo, Hughes," *American Literary History*, 27 (4): 683–716.
Feinsod, H. (2018), "Death Ships: The Cruel Translations of the Interwar Maritime Novel." *Modernism/modernity* Print Plus, 3, cycle 3: https://doi.org/10.26597/mod.0063.
Galvin, R. (2016), "Race," in G. McLeod (ed.), *Wallace Stevens in Context*, 286–96, Cambridge: Cambridge University Press.
Glissant, É. (1997), *Poetics of Relation*, trans. B. Wing. Ann Arbor: University of Michigan Press.
Greene, J. (2009), *The Canal Builders: Making America's Empire at the Panama Canal*, New York: Penguin.
Grinberg Pla, V. (2020), "El tránsito como estrategia de vida y de literature: el Proyecto literario transnacional en resistencia de los intelectuales afrocaribeños Eric Walrond, Claude McKay y Samuel Nation." *Revista Estudios Hispánicos*, 54 (1): 49–72.
Hogan, D. (2021), "Building the Nation in the Bay of Panama: Julio Ardila's Josefina," Unpublished conference paper, Modernism's Working Waterfronts, American Comparative Literature Association Annual Conference.
Hogan, D. (2023), ""All Ways Open to all Men": Anthony Trollope and Mary Seacole in The Central American Transit Zones." *ELH*, 90 (1): 137–165.
Khanna, P. (2016), *Connectography: Mapping the Future of Global Civilization*, New York: Random House.
LeMenager, S. (2014), *Living Oil: Petroleum Culture in the American Century*, Oxford: Oxford University Press.
Lensing, G. (1986), "Mrs. Wallace Stevens' 'Sea Voyage' and 'Sea Surface Full of Clouds,'" *American Poetry*, 3 (3): 76–84.
Linebaugh, P. and M. Rediker (2000), *The Many-Headed Hydra: Sailors, Slaves, Commoners, and the Hidden History of the Revolutionary Atlantic*, Boston: Beacon.
McCullough, D. (1977), *The Path between the Seas: The Creation of the Panama Canal, 1870–1914*, New York: Simon and Schuster.
McKay, C. (1929), *Banjo: A Story without a Plot*, New York: Harper.
McKay, C. (2004), *Complete Poems*, ed. William J. Maxwell, Urbana: University of Illinois Press.
Miller, J., and G. Rogers (2018), "Introduction: Only Disconnect?," *Modernism/Modernity*, Print Plus, 3 (3): https://doi.org/10.26597/mod.0062.
Morse, R. (1989), *New World Soundings: Culture and Ideology in the Americas*, Baltimore, MD: Johns Hopkins University Press.

Mufti, A. (2016), *Forget English! Orientalisms and World Literatures*, Cambridge, MA: Harvard University Press.
Mufti, N. (2017), *Civilizing War: Imperial Politics and the Poetics of National Rupture*, Evanston, IL: Northwestern University Press.
Newton, V. (1984), *The Silver Men: West Indian Labour Migration to Panama, 1850–1914*, Kingston: Institute of Social and Economic Research, University of the West Indies.
Owens, I. D. (2016), "'Hard Reading': US Empire and Black Modernist Aesthetics in Eric Walrond's *Tropic Death*," *MELUS*, 41 (4): 96–115.
Pessoa, F. [Álvaro de Campos] (1915a), "Ode marítima," *Orpheu*, 2: 71.
Pessoa, F. [Álvaro de Campos] (1915b), "Ode triunfal," *Orpheu*, 1: 108.
Pessoa, F. (2006), *A Little Larger than the Entire Universe: Selected Poems*, trans. R. Zenith, New York: Penguin.
Pulido Ritter, L. (2013). La "novela canalera" en Carlos Guillermo "Cubena" Wilson. *Cuadernos Inter.c.a.mbio sobre Centroamérica y el Caribe*, 10 (11): 37–47.
Pratt, M. L. (2008), *Imperial Eyes: Travel Writing and Transculturation*, 2nd edition, New York: Routledge.
Ramos, J. (2001), "Hemispheric Domains: 1898 and the Origins of Latin Americanism," *Journal of Latin American Cultural Studies*, 10 (3): 237–51.
Rodríguez, A. P. (2009). "Nations Divided: U.S. Intervention, Banana Enclaves, and the Panama Canal," In *Dividing the Isthmus. Central American Transnational Histories, Literatures, and Cultures*, 44–75, Austin: University of Texas Press.
Rosenberg, E. S. (2012), "Transnational Currents in a Shrinking World," in E. S. Rosenberg (ed.), *A History of the World*, Vol. 5 of *A World Connecting, 1870–1945*, 815–998, Cambridge, MA: Belknap Press of Harvard University Press.
Senior, O. (2014), *Dying to Better Themselves: West Indians and the Building of the Panama Canal*, Kingston: University of the West Indies Press.
Stevens, W. (1997), *Collected Poetry and Prose*, New York: Library of America.
Walrond, E. (2013), *Tropic Death*, New York: Liveright.
Whalan, M. (2017), "'Oil Was Trumps': John Dos Passos' *U.S.A.*, World War I, and the Growth of the Petromodern State," *American Literary History*, 29 (3): 474–98.
Whitman, W. (2002), *Leaves of Grass and Other Writings*, ed. M. Moon, New York: Norton.
Winkiel, L. (2019), "Introduction." *English Language Notes*, 57 (1): 1–10.

11

Creole Poetics of the Ocean: Carlos Rigby, Ecological Thought, and Caribbean Diasporic Consciousness

Tatiana Argüello

"Inside my blood I carry the sea," says Carlos Rigby (1945–2017), a NiCaribbean poet whose significance far exceeds his renown. Born into an Afro-descendant family from Pearl Lagoon, Carlos Rigby Moses is considered the "great unpublished poet" of the Nicaraguan Caribbean (Castro Jo 2003: 30). Even though his poems have been published in newspapers and anthologies, during his lifetime he never published a book.[1] Instead, a posthumous documentary, *Antojología de Carl Rigby* (2019), by Eduardo Spiegeler and María José Alvarez Sacasa, fills that void via an audiovisual display of Rigby's poetry intertwined with his biography and interview sequences.[2] The title of the documentary, "Antojología," is a neologism that captures Rigby's aesthetic and spirit, as creator of new words. It is a portmanteau of two words in Spanish, "antojo" (whim or strong desire, in particular a food craving) and "antología" (anthology). It is as if the documentary expresses and creates a craving, appetite, or sudden desire of the poet and, for us as appreciators of his poetry, to have an anthology of his poems. The documentary leaves readers with a mouthwatering yet unfulfilled *antojo* and in lieu of a book or anthology offers this rhythmic, visual, and geographic homage that mixes Rigby's poetry, in spoken and written word, interspersed with interview snippets with him, and scenes from

Managua, the Masaya volcano on the Pacific side, and the Caribbean coast and ocean. As a final poetic product, it is as unconventional and original as Rigby's poetry. That such a great poet is unpublished and largely unknown in the self-proclaimed Republic of Poets that is Nicaragua speaks volumes about the marginalization of eastern Nicaragua and its inhabitants. An ecologically and ethnically rich and diverse area, but culturally, economically and politically marginalized, this region once known as the Mosquito or Miskitu Coast, the Mosquitia, the Atlantic Coast, or the Caribbean coastline of Nicaragua, obtained partial autonomy from the Nicaraguan nation-state in 1987. It was split and renamed into the North and South Caribbean Coast Autonomous Region (Pearl Lagoon, Rigby's birth place, is located in the latter of these).

To underscore the significance of Rigby for world literature, we should remember Goethe's idea that national literature and national one-sidedness do not mean much these days. He made this claim in the early nineteenth century, and it is even less applicable in the early twenty-first century (even though some feverishly defend the idea of the nation). It is necessary to think literature beyond national and linguistic boundaries. However, my vision of world literature is indebted to discursive relations that are multidimensional and fragmentary, like Rigby's poetry. This is in some contrast to scholars such as Pheng Cheah (2008), who talks about the capacity of the literary text to generate worlds, or Franco Moretti's (2000) global system focused on European models. Jason Frydman (2014), for example, has paved the way to think about these types of models of global literary circulation in Caribbean texts, which include reciprocity and continuity between the oral and the written, Europe and the non-European. In my case, Indigenous philosophy and Caribbean theories of creolization, particularly Édouard Glissant's rhizomatic perspectives, are powerful critics of cultural nationalism and singular origins, and a point of departure to think Rigby's Caribbean poetry as world literature.[3]

Rigby, as a Caribbean poet and thinker, is connected with the cultural and political effervescence in the mid-1960s in Nicaragua, including the revolution against Somoza's dictatorship and intellectual and bohemian life.[4] From the 1960s until his death, he lived most of his life in the capital, Managua, which is located in the nation's Pacific side. However, Rigby's poetic evocation of the sea—its fluidity, its sounds, and the assemblage formed inside his body—brings the Caribbean Sea "inside," in a process that exceeds and displaces the "Pacific-centered" paradigm in Nicaragua. His ecological poetry imagines a new Nicaraguan identity and shares realities beyond the country's limits. Rigby experiences the ocean as a transformative landscape for individual and collective reflections on identity, ecology, and justice. His work presents an exemplary rethinking of racial and national identity, with an ecological vision that reinvents Nicaragua (and Central American) cultural possibility—he overturns the primacy of culture over nature, and, by doing this, he also overturns the priority of whiteness over Blackness and the center over the periphery.

In this chapter, I focus on his rethinking of the human relationship with the natural world, in both its threatening and sheltering possibilities. Through the study of the ethics and poetics of Carlos Rigby, particularly his epic poem "Sinfonía para los peces en Sim Saima-Sí (B) Mayor" (Symphony for Fish in Sim Saima-Si Mayor [B Major]; 1968) I interpret his Afrodescendant experience of the ocean in an ecological paradigm rather than an anthropocentric one. Previous Caribbean thinkers advocated notions of négritude, the revaluation of Blackness and African descent, and créolité, the countervailing advocacy of diasporic and relational identity, accepting the intermixture of European and African cultures (Bernabé, Chamoiseau and Confiant 1993; Césaire 2001). Rigby critically expands these notions by emphasizing nature and the nonhuman, unsubordinated by human centrality regardless of culture. Rigby's depiction of Afrodescendant communities and their encounter with the sea incarnated as a man counters mestizo anti-Black racism and introduces Caribbean diasporic consciousness. Theoretically, his poems dialogue with Black and Caribbean thought; they evoke Édouard Glissant, who also portrays the ocean as a space that creates new fluid (relational) identities and challenges the center's supremacy over the periphery.[5] Rigby's vision of the sea also bears comparison with other experimental, aesthetical, and philosophical routes, such as Rastafarianism, Surrealism, and the Indigenous perspectivism elaborated by Eduardo Viveiros de Castro.

Scholars have focused on the orality of Rigby's corpus and his cultural significance as a Black Nicaraguan. Many critics notice the performative and ingenious use of language by Rigby—his neologisms, his bilingualism (Spanish and creole English) and orality—and his incorporation of dance and Caribbean rhythms in his live recitals (Alemán Ocampo 2000; Chow 2005; Valle Castillo 1980). Thomas Wayne Edison (2007: 22) notices that Rigby's poetry expresses the transcultural cosmovision of the Nicaraguan Caribbean, incorporating African, European, and Indigenous linguistic and cultural elements, and reflecting the social reality of that region. Edison compares the richness of Rigby's poetry with other great Afro-Caribbean authors, such as Eulalia Bernard (Costa Rica), Joaquín Boleño (Panama), and Nicolás Guillén (Cuba), among others (21). Rigby wrote about the geography of the Caribbean, Palo de Mayo, and he always fought to position the African and Indigenous culture of this region as part of the national culture (Castro Jo 2003: 30–1).[6]

Steven White (2011) values the rich ecological perspective of Rigby's poetry. In his compelling reading of "Symphony for Fish in Sim Saima-Si Major (B Major)," White affirms that the poem "demonstrates a magisterial and intimate knowledge of the natural geography of an often-marginalized region" (515, my translation). The literary critic positions the poem in the same tradition of cyclical poems in which the lyric voice undertakes a trip of dangers and self-discovery, leaving home to gain knowledge, dying sometimes, and then being reborn (e.g., "Le bateau ivre" by Arthur Rimbaud or "The Waste Land" by T. S. Eliot) (516). White also recognizes the affective liaisons of living near the sea, making possible a comparative reading of Rigby's poem with other Caribbean authors, such as Edward Kamau Brathwaite and Derek Walcott (517). For White, the main purpose of the poem is to achieve a final goal after crossing the body of water and rebirth as a new human, receiving the oral tradition of Rigby's culture rooted in the sea (517). White's metaphysical reading of the poem is compelling and I share his view of the poem's philosophical dimension about humans, spirituality, and nature—particularly reflections on God and the meaning of life and death that emerge when the poetic I is in contact with the ocean. Yet White does not explore these relationships in terms of Black consciousness and the European, Indigenous and Afrocentric categories that characterize histories of cultural exchange between the Nicaraguan Caribbean with other creolized and non-creolized communities. The connection of Rigby with Surrealist, Rastafari, creole, and Indigenous ideas shows this plurality of literary exchange and exposes this relationship is not linear but multidimensional, which exposes the fallacy of national genealogy.

Rigby's epic poem, "Symphony for Fish in Sim Saima-Si Major (B Major)," is a song of himself in which he takes on the role of a culture-hero for his people, the Afrodescendant Nicaraguans of the Atlantic Coast. The title of the poem refers to a "Symphony," a form of orchestral music, which usually starts in a light and soft manner with a major key. It is also influenced by Rubén Darío's "Symphony in Grey Major," which also emerges from dialogue between literature and music about the sea (White 2011: 516). The allusion to the "symphony" in Rigby's poem, nevertheless, starts in a less-peaceful way and has a more subversive tone than Darío's pictorial description of a sea scene and a sailor, where everything is still and monotonous including the music. Rigby's poem begins with an ancestral message, the knowledge imparted to him by his grandmother. She begins with a warning about the shark, the figure for all of the fearsome violence and inhuman malevolence of the ocean. However, she also presents the figure of a personified ocean—the ocean becoming visible as an individual man. Subsequently, the poetic I speaks of a journey toward understanding and reconciliation with the ocean; he writes of moving toward Zero to make One. The experience of destitution and negativity, nature without the human, is necessary for him to truly understand what is to be human, immersed in a nonhuman world. Late in the poem, he anticipates and accepts his own death and the existence of unknown monsters, concealed by the depths. He writes that the sea tramples on sacred things; it washes away illusions and hubris attendant to human historical "progress."

While the sea is a place of death, it also is one of fecundity. It provides for the possibility of becoming the "only true semen" (el único semen puro) to arrive at a type of immortality. This is a naturalistic point of view in which the poetic I associates the foam of the sea with fecundity, first in its masculine possibilities (and later with more feminine language). Human continuity and survival can only be achieved by recognition of the sea's triumphant permanence, in excess of any individual life. Rigby realizes that he "must always recognize [him]self as less noble than this body of water" (siempre [ha] de reconocer[se] menos noble que este cuerpo de agua), but this acceptance of the priority of nature brings him closer to God. As a complement to his grandmother's image of the ocean as a man, Rigby also feminizes the sea: He writes of the sensual contortions of the Black women of his culture as effects of the sea's movements, in profound harmony with them. At the conclusion of the poem, the shark is no longer a figure of menace: "The joy of the fish was ours" (La alegría de los peces era nuestra).[7] Rigby's poem achieves an alternative understanding of the human relation with nature, according to which it is impossible and undesirable to dominate nature, and that this respect prepares the way for a more authentic reflection on human identity and possibility.

Regional and Global Routes in Rigby: Surrealism, Rastafarianism, and Indigenous Perspectivism

Carlos Rigby was a writer immersed in multiple cultural constellations, ranging from the cosmopolitan position of the Nicaraguan Caribbean and its bohemian influences from foreign poetry, to Rastafari and re-Indigenizing ideas. The Atlantic coastal region had a more direct contact from the flux of foreign capital, goods, and people than the Pacific, and for this reason Rigby's aesthetic perspective is even more transnational than the norm for Nicaraguan literature. Carlos Castro Jo confirms that Rigby benefited from consuming French authors by asking sailors to bring him books at the Bluff (the port facility at the entrance to Bluefields Lagoon), in a period in which Bluefields had a strong connection with the Caribbean and, therefore, the world.[8] This dynamic is a remnant of the "old good days" in Bluefields, a period in the first quarter of the twentieth century in which there was plenty of work, ships, supplies, and food, and people could rely on foreign goods rather than Nicaraguan products (Sujo Wilson 1991: 33).

It is fruitful to compare Rigby's narrative to a famous example of modernist poetry, *The Song of Maldoror* (1874), by the Uruguayan-French poet Isidore Ducasse, who published under the *nom de plume* Comte de Lautréamont. The poem was a crucial influence on European avant-gardes, particularly Surrealism, and presents a pioneering poetic attempt to destroy conventional understandings of humanism and to replace them with a more profound understanding of natural forces. As for Rigby, the ocean and the shark are pivotal figures for Lautréamont, and an enigmatic figure, a personification of nature, acts to dispel the illusory moralism of modern humans. For example, Lautréamont ([1874] 1999) presents the shocking and grotesque image of a man in sexual congress with a shark, presenting a visceral experience of human acknowledgment of the value of animal predation. Lautréamont also composes a famous hymn to the ocean, commending its immortality and superiority over human ambitions and values (Bachelard [1956] 2012). Rigby's echoes of Lautréamont and consequently other French authors that influenced Ducasse on the mystery of the ocean and its relationship with humans (e.g., Charles Baudelaire's "Man and the Sea") can be traced to the importance that French poetry plays for Nicaraguan poets. As Steven White states in *Modern Nicaraguan Poetry: Dialogues with France and the United States* (1993: 15–16), from modernist Rubén Darío, to avant-garde poets and committed poets like Ernesto Cardenal, we cannot understand contemporary poetry in Nicaragua without analyzing the French and North American literary traditions that influence the national canon. Rigby's poem is much more affirmative than Lautréamont. This is most likely because Lautréamont perceives no serious option other than despair because European modernity tends to foreclose a positive and creative reception of natural power. In contrast, Rigby's Afrodescendant heritage provides him with the cultural space from which to think and act, reassuring him that humans can build a society with a truer understanding of nature's force and vitality.

In addition to modern poetry, Rigby draws from Caribbean religious innovations, particularly Rastafari. This belief system originated in Jamaica in the 1930s, and awareness of aspects of its perspective and practices has spread worldwide particularly because of its prominence in the lyrics and culture of reggae music. Rastafarians draw from traditional Biblical scripture, and Jewish and Christian theological interpretation. However, Rastas apply this allegorically to the experience of the African diaspora. Part of their belief system involves alterations of the traditional understanding of Christian incarnation or *kenosis*, by which God appears as a mortal man. Like other traditions of Black theology, Rastas believe that Christ was a Black man and that the white depiction of Jesus is a deception. Moreover, Rastas believe that suffering humans, especially oppressed Afrodescendant peoples, have a special relationship with God, chosen by Him. Some versions of Rastafari also hold practices of ancestor veneration according to which individual death is illusory, and further that God (an Ethiopian messiah whom they call "Jah") is present within the soul of believers (Murrell 2010: 1–11).

As can be found in other varieties of Black theology (such as James Cone's Black Christian liberation theology, the Nation of Islam and the Five-Percent Nation, and the Black Hebrew Israelites), incarnation becomes collectivized rather than entirely unique; these traditions suggest that the Black peoples as a whole can be identified with God, in excess of the individual historical appearance of Jesus Christ. The influence of Rastafarian ideas in Rigby can be partly understood by the popularity of Jamaica's Marcus Mosiah Garvey, one of the precursors to the Rastafari movement, among English-speaking Black people from the Central American isthmus. Garvey's Universal Negro Improvement Association (UNIA) had active branches from Panama and Costa Rica, on up to Guatemala and Belize—and particularly in Nicaragua, there were UNIA branches in every town from Greytown to Bluefields, Rama and El Bluff, on up to Puerto Cabezas (Vincent 1985: 37).

However, I see Rigby's creative reception of Rastafari much less humanist and patriarchal, and more horizontal and pantheistic than the orthodox variety of it. In his poem, Rigby maintains the idea that God is materially present on earth today. However, for him God is not primarily incarnated in the human population but rather outside of it in the depths and greatness of his creation, particularly in the ocean. As the poetic I reminds us, while being immersed in ocean: "I feel so close to God today in the liquefaction of my feelings" (me siento hoy tan cerca de Dios en la licuefacción de mis sentimientos). For Rigby, an apprehension of the divine within the human is possible, but this apprehension requires a profound meditation on the extra-human and the inhuman because this is also the place of God. In this respect, Rigby is in accord with certain Indigenous ontologies that rearticulate the Caribbean as a place in which Indigenous thought persists. Juan Duchesne Winter (2015: 22) calls this an "eccentric Caribbean" that opens a "cosmopraxis" with a multiplicity of actors. Duchesne Winter writes that Caribbean studies traditionally focus on this region through "insularism," the island model, which erases its indigenous past. He proposes that the eccentric Caribbean open to the Indigenous legacy (re-Indigenization) and rearticulates this region, not only the shore of the sea but also the marginal hinterland. This is in tune with reality in the Nicaraguan Atlantic Coast, which is both sociologically and historically an Indigenous and a Black Caribbean. Afrodescendant creole people live alongside the Indigenous communities of Garífuna, Miskitos, Sumo, and Rama.

Drawing from the Amazonian context, the research of Eduardo Viveiros de Castro has demonstrated that some Indigenous communities believe in radical perspectivism; each entity sees and acts in the world according to its own nature and point of view. Viveiros de Castro writes that this type of metaphysics sees one fundamental type of soul, with multiple distinct natural bodies; there is no human uniqueness to the presence of a soul or a mind ([2009] 2014: 52–3). Similarly, Rigby believes that true knowledge of the ocean depends on recognizing it as a sentient being, one that can act and think just as much as human beings can. Another fundamental aspect of Viveiros de Castro's perspectivism entails a relational status of predator and prey between human and nonhumans, an Amazonian metaphysics of predation; this also appears in the Caribbean Sea. In this sense, Rigby's poem presents an oceanic predatory power at the beginning, by acknowledging marine species including big predators like the aforementioned shark and other fish like barracuda and swordfish who are described in a violent manner. In one passage, the poetic I imagines his body being gnawed and devoured by these fish and comments on this scene as an attractive plot for a movie. It refers a thriller about the horrors of the sea but captures a Eurocentric voyeuristic experience of the sea through mass consumption.

The ocean also expands other conflicts and antagonisms from this multiplicity of natures and bodies in a world of relational objects. Rigby mentions in one verse that humans could hear the "sad biography of the Sea" (la triste biografía del mar) echoing how humans and the sea are dependent on the other and mutually suffer violence. Obviously, the capitalist modes of productions affect the Caribbean Sea and produce ecological disaster and degradation. In addition, the ocean is also a particularly loaded and striking place for the African diaspora, because it is not only a place of natural danger; it is also the setting of the forced migration and enslavement of the Africans who were taken to the Americas. Rigby captures different fearful reactions of men to the sea in his poem, describing "cold-blooded sailors" (marineros de sangre fría). Hence, Rigby's appreciation and respect for the ocean are not only an experience of ahistorical Nature but also the scars and memories of human and nonhuman traumas contemporaneously bundled together in spaces that reject human control. While Rigby does not talk directly about the ecological degradation of the ocean, in his poem there is the constant knitting together of the human and the extra-human relations, in which Caribbean creoles cannot understand themselves without the ocean. As the poem says: "It is on the sea / where should we look at / if we know / the true age of man" (Es sobre el mar / que de debemos mirar / si hemos de conocer / la verdadera Edad del Hombre).

Black and Caribbean Poetics: Glissant and Rigby in World Literature

Traditional Rastafari, like Marcus Garvey's "back to Africa" movement and certain tendencies of the francophone poetic social movement called négritude, holds the ideal of Africa as redemptive and views diasporic life as a condemnation. In contrast, Rigby eschews nostalgia for Africa and affirms the contemporary life of Caribbean and Central American Black people. In this respect, the francophone author of *The Poetics of Relation*, Édouard Glissant ([1990] 2010), can help us to understand Rigby's outlook. Glissant rejects the cultural desire to return to origins of what he calls *retour* (return); he believes that this fixation on beginnings and original purity was itself derived from European metaphysical presuppositions. Glissant responds to a question in Caribbean thought: How to create cultural self-representations and reconcile the history and the future for creole communities originating in a complex process of erasure, conquest, and exploitation such as the Indigenous genocide, the slave ship and trade, the plantations, post-plantation politics and multiple immigrations. There are different positions on how to see creole identity: as a novel fixed essence that has no relationship with the prior order (the Creolité movement), the retention of elements of prior order in addition to embracing new aspects (Kamau Braithwaite), and the retention of certain facets of a premodern past that are no longer accessible for historical and political reasons, yet can be imagined (Stuart Hall) (Roberts 2015: 146).

Instead, Glissant emphasizes that creole communities do not exist in a vacuum, and influenced by Gilles Deleuze and Félix Guatarri's ([1980] 1987) concept of the rhizome, he argues that the ocean is a place of relation according to which multiple heterogeneous elements can interact without the predominance and hierarchy of some entities over others. He believes that the Caribbean is a particularly creative site for human beings because of its cultural variations and archipelagic construction; in this sense, he describes this landscape as a positive mode of thinking that is ongoing, never fixed and ever changing. He says, "[R]hizomatic thought is the principle behind what I called the Poetic of Relation, in which each and every identity is extended through a relationship with the Other" ([1990], 2010: 11).

In the Hispanic Caribbean, on the contrary, conceptualization of Caribbean identities and societies has traditionally emphasized these identities as a final product but not as the ongoing process that Glissant describes. For example, prevalent ideas are those of Caribbean insularism; for example, Antonio Benítez Rojo ([1989] 1996: 1–5) proposes the notion of the "Repeating Island," the island as a symbolic space, a center, which produces everything else including the ocean. Some scholars, such as Guillermina De Ferrari (2007), Juan Duchesne Winter (2015), and Rubén Ríos Ávila (2018), have pointed out that Benítez Rojo's theory creates an abstract notion of the Caribbean, which tends to be "Cubancentric." This conception does not take into consideration concrete particularities and multiple experiences of less hegemonic Caribbean communities, including their connection with the ocean. Rigby shares with Glissant a reconceptualization of Caribbean identities, drawing from the ocean as a place that produces thought. Glissant begins his *Poetics of Relation* with a surrealistic image of a slave ship in the ocean (like Rigby, also influenced by Lautréamont) in which he captures the terror and suffering that captive Africans experienced during the middle passage. He portrays the unknown of the sea with its violence similarly to Rigby, in the sense that the stark journey creates a transformation and a new knowledge that everything is interconnected with each other, and poetry is the only means to capture this intense experience.

In Rigby's poem, this connection appears in different forms of relations. For instance, returning to the influence of music, I can see that his poem is a symphony in a sonata form, following its structure of two main themes in relation to each other: the mystery of the sea and the certitude of the land, with different types of variations or tonalities (sad, bittersweet, or joyful images).[9] The lyric subject knows about his family, his community, and its traditions, including the food and music, from the land, whereas the sea represents everything that cannot be understood. As the poem says "the sea is tamable only in thoughts," reflecting themes such as spirituality, God, death, and the power of nature. Rigby's lyric subject creates lines of flight in which his trip in the ocean gets him away from what Glissant ([1990] 2010) calls "continental thinking," that is systematic, linear, and depending on filiation. Rather, the sea helps him to create an "archipelagan" viewpoint that is open to the multiple unexpected influences. This change of perspective or different modes of thinking is captured in the following verses: "But, what is the truth? / That the waves crash against the boat / Or the boat's crashing against the waves" (Pero, ¿Cuál es la verdad? /¿Qué las olas se arremeten contra el bote / o que el bote se arremete contra las olas?) As I indicated before, the unknown of the violence of the sea is only transformed through the cathartic role of poetry and the poets who play an important role in their communities, for Glissant and Rigby. Glissant says, "We know ourselves as part and as crowd, in an unknown that does not terrify. We cry our cry of poetry. Our boats are open, and we sail them for everyone" ([1990], 2010: 9). Similarly, Rigby mentions:

> We are the race of POETS
> known only among the others
> for our little names of men
> But we are brothers
> ...
> We also have to die
> even if we sing
> In our chains
> like the sea.
>
> (Somos la raza de POETAS
> conocidos únicamente entre los otros
> por nuestros pequeños nombres de hombres
> Pero nosotros hermanos
> ...

también hemos de morir
aunque cantemos
en nuestras cadenas
como el mar.)

By placing Rigby's Caribbean consciousness in dialogue with Glissant's, and other tendencies of Caribbean literature, we find a new avenue for the expansion of world literature. Certainly, many critics have expanded the planetary approach to world literature from European centers to non-Western and postcolonial zones—such as Ngũgĩ wa Thiong'o (1992), Gayatri Chakravorty Spivak (2003), Emily Apter (2013); and, to turn toward Latin America, works by Ignacio Sánchez Prado (2006), and Gesine Müller, Jorge Locane, and Benjamin Loy (2018), among others. In terms of ecological approaches to world literature, there are innovative works on the environmental problems suffered by human and nonhuman communities because of violence that transcends time and geographies ("slow violence") and that often is the result of colonial legacies and its contemporary permutations (Kressner, Mutis, and Pettinaroli 2020). Although my work does not focus on ecological violence, it shares with this ecocritical thinking the emphasis on materiality and physical manifestations of a particular space in order to reconfigure it and create a new spatial consciousness beyond its geographical limits. Oceanic studies have placed the sea and maritime narratives at the center as water worlds full of life (Anderson and Peters 2016). For me, the exploration of the ocean cannot be understood in Rigby's poetry, if it is not as a space that entangles the realities of cultural exchanges in the Global South (Mann and Phaf-Rheinberger 2014, Phaf-Rheinberger 2017).

In the case of Caribbean literature, Silvio Torres-Saillant (1997: 1–12) has mentioned that it has a cohesive place in world literature rooted in the historical dynamics of colonialism, which means that it is both connected to and disconnected from Western tradition. However, Caribbean people have created an authentic and emancipating discourse, in which they are constantly reassessing hegemonic assumptions and categories in their everyday existence, including "universality." Caribbean poetics as world literature—of which Rigby is certainly a part—does not have "a center" as Torres-Saillant mentioned; rather, they are rhizomatic, expansive, and anchored in a particular cultural geography that allows global entanglements such as the cosmopolitan past of the Nicaraguan Caribbean, the reciprocal influence of Caribbean and Indigenous cultures, and the European aesthetic adaptations to local use. The work of Glissant is pivotal to think about these types of new routes in world literature since he gives us tools to reflect about the notion of identity beyond the nation-state and question official history, emphasizing fragments and linguistic constellations (texts, languages, people, cultures) to construct open identities (Bermann 2014: 66–71). Rigby participates in this movement by expanding the official geo-political map of what is Nicaraguan, Central American, or Caribbean literature. He interweaves his narrative with other linguistic communities within the Pacific and the Nicaraguan Caribbean and beyond the isthmus and questions traditional notions of race and nation. As such, he also insists on Blackness in Central America. Indeed, Rigby considers any approach to Nicaraguan identity that does not include the Black experience as fundamentally incomplete. Further, for Rigby, Blackness is not only a question of skin color. The Black experience in Central American carries with it a greater awareness of the significance of the land and the ocean, and their autonomous life beyond human priorities.[10]

Notes

1 While Rigby did not publish collections of his poetry in a book of his authorship, his poems have been included in the Nicaraguan newspapers and journals *La Prensa Literaria* and *Wani*, and anthologies of poetry such as *Poesía Atlántica* (Valle-Castillo 1980), *El siglo de la poesía en Nicaragua: Neovanguardia (1960–1980)* (Valle-Castillo 2005), *Los Hijos del Minotauro. Antología de la poesía contemporánea nicaragüense (1950–2008)* (Yllescas Salinas 2009), and *Nicaragua: el más alto Canto* (Avellán 2012), among others.
2 All the English translations of Rigby's poems that I mention in this article are from the website associated with the documentary, *Antojología de Carl Rigby: Primer Tomo de los Que Vienen*, and available online at www.antojologiadecarlrigby.com.
3 The adjective "rhizomatic" refers to rhizome a term that Glissant borrows from Gilles Deleuze and Félix Guattari. Rhizome is a creative and dynamic model of thinking, in opposition to a tree-root system, which is hierarchical, chronological and constrained. The rhizome has nomadic qualities since it has no beginning or end, but it is always in propagation and growth. For more information, see Deleuze and Guattari ([1980] 1987: 3–25).
4 From 1936 to 1979, Nicaragua had been governed by the authoritarian Somoza dynasty, which functioned as a US client state, and Rigby as well as a layer of other Creoles placed great hope in the victory of the 1979 revolution led by the Sandinista National Liberation Front (FSLN). Edmund T. Gordon (1998: 150–75) calls Creoles supporting and acting in concert with the Pacific FSLN "Black Sandinistas."
5 Rigby (2019) first declares, "I am from the NiCaribbean Coast / I am NiCaribbean" (Yo soy de Nicaribia / nicaribe soy) inventing a new portmanteau word that maintains Nicaraguan national identity alongside Caribbean experience. This is a geographical marker, but the material location produces an embodied experience of the world. I want to conclude by emphasizing this claim. Rigby's identification as "NiCaribbean" suggests that

the territory is open and permeable, like that described by Glissant. Glissant ([1990] 2010) called for a new type of métissage that would valorize the peripheral area of the Caribbean and its Black inhabitants, but not to produce a new closed state and identity—rather, carrying with it the complexities and difference with relation. In doing so, Rigby's perspective might serve not only to empower the Atlantic Creoles and to advocate their inclusion as "full" Nicaraguans but also to make Pacific mestizos more aware of their own Black heritage. Contemporary Nicaraguans must become aware that a simple division between a mestizo Pacific and a Black Caribbean is untenable. Sergio Ramírez (2007), a pioneering Nicaraguan novelist and political figure, demonstrates in his book *Tambor olvidado* (Forgotten Drum) that most Nicaraguan mestizos are partly of African descent in addition to their more widely known Spanish and Indigenous heritage. For this reason, Rigby's reevaluation of African ecological thought represents a vital contribution to the national culture of all Nicaraguans, on both coasts.

6 Palo de mayo (Maypole) refers to the music and dance with Afro-Caribbean rhythms that the communities in the Atlantic Coast perform on the streets to celebrate during the month of May. Carlos Rigby was the coordinator and promoter of *¡Mayo Ya!*, a contemporary festival to celebrate Maypole. One of his most famous poems refers to this festival: "If I were May" (Si fuera mayo). See Antonia MsCoy (2002).

7 This chant for the rebirth of nature and humans' rebirth through nature also appears in poems such as Ernesto Cardenal's "Nueva ecología" (New Ecology) (1985). Both Cardenal and Rigby refer to the positive effects of the Nicaraguan revolution in its flora, fauna, and bodies of water.

8 Email communications with Dr. Carlos Castro Jo. I thank Dr. Castro Jo for kindly sharing with me information on Carlos Rigby's French influence.

9 Classical period symphonies were written in symphonic forms.

10 I thank Director María José Alvarez Sacasa, for commenting on her relationship with Rigby, and Dr. Andrew Ryder, for editing this article and for his theoretical insights on Black theology, Caribbean thought, and Comparative Literature. I appreciate the support of TCU AddRan College for giving me a summer research award that allowed me to work on this project.

References

Alemán Ocampo, C. (2000), "Cultura de poder. Literatura indígena y afrocaribeña en Nicaragua," *Revista Universitaria del Caribe*, 2 (1): 149–76.

Anderson, J. and K. Peters, eds. (2016), *Water Worlds: Human Geographies of the Ocean*, London and New York: Routledge.

Antojología de Carl Rigby (2019), [Film] Dir. Eduardo Spiegeler and María José Alvarez Sacasa, Nicaragua: Luna Films.

Apter, E. (2013), *Against World Literature: On the Politics of Untranslatability*, London: Verso.

Avellán, H., ed. (2012), *Nicaragua: el más alto canto: nueva antología de la poesía nicaragüense*, Managua: Instituto Nicaragüense de Cultura.
Bachelard, G. ([1956] 2012), *Lautréamont*, trans. R. S. Dupree, Dallas: Dallas Institute Publications.
Benítez-Rojo, A. ([1989] 1996), *The Repeating Island: The Caribbean and the Post-modern Perspective*, trans. J. E. Maraniss, 2nd edition, Durham and London: Duke University Press.
Bermann, S. L. (2014), "Édouard Glissant and the Imagination of World Literature: Relation, Creolization, and Translation," in P. F. Bandia (ed.), *Writing and Translating Francophone Discourse: Africa, the Caribbean, Diaspora*, 63–86, Amsterdam: Rodopi.
Bernabé, J., P. Chamoiseau, and R. Confiant (1993), *Éloge de la Créolité / In Praise of Creoleness*, Paris: Gallimard.
Cardenal, E. (1985), *Flights of Victory/Vuelos de Victoria*, trans. M. Zimmerman, Willimantic: Curbstone Press.
Castro Jo, C. (2003), "Raza, conciencia de color y militancia negra en la literatura Nicaragüense," *Wani: Revista del Caribe Nicaragüense*, 33: 21–32.
Césaire, A. (2001), *Notebook of a Return to the Native Land*, trans. and ed. C. Eshleman and A. Smith, Middletown: Wesleyan University Press.
Cheah, P. (2008), "What Is a World? On World Literature as World-Making Activity," *Dædalus*, 137 (3): 26–38.
Chow, J. (2005), "Rostro cultural del Caribe nicaragüense," *Wani: Revista del Caribe Nicaragüense*, 40: 58–62.
De Ferrari, G. (2007), *Vulnerable States: Bodies of Memory in Contemporary Caribbean Fiction*, Charlottesville: University of Virginia Press.
Deleuze, G. and F. Guattari ([1980] 1987), *A Thousand Plateaus: Capitalism and Schizophrenia*, trans. B. Massumi, Minneapolis and London: University of Minnesota Press.
Duchesne Winter, J. (2015), *Caribe, Caribana: cosmografías literarias*, San Juan: Ediciones Callejón.
Edison, T. W. (2007), "La cultura afro-caribeña vista en la poesía: la tradición del Palo de Mayo y en el poema Si yo fuera mayo por Carlos Rigby Moses," *Wani: Revista del Caribe Nicaragüense*, 49: 21–32.
Frydman, J. (2014), *Sounding the Break: African American and Caribbean Routes of World Literature*, Charlottesville: University of Virginia Press.
Glissant, É. ([1990] 2010), *Poetics of Relation*, trans. B. Wing, Ann Arbor: University of Michigan Press.
Gordon, E. T. (1998), *Disparate Diaspora: Identity and Politics in an African Nicaraguan Community*, Austin: University of Texas Press.
Kressner, I., A. M. Mutis, and E. M. Pettinaroli, eds. (2020), *Ecofictions, Ecorealities, and Slow Violence in Latin America and the Latinx World*, New York: Routledge.
Lautréamont, C. de ([1874] 1999), *Les Chants de Maldoror*, Paris: Pocket Classiques.
Mann, M. and I. Phaf-Rheinberger, eds. (2014), *Beyond the Line: Cultural Narratives of the Southern Oceans*, Berlin: Neofelis Verlag.
Moretti, F. (2000), "Conjectures on World Literature," *New Left Review*, 1: 54–68.

MsCoy, A. (2002), "Significado del palo de mayo," *Revista Universitaria del Caribe*, 8 (2): 131–4.

Müller, G., J. J. Locane, and B. Loy, eds. (2018), *Re-Mapping World Literature Writing, Book Markets, and Epistemologies between Latin America and the Global South*, Berlin: De Gruyter Mouton.

Murrell, N. S. (2010), *Afro-Caribbean Religions: An Introduction to Their Historical, Cultural, and Sacred Traditions*, Philadelphia: Temple University Press.

Phaf-Rheinberger, I. (2017), *Modern Slavery and Water Spirituality: A Critical Debate in Africa and Latin America*, Frankfurt: Peter Lang.

Ramírez, S. (2007), *Tambor olvidado*, San José: Santillana.

Rigby, C. ([1968] 2019), "Symphony for Fish in Sim Saima-Si Major (B Major)," *Antojología de Carl Rigby: Primer Tomo de los Que Vienen*. Available online: www.antojologiadecarlrigby.com/en/poetry/symphony-for-fish-in-sim-saima-si-mayor/. Accessed May 5, 2021.

Rigby, C. (2019), "I Am NiCaribbean (version)," *Antojología de Carl Rigby: Primer Tomo de los Que Vienen*. Available online: www.antojologiadecarlrigby.com/en/poetry/i-am-nicaribbean/. Accessed May 5, 2021.

Ríos Ávila, R. (2018), "Pájaro Caribe: Puerto Rico y la poética de la relación," in M. M. del Valle Idárraga and E. M. D. Muñoz (eds.), *Cosmografías sutiles del Caribe y Latinoamérica*, 51–75, Barranquilla: Universidad del Atlántico.

Roberts, N. (2015), *Freedom as Marronage*, Chicago: Chicago University Press.

Sánchez Prado, I. M., ed. (2006), *América Latina en la "literatura mundial,"* Pittsburgh: Instituto Internacional de Literatura Iberoamericana.

Spivak, G. C. (2003), *Death of a Discipline*, New York: Columbia University Press.

Sujo Wilson, H. (1991), "Historia oral de Bluefields," *Wani: Revista del Caribe Nicaragüense*, 9: 25–39.

Thiong'o, N. wa ([1992] 2008), *Moving the Centre: The Struggle for Cultural Freedoms*, London: James Currey.

Torres-Saillant, S. (1997), *Caribbean Poetics: Toward an Aesthetic of West Indian Literature*, Cambridge: Cambridge University Press.

Valle-Castillo, J., ed. (1980), *Poesía atlántica*, Managua: Ministerio de Cultural.

Valle-Castillo, J., ed. (2005), *El siglo de la poesía en Nicaragua: Neovanguardia (1960–1980), Tomo III*, Managua: Fundación Uno.

Vincent, T. (1985), "The Harlem to Bluefields Connection: Sandino's Aid from the Black American Press," *The Black Scholar*, 16 (3): 36–42.

Viveiros de Castro, E. ([2009] 2014), *Cannibal Metaphysics: For a Post-Structural Anthropology*, ed. and trans. P. Skafish, Minneapolis: Univocal Publishing.

White, S. (1993), *Modern Nicaraguan Poetry: Dialogues with France and the United States*, Lewisburg: Bucknell University Press.

White, S. (2011), *Arando el aire: la ecología en la poesía y la música de Nicaragua*, Managua: 400 Elefantes.

Yllescas Salinas, E., ed. (2009), "*Los hijos del Minotauro: Antología de la poesía contemporánea nicaragüense (1950–2008)*," *Trilce*, 23, Managua: Trilce and Itsa.

12

US Central Americans Writing Global South Spaces

Andrew Bentley

This chapter identifies the interrelated threads of US Central American writing, world literature, and the Global South by examining works produced in the diaspora. Central American literature has long held a worldwide resonance, evident in novels that fictionalize Cold War era dictatorships and far-reaching work of regional laureates such as Rigoberta Menchú. The ongoing exodus of migrants, whose movements are ignited by climate change, post-conflict violence, and the Covid-19 pandemic, has further brought Central America into twenty-first-century global consciousness. With growing numbers of Central Americans in the United States and elsewhere outside their countries of origin, their works establish networks of solidarity that extend beyond the geographic limitations of the isthmus, in tune with the struggles of peoples elsewhere in the Global South. Accordingly, in a gesture toward literary world-making of the diaspora, recent US Central American creative works in English navigate and transcend the isthmus. For example, short pieces by Patrick Mullen-Coyoy and Gabriela Ramirez Chavez from the anthology *The Wandering Song: Central American Writing in the United States* (2017) bring Guatemalan perspectives to bear on global themes of internal armed conflicts and migration. The poetry collections *Unaccompanied* (2017) by Javier Zamora and *Catrachos* (2020) by Roy G. Guzmán lay the groundwork for migration with empirical knowledge about militarized frontiers and xenophobia in ways that resonate beyond El Salvador and Honduras. In the process, the works describe Global South spaces, which I understand as areas—indeed, worlds—negatively shaped by military interventions and neoliberal globalization, including within the United States. I posit that the works achieve a world literary standing in which a trans- or even postnational Central American canon is possible.

Transnational Imaginaries

US Central American stories establish discursive configurations of Central Americanness similar to but distinct from related Latin/x American voices. They are bound together by shared histories of US-influenced violence and homegrown racist complicity with that violence from the highest echelons of Central American oligarchies within the isthmus. They are told by displaced refugees of the war years, children of migrants with connections to home vis-à-vis the Central American transnational imaginary, those who endured the trauma of moving northward through Mexico, and people such as myself who have reconnected with Central America in adulthood. They challenge Eurocentric notions of cosmopolitanism in the sense that Pheng Cheah elucidates, with world literature understood as "a form of critical resistance that brings the attention of the wider world to the plight of peoples impacted by global forces and their struggles to safeguard a future for their worlds" (2016: 17). With an eye toward how US Central American writing sheds light on broader implications of the Global South, I draw from Cheah's approach to world literature, focusing on how creative works read under this rubric "generate alternative cartographies that enable a postcolonial people or a collective group to foster relations of solidarity and build a shared world in which self-determination is achieved" (2016: 17). For the purposes of this chapter, I focus on US Central Americans as a collective group rather than a postcolonial people due to their decidedly (neo)colonial life experiences, as visible in U.S. Immigration and Customs Enforcement (ICE) detention facilities, extractivism by mining companies from Canada and the United States on ancestral lands, the treatment of migrants on La Bestia, or the murder of Indigenous environmental activists such as Berta Cáceres, to name but a few examples.

In literary and extraliterary realms, Central American worlds in the diaspora emerge—to name one possibility—through the lenses of Guatemalan, Salvadoran, Honduran, and Nicaraguan experiences of wars and post-conflict eras. These experiences are united by US imperialism and create regional perceptions of countries, peoples, politics, and natural and human-made features of the social landscape. As Ana Patricia Rodríguez asserts, they can also be "deeply grounded in historical contexts yet unbound by place and borders" (2018: 528). The literary pieces generated by these worlds call attention to unique (Central American) experiences of marginalization within (Latinx) frameworks that are themselves marginal to dominant (US American) narratives. Drawing from firsthand experiences, Arturo Arias has remarked that a Guatemalan (or other Central American) writer in the United States or Europe may encounter questions such as "and what is that country? Where is it?" (2008: 27:51). A Mexican or Brazilian author, while undoubtedly still occupying a minority position in these northerly spaces, would be less likely to have to indicate their countries on a map. Thus, US Central American literature intrinsically opens our eyes to a heavily nuanced invisibility. It crosses borders and national experiences, supporting the idea of global citizenship conceived from below and the shared humanity of marginalized peoples across the Global South.

To situate the works under consideration in this chapter within the realm of world literature, a few words are in order on emergent categorizations of Central Americans in the United States and my use of "US Central American" throughout this chapter to distinguish from cultural production on the isthmus. Across borders within the isthmus itself, Mexico, and the United States, the imagined boundaries between countries are increasingly porous as Central American populations continue to grow in cities where they have lived for decades, such as Los Angeles and Washington, DC, as well as the newer Midwest destinations of Iowa and Nebraska (Arias 2012: 5). In response, humanities scholars of Central American origin at US universities—Arturo Arias, Maritza Cárdenas, Yajaira Padilla, and Ana Patricia Rodríguez foremost among them—have grappled with shifting dynamics of mobilized Central American subjectivities. Influenced by new patterns of Central American migration, recent cultural production, and each other's work, they contemplate modes of identification both inside and outside the academy.

The theme of transnationality vies for dominance in the criticism. For instance, Arias does well to remind us how the topographies (and traumas) of Central American migration significantly transformed after 9/11 when border security became tighter with the inception of ICE under the aegis of the Homeland Security Act. To illustrate this point, he examines the infamous 2008 Postville Raid in Iowa, wherein nearly 400 undocumented workers were detained at a meatpacking plant (Arias 2012: 6). Civil war traumas, while still figuring prominently in Central American subject formations, have developed alongside "newer traumas, such as 'the crossing' of the 3,000-mile-long journey from the isthmus to the US border, military service in the Middle East for those with legal resident status, or the daily risk of living without legal papers in the US in an increasingly hostile environment" (Arias 2012: 5). While Arias penned those words nearly a decade before the onset of the global Covid-19 pandemic, the virus has created an additional layer to the "hostile environment" he describes. This is visible, for example, in Instagram posts that show entry denial due to not providing negative test results at inner-Central American borders.[1]

Scholarly texts and social media thus accentuate the evolution of Central American migrations and their representations.

While newer written and visual representations, as well as lived experiences, shed light on violent themes that have been inherent to Central American countries since their independence, they also serve to destabilize nineteenth-century concepts of nation and nationalism. Given recent global advances, coupled with ongoing US influence in every country in the region, the identity marker of "Central American" already denotes a certain transnational status on its own without the addition of either "US" or "-American" (note the hyphen). In this regard, Arias tells us, "As it becomes deterritorialized, Central American discursivity, already a very particular hybrid, acquires new symbolic mediations and experiential flows as it becomes the anchor of a diasporic culture" (2007: 198). In a similar fashion, Yajaira Padilla deconstructs Benedict Anderson's notion of the imagined community in her contemplation of a "Central American transnational imaginary." She traces this phenomenon as "marked by memories of war, settlement in the United States, and crossings through Mexico, in which individual and communal identities are being continuously defined and negotiated" (2013: 151). For Padilla, cultural production both makes the transnational imaginary visible and participates in its ongoing creation as it continues to signal the presence of Central Americans outside the region.

Padilla makes clear that cultural production by and about US Central Americans is a political undertaking that pushes the boundaries of minority representations. With emphasis on conservative categorizations of Central Americans as perpetual "threatening guerrillas" and "illegals" from the Reagan through Trump presidencies, she proposes "non-belonging" as a framework to understand how cultural production explores the transnational imaginary. She argues that the idea of non-belonging registers "both the ways in which US Central Americans (immigrants and subsequent generations alike) have been constituted as Others who don't belong on a symbolic and material level, and the related means by which US Central Americans and others affirm, unsettle, and counteract this exclusionary condition" (2022: 5). US Central Americans create counternarratives to forty years of political discourse that has sought to justify their racist mistreatment and generalize their home countries as a homogeneous, violent landmass "down there." On the contrary, US Central American writing demonstrates community formation that defies their own disenfranchisement.

As such, Ana Patricia Rodríguez originates the term of the transisthmus, "an imaginary yet material space" (2009: 2), which symbolizes intersections of peoples from and beyond the region. For her part, Maritza Cárdenas argues that "Central American" on its own is intrinsically diasporic in nature, since people on the isthmus and elsewhere, in a postnational way, self-identify in regional terms in addition to or in place of national demonyms such as "Guatemalan" and "Salvadoran." However, as she rightfully notes, "it is rare to find someone refer to themselves as 'U.S. Central American' or 'Central American-American'" (Cárdenas 2018: 9), the latter of which Maya Chinchilla first coined in her poetry without the hyphen (2014: 21). Cárdenas argues that these two terms mostly manifest today as analytic constructs in the US academy, rather than in the popular imagination. While I fully concur with this critical assertion, I would go a step further to argue that these neologisms carry a pointedly imperialistic ethos that does not account for Central American diasporic communities elsewhere—in Canada, Mexico, Spain, Australia, or within the isthmus but outside the country of origin. I can foresee similar arguments against "Central American Latinxs" or "Latinxs of Central American origin," and, given its scholarly undertone, "diasporic Central Americans" would likely not enter the vernacular outside learned circles. It is not as though Central Americans arrive in the United States and declare "now I am US Central American," "now I am Latinx/o/a/e," or, even more generally, "now I am in the diaspora."[2] Those in the North still seem to favor a regional shared "Central American" identity as distinguishable from Mexicans or South Americans or a national moniker such as that of the *chapín* (for Guatemalan) or *guanaco* (for Salvadoran).

Certainly, these debates will be the topic of other investigations in the field of Latinx Studies beyond the scope of this chapter. The fact remains that the presence of Central Americans outside their countries of origin, and particularly in the United States, signals the ongoing development of regional, trans-, and postnational identity making. With the hugely influential formulations of Central American scholars, as well as the potential pitfalls of "US Central American" in mind, I cautiously employ the term in this chapter to pinpoint writers whose work is characterized by their physical locations in the geographic North. I acknowledge that their writing itself, while shedding light on the spatial and discursive significance of "US Central American," frequently critiques the imperialistic position that the United States has maintained over the transnational imaginary. These advances are evident in everything from international adoption, detention centers that predate the Trump presidency, resource extraction on ancestral lands, the means through which people reconnect with their homelands via WhatsApp, the trek northward through Mexico, and remittance fees through services such as Western Union. With many of these topics present in the writing, it therefore seems applicable to use "US Central American" to distinguish from works produced in the countries of origin and to stress the systemic dynamics to which the cultural production belongs. That is, by virtue of what I view as its imperialistic tendencies, the term automatically calls attention to the violence that generates the diaspora in the first place and, consequently, its writing, which has become increasingly more globally visible.

The proliferation of US Central American literary pieces published over the last decade in English speaks to this point. They include, among others,

Maya Chinchilla's *The Cha Cha Files: A Chapina Poética* (2014); Cristina Henríquez's *The Book of Unknown Americans* (2014); William Archila's *The Gravedigger's Archaeology* (2015); Adela Najarro's *Split Geography* (2015), *Twice Told Over* (2015), and *My Childrens* (2017); *The Wandering Song: Central American Writing in the United States* (2017), edited by Leticia Hernández Linares, Rubén Martínez, and Héctor Tobar; Cynthia Guardado's *Endeavor* (2017); Javier Zamora's *Unaccompanied* (2017) and *Solito* (2022); Francisco Aragón's *After Rubén* (2020); Ariel Francisco's *A Sinking Ship Is Still a Ship* (2020); Roy G. Guzmán's *Catrachos* (2020); Héctor Tobar's *The Last Great Road Bum* (2020); and Francisco Goldman's *Monkey Boy* (2021). Short stories include Arturo Arias's "Pandora's Box" and Raquel Gutiérrez's "Aquí viene Johnny," both in the anthology *Ambientes: New Queer Latino Writing* (2011), and my own "The *Gringo Chapín* Goes to Guate" (2020), in *Chiricú Journal: Latina/o Literatures, Arts, and Cultures*. By listing these publications of the second and third decades of the twenty-first century, I do not wish to obscure earlier waves of Central American migration to the United States, as evidenced, for example, by Salvadorans who have been present since the 1950s (Hernández-Linares 2017: 10). I would also be remiss not to mention key earlier works than the more recent wave I highlight here, among them *The Long Night of White Chickens* (1992) by Francisco Goldman; *Mama's Girl* (1996) by Veronica Chambers; *Odyssey to the North* (1998) by Mario Bencastro; *Life in the Damn Tropics* (2002) by David Unger; *The Immigrant Museum* (2003) by Quique Avilés; or crime novels by Marcos McPeek Villatoro, published between 2001 and 2011.[3] As Tatiana Argüello tells us, novels of this period dialogue transnationally with more recent work, including those published in Spanish on the isthmus (2018). I would further argue that more recent literature points to new trends in US Central American writing that represents an even broader multiplicity of worldly experiences.

Indeed, as Ana Patricia Rodríguez indicates, "Central American cultural production in the United States is not an entirely recent or stand-alone phenomenon but one built on historical collaborations, solidarity networks, and transnational dialogues established among artists, scholars, and activists" (2009: 163). While the more recent titles I mention build upon long-standing solidarity networks, taken together they are paradigmatic of a recent shift in which US Central American writers, especially those of the second or 1.5 generations, elaborate primarily in English on contemporary themes of adoption, climate change, gang violence, gender and sexuality, xenophobia, and personal viewpoints on migration informed by (social) media outlets or (post)memories of war.[4] In the case of *The Wandering Song* in particular, the authors are cognizant of the fact that they participate in a deeply politicized critical movement that seeks to reverse the erasure of their voices, as Leticia Hernández Linares hints at in the preface (2017: 10). This is further evidenced by the fact that, as the first anthology of its kind combining diasporic voices from all seven Central American countries in English, it appears some forty-five years after *Aztlan: An Anthology of Mexican American Literature* (1972). And, in contrast to earlier writing, more recent works are indicative of intermediality between literature and social media. This is visible through Facebook Live readings by select authors from *The Wandering Song* in Summer 2020 and the subsequent GoFundMe campaign for the book's second printing, as well as Facebook and Instagram posts by authors like Roy G. Guzmán and Javier Zamora to promote their work.[5] Central American Twitter also dialogues productively with literary and film production.[6] Therefore, the concept of US Central Americanness moves across the global currents afforded by social networks, pointing to new directions for the construction of transnational solidarity.[7]

These titles speak to the reversal of Central America as "the invisible hinge between North and South" (2007: xvi), as Arias once called it. One could also argue that the texts bring the "'nonspace' that Central Americans occupy within Latinidad" (Cárdenas 2018: 6), further into grayscale. The wide range of US publishing houses publishing these works—such as small independent venues like Copper Canyon, Kórima, Red Hen, and Tía Chucha, to university presses such as Indiana and Wisconsin—complicate the notion of who or what constitutes the cosmopolitan center. The authors, too, offer new angles from which to develop an understanding of world literature as a form of resistance; we are "peoples impacted by global forces" (Cheah 2016: 17). Chinchilla and Tobar, for example, were born in the United States, while others such as Arias and me were born in Guatemala and divide our personal and professional lives between Central America and the United States. The worldliness of the texts comes to light through influences from the North and South and, indeed, conceive of the spaces where the two converge.

Global South Mappings

US Central American authors, just as those on the isthmus, are practitioners of cosmopolitanism from different angles and loci of enunciation, pointing to a world literature from below, in relation to margins and other ex-centric locations, as this volume shows. In tune with Cheah's approach to world literature, I emphasize the Global South as an apt framework through which to read US Central American literature. On the one hand, "Global South" is a post-Cold War replacement for Third World in consideration of economically disadvantaged countries such as those of Central America. As a critical category of analysis, Anne Garland Mahler asserts that a useful definition of the Global South is a "transnational political imaginary that results from the identification of one's shared conditions with others across the globe, a recognition that produces a 'world of protest'" (2018: 33). In a similar vein, Debra Castillo and Shalini Puri write that the Global South "refers to a locus of solidarity and contestation that seeks futures more democratic than those held out by first world capitalism, developmentalism, and sub-imperialisms within the south" (2016: 6), and Vijay Prashad declares that it is "a world of protest, a whirlwind of creative activity" (2012: 9). The home countries of US Central Americans and their families lie outside the high-income powerhouses of the United States or Europe, are demarcated by their physical locations to the literal south of the imperial powers, and thus neatly fall into the category of Global South. Beyond this simple reconceptualization of the Third World, however, the Global South as understood by US Central Americans emerges in a deterritorialized fashion to articulate social movements and solidarities with peoples in similar— imperialistic, neocolonial, neoliberal, even necropolitical—subject positions across the world.

I approach US Central American writing through the lens of the Global South because, as Castillo and Puri point out, "it has a life outside academia" (2016: 6), which suggests the inclusion of the writers (and their readers) in debates about the work's circulation and reception. In this sense, the critical category contrasts with other terms used in relation to Central America such as EpiCentro (Chinchilla 2007), transisthmus (Rodríguez 2009), or Northern Triangle, which was originally coined for commercial purposes.[8] Correspondingly, I understand Global South spaces as geographically expansive areas, occupied and populated by Central Americans and others, which reflect the negative impacts of neoliberal globalization and ongoing imperialism spearheaded by US foreign policies and their political allies. Global South spaces are areas where the impacts of civil wars, coup d'états (or other armed conflicts or natural disasters), are strongly felt, and where past or present North-South, South-North, or even South-South movements of peoples take place or are imagined, especially across borderlands and heavily militarized zones. Global paradigms such as exile, migration, state or urban violence, and white supremacy are harbingers of these spaces since they stress neoliberal policies and remarkable failures of governance, both in less economically powerful countries and precarious spaces within US borders. Global South spaces generate (even necessitate) the creative imagination of alternative futures. They are omnipresent in Guatemala, in the gang-controlled sectors of Guatemala City as well as commercialized zones dominated by US American capitalism, and its frontiers with El Salvador, Honduras, and Mexico, especially Chiapas. The Global South positions of El Salvador and Honduras are enhanced by the fact that migrants from these countries must pass through the entirety of Guatemala before reaching Mexico, itself characterized by Global South spaces of La Bestia and areas along the migrant trails dominated by narcoactivity such as Tamaulipas.

Given these parameters, it would be fair to say that any of the twenty-first-century US Central American texts I have cited could be the subject of this chapter. I have chosen *The Wandering Song* because of how it unites writing from all countries on the isthmus. While the seven countries have not been affected to the same measure, all of them have been deeply shaped by imperialism and related citizen reactions, which indicate a shared condition as a Global South space. I also note the diversity of genres in the anthology, including essays, autobiographical writing, creative nonfiction, fiction, memoirs, novel excerpts, poetry, and short stories. Voices of women, Indigenous Peoples, LGBTQ+ identifying persons, and Afrodescendants are present, which highlight the periphery from a multitude of angles that are themselves peripheral to dominant heteropatriarchal perspectives. Furthermore, the editors Leticia Hernández Linares, Rubén Martínez, and Héctor Tobar constitute major figures in US Central American writing in their own rights, with Tobar's *The Tattooed Soldier* (1998) most representative of this literary status. The publication date of the anthology, 2017, is poignant because of how it falls in the first year of the Trump presidency, a political gesture to push back against proposed border walls and global xenophobic ideologies promoted by the racist administration. The specific pieces from the anthology under consideration approach migration from a decidedly Global South subject position that moves from Guatemala to the United States and back in their imaginations. In addition, I have chosen *Catrachos* and *Unaccompanied* because they mark the places of El Salvador, Honduras, and their peoples within global flows of migration, which necessarily cross multiple borderlands, each with their inherent Global South qualities. Their life stories thematize (and humanize) border crossing while at the same time confronting the countries of origin as catalysts for placemaking across geographically expansive areas.

The imagination of Central America, both physically embodied and distantly remembered, is a focal point of much of the writing found in *The Wandering Song*, with the work by Patrick Mullen-Coyoy standing out in this regard. The title of his poem, "Where Is Guatemala?" automatically evokes an image of a country and its peoples not firmly anchored in place. He opens by writing:

"Where in Mexico is Guatemala?"
The question hangs in the air, waiting,
For an answer that lies beyond your grasp.

(2017: 180)

On the one hand, the question seems laughable because of how common it is for US Central Americans to have to identify their countries on a map, even in conversation with other Latinxs. Its ignorance notwithstanding, it makes a direct reference to the movement of Guatemala—Guatemalan people, ideas, and thought—through and within Mexico. Guatemala could be located within Mexico, insofar as Guatemala is understood as an epistemology, a broad scope of knowledges not tethered down by geographical forces but rather informed by cultural norms, including those related to exile as a main pillar of Guatemalan thought. That Guatemala/ns are in Mexico is more than a passing reference to an obtuse question asked by people in the North; it is a signal of the spread of the Guatemalan condition and the spread of the South northward. The "souths in the geographic North" (Mahler 2018: 6) are embodied by Guatemalans who are faced with the simple task of explaining their country's location. As Mullen-Coyoy's poem makes clear, his voice struggles with an answer to the question of where Guatemala is located, since it can take on multiple forms, "a place, a feeling—a memory" (2017: 180), or an idea or performance of knowledge elucidated by these categories. In an indirect reference to the "nonspace" that Cárdenas develops in her thinking of US Central Americans adjacent to other Latinx groups, the poem alludes to an unknown location, while simultaneously working to map Guatemala in our imagination. Yet the olfactory dimensions of the country, described as "[s]mog [that] mixes with incense and sawdust to create the sweetest scent—*aire chapín*" (2017: 180), underscore a state of being easily transported beyond borders.

In attempting to answer the question regarding Guatemala's location, it paradoxically seems easier for the poem to identify what the country decidedly is *not* to help place it in our imagination. For example, it is not "something the sociologist-anthropologist-tourist can easily catalogue in their guidebook" (Mullen-Coyoy 2017: 180). The learned anthropologist or sociologist travels to the country to conduct fieldwork and write ethnographies or case studies. While typically not in the same category as a casual tourist, the poem does well to point out these identities together since they often constitute non-Guatemalans writing about the country and its customs from an outsider perspective that must establish and maintain rapport with local populations. In a similar fashion, in direct reference to the shared dimensions of Guatemalan identities at home or in the United States, the text gets at the heart of what it means to embody the "in-between" or "nonspace." It pinpoints how Guatemala, as an idea and epistemology, is "[a] rage against the governments—whether *de aquí o de allá*—that hate your people" (Mullen-Coyoy 2017: 181). In this sense, the text is a site of political thinking that positions the Guatemalan and US governments as catalysts for the development of Guatemala as a feeling, perhaps even superior to its position as a fixed location difficult for outsiders to discern on a map. Indeed, by the end of the short piece the voice seems to surrender, declaring "Hard as I try, I still can't tell you where Guatemala is" (Mullen-Coyoy 2017: 181). With this air of resignation, the poetic voice establishes solidarity with other Guatemalans, Central Americans, and migrants from other parts of the Global South who feel obligated to explain their country's location, an act that cements their subjugation while at the same time placing emphasis on the globalizing forces that warrant what countries are more economically powerful and thus worthy of knowing.

The voice of Gabriela Ramirez Chavez (no accents) in the anthology similarly conceives of Guatemala as a place that extends beyond its geographic contours to occupy a space of memory. She opens "When Mamá Told Me" with a nod to forced disappearance, which was a defining feature of the internal armed conflicts in Guatemala and elsewhere in Central and Latin America in the 1970s and 1980s that still haunts the transnational imaginary. Her work tells us: "When Mamá told me, I didn't understand how someone could just be somewhere and then poof away. I thought it was like when the earth opened up her mouth and swallowed bad people in the Bible, including the kids" (Ramirez Chavez 2017a: 134). Here, a young Ramirez Chavez struggles to conceive of disappearance as a viable way for someone to no longer be with the rest of the family. The biblical reference serves as a strategy for her to understand a defining feature of Guatemala, which continues more than twenty-five years after the end of the conflicts. The poetic voice articulates violence acted upon those who either spoke out against the hyper-militarization of everyday life or were simply in the wrong place at the wrong time, numbering more than 45,000.

The poem continues: "Mamá would say, when I was disobedient and when she hit me lightly with a wooden spoon, how good I have it because I wasn't born in that time. My tío must've disappeared like that" (Ramirez Chavez 2017a: 134). The memory of Ramirez Chavez's tío is evident even in the most everyday interactions with her mamá. Although we do not know for sure if the two are siblings, the memory of the tío haunts the mamá and guides her interaction with her daughter who, from a very comfortable distance, is nevertheless able to discern disappearance as an everyday element of the culture in the South and, by extension, a focal point of her Guatemalan heritage. She conceives of the Global South space as that place where people are surely bound to disappear or otherwise be violently acted upon, as her tío has. Furthermore, the reader is left to surmise that the poem refers to Guatemala, given that this is Ramirez Chavez's country of origin that is not outwardly named. Just as "readers are still at a distance and free to be in some other place" (2013: 251), as Jean Franco cautions observers of Latin American state violence, Ramirez Chavez's status in the North prevents her from being disappeared, while at the same time affording her the opportunity to reflect upon the lingering impacts of disappearance on her family. Her identity as a Guatemalan is shaped by disappearance since it is a clear marker of the continued impact of US foreign policies and homegrown complicity. As in the case of Mullen-Coyoy's writing, the piece tapers off in a resigned tone that accepts disappearance for the time being, while alluding to an alternative future that will exist without it.

To reach that point, Gabriela's voice must scrutinize what disappearance must have looked and felt like for its victims. "Resistance Footage" takes a more participatory role and begins thus: "The first time I see disappearance is in a documentary. A silent clip in which a young man walks past a fenced building. A grey jeep pulls up, two figures jump out. One chokes him from behind, the other traps his arms. I wonder what the man is thinking, when a third figure with a black gun joins them" (Ramirez Chavez 2017b: 135). The documentary footage speaks volumes to how disappearance became a fixture of wartime milieu. On the one hand, the silence dramatically adds more suspense to an already harrowing clip. The man, while likely not Ramirez Chavez's tío, nevertheless sheds light on his experience. The man is completely defenseless and taken off guard, with the violent act characterized by a group effort that has been strategically planned and executed. After going into more detail about the physical violence, the poem continues: "I move the cursor over the videoplayer, drag the white dot across the screen, to watch it all go backwards" (Ramirez Chavez 2017b: 135). With violent Global South spaces firmly in the poetic voice's consciousness, the documentary is a means through which to understand disappearance and effectively the wartime cultures that still surface in the present. The footage serves as a point of departure for Ramirez Chavez to understand her own past; her origins, as with so many other Guatemalans in the diaspora, can be traced to human rights violations. The ability to rewind the video, as if to prevent the forced disappearance from happening in the first place, allows for a participatory role in memory making and the conception of a Global South space that can be reimagined. By moving the cursor backward, the poetic voice advances the notion that the violent dynamics depicted could change in the future, while at the same time confronting the impossibility of completely escaping the subjugated status imposed upon Guatemalans at home or abroad.

Similar scenarios surface in the work of Javier Zamora, who left his grandparents' care in El Salvador to join his parents in the United States at the age of nine. His poem "Second Attempt Crossing" captures the essence of the border itself as violence, while at the same time conceiving of US-Mexico borderlands as a Global South space. With the desert as the backdrop, the poetic voice reveals to us how "someone yelled '¡La Migra!' and everyone ran. In that dried creek where forty of us slept, we turned to each other, and you flew from my side in the dirt. Black-throated sparrows and dawn hitting the tops of mesquites" (Zamora 2017: 9). Recalling this violent episode with Border Patrol agents, the poem at once speaks directly to distant readers and one of Zamora's travel companions who runs out of view to escape capture. Directly from Zamora's point of view, the poem continues: "I said, 'freeze Chino, ¡pará por favor!' So I wouldn't touch their legs that kicked you, you pushed me under your chest, and I've never thanked you. Beautiful Chino—the only name I know to call you by—farewell your tattooed chest: the M, the S, the 13" (Zamora 2017: 9). Here, he presents a positive view of gang members, in sharp contrast to both academic and popular discourses.[9] He observes the extension of ubiquitous militarization of everyday life by another means, a reality Salvadorans know all too well in their home country. US border security unknowingly mimics inherent Central American qualities, which come to the fore via the poetic voice's account of a fading MS13 insignia as an inscription of a group that originated within US borders in the first place. As a goodbye to Chino, Zamora recalls thinking "Farewell your brown arms that shielded me then, that shield me now, from La Migra" (Zamora 2017: 10). Brownness is an ethnic marker of the migrants' Central Americanness, which is obviously all that is important for border officials to consider their presence a punishable offense, while also serving as a source of comfort as subjugated peoples in subjugated spaces are bound together by their desire to reach the ostensible safety of the North. Aside from the arguably Central American qualities of its southern borders, we can consider this a Global South space because of how violently immigration is acted upon and because detention centers function to create forced disappearances of another kind. These sentiments extend much further than memories of El Salvador or even Central America taken as a whole. Yet nostalgia for home also comes to the fore as a guiding principle of Zamora's work.

In a poem simply titled "El Salvador," the poetic voice speaks directly to his distant country of origin: "Salvador, if I return on a summer day, so humid my thumb will clean your beard of salt, and if I touch your volcanic face, kiss your pumice breath, please don't let cops say: *he's gangster*. Don't let gangsters say: *he's wrong barrio*. Your barrios stain you with pollen" (Zamora 2017: 11). The poem immediately allows us to see how migrants' relationships with their country of origin evolve as they encounter multiple Global South spaces and scenarios. The personification of the country is made clear using second-person singular pronouns. Despite having risked his life to leave, Zamora still feels inherently Salvadoran. His direct pleas to the country indicate his desire to have stayed there, given different circumstances and a lack of US interventions that necessitated the departure of him and his family members. At a Global South crossroads, he wants to return to see El Salvador but his parents say, "*[D]on't go; you have tattoos*," which could inadvertently signal a *marero* persona with which he unequivocally does not personally identify yet has humanized through his relationship with Chino.

As the poem continues, we consider whether "postwar" is even an accurate strategy to describe the country, despite how often it is employed to describe El Salvador and its neighbors. Continuing to address the country as a person, the poem goes on:

> Stupid Salvador, you see our black bags, our empty homes, our fear to say: *the war has never stopped*, and still you lie and say: *I'm fine, I'm fine*,

but if I don't brush Abuelita's hair, wash her pots and pans, I cry. Tonight, how I wish you made it easier to love you, Salvador. Make it easier to never have to risk our lives.

(Zamora 2017: 11)

By thinking and writing beyond the nation and multiple national borders, Zamora's poem conceives of being Salvadoran beyond El Salvador in a work that curiously leaves out the "El" of the country's name, even though doing so is considered insulting. Perhaps, paradoxically, its omission signals personification of a flawed country and the poetic voice's frustration with an inability to easily return, emphasizing its permanent Global South status. It highlights an incomplete Salvadoran identity, firmly anchored in neither Central America nor the United States, flowing between the two in the literary imagination.

Similarly, with *Catrachos*, Roy G. Guzmán presents a life story that addresses themes of nostalgia and the (im)probability of return to Central America from a queer Honduran perspective. Crossing lines between public and private, they showcase shared conditions of those whose lives oscillate between the United States and the Global South, including when these movements are restricted to the imagination.[10] One of their poems, "Preparations for a Trip Home," is divided into six parts, each of which is represented by a number with a strikethrough. This postmodern stylistic detail automatically suggests several possibilities, among them memories that are presumed to be one-time events, temporal or spatial distance from the events described, or even sensorial dynamics at the nexus between everyday challenges in the United States and foregone questions of insecurity in Honduras. The poem begins by relaying the trials and tribulations of preparing for a visit to a distant home in the South, moving quickly to a memory of buying tickets for La Chica, the Honduran national lottery. In part 2 [*sic*], the poetic voice details how "[y]ou buy your tickets at the pulpería or any other store at the mall if you can afford a big bowl of seafood soup, un sopón" (Guzmán 2020: 16), explaining how players can gamble lempiras in exchange for household items. It launches into the hopeful possibility if the players win, with the poetic voice, a literary embodiment of Guzmán's own memories, longing for a family telephone instead of a PlayStation, a much more popular choice. The poem continues:

But there were times when you could wager on a telephone & finally have a way to communicate with your brothers en La Yuma [a Honduran colloquialism for the US] without having to use your neighbor's phone— the one neighbor who had lived outside the country & recently came back all sick to live out the rest of her days in Honduras—if you won.

(2020: 16)[11]

Here, the poetic voice provides a prelude to migration to La Yuma (the United States), suggesting that this is the most coveted La Chica prize of all.

As the poem advances, it reveals that Guzmán's parents will make the return visit to Honduras without them due to an inability to miss work. Their mother quips, "You can't trust these zánganos [a regional colloquialism for a lazy person], especially when you're at the airport & they're inspecting every detail in your bag like you just stepped out of prison" (2020: 18). Her observation, which could resonate with someone outside of a minoritized subjectivity, nevertheless gets at the heart of shared experiences of peoples whose very presence counters hegemonic expectations. "These zánganos," whether they are at airline counters or Transportation Security Administration (TSA) agents who invade personal space, are categorized as such on the one hand because they are not likely to recognize Guzmán's mother's Honduran identity. On the other, in her estimation, they are prone to assume that a Latina woman is suspicious, with a propensity to transport illicit goods in her bag. Similar concerns are undoubtedly shared by other Global South ethnic minorities who face multifaceted challenges when crossing borders, even by air. While land border crossings and confrontations with customs agents launch their own sets of challenges, as Zamora's work affirms, the US Central American woman, as with other people of color with roots outside the United States, must convince airport officials that her journey back to her country of birth is also legitimate.

At the same time, as phenomena such as deportation to and within the Global South have repeatedly taught us, the act of returning to one's country is weaponized when the desire is violently ignited from the outside. Another poem from Guzmán's collection is entitled "When a Person Says Go Back to Your Country." In direct dialogue with the title, it begins: "that's exactly what you do, though you can't tell if you'll aggressively run or trip on national borders you'll have to make up for, the declaration so thunderous that even the floor can't hold still" (2020: 46). Here, the poetic voice ponders the difficulties associated with returning home, while remaining determined to defy the aggressor and take their racist suggestion to heart. The phrase "go back to your country" is one that innumerable persons from the Global South beyond Central America have heard, triggered even by the most everyday occurrences such as speaking Spanish (or any number of native languages other than English) in public. In Guzmán's case, the phrase is a painful marker of identity, which serves to create division between them and the aggressor. The poem considers when they will finally be able to heed the unsolicited advice and return to their country on their own terms. In reference to a distant future, the poem tells us: "Because by then you're not an adult but a child aspiring to behave like a breadwinner, & when you can't find this country to which you're asked to return, though *back* has always meant finding an undisclosed place to vanish in, you try to give a retort" (2020: 46).

The inability to find the country of origin stresses the disorientation associated with returns, whether due to passport or visa delays, major changes in infrastructure after prolonged periods away, or the treatment in the airport as Guzmán's mother describes. Just as people's movements out of their countries are violent, so, too are the returns. As the poem observes that "*his* family *can* be remembered" (2020: 46), it seems to internally dialogue with itself, as if to say, for now, Honduras exists only as an unnamed country, both from the perspective of Guzmán and the combative challenger. Despite its morose undertone, the poem achieves an air of solidarity with the shared conditions of migrants who embody similar subjectivities, whose movements out of their countries and their returns—including as they are imagined by others—are forever marked by North-South relations.

Conclusion

The combination of world literature, understood as an effective strategy to portray how marginalized peoples have experienced global phenomena such as migration, and the Global South as a locus of solidarity, elicits a critical framework to categorize US Central American writing. In this chapter, I have explored how understandings of world literature that challenge Eurocentric visions and the Global South as conceived beyond geographical limitations prove particularly salient in US Central American discourses. This development suggests that both critical categories, along with US Central American writing itself, emerge as forms of resistance. The deterritorialized Global South spaces as imagined by writers from El Salvador, Guatemala, and Honduras in the United States necessarily depict shared conditions and scenarios with any number of life experiences, from the necessity to describe a country's location on a map, racist dialogues, or the violent migration process itself. The alternative cartographies of solidarity communicate with a wider world of readers both at a comfortable distance from those realities (but with a disposition to be sympathetic to them) and others away from US/Central American worlds. Migrants from across the Global South—other parts of Latin America, the Caribbean, Africa, South and Southeast Asia, and elsewhere—could very well need to describe their country's location or answer the question "what is it?" as Arias recalls or even "what are you?" as I know from personal experience. The global forces of wartime violence, and the need to revisit them to understand one's own identity, could easily move outside US Central American contexts. Borders and migration as an extension of that violence, and the people summoned to tell the underlying stories, also resonate far beyond the isthmus. To name but two possibilities, they could dialogue productively with experiences of Haitians in makeshift tent communities along the river border at Del Río,

Texas, in September 2021 or ongoing flows of Somali refugees leaving the Horn of Africa to cross the Mediterranean.

In line with the aforementioned, the creative works explored here move US Central American voices into discussions on world-making and canon formation. By illustrating world experiences of the twenty-first century, the works not only create their own networks of solidarity but also present the possibility to intersect with major ongoing social movements of our times. The short poems by Mullen-Coyoy and Ramirez Chavez seek to understand Guatemala's location and its wartime past as a means through which to come to terms with transnational identities written by violence. In the case of Ramirez Chavez's work, it also gestures toward alternative futures where forced disappearance is no longer a fixture of Guatemalan culture on both sides of (or right along) the border(s). In the process, the Guatemalan voices divulge the current development of a transnational political imaginary. In the case of Zamora's poetry, a prolonged unaccompanied identity, coupled with the personification of El Salvador, means that borderland politics, race, and migration are focal points of both the deeply personal and a birth country left behind. Guzmán's work exhibits shared conditions of marginality, communicating that Honduras remains at the forefront of the imagination even (or perhaps especially) when one can imagine return trips back and forth between North and South. Above all, the texts show an ecosystem of cultural production consonant with Global South spaces as worlds of protest that will give way to inclusive futures attuned to Central Americanness beyond the isthmus.

Notes

1   See January 2021 Instagram posts by Guatemalan photojournalist @estebanbiba, some of which depict Hondurans who were denied entry at the border with Guatemala due to their inability to provide negative Covid test results.

2   I am beholden to J. Andrea Carrillo for ongoing conversations about this topic.

3   Houston-based Arte Público Press simultaneously published the original Spanish *Odisea del norte* and its English translation *Odyssey to the North* as separate volumes.

4   For more on memory and postmemory as related to contemporary Latin American Cultural Studies, see Lazarra (2018) or Szurmuk (2012).

5   Guzmán promoted *Catrachos* on Facebook by offering personalized signed copies to those who purchased from them directly. When *Solito* was released, Zamora announced his book tour on Facebook and via the Instagram story feature with registration links to his personal website. His interviews on *The Today Show* and other outlets further illustrate the intermediality between *Solito* and various media.

6   Hashtags such as #CentralAmericanTwitter and accounts like @CentAm_Beauty speak to this point.
7   I thank Tamara Mitchell for bringing this point to my attention.
8   See Chavez and Avalos (2014).
9   See Carter (2022), Levenson (2013), and Ward (2012), among other recent texts on gangs of Central America.
10 My discussions of Guzmán's poems respect their use of they/them/their pronouns.
11 I thank Guzmán for pointing out this Honduran colloquialism.

References

Aragón, F. (2020), *After Rubén*, Pasadena: Red Hen.
Archila, W. (2015), *The Gravedigger's Archaeology*, Pasadena: Red Hen.
Argüello, T. (2018), "War and Its Impact on Central American-American Literature," in *The Oxford Encyclopedia of Latina/o Literature*, Oxford: Oxford University Press.
Arias, A. (2007), *Taking Their Word: Literature and the Signs of Central America*, Minneapolis: Minnesota University Press.
Arias, A. (2008), "UO Today Show #383 Arturo Arias," YouTube video, 28:49, https://youtu.be/O499CFRlinc.
Arias, A. (2011), "Pandora's Box," in L. Lima and F. Picano (eds.), *Ambientes: New Queer Latino Writing*, 27–44, Madison: University of Wisconsin Press.
Arias, A. (2012), "Central American-Americans in the Second Decade of the Twenty-First Century: Old Scars, New Traumas, Disempowering Travails," *Diálogo*, 15 (1): 4–16.
Avilés, Q. (2003), *The Immigrant Museum*, Mexico City: PinStudio y Raíces de Papel.
Bencastro, M. (1998), *Odyssey to the North*, Houston: Arte Público.
Bentley, A. (2020), "The *Gringo Chapín* Goes to Guate," *Chiricú Journal: Latina/o Literatures, Arts, and Cultures*, 5 (1): 88–104.
Biba, E. (2021), "Un niño se para entre #LaCaravanaDeMigrantes y la Policía de Guatemala," Instagram.
Cárdenas, M. (2018), *Constituting Central American-Americans: Transnational Identities and the Politics of Dislocation*, New Brunswick: Rutgers University Press.
Carter, J. H. (2022), *Gothic Sovereignty: Street Gangs and Statecraft in Honduras*, Austin: University of Texas Press.
Chambers, V. (1996), *Mama's Girl*, New York: Riverhead Books.
Chavez, S. and J. Avalos (2014), "The Northern Triangle: The Countries That Don't Cry for Their Dead," *InSight Crime*, https://insightcrime.org/news/analysis/the-northern-triangle-the-countries-that-dont-cry-for-their-dead/#:~:text=The%20Northern%20Triangle%20epithet%20was,agreement%20in%20Nueva%20Ocotepeque%2C%20Honduras.

Cheah, P. (2016), *What Is a World? On Postcolonial Literature as World Literature*, Durham: Duke University Press.
Chinchilla, M. (2007), "Desde el EpiCentro," *EpiCentroAmerica* Blog, http://epicentroamerica.blogspot.com/2007/09/desde-el-epicentro.html.
Chinchilla, M. (2014), *The Cha Cha Files: A Chapina Poética*, San Francisco: Kórima.
Francisco, A. (2020), *A Sinking Ship Is Still a Ship*, DeLand: Burrow.
Franco, J. (2013), *Cruel Modernity*, Durham: Duke University Press.
Goldman, F. (1992), *The Long Night of White Chickens*, New York: Grove.
Goldman, F. (2021), *Monkey Boy*, New York: Grove.
Guardado, C. (2017), *Endeavor*, CreateSpace.
Gutiérrez, R. (2011), "Aquí viene Johnny," in L. Lima and F. Picano (eds.), *Ambientes: New Queer Latino Writing*, 137–43, Madison: University of Wisconsin Press.
Guzmán, R. G. (2020), *Catrachos*, Minneapolis: Graywolf.
Henríquez, C. (2014), *The Book of Unknown Americans*, New York: Vintage Contemporaries.
Hernández-Linares, L. (2017), "Preface: Stories of Our Unincorporated Territories," in L. H. Linares, R. Martínez, and H. Tobar (eds.), *The Wandering Song: Central American Writing in the United States*, 9–11, Los Angeles: Tía Chucha.
Hernández-Linares, L., R. Martínez, and H. Tobar, eds. (2017), *The Wandering Song: Central American Writing in the United States*. Los Angeles: Tía Chucha.
Lazarra, M. (2018), "The Memory Turn," in J. Poblete (ed.), *New Approaches to Latin American Studies: Culture and Power*, 14–31, New York: Routledge.
Levenson, D. T. (2013), *Adiós Niño: The Gangs of Guatemala City and the Politics of Death*, Durham: Duke University Press.
Mahler, A. G. (2018), *From the Tricontinental to the Global South: Race, Radicalism, and Transnational Solidarity*, Durham: Duke University Press.
McPeek Villatoro, M. (2001), *Home Killings: A Romilia Chacón Novel*, Houston: Arte Público.
McPeek Villatoro, M. (2005), *A Venom beneath the Skin: A Romilia Chacón Novel*, Boston: Justin, Charles, & Co.
McPeek Villatoro, M. (2005), *Minos: A Romilia Chacón Novel*, New York: Dell Publishing Company.
McPeek Villatoro, M. (2011), *Blood Daughters: A Romilia Chacón Novel*, Pasadena: Red Hen.
Mullen-Coyoy, P. (2017), "Where Is Guatemala?" in L. H. Linares, R. Martínez, and H. Tobar (eds.), *The Wandering Song: Central American Writing in the United States*, 180–1, Los Angeles: Tía Chucha.
Najarro, A. (2015), *Split Geography*, El Paso: Mouthfeel.
Najarro, A. (2015), *Twice Told Over*, Portland: Unsolicited.
Najarro, A. (2017), *My Childrens*, Portland: Unsolicited.
Padilla, Y. (2013), "The Central American Transnational Imaginary: Defining the Gendered and Transnational Contours of Central American Immigrant Experience," *Latino Studies*, 11 (2): 150–66.
Padilla, Y. (2022), *From Threatening Guerrillas to Forever Illegals: US Central Americans and the Cultural Politics of Non-Belonging*, Austin: University of Texas Press.

Prashad, V. (2012), *The Poorer Nations: A Possible History of the Global South*, London: Verso.
Puri, S. and D. A. Castillo (2016), "Introduction: Conjectures on Undisciplined Research," in S. Puri and D. A. Castillo (eds.), *Theorizing Fieldwork in the Humanities: Methods, Reflections, and Approaches to the Global South*, 1–26, New York: Palgrave Macmillan.
Ramirez Chavez, G. (2017a), "When Mamá Told Me," in L. H. Linares, R. Martínez, and H. Tobar (eds.), *The Wandering Song: Central American Writing in the United States*, 134, Los Angeles: Tía Chucha.
Ramirez Chavez, G. (2017b), "Resistance Footage," in L. H. Linares, R. Martínez, and H. Tobar (eds.), *The Wandering Song: Central American Writing in the United States*, 135, Los Angeles: Tía Chucha.
Rodríguez, A. P. (2009), *Dividing the Isthmus: Central American Transnational Histories, Literatures, and Cultures*, Austin: University of Texas Press.
Rodríguez, A. P. (2018), "Invisible No More: U.S. Central American Literature before and beyond the Age of Neoliberalism," in J. M. González and L. Lomas (eds.), *The Cambridge History of Latina/o American Literature*, 510–31, Cambridge: Cambridge University Press.
Szurmuk, M. "Postmemory," in R. M. Irwin and M. Szurmuk (eds.), *Dictionary of Latin American Cultural Studies*, 258–63, Gainesville: University Press of Florida, 2012.
Tobar, H. (1998), *The Tattooed Soldier*, Picador: New York.
Tobar, H. (2020), *The Last Great Road Bum*, MCD: New York.
Unger, D. (2002), *Life in the Damn Tropics*, Syracuse: Syracuse University Press.
Valez, L. and S. Steiner, eds. (1976), *Aztlán: An Anthology of Mexican American Literature*, New York: Knopf.
Vida, M. (2017), "How #CentralAmericanTwitter Evolved beyond a Hashtag into a Much-Needed Community," *Remezcla*, https://remezcla.com/features/culture/central-american-twitter/.
Ward, T. W. (2012), *Gangsters without Borders: An Ethnography of a Salvadoran Street Gang*, Oxford: Oxford University Press.
Zamora, J. (2017), *Unaccompanied*, Port Townsend: Copper Canyon Press, 2017.
Zamora, J. (2022), *Solito*, New York: Vintage Español.

13

Caravaneros as Citizens of the World

Robert McKee Irwin

In October of 2018, the eyes of the world turned to Honduras, a country in which the world has historically shown little interest, as a large group of migrants gathered in San Pedro Sula, setting out for the United States. Upon hearing about this migrant caravan, Douglas Oviedo, a once homeless youth pastor, left his home in Tegucigalpa, to join it, eventually making it all the way to the Tijuana border. Throughout his journey with the migrant caravan, and through much of the ten months he spent in Tijuana awaiting the outcome of his application for asylum in the United States, the *caravaneros* remained on the world stage, at the center of debates on migration, border control mechanisms, and human rights. While awaiting his court dates in Tijuana, Oviedo wrote *Caravaneros*, a testimonial drama documenting that tumultuous and politically charged journey from the perspective of the migrants who made up the ranks of the caravan. *Caravaneros*, published in 2020 in Mexico, is an epic story told by an extraordinary migrant. In what follows, I will reflect on what this work might represent to Honduran, Central American, or world literature. I will argue, following philosopher Pheng Cheah's (2016) view of world literature as a space of world-making as well as migration studies scholar William Walters's (2015: 16) assertion that "migration, no less than global finance or climate change, is a truly world making phenomenon," that Oviedo's *Caravaneros* should be read as a work of contemporary world literature.

The Migrant Caravans of Fall 2018

I will confess that I am not an impartial observer or detached critic, but rather am a supporting character in this story. I had coincidentally planned a trip to Tijuana to follow up on work I was carrying out for the Humanizing Deportation digital storytelling project, which I have coordinated since its launch in late 2016 (see Irwin 2020a), for mid-November of 2018. Just a few days before my arrival in Tijuana, the first contingents of the migrant caravan (really a series of caravans) arrived in the city.

The media attention to the caravans had been especially pronounced. While the concept of a migrant caravan was not new—past caravans in the region had been staged as political events, including, notably, an annual journey made by mothers of migrants who had disappeared along the migrant trail in Mexico—this was the first time that a large-scale caravan had formed as a vehicle for migration (Irwin and Silva 2020: 20–1).

The caravan took place in a politically volatile and charged (trans)national context in Honduras, Mexico, and the United States. In Honduras, the government of then president Juan Orlando Hernández had been facing protests about fraud and corruption since its inception in 2014. These increased after the president's brother was arrested by the US Drug Enforcement Agency on drug-trafficking charges, including allegations that he had used Honduran military infrastructure to ship drugs to the United States. His arrest in November 2018 (convicted in 2021, Tony Hernández is now serving a life sentence in US federal prison, and Juan Orlando Hernández himself is currently in prison in Honduras, awaiting possible extradition to the United States to face drug-trafficking charges) coincided with the arrival of the caravans at the US border, and political opponents argued that this large-scale emigration was the result of the failures of the current regime, whereas defenders of Orlando Hernández's regime accused the opposition of having organized the caravan as a political ploy. Political maneuvering, misinformation campaigns, and counter accusations ran rampant with regard to the caravan's origins, its composition, and the purported role of external agitators in its leadership.

In Mexico, the caravan's arrival in Tijuana occurred during the last days of the presidency of Enrique Peña Nieto, with president elect Andrés Manuel López Obrador set to take office on December 1. Despite demands from the United States that Mexico impede the migrants from entering Mexico, and from reaching the US border, thousands arrived in Tijuana and other border cities beginning in the latter half of November. While it was the Peña Nieto regime that let them pass, they would soon become a major problem for the incoming president. While migration debates in Mexico had long focused on Mexican emigration to the United States, the caravan generated political agitation in Mexico about Central American migrants. A few days after the first caravan migrants reached Tijuana, with many setting up camp along the border in Friendship Park, at the city's northwestern boundary in Playas de Tijuana, a protest took form along the edge of the migrant camp, demanding their removal. Until that day, protests against migrants had been unheard of in Tijuana, a city built on accelerated internal migration, its population having risen from less than 100,000 in the mid-1950s to over 2,000,000 by the late 2010s. Growing anti-migration sentiment, directly primarily at Central Americans, was taking hold all over Mexico (Irwin and Silva 2020: 23).

Meanwhile, the mounting media spectacle of the caravan took hold as the United States was preparing for midterm congressional elections. US president Donald Trump published frequent allegations on Twitter that the caravan was camouflaging movements of organized crime or terrorist groups, presumably in order to rouse nativist sentiments and drum up votes from his conservative base; meanwhile, opposition rhetoric denounced the Trump administration's callous treatment of refugees, including families escaping threats of violence. Significantly, with the November 6 vote, the democratic opposition took control of the House of Representatives, a significant blow to the White House, which reacted by taking a more severe stance against Central American asylum seekers, including, notably, the January 2019 launch of Migrant Protection Protocols (MPP) that required Central Americans seeking asylum at the US southern border to wait out the often lengthy process of the evaluation of their cases in US immigration court on the Mexican side of the border (Irwin and Silva 2020: 24–8).

These political tensions, most especially those of the latter two contexts, were palpable in November of 2018 when I arrived in Tijuana the morning following the above-mentioned protests in Playas de Tijuana. My stay in the city, which was to be just for a few days, ended up getting extended as massive smoke clouds from wildfires raging in northern California shut down the University of California, Davis, and I decided I would be better off in Tijuana. At that time I made the decision to extend the Humanizing Deportation project, which had until then focused its attention only on deported migrants and their families, to include migrants in transit. I realized that Central American migrants in Mexico were just as vulnerable to deportation and other migration control mechanisms as undocumented immigrants living in the United States. Indeed the very first caravan migrant who published his story on the Humanizing Deportation website ended up getting deported twice in the following months, once from the United States and again from Mexico, after setting out a second time from Honduras. That anonymous migrant published two digital stories, one recorded in Playas de Tijuana on November 18, 2018, and another recorded in Huixtla, Chiapas, some six months later, after he fled Honduras for a third time, following his two deportations (see Irwin 2020b).

Douglas Oviedo, The Bridge

I first met Douglas Oviedo in February of 2019 at Enclave Caracol, a cultural center located in downtown Tijuana. Humanizing Deportation had organized an exhibition of our digital stories there, featuring a series of public events with different community partners. During a question-answer session at the end of our opening reception, a voice rose up from the back of the gallery space. A young bearded man read what appeared to be a manifesto articulating an eloquent defense of the migrant caravans from his telephone. We spoke to him afterward and offered him the platform of Humanizing Deportation to tell his story, resulting in a two-part digital story, *Historias de la caravana* (Oviedo 2019a, 2019b).

Oviedo, who would end up being assigned to the MPP program the very first day of its implementation, became an unusually prominent figure in Tijuana in 2019. Through personal connections with artists and activists, he ended up, during the remaining nine months he spent in Tijuana awaiting the outcome of his asylum case, assuming a leadership role—unheard of for a migrant in transit—in the organization of several cultural events, and, remarkably, the construction of a new shelter for migrant families in Tijuana, Casa Hogar El Puente. Oviedo, who is one of a small fraction of caravan migrants who have been granted asylum (according to the TRAC Immigration Project [2021], about 25 percent of MPP cases have had a positive result), recounts his extraordinary experience as musician and community organizer in Tijuana in two additional segments of *Historias de la caravana* (Irwin and Silva 2020: 29–34; Oviedo 2019c, 2019d).

Another of Oviedo's activities in Tijuana occurred when local arts activist Gaba Cortés, seeing him disheartened at the slow pace of his asylum case, offered him a living subsidy to spend a month writing about his experiences migrating in the caravan. Douglas was granted asylum in September of 2019 and was placed initially in the home of a generous resident of Hercules, California. There, under the auspices of the Humanizing Deportation project, I was able to help Douglas publish *Caravaneros*, which in addition to his own text features a contextualizing introduction that I cowrote with Aída Silva and a brief prologue penned by two of Oviedo's key allies, Adam Elfers and Kei Kurimoto (2020), both US citizens who spent significant time in Tijuana working with Oviedo and other migrants in the months following the arrival of the caravans. They titled their short introductory text, "Douglas Oviedo es un puente" (Douglas Oviedo Is a Bridge).

Migrant Writings as Regional Literature

An inspiration for Oviedo in the writing of *Caravaneros* was Ustin Pascal Dubuisson, a Haitian migrant and arts activist who had arrived in Tijuana in 2016 as part of a large wave of Haitians who had come mostly via South

America to the US border in hopes of obtaining Temporary Protected Status or some other form of legal entry to the United States. Dubuisson had just, in late 2018, published a book *Sobrevivientes*, chronicling his own experience migrating, along with many other Haitians through northern South America into the Central American isthmus and through Mexico to the Tijuana border. Oviedo and Dubuisson had become friends in Tijuana, cohosting the Juntos Somos Más (together we are more) cultural festival in March 2019. The two books are very different: *Sobrevivientes*, narrated in the first person, takes the form of a travel memoir; on the other hand, the plot of *Caravaneros*, which follows the individual stories of a half dozen migrants, is driven mainly by dialogue, resembling more the script of a play or a film. As Oviedo has revealed that the book's main characters are based on real migrants, including himself and others that he met on his journey through Mexico, it also assumes elements of a testimonial narrative (see Irwin et al. 2020). Thus both books are testimonial in nature, as they draw on their authors' lived experiences migrating under precarious circumstances.

Oviedo's *Caravaneros* might be located in a genealogy of testimonial narratives along the Central America-Mexico-United States corridor. While both books were published in Mexico, neither qualifies easily as a Mexican text. Neither author was born or lived for very long in Mexico. Both have gone on to migrate to the United States, but their books have seen limited diffusion in the United States, and while their status may change over time, they don't fit neatly into any category of US American, including African American or Latinx, literature. It would also be difficult to attach either of them to national traditions in Haiti or Honduras. Neither author was likely inspired by any national literary tradition. Oviedo, for his part, lost both his parents to HIV when he was very young, ending up orphaned and homeless as a teenager before finding stability in his life as a youth pastor. He did not complete high school, much less formally study literature or creative writing. While there are no doubt cultural references that might link *Caravaneros* to works of Honduran literature, the only literary affiliation that Oviedo has discussed is *Sobrevivientes* (see Irwin et al. 2020).

This would indicate that *Caravaneros* and *Sobrevivientes* belong in a common genealogy of regional migration literature, which might include texts such as Óscar Martínez's *Los migrantes que no importan* (2010), a chronicle of stories of migrants that Martínez met traveling on La Bestia, or Javier Zamora's poetry collection *Unaccompanied* (2017). A few other texts that might be located in this genealogy of true or semi-fictionalized stories of migration that begin south of the Mexican border include Roberto Lovato's *Unforgetting: A Memoir of Family, Migration, Gangs, and Revolution in the Americas* (2020) and Sonia Nazario's *Enrique's Journey: The Story of a Boy's Dangerous Odyssey to Reunite with His Mother* (2007). Transnational regional literature of this kind may or may not be thought of through a world literature lens. In the case of *Caravaneros*, which has seen very little distribution outside of Mexico and the United

States, its lack of prominence in global markets might imply that a world literature moniker is misplaced. However, it might be helpful here to think about what we mean by world literature.

World Literature and Literary World-Making

Discussions of what qualifies as national literature, or world literature, or even literature are often fraught and do not necessarily lead to anything aside from highly subjective or even abstruse taxonomies that serve mainly for determining the content of literary anthologies, course surveys, or bookstore shelves. On the other hand if the literatures of peripheral places in the world, such as Honduras, might get the attention of scholars or readers through the category of world literature, maybe the exercise of defining the concept is worth pursuing.

Discussions on world literature very frequently revolve around questions that more often open up debates than arrive at definitive answers. In one of the most often-cited studies on world literature in recent decades, a book titled with the question *What Is World Literature?*, David Damrosch asks: "What does it really mean to speak of a world literature? Which literature, whose world?" (2003: 1). These questions, which he explores in detail in his much-cited study, draw attention to challenges in defining these two very common words, "world" and "literature."

Numerous scholars have followed his interrogative approach, revisiting and sometimes rearranging his questions. Indian scholar Supriya Chaudhuri (2021) revises Damrosch's question in her article, "Which World, Whose Literature?" Her interrogation pushes farther than Damrosch in insisting on addressing the question from outside the Western academy, noting that the notion of world tends to get casually conceived in globalized contexts of literary criticism. However the borderless world implicit in many discussions of world literature doesn't synch with the worlds experienced by many. As Chaudhuri observes: "In the world as we have it today, the world that we inhabit but cannot make sense of, the most typical figure is that of the refugee or immigrant waiting behind a fence, herded into a camp, or crowded into a sinking boat" (2021: 90). This reference to the world of precarity experienced by many refugees and migrants resonates with the work of authors such as Dubuisson and Oviedo and begins to hint at how they might fit into a scheme of world literature.

The decolonial questioning of the notion of "world" is further developed by postcolonialist literary scholars Karima Laachir, Sara Marzagora, and Francesca Orsini (2018: 294) who propose "significant geographies"— defined as "the *conceptual, imaginative,* and *real* geographies that texts, authors, and language communities inhabit, produce, and reach, which typically extend outwards without (ever?) having a truly global reach"—as a more productive concept than "world literature." They reject approaches to literature that emphasize "structure at the expense of agency" (292), instead proposing "an approach to world literature that works 'from the ground up'" (293). They seek to underline "how 'the world' is not a given but is produced by different, embodied, located actors" (294). While literature may not be the field to most fully explore the kind of embodied difference that this approach opens up, its interest in the lived experience of social actors, a category that might include migrants such as Oviedo or Dubuisson, sets it at odds with others that understand worlds via more academic or commercial configurations. As they sustain, "[i]t forces us to ask the question 'for whom' that puts 'people' back into the 'world,' unsettling the static idea of the world as a disembodied abstraction" (295), an approach that aligns very much with that of literary and cultural critic Arturo Arias (2007: xi), who signals, following Gayatri Chakravorty Spivak in his approach to Central American literature, that literature, defined broadly, can assume an important role in "elaborating and understanding solidarity across linguistic, national, ethnic, and cultural borders, not to mention even differences in social class."

Philosopher Pheng Cheah returns to the interrogations of Damrosch in his study on cosmopolitanism, *What Is a World*? In a sense his approach is completely at odds with that of Laachir, Marzagora, and Orsini in that it looks not to people but to nonhuman agencies. He puts forward a revised notion of world literature as "a literature that is an active power in the making of worlds, that is both a site of processes of worlding and an agent that participates and intervenes in these processes" (Cheah 2016: 2). For Cheah, literature can represent a "normative force" in which world literature can assume "a modality of cosmopolitanism that responds to the need to remake the world as a place that is open to the emergence of peoples that globalization deprives of world" (19). Combining these divergent approaches, I wish to argue that these interrogations invite us to think of Oviedo and Dubuisson as protagonists of world literature.

Migrants as Citizens of the World

The subtitle of Dubuisson's *Sobrevivientes* is *ciudadanos del mundo* (citizens of the world). His story tells of his own migration journey, which he makes mainly with other Haitians, thousands of whom migrated through Mexico to the US border in 2016 (2018: 134). He begins by pointing out that Haitians do not live in nationalist seclusion but rather live in a world in which transnational connections are central: "[l]a mayoría de los haitianos que viven en Haití dependen de otras personas" (the majority of Haitians living in Haiti depend on other people), meaning on the Haitian diaspora already living and working in the United States, Canada, Chile, Brazil, France, Ecuador, Venezuela, etc. (13).

The epic migration journey that he undertakes leads him from Brazil through Peru, Ecuador, Colombia, Panamá, Costa Rica, Nicaragua, Honduras, Guatemala, and Mexico en route to the United States. While most chapters of the book tell of crossing a single country (each ranging in length from five to twenty-five pages), its longest chapter, situated between those of Colombia and Panama, is forty pages long. "Darien Gap: Sálvase quien pueda" (Save Yourself If You Can) tells of the infamous perilous crossing of the remote expanse of jungle spanning the very northwest of Colombia into southeastern Panama. It is in this, the most terrifying segment of the voyage, that the Haitians seem to interact most with other migrants following the same path, undergoing the same hazards, including wild animals, violent storms, flash flooding, powerful river rapids, and the fetid smell of decaying corpses of migrants they pass along the way (Dubuisson 2018: 66, 69). The migrants with whom they share experiences in this terrifying rainforest come from both nearby: Cuba, Brazil, and very far away: Pakistan, Nepal, Ghana, and "muchos otros países" (many other countries) (46).

While they spend most of this period braving the jungle in vast areas with no signs of human life other than themselves, the few sites of refuge they find along this route are equally horrifying, one a large clearing supervised by Panamanian authorities where migrants were invited to set up tents on muddy, rocky soil, and were kept awake by shots fired by Panamanian guards to scare off wild animals. It is in one of these open air camps that Panamanian soldiers organized a swimming competition, dividing the migrants up by nationality: "Cualquiera que supiera nadar podía defender a su país" (whoever knew how to swim could defend their country). Interestingly, this superficially nationalist game "nos hizo olvidar momentáneamente en dónde estábamos. Por esos instantes pensábamos que éramos una verdadera comunidad" (made us forget momentarily where we were. For those instants we thought we were a true community) that implicitly included not only the migrants but also the Panamanian soldiers, who otherwise tended to treat the migrants with callous harshness (Dubuisson 2018: 55).

The phrase "citizens of the world" that Dubuisson uses as a subtitle appears twice within his narrative, once in his introductory chapter and again at the book's conclusion. On the first occasion, he explains that he means for his story to represent not only his own struggles or those of the Haitian diaspora of the mid-2010s but those of all migrants who, faced with dire living conditions in their homeland, have taken flight in search of a better life. As he puts it: "Esta historia fue vivida por miles de ciudadanos del mundo en búsqueda de una vida mejor en los Estados Unidos" (2018: 13) (This story was lived by thousands of citizens of the world in search of a better life in the United States). His final chapter opens with a commentary on each of the different borders he crossed and ends with words of advice to his readers: to live their lives based on principles of "Paciencia, Amor, Unión y Respeto" (patience, love, union, and respect). He invites everyone to not get hung up on money or fancy cars or be held back by fears: "Escojamos una razón valiosa para vivir, convirtámonos en ciudadanos del mundo y el éxito será para todos" (154) (Let's choose a worthwhile reason to live, making ourselves into citizens of the world, and success will be everyone's). His invocations here are of unity (common experience of migrants) and virtue (universal values).

Interestingly both discussions lead him to the notion of "citizens of the world"—recalling the thinking of another migrant activist, Nancy Landa, a young deported Mexican whose blog *Mundo Citizen* (2013–20), much of it written from Tijuana, drew significant attention to the plight of childhood arrival migrants. Dubuisson appears to have written this account of his migration not to get it off his chest, nor necessarily to leave a historical record of this particular migrant stream. He has an agenda that he wishes to present to migrants, allies, or anyone else that is motivated to read his book, to present his vision of the world, a world of shared circumstances (many are driven to migrate), of shared values (many aspire to be good people), and also a world in which everyone is a citizen, a concept that implies basic rights, including a right to cross borders and seek better circumstances. His is not a world of open borders, as some border crossers—for example, smugglers, human traffickers, organized criminal networks—may not be motivated by his tenets of "patience, love, union, and respect." His project of world-making is instead rooted in universally esteemed values. *Sobrevivientes: ciudadanos del mundo* is much more than a travelogue; it is a text that aspires to promote a better world, one that not only includes but respects the struggles of migrants, indeed accommodating migrants, not as undocumented aliens, but rather with the status of citizens.

Caravaneros

My argument is that *Sobrevivientes* is a text of world literature, not necessarily because its protagonists are designated as "citizens of the world" but rather because it is a novel of world-making, a novel what aims to defy current regimes of global economies, racial capitalism, neoliberal exclusions, and nativist populism, fomenting instead a world rooted in transnational solidarity. Oviedo, no doubt inspired by Dubuisson's ability to not only accommodate himself as a Haitian migrant in Tijuana but also become a respected activist of migration rights there, set out to write his own book. While he does not replicate Dubuisson's terminology, his writing and activism have much in common with those of his Haitian friend.

All the migrant protagonists of *Caravaneros* are all Hondurans, although the caravan is portrayed as incorporating migrants from El Salvador, Guatemala, and Nicaragua as well. El Pastor, one of the caravan's leaders, who Oviedo has admitted is based on himself (Irwin et al. 2021), helps organize the migrants as they prepare to negotiate entry into Mexico, indicating that they will display the flags of these four countries and that of Mexico, confirming that they have "dejado de ser una caravana de catrachos y nos convertimos en una caravana centroamericana" (ceased to be a caravan of Hondurans and become a Central American caravan) (Oviedo 2020: 71), making clear that this is a shared migration project that should not be reduced to a national phenomenon or even a series of common national mobilizations but rather a regional dynamic.

Soon afterward, as they cross into Mexico, although everyone continues to be identifiable by their accent—Hondurans as "catrachos," Salvadorans as "guanacos," Nicaraguans as "nicas," the Guatemalans as "chapines"—the omniscient narrator observes: "Muy orgullosos de su país, pero en México todos ahora son MIGRANTES" (Oviedo 2020: 90) (All very proud of their country, but in Mexico they are all now MIGRANTS). The difference here is subtle but important: as they move farther from their birthlands, the national fades to regional and regional to universal. El Pastor reiterates this shift several days later in Veracruz: "aquí en México ustedes dejaron de ser salvadoreños, nosotros dejamos de ser hondureños, guatemaltecos, nicaragüenses para ser migrantes, que no se te olvide que eso somos: migrantes" (115) (here in Mexico you stopped being Salvadorans, we ceased being Hondurans, Guatemalans, Nicaraguans and became migrants, don't forget that's what we are migrants).

The shift to universal terminology also shows up in several moments when the caravan begins to feel the strength of its numbers and express a political rhetoric in the form of collectively shouted slogans. As they pass through a zone known for the aggressive patrols of Mexican migration agents, who arbitrarily detain and deport any migrant they can catch, they begin to chant phrases such as "Alerta, alerta, alerta al que camina, la lucha del migrante por América Latina, ¿por qué nos matan? ¿por qué nos asesinan? si somos la esperanza de América Latina" (Sound the alarm of the struggle of the migrant for Latin America, why do they kill us, why do they assassinate us if we are the hope of Latin America?), "Manchadas de rojo están las fronteras porque ahí se mata a la clase obrera" (The borders are stained red because there they kill the working class!), and "Los migrantes no somos criminales, somos trabajadores internacionales" (Migrants are not criminals, we are international workers), slogans that the migrants repeat once they have arrived in Tijuana and stage a march toward the border (Oviedo 2020: 95, 145). As the migrants unite through a shared political rhetoric, again their national identifications fade, as they become migrants, laborers, the working class, the hope of Latin America.

The theme of unity resounds throughout the book, as the migrants of the caravan feel their strength of numbers. When they need to separate into buses, sometimes following different routes, it is always important for them to reunite later on. Likewise, it is important that they all arrive in Tijuana. Their collectivity is what makes them controversial, implying a power in numbers seen as threatening in some sectors, but it also protects them, reassures them, and inspires them to move onward.

Early on as they wait to cross the border into Mexico, a character called "Caravana" representing their collective voice reminds them, "Por favor, no se vayan solos. Tenemos información que en México están deportando a todos aquellos que van solitarios. Pues no nos arriesgaremos. Recuerden, venimos juntos y es necesario seguir juntos" (Oviedo 2020: 61) (Please don't go alone. We have information that in Mexico they'll deport those who are by themselves. So we won't risk it. Remember, we came together and we need to stay together). Soon thereafter, in one of several public prayers improvised by El Pastor, he summons God: "Tú no nos trajiste para estar en discordia los unos con los otros, sino para estar unidos y de esa forma poder seguir nuestro camino" (67) (You did not bring us here to be in discord against one another, but rather to be united and in that way be able to follow our path). Later, as they enter Chiapas, the narrator notes: "Nadie se ha quedado atrás. Todos unidos con sed de más triunfos" (95) (No one has been left behind. They are all united with a thirst for more triumphs). Once in Mexico City, where social service organizations offer them a warm reception, the narrator observes: "Todos están alegres. Ni el clima les quita las esperanzas de avanzar y llegar juntos hasta el final" (119) (Everyone is happy. Not even the weather diminishes their hope in moving forward and arriving together at their destination). A few days later, when setting out from Mexico City, after El Pastor leads an emotional rendition of the inspiring "Victory Hymn," the mood of the caravan is optimistic: "La alegría es aún más grande. De nuevo todos juntos. Los abrazos, los apretones de mano fueron aún más importantes que en todo el trayecto anterior. Listos para continuar su viaje, todos unidos, la caravana está completa" (132) (The joy is greater. Once again everyone is joined. The hugs, handshakes are more important than in any earlier segment. Ready to continue on, all united, the caravan is complete). Likewise the concept of unity is repeated as the caravan prepares for its last movement from Mexicali to Tijuana: "Ahora, todos juntos, se toman de la mano para ser más fuertes. Darán su último paso unidos y que sepa Estados Unidos que la caravana llegó a la frontera" (140) (Now, all joined together, they join hands to be stronger. They'll unite in taking their last step so that the United States will know that the caravan arrived at the border). Once in Tijuana, the narrator reports that optimism again rises among the weary migrants: "La alegría, la sonrisa, han vuelto a sus rostros. Se sienten como en casa .... Al estar todos juntos nada más les importa .... De verdad que son una gran comunidad" (149) (Joy, smiles return to their faces. They feel at home .... Being all together, nothing else is important .... It is true that they are a grand community).

Unity and togetherness indeed are key themes of the story, and these same keywords would come to define Douglas Oviedo during his extended stay in Tijuana. The Juntos Somos Más cultural festival that he co-organized with Ustin Dubuisson in March of 2019 highlights that the concepts of unity and togetherness across cultures that Oviedo promotes are meant to join all struggling migrants, drawing cosponsorships of a wide range of local organizations that operate with transnational vision in the border zone of Tijuana and San Diego. As Oviedo puts it in the final installment of *Historias de la caravana*, referring to a concert he and his musical collaborators had organized in Playas de Tijuana in early September, about a week prior to his final asylum court date:

> de ese evento lo que realmente tenía como propósito era unir al mundo: unir a las familias, unir a Centro América y a México y Estados Unidos, a través de la música. Y darnos cuenta de como seres humanos todos somos iguales, no tenemos que vernos con racismo ni con un tipo de división sino que al contrario, tenemos que ser más unidos (2019d) (the event's goal was to unite everyone: families, Central America, Mexico, and the United States, through music, and let everyone know that as human beings we're all equal, we don't need racism or any other division; instead we need to be more united).

However, it is in the collaborative project that Oviedo spearheaded to build the Casa Hogar El Puente migrant shelter in Tijuana that his world-building vision is most clear. In an interview realized at the shelter's inaugural celebration, just prior to Oviedo's admission to the United States, he stated, "las personas que migramos buscamos siempre un mundo mejor" (those of us who migrate are always looking for a better world) (Inauguran albergue 2019). And in another interview soon after that, in California, he comments on the notion of borders: "Una frontera significa un límite, como dividir el mundo. Para mí, es provocar que haya racismo, que haya discriminación y xenofobia" (A border signifies a limit, a way of dividing the world. I see it as provoking racism, discrimination and xenophobia), adding as the final message of the interview: "Todos nacimos en esta Tierra y somos creados para vivir en esta Tierra" (We all were born on this Earth and are created to live on this Earth) (Oviedo 2019e).

Oviedo's migrants, the protagonists of *Caravaneros*, like those of *Sobrevivientes*, are citizens of the world. As they move across the hemisphere, they not only pass by, but they create, they collaborate, they make a mark, and they transform the world around them. Migration, for migrants such as Dubuisson and Oviedo, is a process of transforming the world, of world-making. I approach these texts, these authors, not from the perspective of the academy, or of the publishing industry, but rather from that of the works themselves and their authors. This approach reflects Chaudhuri's (2021) thoughts on where the worlds of migrants might figure in constructs of world literature, or the "ground up" thinking proposed by Laachir, Marzagora, and Orsini (2018) that looks to the worlds produced by embodied actors, such as Dubuisson and Oviedo. It also exemplifies Cheah's (2016: 211) vision of world literature as a "world-making" enterprise that reflects a spirit of "cosmopolitanism" that is not limited to what he sees as world literature's historical "mesmerizing focus" on the North Atlantic. It also offers a key to understanding the writings of authors such as Oviedo by recognizing that "literature can play an important role in announcing the advent of new collective subjects and giving public phenomenality to their ongoing attempts to remake the world" (Cheah 2016: 210). *Caravaneros* not only documents the experience of the caravan migrants but also offers a caravan migrant's vision for a better world, a world in which he and fellow migrants have a place.

Cheah, along with these other critics who seek to define world literature from a postcolonial posture, privileges cosmopolitan positionings from below, from the south, from the working classes, from the experiences of migrants and refugees. Importantly, his definition of cosmopolitanism is not limited to elite world travelers but includes those who encounter different worlds from a defensive position but do not fold under pressure, instead asserting their ideas for remaking the world through literary expression. Considering the position of migrants in the contemporary contexts of heavily fortified border regimes, Cheah's position recalls that of migration scholars Dimitri Papadopoulos, Niamh Stephenson, and Vassilis Tsianos (2008: 211) regarding migrants and world-making: "Even if migration sometimes starts as a form of dislocation (forced by poverty, patriarchal exploitation, war, famine), its target is not relocation but the active transformation of social space." Oviedo's world is not defined by borders, but by bridges, by a spirit of human unity in which people celebrate that "together we are more." In Cheah's view, "[t]he world in a normative sense refers to the being-with of all peoples, groups, and individuals. It is the original openness that gives us accessibility to others so that we can be together" (2016: 18–19).

Conclusion

The testimonial literature of migration might best be understood as its own stateless genre, especially when its authors not only write about the transnational contexts of their migration routes but do so while still in the process of migrating. For Honduras, with roughly 10 percent of its population living abroad, and many fleeing northward every day, migration is an essential element of contemporary national culture. However, the inevitably transnational contexts of migration literature make it difficult to think about this phenomenon in national terms. *Caravaneros*, set mostly in Mexico, written and published in Mexico by an emigrant author living in the United States—and available for purchase only in Mexico and the United States, seems only very peripherally Honduran. Some might argue that this tale of emigration should not be considered at all in the context of a discussion on Central American literature, into which it makes no claims of linking to a tradition, whether national or regional. At the same time, being published outside of the isthmus is also one characteristic quite common to Central American literature, given the relative weakness of its publishing industries and markets. So maybe *Caravaneros* is instead border literature, or even Latinx literature, or yet another, more recent example of what Ana Patricia Rodríguez calls "transisthmian narratives" (2009). I won't try to figure that out. But, read through intertextual links with *Sobrevivientes*, along with its author's larger public actions and statements, it is surely a text of world literature.

Presently Oviedo faces challenges in adapting to life in the United States. Six months after he was granted asylum, the country went into pandemic lockdown. Oviedo, like many recently arrived migrants, has subsisted as a day laborer and faced major setbacks as he tried to set up his own house-painting enterprise and has struggled to make ends meet. Moving from California to Texas, he has so far been unable to establish the deep community bonds he formed while staying in Tijuana. Nonetheless his book came out the summer of 2020, and he's been invited to promote it in Mexico City, Tijuana, California, and Texas. None of his Tijuana friends doubt that one day he'll get established and resume his world-making activities here in the United States. But for now we can read his migration story and learn from his contribution to world literature.

References

Arias, A. (2007), *Taking Their Word: Literature and the Signs of Central America*, Minneapolis and London: University of Minnesota Press.

Chaudhuri, S. (2021), "Which World, Whose Literature?," *Thesis Eleven*, 162 (1): 75–93.

Cheah, P. (2016), *What Is a World?: On Postcolonial Literature as World Literature*, Durham and London: Duke University Press.

Damrosch, D. (2003), *What Is World Literature?*, Princeton and Oxford: Princeton University Press.

Dubuisson, U. P. (2018), *Sobrevivientes: ciudadanos del mundo*, Tijuana: ILCSA Ediciones.

Elfers, A. and K. Kurimoto (2020), "Prólogo: Douglas Oviedo es un puente," prologue to Douglas Oviedo, *Caravaneros*, 7–14, Mexico City: Festina.
"Inauguran albergue para migrantes en situación de asilo" (2019), editorial, *Zeta Tijuana*, September 14. Available online: https://zetatijuana.com/2019/09/inauguran-albergue-para-migrantes-en-situacion-de-asilo/.
Irwin, R. M. (2020a), "Digital Resources: The Humanizing Deportation Archive," in W. H. Beezley (ed.), *Oxford Research Encyclopedia of Latin American History*, https://doi.org/10.1093/acrefore/9780199366439.013.855.
Irwin, R. M. (2020b), "Thickening Borders across Mexico: Follow-Up Stories from the Caravan," *Latinx Talk*. Available online: https://latinxtalk.org/2020/02/04/thickening-borders-across-mexico-follow-up-stories-from-the-caravan/.
Irwin, R. M. and A. Silva (2020), "Introducción: La historia insólita de la caravana migrante y del hondureño Douglas Oviedo," introduction to Douglas Oviedo, *Caravaneros*, 15–41, Mexico City: Festina.
Irwin, R. M., D. Oviedo, D. Castillo, J. Medina and S. A. Hart (2021), "Presentación del libro *Caravaneros*," [video] recording of Una conversación con el migrante Douglas Oviedo sobre su recién publicado drama testimonial *Caravaneros*, UC Davis, Global Migration Center, November 30, 2020. YouTube, February 19, 1:37:28, https://www.youtube.com/watch?v=Q47FGsl41Go.
Laachir, K., S. Marzagora, and F. Orsini (2018), "Significant Geographies: In Lieu of World Literature," *Journal of World Literature*, 3: 290–310.
Landa, N. (2013–20), *Mundo Citizen*, https://mundocitizen.com/about-mundocitizen/.
Lovato, R. (2020), *Unforgetting: A Memoir of Family, Migration, Gangs, and Revolution in the Americas*, New York: HarperCollins.
Martínez, Ó. (2010), *Los migrantes que no importan*, Barcelona: Icaria.
Nazario, S. (2007), *Enrique's Journey: The Story of a Boy's Dangerous Odyssey to Reunite with His Mother*, New York: Random House.
Oviedo, D. (2019a), "166a. Historias de la caravana I," *Humanizando la Deportación*, http://humanizandoladeportacion.ucdavis.edu/es/2019/05/29/166a-historias-de-la-caravana-parte-i/.
Oviedo, D. (2019b), "166b. Historias de la caravana II," *Humanizando la Deportación*, http://humanizandoladeportacion.ucdavis.edu/es/2019/05/29/166b-historias-de-la-caravana-parte-ii/.
Oviedo, D. (2019c), "166c. Historias de la caravana III," *Humanizando la Deportación*, http://humanizandoladeportacion.ucdavis.edu/es/2019/12/03/166c-historias-de-la-caravana-parte-iii/.
Oviedo, D. (2019d), "166d. Historias de la caravana IV," *Humanizando la Deportación*, http://humanizandoladeportacion.ucdavis.edu/es/2019/12/03/166d-historias-de-la-caravana-parte-iv/.
Oviedo, D. (2019e), "Perfil de un migrante," *El Migrante* (20), October 7. Available online: https://internews.org/sites/default/files/2020-02/El_Migrante_20.pdf.
Oviedo, D. (2020), *Caravaneros*, Mexico City: Festina.
Papadopoulos, D., N. Stephenson, and V. Tsianos (2008), *Escape Routes: Control and Subversion in the 21st Century*, London: Pluto Press.
Rodríguez, A. P. (2009), *Dividing the Isthmus: Central American Transnational Histories, Literatures, and Cultures*, Austin: University of Texas Press.

TRAC (Transactional Records Access Clearinghouse) (2021), "Details on MPP (Remain in Mexico) Deportation Proceedings—All Cases," TRAC Immigration, Syracuse University. Available online: https://trac.syr.edu/phptools/immigration/mpp4/.

Walters, W. (2015), "Reflections on Migration and Governmentality," *Movements: Journal for Critical Migration and Border Studies*, 1 (1): 1–25.

Zamora, J. (2017), *Unaccompanied*, Port Townsend: Copper Canyon Press.

NOTES ON CONTRIBUTORS

Tatiana Argüello (PhD in Hispanic Studies, University of Pittsburgh) is Associate Professor of Spanish and Hispanic Studies at Texas Christian University. She specializes in literature and cultural studies of Central America and its diaspora, particularly modernist and avant-garde poetry, war and violence, Indigenous experience, and questions of ecology and the nonhuman. She has published her work in various peer-reviewed journals and academic publishing houses. She is the co-editor of a special dossier on "Posthuman and Non-Human Approaches to Central American Culture and Literature," *Istmo: Revista virtual de estudios literarios y culturales centroamericanos* 34 (2017). She is currently cowriting a book manuscript that reexamines notions of race and gender through ecological thought in the writings of literary and philosophical figures from the Mesoamerican region.

Andrew Bentley (PhD in Hispanic Cultural Studies from Michigan State University) specializes in in contemporary Latin American and Latinx cultural production with an emphasis on Central America and its diasporas. He examines how transnational Central American peoples craft knowledges, memory, and solidary movements in literature, social media, and urban space. In particular, he is interested in how platforms such as Instagram function to make visible a world beyond neoliberal capitalism. His work on these topics has appeared in *Istmo*, *Latinx Talk*, *Revista de Estudios de Género y Sexualidades*, and *Romance Notes*, as well as in Facebook Live discussions and the podcast *Collaborative Edges*. He has also published creative work in *The Wandering Song: Central American Writing in the United States* and *Chiricú Journal*.

Gloria Elizabeth Chacón (PhD in Literature, UC Santa Cruz) is Associate Professor of Literature at the University of California, San Diego. Her research areas include Indigenous literatures of the Americas, Chicanx/Latinx literary and cultural movements, Central American poetics and politics, US Central Americans, and Latin American literary and cultural theories. She is the author of *Indigenous Cosmolectics: Kab'awil and the Making of Maya and Zapotec Literatures* (2018), co-editor of *Indigenous Interfaces: Spaces, Technology, and Social Networks in Mexico and Central America* (2019) and *Teaching Central American literature in a Global Context* (MLA 2022).

Sophie Esch (PhD in Spanish and Portuguese, Tulane University) is Associate Professor of Central American and Mexican literature and culture at Rice University. She is the author of the award-winning *Modernity at Gunpoint: Firearms, Politics, and Culture in Mexico and Central America* (2018) and the editor of a special dossier on "Central American Literature: Passages: Routes of Migration and Memory in Central American Literature," *Revista de Estudios Hispánicos* 54/1 (2020).

Harris Feinsod is Associate Professor of English and Comparative Literature at Northwestern University. He is author of *The Poetry of the Americas: From Good Neighbors to Countercultures* (2017), co-translator of Oliverio Girondo's *Decals: Complete Early Poems* (2018), and director of Open Door Archive (opendoor.northwestern.edu). His current research on the global literary history of the modernist seaways appears in *American Literary History*, *Comparative Literature*, *ELN*, and *Modernism/Modernity*, as well as *The Baffler* and *n+1*.

Carolyn Fornoff is Assistant Professor of Latin American studies at Cornell University. She has coedited two volumes in the environmental humanities: *Timescales: Thinking across Ecological Temporalities* (University of Minnesota Press, 2020) and *Pushing Past the Human in Latin American Cinema* (SUNY Press, 2021).

Carlos F. Grigsby is an Alexander von Humboldt Postdoctoral Fellow at the University of Cologne. He was formerly a stipendiary lecturer in Spanish at St. Catherine's College of the University of Oxford, where he also completed his doctorate, titled "Rediscovering Rubén Darío through Translation." His work has appeared in journals such as the *Bulletin of Spanish Studies* and *MLR*. His present research focuses on Central American literature vis-à-vis World Literature(s). Aside from his academic work, he is also a poet and translator.

Tamara de Inés Antón (PhD from the University of Manchester, UK) is a lecturer and academic coordinator of the MA in Translation (Spanish/French) at the University of the West Indies (Mona). She is an early-career academic with research interests in the intersection between gender studies, the sociology of translation, and Central American women's writing. She is also fully invested in the teaching of translation and carries out research in this field.

Robert McKee Irwin (PhD in Comparative Literature, NYU) is Professor in the Department of Spanish and Portuguese at the University of California, Davis, where he is also the deputy director of the Global Migration Center. He is (co)author or (co)editor of numerous scholarly monographs and articles on issues of masculinity, borders, migration, and cultural industries in the context of greater Mexico and Latin America. Since 2016, he has coordinated the digital storytelling project *Humanizando la Deportación*. He also cowrote the critical introduction to Douglas Oviedo's *Caravaneros* (2020).

Tamara L. Mitchell (PhD in Spanish, Indiana University Bloomington) is Assistant Professor of Hispanic Studies at the University of British Columbia, Vancouver. Her research examines the relationship among aesthetics, politics, and the literary tradition, with a focus on contemporary Mexican and Central American narrative fiction. Her work has appeared in *Revista de Estudios Hispánicos*, *Revista Canadiense de Estudios Hispánicos*, *Modern Language Notes*, *Chasqui*, and *CR: New Centennial Review*. Her current book project interrogates what becomes of the Latin American novel as national modernity gives way to neoliberal globalization with special attention to Central American and Mexican writers.

Magdalena Perkowska (PhD in Spanish, Rutgers University) is Professor of Latin American Literature at Hunter College and the Graduate Center of the City University of New York. Her areas of specialization include Latin American narrative of the twentieth and twenty-first centuries, with emphasis on Central America, literary and cultural theory, visual and memory studies. She is the author of *Historias híbridas* (2008) and *Pliegues visuales* (2013). She edited a special issue of *Istmo* (2014) and coedited *Tiranas ficciones* (2018) and *Escritura(s) en femenino en las literaturas centroamericanas* (2022). Perkowska is currently working on a new book on affect(s) in post-war and post-utopian fiction and film from Central America.

Rita M. Palacios, Guatemala-born refugee settler (PhD in Latin American Literature, University of Toronto) is Professor of Liberal Studies at Conestoga College Institute of Technology and Advanced Learning in Kitchener, Ontario. Her work examines contemporary Maya literature from a cultural and gender studies perspective. She is the coauthor of *Unwriting Maya Literature* (University of Arizona Press, 2019) and is contributing editor (Central American Poetry) for the *Handbook of Latin American Studies* (Library of Congress).

Yansi Pérez (PhD in Spanish, Princeton University) is Associate Provost and Professor of Spanish and Latin American Studies at Carleton College. As a recipient of the Frederick Burkhardt Residential Fellowship by the American Council of Learned Societies, she was a visiting scholar at the Central American Studies Department at the California State University, Northridge. She has published about Roque Dalton, Horacio Castellanos Moya, and Claudia Hernández, among others. Her book *Más allá del* *duelo* was published in 2019. Currently, she is working on a project titled "A Cartography of Material Memory of the Central American Diaspora in Los Angeles."

Ignacio Sarmiento Panez (PhD in Spanish, Tulane University) is Assistant Professor of Spanish and Latin American History at the State University of New York at Fredonia. His book project, *Specters of War. The Battle of Mourning in Postwar Central America*, studies various expressions of mourning in postwar El Salvador and Guatemala, with an emphasis on fiction, theatre, and sites of memory. He co-edited the volumes *Central American Migrations in the 21st Century* (University of Arizona Press, 2023) and *(Re)Imaginar Centroamérica en el siglo XXI* (Uruk Editores, 2017), and the special issue "(En)Visioning Central American Migration: Views From the Diaspora" (2022) for the journal *Label Me Latino/a*.

Paul M. Worley, settler (PhD in Comparative Literature at UNC-Chapel Hill), is Professor of Spanish and Chair at Appalachian State University. He is the author of *Telling and Being Told: Storytelling and Cultural Control in Contemporary Yucatec Maya Literatures* (2013) and coauthor of *Unwriting Maya Literature* (2019). A Fulbright Scholar, in addition to his academic work, he has translated selected works by Indigenous authors such as Hubert Malina, Adriana López, and Ruperta Bautista and serves as poetry editor for the *North Dakota Quarterly*.

INDEX

academics 2, 42, 72
Aching, G. 105
Ak'abal, H. 9–10, 13, 29, 174–86
   Grito en la sombra (Scream in the Shadow) 185
   "No'j/consejo" (Advice) 186
Alcides Orellana, R. 127
Alegría, C. 67–9, 75
Ali, T. 95
Alonso, A. 148
Anderson, B. 24, 226
Antojología de Carl Rigby (Spiegeler and Sacasa) 207
Apollinaire, G. 103–4, 195
Apter, E. 160, 165–6
Árbenz, J. 44, 145
Arguedas, J. M. 105, 117 n.4
Argüello, T. 13, 228
Arias, A. 6, 56, 65, 82, 225–6, 229, 238, 249
Armas, A. d. 115–16
Auerbach, E. 6, 191–3
Ávalos, J. 125–6

Baax ka mentik 32
Baker, M. 69
Bañales, V. 75
Barbas-Rhoden, L. 68
Basile, T. 162
Bautista, R. 20
Belize 31–2, 213
Benítez-Rojo, A. 215
Bernhard, T. 155–8
Blanchot, M. 148
Brathwaite, E. K. 210
brevity 7, 29, 42–3, 46
Brodzki, B. 66
Buiza, N. 156
Burgos, E. 72–3

Camus, A. 136
Canal Zone. *See* Panama Canal Zone
Canetti, E. 158
Cardenal, E. 212, 219 n.7
Cárdenas, M. 226–7, 232
Caribbean 207–18
Carillo, G. 5
Carrasco, C. 157
Casanova, P. 9–10, 41–3, 46–7, 67–8, 70, 81–2, 106
   La république mondiale des letters 9, 105–6
   The World Republic of Letters 81
Cassin, B. 165–6
Castellanos Moya, H. 12, 82, 127, 155–60, 162, 164–5, 167–8, 168 nn.2–3
   El asco 127, 155–8
   Entre paréntesis 157
   La diáspora 12, 156–7, 159–62, 164–8
   Roque Dalton: correspondencia clandestina y otros ensayos 159
Caste War 31
Castillo, D. 230
Catrachos (Guzmán) 223, 228, 231, 236, 239 n.5
Cendrars 200–1
Cendrars, B. 7, 191, 194–9, 201
Chacón, G. 12–13
Chan, A. 31–2
Chaudhuri, S. 248, 255
Chávez, R. 27–9
Cheah, P. 3, 24, 140–1, 153 n.13, 181, 208, 224, 229, 243, 249, 255
The Cherokee Nation: A History (Conley) 23
Chiaravalloti, F. 83
Chinchilla, M. 226–7, 229, 232

civil war 49–50, 55, 126–7, 151 n.2, 156, 160, 162, 179, 225, 230
Cold War 8, 12, 69, 123, 126, 130, 134, 142, 146, 157–8, 164–5, 167–8, 202, 223, 229
The Communist International 139, 146, 150
Communist Manifesto (Marx and Engels) 103, 153 n.9
complexity 43–7, 51, 55, 75, 106, 183
Conley, Robert J. 23
Corral, W. H. 40, 42–3
Cortázar, J. 105, 117 n.4
Cortez, B. 169 n.8
cosmolectics 10–12, 174, 178, 180–6
cosmopolitanism 2, 8, 12–13, 103–7, 109–12, 116, 117 n.4, 121, 123, 129, 136, 140, 151, 175–7, 180, 193, 224, 229, 249, 255
Coy, N. 27, 32–4, 35 n.4
   Kikotem: Historias, cuentos, poesía del pueblo maya kaqchikel 33–4
   "Rumuxu'x ri Meq'en ya'/ El ombligo de Meq'en ya'" 33
Craft, L. J. 52
Craveri, M. 31
Creegan Miller, T. D. 30
Cuba 131, 145, 152 n.6
Cumes, A. E. 19–20, 23

Dalton, R. 12–13, 122–3, 126–9, 140–51, 152 n.4, 152 n.7, 159, 161, 163, 168
   Las historias prohibidas del Pulgarcito (The Banned Histories of Tom Thumb) 142, 149
   Pobrecito poeta que era yo (Poor Little Poet that I Was) 148–9
   "Poema de amor" (Love Poem) 149–50
Damrosch, D. 5–6, 10, 42, 82, 86, 95, 107, 180, 248–9
   What Is World Literature? 5, 248
Darío, R. 5, 7, 12, 82, 103–16, 117 n.9, 121, 210, 212

Cantos de vida y esperanza 104, 111
civilized *(civilizadas)* 114
crónicas 107, 109, 111–13, 116
El canto errante 111–12, 116
España contemporánea 109
French culture 112–16
"La exposición: los hispanoamericanos" (The Exhibition: The Spanish Americans) 113
"La Sociedad de Escritores de Buenos Aires" (The Writers' Society of Buenos Aires) 114
Prosas profanas 104–5, 107, 112, 117 n.15
"Symphony in Grey Major" 210
Debray, R. 145
de Certeau, M. 132
Deleuze, G. 215
Derrida, J. 66
Diccionario de la lengua española 166, 168 n.5
Dimock, W. C. 129–30
Doubrovsky, S. 94
Dubuisson, U. P. 246–51, 254–5
Duchesne Winter, J. 213, 215
Dulfano, I. 72
Durrell, L. 148–9, 159

Easterling, K. 195
eccentric Caribbean 213
Edison, T. W. 209
Elfers, A. 246
ellipsis 51, 55
El Salvador 11–12, 49–50, 52–4, 69–70, 121–3, 125–8, 130, 134, 136, 142, 148–51, 156, 160–4, 166–8, 168 n.5, 223, 230–1, 234–6, 238–9, 252
Engels, F. 103, 153 n.9
Escamilla, J. L. 162
Esch, S. 161
Export Processing Zone (EPZ) 195
Extinction (Bernhard) 155–6

Farabundo Martí National Liberation Front (FMLN) 158, 167
Feinsod, H. 13

Flakoll, D. J. 11, 67–70
Fornoff, C. 12
Franco, J. 8–9
Free Trade Zone (FTZ) 195
Frydman, J. 208
Fuentes, C. 57 n.10

Galich, F. 8, 57 n.8
Garvey, M. M. 213–14
Gellner, E. 24
Getachew, A. 24
Glissant, É. 13, 199, 208–9, 215–17, 218 n.3, 219 n.5
global, globalization 1–3, 6, 9, 20, 23–4, 26–7, 32, 35, 52–4, 83–4, 89–95, 103–6, 116, 117 n.4, 121–4, 129–31, 134, 136, 140–2, 146, 152 n.7, 156–7, 175, 177–8, 181–3, 185–6, 191, 195, 197–8, 202, 208, 223–6, 229–31, 248–9
Global South 2, 13, 217, 223–5, 229–39
Goethe, J. W. v. 1, 7, 23, 140, 158–9, 175, 208
Gómez Carrillo, E. 5, 121
Gourmont, R. d. 114
The Great Primordial Wharf (O Grande Cais Anterior) 192–4
Grigsby, C. F. 12, 118 n.17
Guatarri, F. 215
Guatemala 6, 8–12, 26, 28, 30, 43–5, 53–4, 65, 72, 83–4, 86, 90, 93–5, 96 n.5, 175–9, 181, 185, 229–34, 252
Guinea, G. 175, 179, 184
Guzmán, R. G. 223, 229, 236–9, 239 n.5

Habib, A. 166
Halfon, E. 11, 57 n.11, 96 n.3
  Duelo 82, 84–9
  El boxeador polaco 82, 85–9
  expressive logic 95, 96 n.1
  Mañana nunca lo hablamos 84, 90, 93
  Monasterio 82, 85–9
  Monastery 83–4, 86–7, 90
  Mourning 83–4, 86–7, 89–90, 92
  The Polish Boxer 83, 86–7, 90, 92, 95
  puzzle 86, 89
  Signor Hoffman 82, 85–90
Harney, G. J. 140
Heller-Roazen, D. 143, 146
Herlihy, P. 25
Hernández, C. 11, 39–42, 49–56, 57 n.11, 57 n.13
  Causas naturales 50–1
  De fronteras 50–4
  El verbo J 55, 57 n.14
  "La han despedido de nuevo" (They Have Fired Her Again) 53–4
  Mediodía de frontera 53
  "Molestias de tener un rinoceronte" (Annoyances of Having a Rhinoceros) 51
  Olvida uno 52, 54
  Otras ciudades 50
  Roza, tumba, quema 49, 55, 57 n.14
  Tomar tu mano 55, 57 n.14
Hernández Linares, L. 228
Honduras 150–1, 223, 230–1, 236–9, 243–5, 247–8, 250, 255
Hopkinson, A. 69–70
Huezo Mixco, M. 126
Hugo, V. 113
Huyssen, A. 91–2, 95

indigeneity 26, 32, 52, 121–2, 176–7, 181
Indigenous languages 178–82, 185
Inés de Antón, T. 11, 13
intertextuality 46–9, 156–7, 160–5
I, Rigoberta Menchú 71–7
Irwin, R. M. 13
isthmus 5, 7–8, 13, 56, 123, 129–36, 158, 223–31, 238–9, 247, 256
Ixim 30

The Joke (Kundera) 164–5
Jones, E. 139
Journal of World Literature (Moberg and Damrosch) 180
Judaism 83–5

Kokotovic, M. 50
Kundera, M. 12, 157–60, 163–5
Kurimoto, K. 246

Laclau, E. 142
Lámbarry, A. 43, 48
Landa, N. 251
Lars, C. 124
Lautréamont, C. d. 211–12, 215
Lemus, J. M. 125
Levy, L. 83
Liboiron, M. 35 n.2
Libros, L. 57 n.14
Linebaugh, P. 196
literatura mundial 3–4
Luiselli, V. 26, 105, 117 n.4

Mahler, A. G. 229
Maier, L. S. 72
Marín, L. 75
Marx, K. 1, 141, 149, 152 n.9
Mathews, I. 72
Maya 45
   Belizean 31–2
   cosmovision 33
   indigeneity 26
   K'iche'/Kaqchikel 28–9, 65, 72–3, 174, 179–81, 183, 185–6
   population 93
   textile 11, 19, 21, 34, 185
   ts'íib 19
   urbanity 30
   woman 28–9, 33
McKay, C. 191, 193, 198–9
   "Peasants' Ways o' Thinkin'" 198
Medeiros, P. de 40
Me llamo Rigoberta Menchú 72–3
memory 8, 11, 83–4, 89–94, 133, 174–5, 232–4, 239 n.4
Menchú, R. 5–6, 11, 65, 68, 71–7, 223
   testimonio 64–9, 71–2, 75–7, 162
Menen Desleal, Á. 12, 121–36
   to Committed Generation 123–9
   "Hacer el amor en el refugio atómico" (Making Love in the Atomic Shelter) 131
   speculative fiction 128, 134–6
   "Una carta de familia" (A Family Letter) 126
   "Una cuerda de nylon y oro" (A Cord of Nylon and Gold), 133–4
Mexico 13, 26, 43–4, 46, 49, 127, 134, 147, 161–2, 224–7, 230–2, 243–5, 247, 249–50, 252–4, 256
migrant caravans of fall 2018 244–5
Migrant Protection Protocols (MPP) 245–6
Mingas de la palabra (Rocha Vivas) 22
minority 27, 41, 90, 179–81, 186, 225–6, 237
minor literature 41, 42, 180
Mitchell, T. L. 12–13
Moberg, R. 180
modernismo 104–5, 110
modernistas 103–7, 112–13, 116, 118 n.17
Molloy, S. 109, 112
Momostecan poncho 178, 185
Monsiváis, C. 147
Montaldo, G. 105
Monterroso, A. 3–5, 8–9, 11, 13, 39–50, 52, 55–6, 56 n.6
   La oveja negra y demás fábulas 4
   Lo demás es silencio 46
   Movimiento perpetuo 45, 48
   Obras completas (y otros cuentos) 44, 48
Moreiras, A. 162
Moretti, F. 2, 39, 81–2, 89, 91, 95, 208
   "Conjectures on World Literature" 39, 81, 89
   "More Conjectures" 39
Morris, W. 21
Mullen-Coyoy, P. 223, 231–3, 239
Mundo Citizen (Landa) 251
Murau, Franz-Josef 155–6
The Myth of Sisyphus (Camus) 136

Nance, K. A. 64
Nancy, J. L. 148
Nationalist Republican Alliance (ARENA) 158, 167

Nicaragua 8, 12, 197, 208–13, 218 n.4, 252
NiCaribbean 207, 218–19 n.5
Nickels, J. 25, 174
No me agarran viva (Alegría and Flakoll) 66–71

ocean 50, 54, 155, 192–3, 201, 208–18
Ollé, M. L. 175, 180, 182
On Populist Reason (Laclau) 142
Orlando Hernández, J. 244
Ortiz Wallner, A. 8, 50, 162
Oveja negra 47
Oviedo, D. 13, 153 n.15, 243, 246–9, 251–6
  Caravaneros (Caravan Members) 13, 153 n.15, 243, 246–8, 251–6
  Historias de la caravana 246, 254

Padilla, Y. 226
Palacios, R. M. 11
Palo de mayo (Maypole) 209, 219 n.6
Panama Canal Zone 191–9, 201–3 nn.1–3
The Panama panic 194–6
Paz, O. 104–5
Pérez, Y. 12
peripheral, periphery 9, 13, 19, 35, 40–4, 53, 56, 63, 67, 72–3, 77, 81–3, 130–1, 156–9, 164–8, 180–1, 209, 231, 256
Pessoa, F. 191–3
planetary 12, 122–3, 129–33, 135–6, 174, 177–8, 196, 217
The Poetics of Relation (Glissant) 215
Popol Wuj (Book of Council) (Quiroa) 177
Popul Vuh 47
Prashad, V. 230
Prose, F. 83
Puri, S. 230

Rama, Á. 44, 46, 105, 112, 117 n.3
Ramirez Chavez, G. 223, 233–4, 239
Ramírez, S. 125, 219 n.5
Rancière, J. 143, 152 n.5

Rediker, M. 196
Reinhardt, M. A. 166
Rey Rosa, R. 57 n.11
rhizomatic 208, 217–18
Rigby, C. 13, 207–18, 218–19 n.5, 218 nn.1–2, 219 nn.6–7
  The Song of Maldoror 211–12
  "Symphony for Fish in Sim Saima-Si Major (B Major)" 210
Rimbaud, A. 116, 210
Rivas, C. 127–8
Rocha Vivas, M. 22
Rodó, J. E. 104–5
Rodríguez, A. P. 1, 224–6, 228, 256
Ruíz, M. 26

Sacasa, M. J. A. 207
Said, E. 6
Said, M. 6
Salvadoran Imaginaries (Rivas) 127–8
Sánchez, J. 175, 182
Sánchez Prado, I. M. 2, 3, 26, 45, 82, 127, 134, 156, 168 n.3, 217
"San Estevan Versus Yo Creek" (Craveri) 31–2
Schachter, A. 83
Schröder, G. 92
"Sea Surface Full of Clouds" (Lensing) 200–2
self-translation 183
Shea, M. 39–42
Singer, A. 83
Siskind, M. 3, 5, 12, 105–6, 109, 112–13, 129, 152 n.7
The Slow Cyclone 196–8
Sobrevivientes (Dubuisson) 247, 249, 251, 254, 256
Sommer, D. 73
source text (ST) 68–74, 76
Spiegeler, E. 207
Spivak, G. C. 65, 249
SS Kroonland 200, 202, 203 n.3
subaltern, subalternity 7, 65–7, 71, 73, 122
subaltern letrado 46, 48, 57 n.8

subversive 65, 69, 210
The Suction Sea 198–200

"Taberna" (Tavern) (Dalton) 141–3
Taking Their Word (Arias) 6
target text (TT) 68–74, 76
The Tattooed Soldier (Tobar) 231
Tedlock, B. 22
They Won't Take Me Alive (Alegría) 68–9, 71, 75
Time and the Highland Maya (Tedlock) 22
Tobar, H. 229, 231
Tonalmeyotl, M. 26–7
Torres, E. 46
Torres-Saillant, S. 217
translation 6–7, 63–74, 76–7, 82–3, 86–9, 91, 95, 106–7, 114, 117 n.10, 143, 151, 153 n.11, 160, 166, 174–5, 177–80, 183–4
transnational imaginary 224–9, 233
Transportation Security Administration (TSA) 237
Traverso, E. 91–2
tronar 165–8, 168 n.5
Trump, D. 226–7, 231, 245
Tzoc Bucup, M. 29–30, 34

Unaccompanied (Zamora) 223, 231, 239, 247
universal 108–9
Universal Negro Improvement Association (UNIA) 213
untranslatability 12, 63, 165–8

Unwriting Maya Literature (Worley and Palacios) 19–22
US Central Americans 223–32, 237–9

Viveiros de Castro, E. 109, 209, 213–14

Walcott, D. 210
Walrond, E. 191, 198–202, 202–3 n.2
Walters, W. 243
The Wandering Song (Hernández Linares) 228–9, 231
Warwick Research Collective (WReC) 2–3, 9
Weaver, J. 20
Weisenfeld, G. 132–3
Weltliteratur (world literature) 1–2, 6–7, 103, 157–60
What Is a World? On Postcolonial Literature as World Literature (Cheah) 3, 140, 181
White, S. 209–10, 212
  Modern Nicaraguan Poetry Dialogues with France and the United States 212
Worley, P. M. 11
Wuj (Tzoc) 29–30

xocom balumil 11, 19–24, 27, 29, 32, 34–5, 35 n.1

Zamora, J. 223, 228–9, 234–7, 239, 239 n.5, 247
Zola, E. 194

www.ingramcontent.com/pod-product-compliance
Lightning Source LLC
Chambersburg PA
CBHW070022010526
44117CB00011B/1672